John Moria

Not the Whole Story

JOHN MORIARTY

NOT THE WHOLE STORY

Mary McGillicuddy

THE LILLIPUT PRESS

John Moriarty: Not the Whole Story

First published in 2018 by Mary McGillicuddy in association with The Lilliput Press

ISBN 978-1-843-51748-1

Typeset by Dominic Carroll, Ardfield, Co. Cork
Printed and bound in Spain by GraphyCems, Villatuerta, Navarra

'What we are between birth and death is not the whole story;
what we are in the universe is not the whole story;
the universe itself is not the whole story.'
John Moriarty

For Owen,
in the hope that you are forever walking on.
And for John,
whose legacy has the capacity to mind us all.

CONTENTS

ACKNOWLEDGMENTS

It occurred to me only recently how very fitting it is that this book should be published in the year of the fiftieth anniversary of the Viscount aircraft crash off Tuskar Rock in 1968. I was 12 and the grief of our parish provoked a peculiar question for me – not, as might be expected, how could God let this happen, but why all the grief if this was God's will? My uncle, Jerry Collins, provided an answer that I didn't understand at the time. He said that I was really asking about "free will, and that this is something that is very controversial." That concept of free will puzzled and intrigued me then and in a strange and roundabout way led to this book. Thank you, Jerry.

Equally my mother and father, Mick and Jose O'Sullivan, and my grandfather, Tom Collins, who encouraged education, reading and open-mindedness while rooting their family in a world of rich and ordinary life. Thank you, Mam, Dad and Grandad.

Years down the line, Jerry's answer having led me to a place of radical disbelief in any god or any religious system, I eventually encountered the teaching of John Moriarty and for this I must thank a fellow teacher and great friend, Pat O'Loughlin, who simply insisted that I listen. Thank you, Pat.

Listening eventually led to reading John's books and to an appreciation of the importance of what he has to offer modern culture; also to a fear that his work might be neglected. With this in mind and with the encouragement of the extended Moriarty family, in particular his nieces Nita Barrett and Amanda Carmody, the book began to germinate. Thank you, Moriartys, and in particular, thank you, Amanda.

Chapter by slow chapter, as the writing progressed, I conscripted a group of readers, a target audience so to speak, who were tasked with providing feedback – was it true to John, could you hear his voice, was it clear, readable, a good story? These readers were the people who kept me going: Amanda Carmody, Sarah McGillicuddy, Pat O'Loughlin, Nóirín Tanner, Fr. Pat Moore, Sister Noreen Foley, Seán McGillicuddy, Sister Frances Day, Brother John Aherne, and also the Ballyheigue Reading Group that includes Kathy Cunningham, Maria Hayes, Mick

Joyce, Josephine Fitzgibbon, Mary Lyne, Ger McMahon and Amanda Carmody. We got there! Thank you all.

There is one other who, although not directly involved, was nonetheless pivotal. The sudden death of my aunt Eileen Cripps in April 2017 was both a shock and a catalyst; her death cataclysmed me into action – she is responsible for nailing me to the desk until the job was done. She would enjoy that! Thank you, Eileen.

Many others provided help and support, John's great friend Lynne Hill from his Connemara days; Brendan Touhy who gave me access to wonderful interviews; Dee Bradshaw who provided film footage of John in action at a number of his talks; and Brendan O' Donoghue who gave me an 'imprimatur' when it was badly needed. I particularly want to thank Dolores O' Connor for sharing and allowing me to use her moving account of John's death.

Writing a book is one thing, getting it published is quite another. For this I must thank Antony Farrell of Lilliput Press for his advice and assistance and for allowing me to publish in association with Lilliput – this means a lot. Hugh Stancliffe, publisher, printer and friend, has guided me through the entire process and has been invaluable. Dominic Carroll, book designer, typesetter and man of extreme patience, has done a wonderful job in polishing what was an untidy manuscript. A sincere thanks to both Hugh and Dominic. Needless to say, any remaining untidiness is mine alone.

My immediate family, Jackie, Sarah and Seán, have put up with my distractedness, melt-downs, highs and lows over this book for quite a while now – they have been great – but I suppose they understood at all times that it has been a book for our Owen, my son who died in an accident on June 1st 2008 while I was in attendance at John Moriarty's first anniversary Mass. John had died on June 1st 2007. To have this book published and launched on June 1st 2018 feels like a small miracle; it is also my tribute to both of them and my way of keeping us all together *ar shlí na fírinne.*

INTRODUCTION

To be in the presence of John Moriarty, either casually or in attendance at one of his 'talks', was an unforgettable experience. A tall man, unconventionally dressed, with, in the words of Paul Durcan 'his mane of curling hair and the pain of humanity in his face', he would approach the microphone and start to speak. No notes, no power point. The man was the message. He told stories, stories about ordinary happenings, ordinary but rich in wisdom and wonder and humour, and out of those stories he conjured a vision of a different way of being in the world. He spoke of 'the great and sacred earth', of coming home to that earth, of living on it with passion and compassion towards every living thing. He spoke of the tremendous beauty of a cowslip coming up out of the black earth, of the tremendous beauty of the Gleannta Du Cheoig in Connemara, of what he called 'silver branch perception'. He said that we live in a world of miracles if only we had eyes to see. He told us that we live in Divine Ground. He told us that science was only half the story, that philosophy was only half the story, that religion itself was only half the story, but that it was all a tremendous story. He told us that, living in the modern world, we had lost our sense of soul and that this was the greatest possible loss. In his speaking and in his passion, he reawakened that sense of soul in us. Listening to him could reawaken hope. Listening to him one got a glimpse of a world 'always and in everything eruptively divine'. His was a powerful and profound message.

One left the talk, determined to learn a bit more, to read his books, to follow this story. And that's where the problem might arise. Tommy Tiernan, in an interview with John, admitted "I bought one of your books ... I found it impenetrable" and that has been a common experience. In fairness, and with great humour, John was more than ready to acknowledge this. During a talk, giving the background to the writing of his book *Nostos,* which he described as 'a kind of autobiography', he explained:

"I'd been about thirteen years in Connemara, living alone quietly, suddenly Andy O'Mahony, from RTÉ, came in through the door one day and asked me to do an interview, and I was on radio a couple of weeks later. The next day in

Moyvane, where I come from, Gabriel Fitzmaurice was walking down one side of the street and my sister Brenda was walking up the other ... Gabriel asked her if she had heard the programme and what she thought of it. 'Well' she said 'I heard Andy O'Mahony saying at the beginning of the programme that this is John Moriarty from Moyvane in North Kerry, and that was the last thing that I understood.' When my book *Dreamtime* came out a couple of years later, well, she took a look at it anyway, and then her comment was 'Jesus, Mary and Joseph, John, I'm going to have to stick with books about British royalty and the Pope.'"

Given this type of reaction, and it was widespread if not quite so direct and colourful, his friend, the writer and cartographer Tim Robinson, eventually persuaded him to write an autobiography. John's initial reaction was reluctance, even revulsion, at the thought of putting himself on display but Tim persisted. Tim's advice was 'to put the ideas in the context in which they emerged in your life and people will be getting the ideas one by one and then they'll have some chance of understanding them'. For some reason, hearing it put like that, he didn't feel the same resistance, and 'the next morning, it was the longest day of the year, I came down, made the sign of the cross on myself and I started writing ... and this is what emerged ... seven hundred pages, and as I was writing it I was saying, no-one, no-one, no-one is ever going to stay with this ... they'll get so sick of me after a hundred pages that they'll pitch it at the wall, they won't even want it in the house ...' That is not the reaction that *Nostos* provoked, but there is no doubt that it is still not an easy read, not always penetrable without a considerable effort, and so not the book to recommend to someone coming to John Moriarty for the first time, without the benefit of his talks, without the benefit of his inspiring and elucidating presence.

My journey into the writings of John Moriarty began nearly twenty years ago and it started with *Nostos*. I had heard him interviewed, had attended some few talks and found him fascinating, but had never been able to make any hand of the books. They were just too intimidating. Then a friend of mine, Mary B, handed me *Nostos* and said that there was a passage in it about her sister Bridie and that it had them all confused "cos Bridie says she was never under a bush with John Moriarty". Bridie was Sister Bridie, then a Presentation nun, and I was intrigued. What had John and Bridie been up to? And whatever it was, what was it doing in the book? So I started to read, slowly and with careful attention, stopping to look up the obscure references and gradually becoming hooked. 'Hooked' is the only way I can describe it. There is an excitement to be found in the kind of reading that John's work demands. The initial bewilderment or frustration, the grappling to find the meaning, and then the 'eureka' moment, when you get what he means and there is a sense of illumination, and sometimes, depending on the passage, an uplift of spirit that goes beyond one's normal everyday experience of reading and comprehending.

And that was something I wanted to share. I would ring people and make them listen to the more comprehensible passages; on one occasion I subjected my mother to a lengthy telephone reading and was very disappointed that she didn't quite get it. But when I told her the stories she was interested. This became the pattern, people were still hitting a wall when it came to the books. *Nostos* had not fully done what Tim Robinson had hoped, at least not for general readers, but people still wanted to know more. One day, shortly after John died, in conversation with his niece Nita Barrett, she planted the idea that I might write about him, might tell his story "so that we'll all be able to read about him 'cos we have nothing, now that he's gone. I mean it's great to have the books like, but it would be great to have something that we could understand". My reaction was swift. "Jesus, Nita, it's undoable", but the thought was planted and, like John's image of the bush that continues to grow on barren rock in spite of the prevailing wind and rain, the idea simply would not let me go. And so began the process that has eventually become this book, an effort to tell John's story, to interpret his ideas and share his message, closely following his two volumes of autobiography, *Nostos* and *What the Curlew Said*. It somehow feels as if John Moriarty has been knocking at the door of my life for a good many years. What follows is my answer, one that I hope will do him some justice, even though it is in no way, and does not strive to be, the whole story.

1

'A WORLD BELOW HISTORY'

Parents; neighbours; lamplight; Christmas in the cowstall; Jameen Kissane; contradictions; piseógs; a hint of Paradise.

John Moriarty was born on the 2nd February 1938 in the parish of Moyvane in North Kerry, a place once described by another Moyvane native, the poet Gabriel Fitzmaurice, as 'a small, sleepy straggle of a village about 7 miles from Listowel in North Kerry, and off the main road.'[1] Off the main road is a phrase that could describe John's entire life but his own schoolboy address, as he wrote it in one of his national school copybooks was – J. S. Moriarty, Leitrim Middle, the Bally Road, Moyvane, North Kerry, Munster, Ireland, Europe, the Earth, the Milky Way, and finally, in the event of extra-gallactic post, the Universe.

In spite of the grandeur of such an address small holdings were the order of the day and the Moriarty farm, about a half mile outside the village, was a meagre 27 acres, a mixture of bog and pasture which usually supported no more than eleven cows, a few hens, a pig or two and an ass and cart. It was a world of hard work, of turf-cutting, of sowing and reaping, of milking and calving, of cow-stalls and hen houses and piggeries, of fairs and the creamery and the pub, of bread-baking and washing clothes by hand and outside toilets; a world of emigration, of poverty and of inequality. It was also a world of great riches, a world in which every field had a name; a world of lamplight and firelight; a world of neighbourliness, of story-telling and big talk, of small talk and gossip; a world of Mass and the sacraments, a world of superstition, púcas and piseógs. A world, in short, that was both hard and soft, simple and complex, sheltering and unsheltering, open and closed.

It was, as John described it in later years, a world below history.

Cutting turf every year in the bog, we worked our way down into a world no human being had ever set foot on. ... The preserved tree trunks and stumps we'd

1

uncover we called bogdeal. Sometimes the bark of a trunk we'd uncover would be as distinct as it was on the day it fell, frightening birds or deer into flight. Of one thing we could be sure, and that was that it fell long before even the most mythic of our ancestors walked here. I didn't know in any very conscious way then but I know now that this sacrament[2] of going down below history had, by the time I was ten years old, given a direction, never afterwards much altered, to my life. (*Nostos*, p. 7)

This sense of the sacramental nature of exploring the depths, the depths of ourselves, of our past and of our origins, is at the core of John's vision and is echoed again and again in his writings. To understand and to heal, both ourselves and the world in which we live, we must unearth, examine and re-imagine the 'bogdeal' of our past. This is the core of his journey.

John was the fourth child of Jimmy Moriarty from Baile an Lochaigh near Dingle and Mary O'Brien from Barragougeen, a townland near Moyvane on the Kerry/ Limerick border between the villages of Glin and Tarbert. John's arrival into this world of soft light, deep shadow and old rituals was not without drama. His oldest sister Madeleine tells the family story attached to his birth. She remembers her mother telling of her intention to call the new baby Stephen, but of having a dream in which she was told to call him John; also, and always remembered and retold, was the fact that at the time of his birth, the window of the room in which he was born shattered by itself. These were Mary's own stories, never referred to by John, but of interest perhaps because they testify to a world in which there was always potential for otherness, for odd unexplained incidents that were accepted as part of the mystery and way of the world. Mary always said that if ever she dreamt of her own Uncle Stephen she would know 'there was trouble coming'. She often told of one such dream she had during her time in America; she had received a letter from home to tell of her brother Sonny's plans to join her there, she was to meet him from the boat. On the appointed day she did not go; she knew instinctively that he had not travelled. Weeks later she received a letter telling her of his death. Again, a story John would have been familiar with but never mentioned in any of his writings or lectures. Interestingly though, it is perhaps somewhere in the background of an idea John put forward many years later in his book *Dreamtime* where he imagines the next step in evolution as the possible emergence of 'world-soul telepathy, of world clairaudience and clairvoyance'.[3]

John's father, Jimmy Moriarty, Jimmy Phead, was born on 29 July 1903 in a village called Baile an Lochaigh close to Mount Brandon on the Dingle peninsula and was the youngest of nine children. He grew up speaking Irish and by the time he was seven years of age both of his parents had died. One of his earliest memories, later recounted to his own family, was an image of himself as a small boy, waiting for his mother to come home from Dingle. She was an invalid and had to make frequent trips to the doctor. He remembered the anxiety of waiting for her, and of climbing the hill at the front of the house, of watching for her and finally of seeing her coming home the road from Dingle in the ass and cart. Not too long after that she was dead and the image, the lonesomeness of the image of waiting for her to come home, stayed with him for the rest of his life.

Jimmy's childhood effectively ended with the death of his parents. As was customary, the home-place went to one of his older brothers and the other members of the family either emigrated or went into service. In Jimmy's case this meant the life of a farm boy, working for local farmers for little more than bed and board. The GAA broadcaster and writer Micheál Ó Muircheartaigh remembers Jimmy's family, in particular one of his nephews Tony, who "spent a while working with the Kellihers in our village where he was extremely popular as a fine storyteller and a good singer as well",[4] gifts that were also inherited by John.

Jimmy's own memories of this time were mixed.

> Learning hardly anything at all in school by day, he went ag bothántaíocht[5] by night and it was there in this or that neighbouring bothán, sitting on the floor before the fire and listening to the old stories, that he learned almost all of what he knew about himself and his world. Nightly he dropped down out of Irish history into Ireland's Dreamtime. (*What the Curlew Said*, p. 150)

In spite of the richness of this world of song and story, one of his stints at farm work brought hardship and hunger and years later, to his own family, he told of stealing eggs and drinking them because it was "a *'mane'* house". Ultimately he worked for a farmer where he was treated fairly and paid two shillings a week, which was saved for him by the woman of the house; once he was fed and had a place to stay he had no need of money. Eventually, it was this money that bought him his passage to America. It also bought him his first pair of new shoes and a suit for the journey. When he left Dingle in 1921, aged 17, he spoke mostly Irish, had little formal education and did not know how to sign his name in English.

> Then one morning, boarding it in Dingle, he took a train out of his language, out of his dreamtime, and after working briefly for a French farmer in Ontario he ended up working industrially making tyres in a factory called the Fisk Rubber, in Springfield in Massachussets. In his own words, he couldn't at that time read H on the side of a bag and the first time he was asked to sign his name to a document and he couldn't, the cold sweat of shame and embarrassment, he

would say, came out through him. And so it was that Jimmy Phead, loved by all the old women in Ballinloughig, chiefly because his father and mother had died when he was still so young, now he, the lad who had grown up in a largely oral culture, had become a bureaucratic X. (*What the Curlew Said*, p. 151)

Springfield, Massachusetts, was for years a favoured destination of Kerry emigrants; two of his sisters had already made the journey and although he did not have any specific address for them, it was there, in his new suit and his new shoes, that Jimmy headed. On arrival in Springfield, his own story has it that he stood for two entire days at a busy intersection until he met someone he knew from home who could direct him to his sisters. In later years he would recite the progress of his journey. Belfast, Quebec, Montreal, Toronto, Hamilton, Buffalo, Syracuse, Albany and Springfield; a long and lonely way from Baile an Lochaigh.

Jimmy eventually found work and for the next few years repeated the pattern of hard work, of frugal living and of saving his money that had already been established in Dingle. According to his son Chris at one time he held down three jobs, and eventually invested some of his savings in oil company shares, a small investment that came to have a big influence on John's life in later years. Meanwhile, Mary O'Brien from Barragougeen was planning her own journey. She also came from a large family. Born on 16 January 1904, she was one of ten children reared in a two room cottage. There was however a great love of learning and a background of education in that house. Mary's mother came from a family of Kennellys, long associated with a local hedge-school[6] and Mary did receive more formal education than Jimmy in that she completed National School. In the early decades of the twentieth century the national school curriculum was far wider than it is now and it was quite common for children to remain in attendance until age 15. Tarbert poet Thomas MacGreevey did not leave National School until he was 16 and later recalled "Before I gave up I was doing the later books of Euclid and Logarithms, trigonometry, and permutations and combinations."[7]

So Mary O'Brien, having attended Ballygoughlin National School, would have been well educated by the standard of the time. John recounts, "She was hugely and fantastically intelligent and none of us could ever match her. She was the one who would pick up the paper and read it in front of the double-wick paraffin lamp and the mirror behind it to throw the light forward. She would read for the neighbours all about the murder trials and with barrister's language and all thrown in she would be as good as Ann Doyle herself on the television. But isn't it strange, if you met her on a fair day in the Square in Listowel, she would not be half the woman. But at home and in company she could not be matched. There was once when she brought a laudatory discussion on the new priest to an abrupt end by claiming that she could have washed up after a *meitheal*[8] in less time than it was taking him to wipe one chalice."[9] In his autobiography *Nostos* John had this to say: "Ours was a house of talk. Big talk. Talk that never sickened into politeness, not even in the presence of holy things."[10]

That was all in the future but even in her teens Mary displayed a spirited independence. This is clear from a family story about sending for the priest to minister to her ill father. The parish rule was that sick calls had to be requested before eleven o clock in the morning. The call had not been made on time and when the priest arrived he was "like a divil", giving out about the inconvenience and the failure to comply with the rules. Mary, utterly refusing due deference, "quenched the candles and threw him out by the scruff of the neck."[11] A few years later, after she had emigrated to America, the same priest would enquire from her father on the progress of "your virago of a daughter". That independence of mind and challenging spirit stayed with her throughout her life and was inherited by John and indeed by all of her children.

Mary went from National School to a job 'in service', working in one of the local houses as a servant, but soon became dissatisfied. She decided to try her luck in America and set her course for Springfield Massachusetts, again because of local and family connections already there. That was in 1923 and within six years she had met and married Jimmy Moriarty. She herself told John the story of how she saw him on the street with a group she knew to be from home.

> I was milking the cows with her one morning while he was in hospital and she said, "Tis forty seven years ago today that I met Jimmy. It was St. Patrick's Day and Mrs. Basset had given me the day off and I was walking down the street with Mary Bolger and the handsomest man I had seen that day passed us on the sidewalk and I asked Mary did she know who he was and she said, 'He's Mororty from out West in the Dingle Peninsula and he has the first shilling he earned here in Springfield', and didn't I see him again that night at a dance and over he came and asked me out.' (*What the Curlew Said*, p. 153)

In more fractious moments that story would change and she would claim that she was warned to have nothing to do with him 'because he's the meanest thing. He has the first penny he ever made.' In later years Jimmy used to say, "she followed me because she knew I had money" and at least one part of that was true, he did have money, he had saved most of his pay and also had invested in company shares. The illiterate, penniless farm boy had been making good.

Whatever the initial basis for the relationship between them, Jimmy and Mary's marriage lasted for the next 51 years, often stormy and tempestuous, but always passionate and alive. Behind it all they were, to quote their daughter Brenda, "always mad about one another", an opinion slightly qualified by her sister Phyllis "even if they had a *quare* way of showing it". They married in Springfield in 1929 and their first child, Madeleine, was born in 1930. Mary had never settled in America and in 1932 she and her little girl sailed for home, equipped with Jimmy's savings and Mary's dream of buying their own place. While Jimmy remained, working 'round the clock' in Springfield, Mary bought the house and 27 acres for eleven hundred pounds. This became the family home. In February 1933 Jimmy came home to Moyvane, one of his proudest stories in later years being the fact that his original journey from Dingle to Belfast had taken him through Listowel, the train passing the very fields that he and Mary now owned.

Life then settled into the rhythm of a small farm. Chris, Babs, John, Brenda and Phyllis were born between 1933 and 1945, making it a lively and busy house, with the daily routines of child-minding, cooking, washing, bread-baking, milking and managing, all being done without the aid of electricity. In *Nostos* John describes one of Mary's daily rituals:

> Every evening, at nightfall, my mother would take the lamp down from its nail on the wall, she would fill it, she would trim its wicks and clean its glass globe and then, with a taper she would bring the light of the fire to it. Winding down the wicks to their best height, she would fit the globe back on and, it being a sacrament of light she was now holding, she would hang it on the wall, there where its nail was, half way between the Sacred Heart picture and the small yard window. (*Nostos*, p. 47)

In another story he describes his father enacting a similar ritual:

> When I was young, a little child imagining the big world, the world was full of fairies, full of púcas, and full of strangers and full of all kinds of presences and radiances which you mightn't know the names of, or know how to handle. I would see my father on a dark winter's night, he would take down his lantern and he would light it, if it was a wild night he would unscrew, he would wind it back until there was just a little spark of light, and sometimes I would just see half his face in the light of the kitchen and the other half would be in the darkness and I often wondered about him walking out into that dark and that he wasn't afraid. And he would cross the wild yard and he would go over and hang the lantern up on a nail in a rafter and then he would wind it up and he'd have good light now again and he would feed the cows hay and having fed the cows, these were short-horn cows, not the fresians that we have now,

these were wonderful shorthorn cows, with their lovely fur, their lovely coats
... when my father would go over and feed them hay in the night, he would sit
on his three-legged stool, behind them, and he would smoke his last cigarette
of the day there.[12]

This world where light and darkness were 'partners in a dance' was to have a
deep influence on John's mature vision.

In our house it didn't make sense to talk about an enmity between light and
dark ... What we saw, particularly when the fire blazed, is that they were
partners in a dance, Gypsy partners in a Gypsy dance. (*Nostos*, p. 47)

Neither did it make sense to imagine a world in which animals were seen only for
their economic value. Jimmy Moriarty's attachment to his cows was both profound
and problematic. Jimmy was no farmer; 'a fierce worker', in the words of one of the
neighbours, 'but no method', with an endearing if impractical tendency to treat all of
his animals as pets. The cows all had names ... Polly, Hanrahans, the Big Red ... and
John remembers the gentleness with which they were treated. 'Coming up the road
with the cows my father always walked at their rhythm. ..he fell into their rhythm and
some kind of wonderful wisdom came to my father walking up and down behind
those cows, the wisdom of the cow, the wisdom of animal nature came to him.'[13]

Jimmy couldn't sell a calf or kill a hen, all that work fell to Mary; Phyllis gives
an insight into the depth of his attachment to the animals

I remember a cow, I'll never forget this. One day they were in the bog cutting
turf and there was a cow ready to calf. We used to let the cows down to the river
to drink water and leave them there for a few hours. 'Twas frosty and he told
myself and my mother not to let the cow out. However, we did let the cow out
and the cow died of a heart attack below by the river. My father was in bed for
a week. He never got up. He was in bed for a full week. We never again heard
the end of that. 'Twas pathetic. But my mother was practical. She had to make
the money out of it.

That primal connection to the world of animals constantly recurs in John's writings.
One of his earliest memories, a story he told again and again, concerns a Christmas
Eve when he was six or seven.

... this was Christmas Eve and Madeleine, my oldest sister was singing 'Silent
Night, Holy Night', and Chris had brought in two bags of turf from the shed,

and Babs had brought two buckets of water from the well, and already, its flame perfectly calm, the lamp was giving more light than the fire, with its raptures big and small. But lamplight and firelight, that was every night.

Tonight was different.

Looking at the crib in the deep sill of our front window, I could see that the light of heaven was in our house.

It was a night of wonders.

Tonight, all night, the gates of heaven would be open above us.

Riding animals higher than our horse, and wearing glittering vestments, the three Wise Men might pass through our yard tonight and if they did our father would show us tracks in the morning. Plain as could be, we saw them last Christmas morning.

And Santa Claus would come and he would bring us what we asked for. To Babs he would bring a blouse. To me he would bring a game of Snakes and Ladders. And to Brenda and Phyllis he would bring dolls.

And soon we would have supper with currant cake.

There was no denying it, it was wonderful, and in a glow of fellow feeling with all our animals I went out and crossed our yard to the cowstall.

Pushing open the door, I looked in and at first I just couldn't believe what I was seeing ... What I saw was what I would see on any other night, eleven shorthorn cows, some of them standing, some of them lying down, some of them eating hay, some of them chewing the cud, and two of them turning to look at me.

Devastated, I had to admit that it was an ordinary night in the stall.

Coming back across the yard I looked at the fowl house and the piggery and the darkness, and the silence that had settled on them couldn't say it more clearly. Christmas didn't happen in the outhouses. Christmas didn't happen to the animals. The animals were left out. And since the animals were left out, so, inside me somewhere, was I. (*Nostos*, pp. 5–6)

Odd as it may seem, Jimmy's cows provoked John's first philosophical question. In bed later that night he wondered how Christmas could exist if the cows didn't know about it, if there was no Christmas Eve in the cow stall? While it may seem like a childish question, not worth a second thought to those who accept the world at face value, it became a fundamental preoccupation in all of John's later thinking. For him it led to all of the bigger questions, how we as human beings make sense of the world, how we shape it to suit our needs, the stories we tell about our origins, it led him to questions about the Christmas story itself; in short it began a journey far longer than Jimmy's journey from Dingle to Springfield and back home to

Moyvane, it began a journey that John came to believe we must all ultimately make if we, and the world we live in, are to flourish; a journey home to the animals and to the earth, to the sacramental unity of all beings and of all things.

During John's childhood Moriarty's was what was known as a 'calling house', a house of great talk, an open house where neighbours gathered to chat, to argue, to tell stories, to share their lives.

'A lot of people used come into our house. It was mostly because of my mother that people used to come into our house. My mother, a big woman, not physically that big, she was tall, but there was something about her, you had this sense that she was enormous, because she was so psychologically big and psychologically real, we always had the sense that she was huge, but 'twas psychologically that she was big. I don't know how any of us ever survived my mother like, to grow up with such an enormous reality around you all the time, how did we ever survive the presence of my mother in that house, how did my father survive the presence of this huge wonderful woman? People used come in the night, the night walkers used come, and she'd read the paper for all these men, she was a great presence in the world.

There'd be donkeys and carts and horses and carts going up and down the road, going up and down to the creamery, going up and down to the village. And many of these horses, without any direction at all from their drivers, would naturally come into our yard because they were so used to it. I remember summer days when Moss Hartnett would be coming down with his horse and his milk churn, and he would want to go home because he would have hay to cut or turf to cut or something like that, and he would desperately have to wrestle with the horse to stop the horse from going in, but almost always he lost that battle. And he would have to come in then and sit down and they would discuss the world and the politics and everything with my mother. So it was that kind of house.'[14]

Among those callers was Jameen Kissane, whose nightly visits were part of the fabric of their lives. His influence, the stories he told, made a lasting impression.

Every evening as darkness was falling Jameen Kissane would come to our house. To us, Jameen was as old as the fog, and as wise as the bushes. Given how he lived, and the few clothes he lived in, the long months of winter were hard on him. It was a comfort to him to come in and sit in the corner under our chimney breast. There he was out of the way of the draught, and there also he got the full benefit of the fire. But it wasn't only the fire that revived him.

On the hearth, in front of him, at this time of the evening, there would be a three-legged cast-iron oven with coals beneath it and coals on its lid. The last loaf of the day was being baked. And at that time too, just before supper, the kettle, also of cast-iron, would be spitting from within the flames that engulfed it on every side.

A tall thin man with a small appetite, Jameen would eat by the fire.

A sense I had of him was that if bogdeal could talk, it would talk as Jameen talked.

Certainly it was out of a past as old as bogdeal that he talked, and that suited the kind of fireplace we all sat at. (*Nostos*, p. 8)

And that was where stories were told, stories as old as time, stories from a world 'below history', stories from and about an 'Otherworld', being kept alive in a kitchen that, with its lamplight and firelight, its acceptance of the soft interplay of light and dark, was in ways 'in séance' with a past that predated the Iron Age. There was of course iron in the house and in the yard and in the world outside, 'but we didn't have a mind to go with it'.

One night Jameen picked up a boot of mine and saw that it needed a new half-sole. He asked me to bring him the hammer, the last, the tack and a strip of leather from the right drawer of the dresser. Instantly and emphatically my mother said no, pointing to a hen hatching eggs in a wooden butter box under the table. No, she said, that will have to wait for another night. Didn't we know, she asked, that the sound of hammering might kill the chicks in the eggs. Again, three or four days later, hearing Chris hammering outside in the hayshed, she went to the door and called out to him to stop, at once.

In our house we lived from the belief that the sound of iron on iron was lethal.

In our house the metallurgical ages gave way to a hatching hen. (*Nostos*, p. 8)

This was a world in which animals belonged, Jimmy's cows and Mary's hens were in one sense 'accomodated' but it was also a world of enormous contradictions, a world in which

'Regularly, my mother would sharpen an already sharp knife on the concrete floor, knocking sparks out of it as she did so. She would go out to the fowl-house and come back with an outraged, red, squawking cock. Wedging him between her thighs, she would pluck the throat feathers and then, cutting off his gloriously combed and wattled head, she would let the sometimes spasming, spattering rope of blood flow down into a bowl where it would settle into an accusation all the more dreadful because it was so serene. (*Nostos*, p. 15)

Killing the pig was frightfulness. Jack Scanlan, the gentlest man on the Bally Road, he was the pigkiller. He'd come into the house with a big knife and a big hook. Himself and a couple of other men would go out to the piggery. Catching a pig by the ears Jack's assistants would pin it to the wall while Jack hooked it, underneath, between its jawbones. Ropes were tied to its legs front and back. And then pulling relentlessly on the hook and ropes the men gave it no choice but to walk their way. Not far from the front door of the dwelling house it was tumbled over onto its side. The underside of its neck near its collarbones was scalded with boiling water, the hair thereabouts was shaved by Jack with his big knife and then ... the neck was opened and the knife pushed in till it opened the heart. That night the pig would be hanging from a big cross beam in our big farmhouse kitchen. (*Turtle was Gone a Long Time*, vol. 1, p. 19)

And so for John, arising from this casual acceptance of the horror of killing, there were further enormities to be addressed. How do we survive in a universe that has such a capacity for cruelty and for killing, not only of animals, but of one another? In the young boy's mind, as yet at an unconscious level, the killing of the pig and the killing of the cock were powerful rituals enacted at home. But, there was also another powerful ritual at work in his life, the ritual of the Mass, with at its core, the shocking image of the tortured and crucified Jesus. This ritual, in spite of its central horror, carried a profound promise of healing and salvation. It provided, for those who chose to think about it, a way of managing the suffering encountered in the world. It also, in its biblical foundation, gave justification for the way in which human beings treat the rest of creation. John was later to write of 'the sheltering hypnosis of habit and familiarity', of the need for 'a religion to cover our tracks to Ned Stack's butcher's stall'. It was not only exposure to the killing at the heart of human survival that was a disturbing feature of this world.

One day, opening a wyand of hay in the West Field, my father found four bad eggs at the heart of it. This, as it would to any neighbour for miles around, brought the cold sweat out through him. But he had to stand his ground. He had to deal with this evil, because this was 'piseógs'[15] a kind of witchcraft, certainly something more wicked than mere superstition.

Settling a bed of hay on the four prongs of his fork, he took the eggs, praying as he did so, and laid them on it. Then, careful that no egg would fall off, he walked towards the river. And the river, he was so glad to tell us when he came home, had taken the awful thing out of our land ...

Dimly we were aware that this form of witchcraft was based on the belief that like creates like. The bad eggs or the bad butter or the bad meat that someone placed in a field would turn the cattle that grazed that field into its image and likeness. Before long those cattle would themselves be bad meat. In other words, this didn't work by the physical transmission of physical bacteria. It worked by the ritual power of sympathetic magic ...

This kind of witchcraft was as common to our locality as its bushes were. No year went by but some awful new story did the rounds. One story had it that a woman opened her door one morning and a skinned calf fell inward across her threshold. Another story had it that a priest who openly confronted the evil had, within a week, to confront it, in truly sensational form, within his own church ... on Saturday night, when he went into his confession box to hear and forgive the sins of the people, he sat down on thirteen rotten eggs. (*Nostos*, pp. 8, 9, 14)

John remembers being afraid after that to go to the West Field. It was Jameen Kissane who eventually brought some comfort. He arrived at Moriarty's at his usual time one evening and told that he had found bad butter in the field behind his house. Curious with fear and wonder the children wanted to know what he did with it. 'What did I do with it?' echoed Jameen, 'sure what would I do with it, I brought it in and I ate it'.

For weeks afterwards, coming as he did every night to our house, we were afraid of him. He had eaten evil. He had eaten the witchcraft of the ages. He must be contagious. He must be avoided ... but to our astonishment no harm settled on him. (*Nostos*, p. 10)

Not only did he not die, Jameen helped them to have some understanding of this sinister superstition. He explained that some people believed that there is 'a certain amount of bad luck in the world, and it must fall on people. Not all people, but on many people. In the way that bread and wine are the elements of the Eucharist, the bad meat and bad eggs are like the elements of a dark sacrament, a sacrament in which some people attempt to divert the bad luck that might fall on themselves onto others'.[16] So there was an explanation. The piseógs need not be feared and the world could be a little bit more manageable. John tells the story of an old tradition, practised in Wales when someone died. A meal would be prepared and then offered to some tramp who might be walking the roads. In the ritual of eating the meal, it was believed that the tramp was eating, and therefore purging, the sins of the dead person. This tramp was called the Sin Eater. Jameen had become their Sin Eater. He was helping to make sense of their world. The wider world was also posing very large questions.

> I would remember a morning at home in North Kerry. The war over, my father had come home from London. As was their wont, some neighbours came in on their way home from the creamery and, more than anything else, they wanted to know what the blitz was like. Having talked to them about it, he went on to talk about a film called *Belsen* that he had recently seen. Seven years of age at the time, what I couldn't take in was an image of human dripping flowing along stone channels. I knew what dripping was. In our house it was the lard of a pig melted on a frying pan, a liquid to cook rashers and eggs in. But human dripping? Human beings melted down? Their lard flowing in channels? The idea sat like a stone that I couldn't digest in the middle of my mind. (*What the Curlew Said*, p. 118)

'A stone that I couldn't digest in the middle of my mind.' Where was he to find a Sin Eater who could handle that? It was an image and a question that remained with him for the rest of his life.

John once made the point that he had had 'a wild childhood' but it was wild only in the sense that it was free; once school was ended and the various chores were attended to, the children would be off, over the fields, down the river, exploring, finding things to occupy themselves, looking for and making fun, and quite often making mischief.

> Often, we would hear people saying that the countryside we lived in wasn't fit for man or beast. Mary Ann Danny O' was famous because, talking one day to a woman who had called to see her, she said, 'Isn't it a lonely place I am living in, and isn't it lonely I am myself looking out this door and seeing nothing coming towards me always but the blowin' wind and the wet rain?'
>
> Maag Mahony, who lived in Poll, a place almost as desolate, agreed. 'Yes', Maag said, 'there are days when I look through my door and the only thing I can say about the wind is that it is blowin' and the only thing I can say about the rain is that it is wet'.
>
> We knew Mary Ann Danny O'. And yet, however much we tried, we couldn't imagine her. We couldn't imagine how she lived where she did. If only someone could, it would have been a mercy to have turned her into a bush. But then there are limits too to what a bush will put up with.

We didn't send a horse and cart for Mary Ann Danny O'.

We didn't take her in, this woman who lived where a snipe wouldn't live.

We knew the way to her house and we blackguarded her, a rabble of us, pounding her front door and then her back door with our fists, a yellow tangle of us making faces at her and screeching at her through her small lace-curtained, cobwebbed windows.

One day as we ran off in delighted triumph, I looked back and saw the white head of her, just the white head, craning forward in her doorway.

To this day I've seen nothing that so questions the right of the universe to exist, as it exists. (*Nostos*, pp. 10–11)

Here, again, out of a boyhood escapade came one of the big universal questions; seeing the old, frightened, white head of Mary Ann Danny O', and remembering it long afterwards, John was faced with the existence of misery and loneliness in the world, and the capacity for uncaring thoughtless cruelty in the face of that loneliness. Could anything be more bleak? Who or what could alleviate or explain or justify such situations and such impulses? And yet:

How strange it was that we who so happily tormented Mary Ann were so tender towards nesting birds ... By the middle of May ... Tom Welsh and myself had discovered forty-six nests, and these were the nests that were difficult to find, the nests of blackbirds, thrushes, wagtails, wrens, robins, larks, wild duck, snipe and, most difficult of all, the nests of goldfinches – three of them in Paddy Aherne's orchard. ... Never once, by too sudden an approach, did we frighten a bird off her eggs. Never once, by lingering too long, did we make a hatching bird uneasy. Never once, by over-forcing our way to a nest, did we leave evidence of intrusion behind us. Rather than cause the slightest upset, we were happy to walk away not knowing what we would otherwise have liked to have known. And this paid off, because, to a quite remarkable degree it fostered an intuitive sense of our surroundings in us. It was as if our oldest ancestors had whispered to us. In the stealth of our walking and, above all, in a kind of complicity with things, we were on the way to becoming good hunters. (*Nostos*, pp. 10–11)

Tenderness to the nesting birds and cruelty to Mary Ann Danny O'; piseógs and neighbourliness; good sacraments and bad sacraments; accommodating the hatching hen, killing the pig; human dripping, human tenderness; Christmas in the kitchen, an ordinary night in the cowstall ... this was a world of elemental contradictions and mysteries. A local story of a neighbour known as the Hard Man seemed to indicate a way forward:

Out in the bogs one evening, the Hard Man loosed his hound after a big, heavy-looking hare. Coming to the place of carnage, he saw that the hare had been ripped open and her four babies had fallen out. On the football field and at fairs and dances, the Hard Man was able, and made sure he was known to be able, to look after himself. He had never come second best out of a fight. But now, seeing the hare's four babies, he was troubled and instead of leaving them to the hound, he picked them up and brought them home, and by a miracle of patient kindness he found a way of feeding them and caring for them and they lived. And the Hard Man himself – well it wasn't only that he didn't loose his hound at hares any more. (*Nostos*, p. 12)

And Jameen Kissane had pointed them in the same direction:

Is there wickedness as well as bad luck in the world? we asked him.
    The only good answer to that will come to ye in prayer, he said. But in the meantime, he continued, make sure ye don't persecute anyone, or anything. (*Nostos*, p. 13)

So Mary Ann Danny O' would be left alone and the eels that they used to hunt with table forks in the river 'got a better time of it' and, in the meantime, other growing and awareness was happening.

One Sunday evening everyone but me went to Holy Hour in the church. I stayed behind to have a good fire on for Jameen when he came in.
    I made tea for him and cut and buttered two slices of bread for him. Then I sat in the corner opposite him.
    I was proud that he was talking to me. About how many of our cows had calved. About how much turf we had left. About what I would do when I was finished in primary school.
    He asked me if I felt a new power in my body.
    In alarm, which I tried to hide, I said that I did.
    Don't be afraid of that, he said. That is natural. Grow with that and it will make a man of you.
    After that I was easier in myself than I had been for the past six months or so. (*Nostos*, p. 13)

Other mysteries were presenting themselves as well, perhaps the bleakness of the blowin' wind and the wet rain had another dimension, one that could be experienced in the Hill Meadow ...

More often than not now, I'd go off through the fields on my own. There were fields that I loved. Fields with a sward of natural, wild herbs. In the Hill Meadow I saw hints of Paradise. It was the only name I had for the flowers that grew there, primroses and cowslips in the dry parts of it and in the more marshy parts, buttercups and orchids.

And I wondered.

How could something so yellow as a buttercup come up out of brown soil? How could something so purple as an orchid come up out of it? How could something so perfect as a cowslip come up out of it?

Where did the colour and the perfection come from?

And what else was down there?

What else was I walking on?

To me to inhale the fragrance of a primrose was a Eucharist.

A Eucharist[17] without suggestion of bloodshed or blood.

Sometimes I'd inhale the fragrance down to the very soles of my feet. Then I could walk the earth without hurting it. Then I could walk in Paradise. Right here, in our Hill Meadow, I could walk in Paradise. (*Nostos*, pp. 13–14)

2

'HORIZONS OF LONGING'

Learning and growing; St. Michael's College; myths; puberty; bog-sadness; the shelter of religion; encountering Darwin; Training College.

Education comes in strange ways and from strange places. Schools can do their utmost but very often it is the lessons learned outside of them that have the greatest impact. John maintained that it was Snakes and Ladders, the game he got from Santa in the same year that he realised there was no Christmas in the cowstall, that provided a model for understanding the world. It seemed to him that everything had to do with the random throw of the dice.

> Their throw of the dice brought the McGraths[1] to the foot of a ladder. Our throw brought us to the mouth of a snake. The ladder carried them up in the world, the snake carried us down in it. And that's why they had more land than we had. That's why they had more cows, more milk to bring to the Creamery in Newtown,[2] and more calves to sell at the fair in Listowel. That's why Santa Claus brought them bigger and better toys at Christmas. That's why when the Church collections were read from the altar, they were high up in the list and we were low down in it. And even though in school we were … being taught that things were as bad as they were because of a rebellious will in human beings, we nonetheless felt that in some way or another chance was also at work. (*Nostos*, pp. 6, 12)

Much else was learned outside the classroom.

> I knew how to harness an ass, putting on the winkers, the collar and hames, the straddle and breeching. I knew how to handle the ass himself, backing him between the shafts of the cart. If I had to, having seen it done so often in

Paddy Horan's forge, I could make the shoes and shoe a horse, being careful as I hammered them in to keep the nails away from the quick at the heart of the hoof. Using my two front fingers as a surrogate pap, I had taught day old calves to drink milk from a bucket. I had taken cows in heat to McGrath's bull and I knew when they were bulled. I could cut and save turf. I could save hay. I could plant spuds and cabbage. I could distinguish all the birds resident and migrant that came to our fields. Putting one of the fingers that had been a surrogate pap, feeling the difference between the tongue curling round them and the ridged roof of the mouth, putting it in now through the hole of a wren's nest I felt five eggs and putting it in again a few days later I felt five chicks and that more than anything else taught me the wonder and unexpectedness of the world. Never once did we hear a foreign fairy tale, such as you'd find in the books of Andersen and Grimm, and in a sense we didn't need to because we had Maag Mahony and Mary Ann Danny O' and Jameen Kissane, he coming through our door every night, and as well as being as old as the fog, as well as being forever, they, all three of them, were as strange as folk tales and, they being in it, who could take the world for granted.

And every time we found bad meat in the land or bad eggs in a wyand of hay we knew that as well as the wonder that was in it there was evil in the world ... we were vastly knowledgeable, and knowing, so much so that if the entire adult population suddenly died out one night, we would be out there driving in the cows to milk them, we could take over. We didn't have the fairy stories of the world available to us at a click but, the hundred watt bulb not yet installed, we would every evening sink down into the shadowy, twilight mind out of which such stories are born.

As between Walt Disney and Jameen Kissane, I'd choose Jameen any day, and if a sense of life beyond the bounds of where mind is possible, if either or both of these is what I at any time need, then I only have to remember Maag Mahony and Mary Ann Danny O'. (*What the Curlew Said*, pp. 225–6)

'The wonder and unexpectedness of the world ... the shadowy twilight mind out of which stories are born ... a sense of life beyond the bounds of where mind is possible' ... the primary school curriculum in 1940s Ireland was no match for all of this. The big talk, the lamplight, the stories told by Jameen and the freedom of the fields outside made it impossible to give serious heed to a teacher talking about prepositions or fractions, impossible to sit in a bare desk and give serious heed to a man talking about a golden age, a silver age, a bronze age and an iron age'. (*Nostos*, p. 8)

Of the years between five and twelve John would later say "I was nowhere present to education. Nowhere present at all to what was happening in the classroom. I don't know why. I still haven't figured it out. But I was meant for the land anyway and by the time I got to sixth class I was so securely at the back of that class that no one would even challenge me for the position. That was secure like."[3] He remembered National School only as a place of 'uncompromising severity' where on a daily basis he was slapped for being stupid and was never once called by his first name, it was always either 'Moriarty' or 'bostoon'.[4] Most of the punishment arose because of his panic and consequent failure when confronted by mental arithmetic. Years later, hearing from his five year old niece Amanda that she loved school,

> 'That astonished me. I'm 54 now and for anyone my age school tended to be a punitive experience ... remember the old terrible schools with the windowsills around five feet up in case any child looked out and saw a green field or a bit of loveliness out there. They were places of detention and for me it was a particularly awful experience, it was a place of punishment and when I heard this little girl saying I love it, I was genuinely astonished.'[5]

On the day he went to sit his Primary Cert he was met by the teacher who demanded to know what he, a guaranteed failure and therefore an unwelcome statistic, was doing there. His answer was simple, 'My mother wouldn't lave me at home'. To his own great surprise he subsequently passed the exam.

He left national school believing that he was 'backward' and with no enthusiasm for continuing his schooling. However, in September 1951, with the encouragement of his sister Madeleine and following in the footsteps of his brother Chris, he reluctantly enrolled in St. Michael's College in Listowel. His first day remained ingrained in his memory. Madeleine, whom he would later credit for having changed his life, resurrected a rusty ladies bicycle from one of the sheds, and provided him with a copybook, a pencil, two slices of brown bread and a bottle of milk. Too 'stupefied and dumbfounded'[6] to object he set off for Listowel, unsure of the way and peddling furiously to keep up with Chris, who on his proper man's bike and embarrassed by the encumbrance of a younger brother on a rusty bike, was doing his best to lose him. In spite of this, and unexpected as his arrival at the school was, he was accepted as a first year student and, following assessment, was assigned to the 'A' class. However

> I continued to believe that I must be stupid because I couldn't figure out why minus multiplied by minus yielded a plus. And there was something else. When I multiplied three by three I got nine, something bigger than the two numbers I started off with. So that was fair enough, multiplication meant increase. But

then, Paddy Rochford, our maths teacher, asked me what a half multiplied by a half came to. With great confidence I said one. No, he said, it comes to a quarter. I could only take his word for it, because having got used to the idea that multiplication meant increase I must also get used to the idea that it can also mean a decrease. I hadn't at that time heard of Alice, but there were some classes where we did go down a rabbit hole, down into a world where, without warning, things would behave very strangely. What was so surprising was that no one else was surprised. So the problem was not in things. It was in me. I must be stupid. (*Nostos*, p. 76)

By the end of the first term he was determined to leave.

That Christmas, turning my hand to everything and anything, I worked as hard as I could on the farm. What I was trying to do was to so impress my parents that they would ask me to stay at home, but it didn't work. I wasn't yet fourteen, the age at which I could legally quit, and anyway there wouldn't be much going on during the bad months ahead, so my mother thought it would be better if I stuck it out for three more months'. (*Nostos*, p. 75)

But it was in that three months that everything changed:

One day it was my turn to go to the blackboard and translate a sentence into Greek that Timmy O'Connor our teacher would call out to me. The idea was that the other boys would keep a look out for mistakes and pounce on them as they occurred, clamourously raising their hands. Given my reputation, they quite naturally expected that I would provide them with rich quarry, and as I picked up the chalk stick their excitement was palpable. Miraculously, I got to the fifth word before I heard it, an excited voice calling 'Sir, Sir'. Instantly, as though following the lead and wanting to get in on the fun, everyone had picked up the scent and the hunt was on. It was like being caught in hail shower out in the open, a hail shower of 'Sirs', of 'Sir' 'Sir' 'Sir' – hopping off me. Knowing that I would be out of the place in a couple of weeks I kept going, all the way to the end. Then I turned and faced what I hoped would be my last humiliation. The odd thing was that I believed in my own mind that I had got it right.

Timmy O Connor only bothered to ask the first few boys in the first row to tell him what they saw wrong with it.

It was obvious from the tone of his voice that something quite unexpected was about to happen.

And it did happen.

'Ye are all wrong', he said, 'and he is right'.

When at the end of the Easter holidays my mother asked me to stay at home I said no.

She looked at me in great surprise.

'I've got the hang of this thing', I said, 'so I'd like to go on'.

A Greek sentence had thrown a life-line to me, and from that day on the road to Listowel wasn't only the road to the monthly fair or to McKenna's hardware shop or to Whelan's shoe shop or to Leahy's clothes shop, it was the road to Athens, Jerusalem and Rome ... (*Nostos*, pp. 75–76)

A road that, in one way or another, he would walk for the rest of his life. And it was in this class also that John was introduced to the Greek myths, stories of gods and goddesses, with which Timmy O'Connor would enliven his classes. These stories took deep root in his imagination and were as immediate to him as the local stories that were being told on a nightly basis in his own home.

I was only three weeks in St. Michael's when, for the first time, I heard a Greek myth. It was the myth of Perseus and Medousa ...[7]

From the day I first heard this myth ... I pitied Medousa more than I admired Perseus. What a dreadful doom I thought: everywhere she sits, a cemetery of things turned to stone surrounds her ... Cycling home from St. Michael's that evening, even though the wind and rain were against me, I felt they were with me. And once at home I could hardly wait till Jameen Kissane came in. Always it was Jameen who had the stories but tonight it would be different. Tonight I'd be telling the story, and it wouldn't be any of the stories we'd heard over and over again, the story of her horse pushing at her door the night Maag Mahony was being waked, or the story of Pat Bunce crossing the Barragogeen bogs from Aughrim one night. Although he could see nothing Pat heard the murmuring voices of the dead from all the townlands round about. Tomorrow, they murmured, acres of them murmured. To morrow to morrow to morrow to morrow to morrow. Next day, no one expecting it, no one knowing why, Pat's father died.

It was an outlandish story, the story of Perseus and Medousa. And yet by the time I had finished telling it, it seemed to suit our fireside. Under the silence of the thatch, added to every four years, and under the great chimney breast, our fireside was able for anything as long as there was wonder in it. (*Nostos*, pp. 92, 96–7)

In Timmy O'Connor's class John also had his first encounter with the Greek tragedies, more stories of human beings trying to come to terms with the horror of human suffering and the apparent indifference, even the active cruelty, of their various gods. The play *Iphigenia at Aulis* by the Greek playwright Euripides tells the story of Agamemnon, king of Mycenae and hero of the Trojan wars, and of his decision to sacrifice his daughter Iphigenia to appease the goddess Artemis. In return Artemis would allow the Greek fleet to sail on to glory in battle. So Iphigenia was sacrificed to enable a still greater slaughter. How real Agamemnon's bloody sacrifice seemed when one could identify with it in the yard at home.

Outside on a little rise in the yard, I had often held the basin to the red throat-torrent from a pig we were killing, held it till her last gurgle, held it till her last unsqualing collapse into cuttable meat.

Into meat so quietly cuttable that this too was a horror of accusation .

As accusation the quiet was more frightful than the squeal.

What was it like, the silence of Iphigenia after her last gurgle?

What was it like, the silence of Christ after his last gurgle?

How did the mountains survive such silence? How did the stars survive it?

One thing was sure it is a tough universe we live in.

Or was it that the universe has decided to go blind and go deaf? Is that the only way it can cope with being what it is?

I couldn't say. Not then. Not for a long time after. (*Nostos*, p. 15)

Two things were happening as John learned about the cultures of ancient Greece and Rome. Firstly, he was internalising the stories to such an extent that ever afterwards in his writing he would refer to them with utter ease and familiarity, causing considerable difficulty for the general reader, but giving John an extensive source of reference and imagery with which to make big philosophical questions concrete, in so far as that can be done. The Medousa story is invoked time and again; Medousa would later become a metaphor for a world view that cannot see or accept wonder and miracle, while Perseus, slayer of Medousa, becomes metaphor for the human capacity for violence, killing and repression.

Secondly, and even more importantly in terms of his intellectual development, those myths and stories were provoking profound questions. In their light he was interrogating the world in which he lived, comparing Greek myths with local stories and already recognising that maybe there was more than one way of being in the world, maybe it didn't always have to be the way of Agamemnon. Maybe the world of the Hard Man and the baby hares could get a look in.

> If only Agamemnon had reared the babies of the hare destroyed by eagles
> at Aulis, if only he, a hard man also, had said, to hell with the war and had
> taken them home to Mycenae and reared them, reared them with the help
> of Clytemnestra, and with the help of their children, Iphegenia, Electra and
> Orestes – if as a family they had reared the hare's babies in their doomed
> house, then Western history might have run a different course and we wouldn't
> now, three thousand years later, be reading a book called *Silent Spring*[8]
> (*Nostos*, p. 129)

When he was twenty two John spent a summer travelling in Greece, exploring
its ancient culture first hand, and in the course of his solitary ramblings he tells of
a momentary encounter with a very beautiful Greek girl. They simply pass each
other on the road but they exchange a look and a greeting and it saddens him to
think that after five years at school studying Greek he did not have the vocabulary
to chat to her, to express admiration or affection.

> By the time I left St. Michael's I knew the vocabulary of weapons and war in
> four languages, two of them dead and one of them dying. But then, maybe
> that's who we are as a species, maybe the language of commerce and war comes
> altogether more easily and more naturally to us than does the language of affec-
> tion and love. (*Nostos*, p. 128).

The language of affection and love, the vocabulary to express feelings, where were
these to be found in the official Ireland of the 1940s and 1950s? School and church
were preaching a fiercely puritanical and harmful message about the sexual instinct,
but this was fortunately counteracted by a far healthier earthiness in his own home,
an acceptance of and joking about 'coortin' couples, an acknowledgement in the
laughter that sex was totally natural. There would be great fun recounting the
hideaways that couples found after the crossroads dances; in bad weather Jameen
Kissane's hay-barn was a favourite haunt and John's mother loved to tell of Jameen's
surprise when, going to the barn one particular night, 'Lord save us Mary, I went
in last night to get a 'gabháil' of hay for th'oul cows and everywhere I put my hand,
I caught a leg'.

So the fun of sex and the laughter of sex survived in spite of the fanatical
morality that existed at another level. And John was not short of his own romantic
fantasies. He remembers long August days working in the bog, filling and emptying
the rails of turf, handling almost each and every sod, 'I didn't see one of them.
What I was seeing was convent girls ... that there was an old forest floor ten feet
under me meant nothing to me now. I wanted to walk among living pines, not

dead pines, and I wanted to walk among them with Bridie Sullivan'. While turning turf he was working out an imaginary and perfect encounter with Bridie. In his daydream they would meet quite accidentally, both cycling home from school in Listowel, and a convenient shower would oblige them to take shelter under a bush 'and I'd be all poetry to her'. He would recite Milton's *Il Pensoroso*, just to prove how serious-minded he was, and she would know from that, because the poem would tell her, that he was going off to a cloister to become a monk! She would advise him to wait for a few years, he was needed on the local football team, and he would agree to think about that, and they would agree to meet on the next Sunday coming home from Listowel, and then, as he was cycling away from her he would sing a love song, and this would tell her how he felt about her.

> The heath was green on Carraig Donn,
> Bright shone the sun o'er Ard na Lee,
> The dark green trees bent trembling down
> To kiss the slumbering Owenabwee,
> That happy day 'twas but last May,
> 'Tis like a dream to me,
> When Donall swore, aye o'er and o'er,
> We'd part no more, a stór mo chroí.

In reality, I was in the bog alone drawing out turf with an ass and cart and however intense and persistent the longings I never for a moment gave myself a chance with Bridie. I didn't even tell her or so much as contrive a meeting alone with her. But she was on my mind to such as an extent that I never actually noticed that every time I went to Newtown I met Betty Guiney. On the Sundays after Mass a gang of us would be hanging around Brosnan's Corner and she'd come to her door and call me over and ask me if I was going to the dance in Listowel tonight.

By seven o' clock Betty would be on the bar of my bike and, wind or rain, winter or summer, we'd cycle the seven miles to the dance in Listowel ...

My problem was that for my first ten years in school, I was at the back of the class. In the end I came to see myself as my teachers saw me and as everyone in my class saw me. Without knowing it, I made a compact with being last. And when, eventually, my exam results showed that I was first, I regarded it as a fraud. Nothing so trivial as a fact could give the lie to an old sense of myself.

Being last, it never occurred to me to put two and two together and conclude that Betty Guiney was fond of me. Even when she was on the bar of my bike and we were alone coming home from a dance in Listowel, and her hair was blowing back in my face, I never once leaned forward into it. (*Nostos*, pp. 17–18)

Even if there was no success with either Bridie or Betty, there were other achievements. Academically he was doing well at school, and there was also Gaelic football. In 1955/6 John was 'centreback and captain on the St. Michael's team that won the Kerry schools Dunloe Cup.'[9] He was tall and fit and skilful and enjoyed the outlet that football provided. These teenage years, from age fourteen to seventeen, were years of great and troubled growing. They were years of awakened sexual longing, of innocent daydreams, of expanding thinking, of trying to manage his sense of a pervasive loneliness in the world and, for want of any other way of dealing with things, of singing songs.

By the time I was fourteen I had cycled the road to Listowel into a particular sense of myself. To begin with, it was the road past Jack Scanlan's, Danny Shaun's, Richie Fitz's, Con Lynch's, Jim Joy's, Willie Welsh's, Paddy Culhane's, Molly Finucane's, Moss Keane's, Ned Spillane's. Between Spillanes and Flavin's at Dearg Owen Cross I crossed out of what we would all have thought of as our near neighbourhood, and somewhere there I would stop singing. The songs I sang had big, wide, open longings in them and that is why I sang them. I wanted the horizons of longing in those songs to lie down with the horizon of our world and make it less lonely. Singing those songs in the way that I sang them, I was trying to rescue a people up into their longings. I was trying to tell them that there was something more than bog sadness in the world. I was trying to tell them that there is something more than the blowing wind and the wet rain. (*Nostos*, p. 24)

In singing songs, he was 'trying to make the world less lonely'. This deep compassion for the suffering of others, both of his human neighbours and of the animals in his father's cowshed, was at the very core of his being and was possibly the driving force of his entire life. 'I was trying to rescue a people ... to tell them there was something more than bog-sadness in the world.' He did not attempt, or did not have the capacity, to protect himself from this sense of 'bog-sadness', in fact the image of the white, frightened head of Mary Ann Danny O', the sympathy that he felt for her and the personal pain it caused him, were ingrained in him for the rest of his life. For now, in order to counteract all of this pain and loneliness, the only response he had was to sing his songs, as loudly as he could, in an effort to make some difference, to provide some hope and healing and perhaps to ease his own pain. In the school that he was cycling towards he found some refuge from these bleak horizons in the poetry that he was studying – the pastoral idealised rural world of Milton's *Lycidas* and the romanticism of Wordsworth's Lucy poems where the natural world is a world of 'glade and bower', of 'floating clouds', where 'rivulets dance' and even storms have 'grace'.[10] But, in John's world:

> Mornings there were, when cycling between two bogs, I could see that it was all a lie.
>
> But I needed the lie.
>
> I needed to walk in his world with Lycidas.
>
> I needed to live next door to Lucy.
>
> I couldn't be always thinking about bad eggs in the hay, or bad meat in the Bridge Field. I couldn't always be thinking of a skinned calf falling across a woman's threshold. I couldn't always be thinking of a priest sitting down on thirteen rotten eggs within his own confession box. I couldn't always be thinking of the pig's last gurgle. I couldn't always be thinking of a young cock's head, gloriously combed and wattled, lying there like a living hallucination on our concrete kitchen floor.
>
> Walking with Lycidas. Living with Lucy.
>
> In reality, I'd find myself walking a stretch of his road with Paddy Culhane.
>
> In reality, I lived a few sad fields away from Mary Ann Danny O'.
>
> And nature had never called either the one or the other of them her darling.
>
> Instead, from inside them and from outside them, nature had havocked them and it showed.
>
> Passing his scraw hut in the morning, I would sometimes wonder about Paddy Culhane.
>
> Can anything lift his heart? I'd wonder.
>
> I'd wonder, but I wouldn't stop singing …
>
> It was a terrible thought, but I thought it: maybe Paddy Culhane and Mary Ann Danny O' have gone so far down that even the Mass with all its Gethsemane and Good Friday depths can no longer reach them or even see them.
>
> The thought of depths too deep for Christ, too deep for God, that was a thought I couldn't live with. (*Nostos*, p. 26)

So, while the refuge that was English poetry was sometimes a bit threadbare, and singing songs not particularly effective, the larger refuge, the sheltering refuge of a great religion, was still available to him, even while he was wondering if it could bring much comfort to Paddy Culhane and Mary Ann Danny O'. It was not that he was particularly pious, if anything there was a healthy irreverence in the house, but what his school catechism gave him was a story and a structure that made sense of the world. According to that story, in 4004 B.C. God created the world. It was 'a tidy world', 'a drama in five acts, the acts being Creation, Fall, Revelation, Redemption and Last Things', and along with the sacraments and the ten commandments, this was the framework within which people lived. The sacraments brought a sense of splendour and wonder into otherwise ordinary lives and the commandments according to John 'could be compared to traffic rules', if you obeyed these rules you would eventually be rewarded with eternal bliss, if you did not obey you ran the risk of damnation. It was a simple story and it sufficed, at least until he was seventeen. It was then that the cataclysm happened. A classmate, Jack Brennan, acquired a copy of Darwin's *The Origin of Species,* banned in Ireland at that time and consequently of enormous interest to seventeen year old students in St. Michael's. John took it home and began to read.

> My father was sitting at the far side of the kitchen. Sometimes my father and his dog wouldn't only look at each other, they would seem to sit there conjuring each other across a limit of what was not normally possible between an animal and a human being. That is what they were doing now and I was happy to leave them to it, because for ten hours a day for the past three days, Darwin was guiding me into disaster. (*Nostos*, p. 18)

Coming to the geological chapters in the book, the enormity of what he was reading hit him, it was not four thousand years since Creation, it was hundreds of millions of years, and suddenly 'my world, like a boat, was opening at the seams, and it was taking in water, abyssal water'.

> I had grown up believing that the world had been made by a loving, providentially caring God in 4004 BC. ... now ... I hung in infinite time and in what quite possibly was also infinite space. Add me to whatever surrounded me and it wasn't richer, subtract me from it and it wasn't poorer. In whatever it was I was surrounded by I was neither minus nor plus. I was nothing. (*What the Curlew Said*, p308)

He wondered if, in the face of such vastness, he could hold onto his mind.

> It occurred to me that I should read the passage to my father, but looking across at him, I sensed that a gulf had opened between us.
> I got up and went out into the yard. It was a wild night, the wind squalling from the west, and now, for the first time in my life, I found myself hanging in a kind of infinite isolation in infinite space, and there was nothing, nothing, nothing I could now, or ever, do about it.

Providentially, I believe, giving my mind something normal to be normal with, I saw a piece of paper blowing across the yard. Instinctively I followed it, across the lawn, across the road, and it was only when a twisting gust of wind lifted it and carried it up over the hedge into Welsh's field that I stopped, in one way stopped, because years later, I was still following it in my mind, hoping that it would guide me past the lost God to a God I could once again believe in.

It was my calamity that I had fallen out of my story. I had fallen out of a world into a universe that seemed infinitely indifferent, even hostile, to my purposes and yearnings.

And the killingly lonely thing was, I didn't know of anyone else to whom this had happened. As far as I could see, it was an utterly unique calamity. It only deepened my calamity whenever I attempted to talk to someone about it. (*Nostos*, pp. 20–21)

The extent of his distress was noticeable. The heart for football went out of him and weeks later the president of St. Michael's, Fr. Dan Long, confronted him, asking if anything was up with him because he looked so distraught. He didn't talk to him, because he knew that no help could come from within 'the old orthodoxies'. 'I didn't tell him that, having crashed into Professor Ramsay's sums, my world, my biblical world, had gone to the bottom.' He felt there was no help anywhere, and in one sense he says, felt even more bereft than Job 'because all else having failed, there was no God that I could appeal to'. In a history lesson he found an image for his distress. The destruction of the Aztec empire by Cortez and his men began in 1519 AD but in the Aztec calendar this became Year One Reed. 'It was the year in which they lost their religion, their culture, their world. Something like that has happened to me, I thought. I've undergone a Year One Reed.' This insight, 'that I had fallen out of my story' was in a sense to possess him for the rest of his life.[11]

What I didn't know then … is that something not entirely unlike what had happened to me had happened to hundreds of millions of people across the planet. Native Americans, north and south, had been made to fall out of their stories. Australian Aborigines were made to fall out of their stories as were most of the peoples of the Pacific. The story that Europeans had found shelter and meaning in had opened at the seams and was drawing sinking abyssal water. All across the Soviet Union peoples had been made to fall out of their traditional stories. Similarly in China and in Vietnam.

People falling out of their story, that for most human beings was the story of our time. (*What the Curlew Said*, pp. 308–9)

He continued in this calamitous state, alone and not talking to anyone about it 'for three dreadful years'.

Those three years were eventful in many ways. He sat the Leaving Certificate with little or no idea of what he would do with himself after it. At that time, for young men in rural Ireland who were educated to Leaving Cert level, but from outside the professional classes, there were few opportunities. The Civil Service, the police force, or the 'call to teacher training'[12] were the usual career paths. The really coveted one was 'the call to training'. If you got that it was perceived that 'you were made for life'. Yet again, to his own surprise, John got and accepted the 'call' to St. Patrick's Teacher Training College in Dublin. Even in his lengthy autobiography *Nostos* John wrote very little about the two years he spent there, certainly the existential questions he was now asking were not being addressed. John McGahern, who had been a student in this very Catholic establishment four years earlier, complained about the prevailing atmosphere of 'anti-intellectualism'. John remarked years later that his abiding memory of the place was of his own loneliness. He didn't meet anyone else that had 'fallen overboard in the way that I had fallen overboard ... but I joined in the world and played football' and since 'no-one copped on and said you're in the wrong place John,' he passed his exams and qualified as a national school teacher.

He did take on one or two teaching positions, but very soon he began to realise 'sure, Jesus, I'm not cut out for this at all, not because I wouldn't like the kids but because of the hunger that's in me, the hunger for knowledge, the hunger for something ... ', and much to the disappointment of Mary Moriarty he arrived home and went footing turf in the bog with his father. He had by now realised that the answers to the questions he was struggling with could possibly be found in books, already he had found both encouragement and relief in Herman Melville's *Moby Dick*, which he read during the Christmas holidays in his first year at training college.

> Given what ailed me I could be given no better Christmas gift than this, the knowledge that someone else had experienced the shudder and the horror, the knowledge that someone else's world had opened at the seams and left him to fend for himself in the purely unseeing, purely unknowing overwhelming of Saturn's grey chaos.[13]

What *Moby Dick* enabled him to see was that 'I wasn't eccentric and I wasn't daft'. It also contributed to the hunger that was in him, if there was one book out there that was addressing the big questions, there must be more, there must be places where he could devote himself to following that piece of paper so tantalisingly carried away from him by the 'blowin' wind'. So that day in the bog, while eating their lunch in the high heather, John asked his father the extraordinary question.

'Would you give me the money to go to University?'

He was as surprised by the question as I was, because people from our background wouldn't think of going to university.

'Is that what you want?' he asked, holding his nerve.

'Yes'

'So you don't like the teaching?'

'It isn't so much that. It's a hunger that's in me.'

'Did you ever change your mind about settling on the land? If you did we could buy a second farm. There's one going at the moment, sixty acres for seventeen hundred pounds.'

'No. That doesn't interest me.'

'So it's university, is it?'

'Yes.'

'How much will it cost?'

'Three hundred pounds a year for three years. Nine hundred pounds.'

'That's alright then. We'll cycle to Listowel tomorrow.' (*Nostos*, pp. 23–24)

The shares that Jimmy had bought in the Standard Oil Company over thirty years previously were finally going to be cashed. These had always been untouchable, even in the years when things were going so badly on the farm that Jimmy had to go to England to work for part of the year, leaving Mary to manage all the work of home and farm; even when it broke his heart to leave his children (unable to say goodbye, he would get up in the night and head for Listowel, and in the morning when the children got up he would be gone); even then, the shares were for the future, and now, without any fuss, it seemed the time had come to cash them in. Jimmy recognised and accepted John's 'hunger'; this, after all, was the man who had spent his own life '*ag smaoineamh is ag machnamh dom féin*', thinking deeply to himself, over in his cowstall; the man who, coming in to the fire one evening having given his cows their last sop of hay for the night, said 'D'ya know John, I've come to th'end of thinkin' and I shtill haven't found th'answers'. So Jimmy understood. Understandably Mary had a very different attitude. She had no patience with this son of hers who should by now have a good job and be doing well for himself, and she certainly did not agree with the proposed waste of money. This time however she was overruled. In spite of her protests, the following day, dressed in their Sunday clothes, John and his father set off on their bikes for the bank in Listowel. The road to Listowel was yet again the beginning of one journey and the end of another.

Cycling past the stretch of bog on our right, Bridie Sullivan's house came into sight. I wouldn't be contriving to meet Bridie today and it wasn't very likely that Betty Guiney's bright hair would ever again blow back in my face. Betty was in England training to be a nurse and Bridie had entered a convent. And as for myself, well, having taken to wearing my hair long and having taken to books as much as I had, my mother told Gret Welsh that I didn't even look like a fact of life.

Reaching the brow of Donall Bill's hill, we knew from a long way off, from the bent gait of her on her bike, we knew that this was Mary Hegarty coming towards us.

To look at her, you would think that Mary Hegarty hadn't only been left behind by the modern world. She had been left behind by the ancient world as well ... It occurred to me once that she came into the world before fairy stories came into it ... And yet, there she was ... toiling up towards us on her bike, her little bag of shopping hanging from the handlebars.

Mary went to Mass every morning in the convent. Afterwards she'd have tea and toast with the nuns. And then, half-buried in ill-fitting hand-me-downs, she would cycle home.

I was always slightly afraid of Mary.

In conversation with her one day in her house she explained to me why she always sat so far back from her fire. That way, she said, it won't seem so cold when I go out.

She asked me if I'd like some Lourdes water.

I said I would.

'When did you go to Lourdes, Mary?' I asked.

'I do go every year. I do go by plane, for I love flyin'.'

If she had to, Mary would walk. Looking neither right nor left, to the centre of hell or to the centre of heaven, and having done what she'd had to do she'd come home unharmed ... Mary's sanctity made the sanctity of the recognised saints seem somehow suspect. (*Nostos*, p. 29)

Seeing her had set John to wondering about what Mary would make of the 'new sums' that were so bothering him, Bishop Ussher's calculations that put the world at 4004 years old, or the geologist Professor Ramsay's seemingly infinite ages. Somehow, it seemed unlikely that they could affect her at all.

'What is her secret?' I asked my father. We were sitting waiting to be served in John B. Keane's bar after we had concluded our transaction in the bank.

'Her secret', he said, 'is that she has never wanted to be a tree where only a bush will grow.'

Something in his tone of voice and in the way he looked at me suggested that his answer to my question was a warning, only very slightly disguised. (*Nostos*, p. 30)

3

'CHRIST, WHAT'S HAPPENING TO ME?'

UCD; disinherited and destitute; the sickness of the modern age; Cartesian clarity; ancient darkness; kathodos; Pasiphae and the Minotaur; the beast within.

Once enrolled in UCD John found a place to stay at 6, Church Avenue, Rathmines. The irony of the address was not lost on him, promising a kind of religious shelter he no longer believed was possible. He had been looking for something like a monastic cell, and this at least it did provide. The room was at 'earth level' at the back of the house away from the street and he sensed that 'when I wanted it I'd find silence and solitude here'. His room looked out on an enclosed garden and in that garden was a solitary apple tree. It was very much a city tree, pruned and elegant, so different to the old, wild lichened apple trees in Paddy Aherne's orchard, a long way from the weird and wonderful bogs and bushes of North Kerry and he wondered what he was doing to himself. Why was he here and not there, and in answer he realised that he was still following the scrap of paper that had blown across the yard on the night he had been devastated by reading Darwin. He was here and not there because he was relentlessly looking for answers.

During the two years in St. Pat's and working during the holidays in London he had had access to books and had read extensively. In his quest for understanding he had read history, he had read science, he had read psychology; he was familiar with the theories of Albert Einstein and Sigmund Freud but he was no nearer to an understanding of the universe that could make that universe bearable. Science and psychology, Einstein's infinite space and Freud's concept of ego, id and superego, were a terrifying explanation of man and his destiny. Their theories brought no comfort, no sheltering. The sense of catastrophe that he experienced on reading Darwin had only been further compounded. The bleakness of the new world view was shockingly articulated for him by the astronomer Sir James Jeans:

'We have tumbled, as though through error, into a world which by all the evidence was not intended for us. We cling to a fragment of a grain of sand until such time as the chill of death shall return us to primal matter. We strut for a tiny moment upon a tiny stage, well knowing that all our aspirations are doomed to ultimate failure, and that everything we have achieved will perish with our race leaving the universe as though we had never existed. The universe is indifferent and even hostile to every kind of life.'[1]

'This', John would say, 'was worse, much worse, than finding bad eggs in our hay. This was the second law of thermodynamics,[2] and there was no Jameen Kissane who could eat and digest this bone. And there was no God. And there was therefore no deliverance.' (*Nostos*, p. 31)

This was not a realisation he could easily live with and it added to his sense of destitution. 'Our universe is going to burn out, literally burn out, and there will be a final total cold, a cold that will be absolutely inhospitable to life. All our achievements, our music, our loves, our hates, everything we read and appreciate, Shakespeare, Yeats ... all of that will vanish and it will be as though we had never existed. The whole thing is going to end up in a kind of nihil, a kind of nothing. Add me to the universe and the universe isn't any richer, subtract me from the universe and the universe isn't any poorer, I have no significance. My love for the woman I might secretly have hopes about, that isn't significant, none of my moods or passions or thoughts is significant, they are all under sentence of annihilation ... That, for me, was a difficult place to be. It was a place that you might go mad in, this endless machine of a universe. And it was a machine, and the orthodox way, the respectable way of talking about the universe was that it was a purely mechanical system, destined for annihilation.'[3]

So far, his reading had only confirmed the sense of himself, already imagined in history class in St. Michael's: 'I was an Aztec. A European Aztec.' Just as the Aztecs had been disinherited, he had been disinherited, and it didn't matter that the religious view he had grown up with might have been a delusion, it was nonetheless a delusion that provided a shelter, it gave purpose and significance:

Disinheritance from delusion is still disinheritance. And it is when disinheritance is radical that the truly dreadful can happen. With that I felt that I had the key to what happened in Europe in the last three centuries. Europeans didn't only disinherit Aztecs and Incas. Continuously, since the sixteenth century, we have been disinheriting ourselves. (*Nostos*, p. 23)

'We have been disinheriting ourselves'. Our science, our psychology, our philosophy, having undermined the religious account of the world, had replaced that account with theories based on reason and scientific thinking. This, in John's view, was an extraordinary impoverishment, not because the theories were incorrect, but because the world view that they present is terrifying for us to grasp and, in his view, detrimental to our humanity and possibly to our sanity. 'The most awful thing you can suffer from', he would often say, is to suffer from complete meaninglessness.' He thought again of Mary Hegarty, of how Mary survived

> Mary had never heard of Ptolemy, she had never heard of Plotinus, and other than that there was a plough in it she knew little else about the night sky. In relation to what for her was important, Mary had no further figuring out to do. Down here was the earth, up there was the heavens. Down here was exile, up there was the life of glory ... Whatever the weather, Mary always made it to Mass, and I only had to imagine her cycling past Donall Bill's on Christmas morning to see what I'd lost the night I'd collided with the new sums. Having the Mass to go to and having a rosary beads in the pocket of her hand-me-down apron, Mary was fit.
>
> In the brutal Darwinian sense she was fit, and she would come through. Having collided with the sums I couldn't say the same for myself. Nor could I indeed say the same for humanity generally. There is a necessary amnesia to what is the case psychologically inside us and to what is the case astronomically outside us. (*Nostos*, pp. 38–40)

Mary survived because she had the shelter of traditional religion and story, her world made sense. For those without that story the only way to survive was with a 'necessary amnesia', a blocking out of what Freud tells us we psychologically are and also of what science tells us about the universe in which we live. John did not have that capacity for amnesia, and as there was no possibility of going back to the pre-Darwinian world of his childhood, the church that so sheltered Mary Hegarty could no longer shelter him. The really sad thing, he felt, was that the Christian Church 'had refused to embark on the modern voyage'.[4]

It had been refusing it ever since 'it refused to look through Galileo's telescope, calling it a devil's tube,[5] ever since it had seen to it that Giordano Bruno was burned at the stake, ever since it had, initially at least, refused Darwin's voyage to the Galapagos Islands. In John's view, this refusal to grapple with the new knowledge has had extremely serious consequences. Those who could no longer accept the traditional Christian world view fell away from the Church, and 'therefore, tended also to fall away from Christ. I did.'[6] So, for John, there was in a sense a triple dilemma; he had lost the story that said that the world is a harmonious cosmos created by God; he had to contend with an infinite universe that 'started with a Big Bang and would end with a Big Crunch'; and consequently religion in general and Christianity in particular no longer had any sheltering to offer him. He truly was man overboard.

But he did now recognise that he was not in a unique position. His reading had led him beyond Melville and *Moby Dick*; he had found 'Kepler's horror at finding himself wide awake in a universe that had neither centre nor circumference'; he had found Blaise Pascal who reflected that 'man is equally incapable of seeing the nothingness from which he came, and the infinite in which he is engulfed' and who admitted 'the eternal silence of those infinite spaces strikes me with terror'; he had found Matthew Arnold's poem *Dover Beach*:

> The Sea of Faith
> Was once, too, at the full, and round earth's shore
> Lay like the folds of a bright girdle furled.
> But now I only hear
> Its melancholy, long, withdrawing roar,
> Retreating, to the breath
> Of the night wind, down the vast edges drear
> And naked shingles of the world.

He now believed that he was suffering from what he called 'the sickness of the modern age'[7] and would often think of something Christ had said: 'the birds of the air have nests, foxes have holes, but the son of man has no where to lay his head.'[8] For John this meant that he himself had 'no where *inside* his head to lay his head', there were simply no answers. It was in this condition that he approached his studies in philosophy and logic in UCD, in the hope that he would find some remedy, 'somewhere to lay his head'. Coming from the wilds of North Kerry, regardless of how bleak and wet and windy they were, made Dublin a difficult place in which to live.

> Dublin has its moments, people would say. So far I hadn't encountered them. The river had given up. It no longer brought anything of the gentle wildness of the Wicklow hillsides and bogs down into the city ... it was a mortuary slab between granite embankments ... Having its bubbling crystal source in the Wicklow hills, the Liffey was in pure trouble by the time it reached Kingsbridge ...
> And it frightened me to think that after so many years in school our minds were as engineered as canal water was. And remembering a suburban garden I had seen, it didn't entirely comfort me to think that, in the course of our

institutional growing, we too had been subjected to the savageries of Euclidean shaping, to the savageries in our deepest inwardness, of psychic topiary.[9] (*Nostos*, pp. 41–2)

Nor was there any reprieve from ugliness in the architecture of UCD.

Approaching it on that first morning in early October, the main university building... hurt me in my chest and in my spirit.

And the killing thing was it was made of limestone.

Limestone suggested the Burren ...

In the Burren in North Clare the carboniferous is full of wild grykes and in the deep shelter of them there are flowers that seem to say – at least to me they seem to say – that inside us somewhere Paradise has never been lost. (*Nostos*, pp. 32, 45)

But there was no sign of Paradise in this apparently soulless building, and there was no sign of any soul left in the river, and the canal made him shudder in that it suggested an even deeper trouble, of minds being engineered by schooling, by education, by the destructive, deadening impact of 'human intention and purpose'. This was not a nourishing and healing environment. And unfortunately, life inside the building was no better.

Having found, from early on, that the university lecturers were addressing themselves to questions that didn't much interest me, I had decided to go my own way. (*Nostos*, p. 35)

He elaborated on this sense of dissatisfaction in a talk given in 1983. Almost every experience in Dublin gave him a sense of a world that was trying to suffocate him. It was not alone the manicured hedges, the citified solitary apple tree, the eight-by-eight bedsit and the lack of wild spaces that contributed to this feeling. It was the sense of getting 'tidy answers to tidy questions. The kind of questions that I want to ask are much more awkward like 'is pain fundamental to the structure of the universe?' but to ask that would be bad manners ... the kind of questions that I need to ask I can't ask ... it seemed to me that I wasn't gaining anything by coming to Dublin to study philosophy, I was losing things.'[10] He felt he was becoming small and that he would have to battle against what he dubbed 'the bedsitter mentality' he was in danger of developing. He was also battling against the seductive world of appearances, of buying into social expectations, of becoming 'an accomplice with all the agencies and forces and mechanisms within my society that would make me small.' One of the biggest battles was against what he called 'Cartesian clarity', a phrase he used to describe modern philosophical thinking that insisted that all knowledge was based on intellectual reasoning alone.

> I resisted the call to Cartesian clarity. In an argument one day with three other students, I had insisted that there is a night knowing, a knowing not narrowed by ... intellect ... I was trying to tell them that there was much to which they were blinded by their own brightness. It had never occurred to them that intelligence as intellectually conscripted as theirs could be an eclipse ...
>
> Very obviously, I had at this hour of my life neither the patience nor the temperament to be a good and dutiful student. I wasn't, quite simply, well-bred enough for seminars ... any room that I couldn't talk about Mary Hegarty in, couldn't talk about Mary Ann Danny O' in, was a room I couldn't flourish in. (*Nostos*, pp. 39, 47)

What John is resisting here is a call into a world which appeared to take no account of his experience of life as he had known it in North Kerry, a world where what he calls 'night knowing' had its proper place, where it was accepted that there were things that went beyond the realms of reason, of logic and of argument. A world where light and dark could intermingle and where shadows could contain and accommodate both mysteries and miracles.

> It was a great good fortune that I grew up in a house that had an open turf fire and a paraffin lamp. That meant the darkness was never banished, not even when the fire blazed and the lamp burned with a perfectly steady, flat-topped double flame. And I'm not just talking about the darkness in our house. I am talking about whatever ancient darkness was in our minds. That ancient darkness wasn't synonymous with ignorance. It was neither the source nor the seat of ignorance ... In our house it didn't make sense to talk about an enmity between light and dark. (*Nostos*, p. 47)

'Whatever ancient darkness was in our minds ... was neither the seat nor the source of ignorance...' Of this he was convinced, and at a level that was as deep as the darkness itself, at a level deeper than reason, he believed that we have to work with, and not against, this darkness. In fact we have to go down into it moving very cautiously and carrying only a very soft light. Philosophies that sought either to banish it or to brighten it prematurely would cause nothing but trouble. Philosophies that relied solely on the reasoning, logical, proof-driven, progress-loving side of our minds would only do more harm than good. This intuitive sense of ancient, mysterious darkness, rich in possibility but beyond understanding by the power of reason alone, would fascinate and inspire him throughout his life. Perhaps Rilke is expressing a similar sense:

> You darkness, that I come from,
> I love you more than all the fires
> that fence in the world,
> for the fire makes
> a circle of light for everyone,
> and then no one outside learns of you.
>
> But the darkness pulls in everything:
> shapes and fires, animals and myself,
> how easily it gathers them! –
> powers and people –
> and it is possible a great energy
> is moving near me.
> I have faith in nights.[11]

However the academic world of UCD was not receptive to John's sense that there could be a troubled but healing darkness, it was not receptive to stories about Mary Hegarty and Mary Ann Danny O', it did not want to hear about a river that had lost its soul, and it gave scant regard to the world of story and myth. In St. Michael's in Listowel, the Greek myths had fascinated him and the fascination had continued. He says of them that 'they gave me the language with which to name myself to myself, without them I would be 'a landfish, languageless'.[12] Clearly he was an outsider. Fortunately, he was an outsider with a healthy disregard for even the most respected authority, and with a remarkable loyalty to the reality of his Moyvane childhood, he found no option but to steer his own course.

> In this I had something in common with quite a few others. ... on most mornings some 4 or 5 of us would meet and we would live for a charmed hour or two by the light of our own slightly bleeding desires. Almost always after lunch I would break away and go by routes direct or indirect to the National Library ... If at the end of a day's reading I had a new image or a new metaphor to walk up Rathmines Road with I was happy. I much preferred to go home with a metaphor than to go home with an argument. (*Nostos*, pp. 35, 40)

That first year in UCD, he did live 'like a Carthusian' in his room on the

Rathmines Road. He would return home at about five in the evening, bringing the new images from his day's reading with him. Then he would spend time in the silence and solitude of his room, 'in séance' not only with the new images but with 'my own depths', or allowing 'my depths to be in séance with me'. By now he was writing stories and poems and this environment suited him. He was suffering from dejection, from disillusioning, from a sense of godlessness and there were times when he was aware of 'menacing inwardness'[13] which both troubled and fascinated him. To explain it he returned to a word he had learned in his Greek class in school. '*Kathodos*', the word for the road down into the underworld, came to describe this process of looking inwards, of exploring his psyche and of what might possibly lie beneath or beyond psyche. 'For me, because it was the road to my room, Rathmines Road, was a kind of *kathodos*.'[14]

This *kathodos*, this journey into himself, was also overshadowed by Darwin and *The Origin of Species*. The theory of evolution had shattered the concept of the Biblical God, and consequently shattered the concept of man made in the image and likeness and goodness of that God. Man had evolved from the animals, and animal nature was instinctively and dangerously alive in him. In a talk given after the publication of *Nostos*, John had this to say about what he calls 'the beast within': 'I know what might happen if the beast was ever at large in myself. It's there in the headlines of every paper. It probably heads every news bulletin that we hear around the world. The beast at large in the human. We have this sense from the Bible that we were a special creation on the sixth day, but now the theory of evolution has questioned that ... I now know that I have the eye teeth of an ape, of a carnivore, I eat the way carnivores eat; the sexual instinct, the reproductive instinct, I share with animals. I breathe in the way animals breathe, I sleep the way animals sleep, most of me, most of who I am, I have in common with the animals. The animal, in other words, is alive and well in me ... The animal we can live with mostly, but when the animal becomes beast in us we are in huge trouble. Because when the beast is at large great havoc can be done, havoc in society, havoc in marriages, havoc everywhere, havoc, when the beast is at large.'[15]

Here again he was dealing with enormous issues. There was no God and there was therefore no soul, no sin, no devil, no heaven, no hell, and no redemption. Human beings are animals in a godless universe and while as a species they might classify themselves as *Homo sapiens sapiens*, and glory in Aristotle's definition of man as a rational animal, there was nothing sapient or wise or rational about their behaviour towards each other or towards the earth. He was reading philosophy, he was reading history. He had found Nietzsche, who had not only declared the death of God, but who also said 'I have discovered for myself that the old human and animal life, indeed the entire prehistory and past of all sentient being, works on, loves on, hates on, thinks on, in me.' In *Dreamtime* he himself put it succinctly, 'I am all too aware a carnivore's dentition beat the Beatitudes to a place in my head.'[16] Thinking of the Coliseum, of the Inquisition, of the bloody aftermath of revolutions in France and in Russia, of human beings mixed to anonymity in the mud of Flanders, thinking of Dresden, of Katyn Forest, of Auschwitz with its *nacht und nebel* trains, he realised that human beings, in their so called civilizations, are guilty of 'savagery more frightful because more poisoned than anything we are likely to encounter in the wild' (*Nostos*, p. vii).

This was a feature of the 'menacing inwardness' with which he was grappling. Strangely, this awareness co-existed with that other sense of inner depth mentioned earlier, the 'ancient darkness in our minds', a darkness that reason could not penetrate and that animal nature did not affect, something that went beyond 'the end of the psyche'. To explain all of this fully he had to resort to the Greek myths. One of the stories that recurs again and again in his writings is that of Pasiphae and the bull. Pasiphae was a goddess, daughter of the Sun and married to King Minos of Crete. Because of a curse placed on her by Poseidon, the god of the sea, she had regressed to animal nature in her, and was overcome with lust for, and mated with, a magnificent white bull that had been sent as a gift from the gods. Their offspring was the Minotaur, a bull-chested, bull-shouldered, bull-headed child. In shame at her lust and at her infidelity, and seeking a hiding-place for him she went to the skilful Daedalus. His solution was an ingenious creation:

> He would excavate an a-mazing labyrinth under the city and in the last and deepest cavern of it he would impound the monster ... Thus suppressed, the Minotaur turned turbulent. Sometimes, his anger and his frustration building to earthquake intensity, he would shake civilisation ... (*Nostos*, p. 116)

To appease him he must be fed or he would destroy the Cretan world; his fodder must be human and so, from his subject peoples, King Minos demanded virginal boys and girls as meat for the monster. In a particular year when it was the turn of Athens to dispatch this heartbreaking cargo, the young king, Theseus, decided to act. He joined the sacrificial ship and set out to kill the Minotaur. He faced a double task, he must not only slay the beast but he must negotiate the intricacies of the Labyrinth, from whose complicated depths no-one, notwithstanding the beast, had ever re-emerged. Luck was with him. Ariadne, eldest daughter of Pasiphae, and therefore half-sister to the Minotaur, fell in love with Theseus and advised that, as well as his sword, he take with him a ball of thread, unwinding it as he entered and rewinding it to retrace his way out. Thus equipped, with sword and thread, he killed the Minotaur. In retelling the story, John imagines a conversation between Theseus and Ariadne. In it, Ariadne accepts that her brother, the Minotaur, poses an enormous threat but has reservations about the murderous solution.

> 'The road to the Labyrinth calls for a new kind of heroism ... so you aren't the best man for this task. You are merely the best there is, at the moment. And your solution, which is murder, that too is merely the best there is, at the moment.'
> 'So you think it's murder, do you?'
> 'It is murder, yes. And the pity of it is, a murdered Minotaur isn't the end of the Minotaur.'
> 'Tell me why not.'
> 'To kill a monster is to sow him back into the earth. With each new killing he becomes more copiously virulent ... (*Nostos*, pp. 117–18)

He has Ariadne go on to say that what has come into full view in the Minotaur, animal savagery, is latent in every human being 'and the degree of latency depends only on the situations we have or haven't found ourselves in.' In his preface to *Nostos*, John explained that there are three types of myths – myths that are self portraits of our instincts; creation myths; and myths that institute the basic elements of culture. The myth of Pasiphae and the Minotaur is of the first type, it is an exploration of what he elsewhere calls our lower nature, animal nature in us, or to put it more scientifically, 'all that we phylogenetically are', all that we have inherited from our evolutionary past.

Pasiphae, the Minotaur, Theseus and Ariadne are all aspects of every individual; the myth enacts impulses and drives that are inherent, universal, and potentially dangerous, impulses which need to be understood and integrated if they are not to become utterly destructive. For John, every aspect of the Pasiphae myth becomes a metaphor to explain himself and humanity in general. The story illustrates the consequences of serious selfishness and transgression, of giving in to an animal impulse – Pasiphae; of the then disastrous attempt to suppress or manipulate the outcome of such transgression- the Minotaur – something of which we are ashamed becomes hidden but will erupt intermittently in our lives and cause terrible damage; and Theseus is that aspect of the individual, or the culture, that attempts to completely annihilate and deny all that is animal in us. In Ariadne's final words of warning, the savage retribution exacted by Theseus, is frighteningly not the end of the story: 'a murdered Minotaur is not the end of the Minotaur'. What is repressed will not heal but fester. On top of all of these, or perhaps beneath them, is the metaphor of the Labyrinth, a maze so complicated that it was utterly impossible to negotiate its depths. For John, it became the symbol for the human psyche and Ariadne's ball of thread became the faculties (sometimes our senses, sometimes intuition, sometimes logical reasoning) with which we attempt to understand ourselves and our world. To healthily negotiate the labyrinth a thread becomes infinitely more useful and powerful than a sword.

This was the labyrinth of the self that he was exploring in his room on the Rathmines road, where he was coming face-to-face with the totality of human nature, but he suspected that there was also something else going on, a dimension of the self that Ariadne's ball of thread could never reach.

> 'And as for the ball of thread Ariadne had given to Theseus –fully unwound it would only reach the end of the Labyrinth, but I had long ago seen, – in a dream I had seen –that the end of the Labyrinth isn't the end of the psyche and the end of the psyche isn't the end of what we inwardly are. (*Nostos*, p. 53)

He was convinced that there is more to human beings than everyday consciousness can know. When the light of the mind gives out, that's where the wonder begins, where what he called the 'mirum' begins. Wonder, 'mirum' in the 'deep below all depths'; the potential as well as the danger of what lies within; the danger of expression and the danger of repression; these concerns were to occupy him for the rest of his life. He recognised, even then, in his very early twenties, that in all of this 'I was responding to a need. A need altogether deeper sometimes than my need for human companionship' and he spent many evening hours in the silence of his room 'in séance' with what he sensed as a rich darkness. Fortunately however, both for his sanity and his sense of perspective, there was a safety valve, and the practical common sense of his mother breaking out in him, he admits 'mostly though, I was aware of menace, and whenever I felt threatened, I gave up.'[17]

In spite then of the inhospitable city environment and of the semi-reclusive aspect of some of his time there, the years in UCD, from 1959 to 1962, were enormously enriching, both intellectually and socially. The 'Carthusian cell' on the Rathmines Road was not always monastic; there was a wide circle of friends, there were dances, there were sessions in Neary's and McDaid's, there were profound and interminable philosophical conversations, there were poetic contributions to student magazines, there were summers spent working in London, there was long hair and a flowing overcoat, and there was 'Lydia Carlyle'.

It will be remembered that in his teens, when it came to his relationships with women, John had been both hopelessly romantic and gloriously unsuccessful. This was partly because of his old sense of himself as a failure, of always being at the back of the class, but it was also due to the indoctrination of Church and of school.

In spite of a farming background, in spite of the healthy earthiness and humour of his home, in spite of the timely advice of Jameen Kissane, somewhere powerfully at the back of his mind was the deeply internalised message that instinctive energies and impulses were incompatible with Christian living, that these were part of something called 'lower nature' and best repressed. He remembered at seventeen or eighteen imagining himself standing outside the church and calling out 'Is there welcome for me in this house?' And the answer he imagined coming back to him from those inside was 'In so far as you're good, there's welcome for you in this house.' This was an instinctively crippling message and, for a few years, the source of a turbulent struggle. The church that could not accommodate Galileo, Copernicus, Newton, Darwin and so many more, could not accommodate human sexuality either.

This struggle was finally overcome during one of his summers in London. He had taken a job working on the conveyor belt in Wall's ice-cream factory in North Acton and found accommodation in Shepherd's Bush. Any free time was spent scouring bookshops, frequenting the British Museum, the Planetarium and the Natural History Museum while also attempting to fathom the world of the poet William Blake. This was the author of *Songs of Innocence and Experience* and in spite of all its warnings on the outcome of 'experience', John was in search of sexual experience at least, as he would laughingly say years later, 'I didn't only go to London for culture, like.' One evening, with that in mind, he took the number of a London call girl from a public notice board and eventually made the call.

> When I did phone her, she asked me, as though we had known each other all our lives, to bring her some chips.
>
> She was a woman you'd hope would give you a second look at a party and from the beginning I felt that she had an easy-going, almost sumptuous hospitality to human need.
>
> After talking for a couple of hours, we both knew that what we expected would happen, couldn't now happen. Something spoken but not yet openly spoken between us had to be protected, and she knew how, saying it is late, but I see you have my phone number on the cover of your book. (*Nostos*, p. 55)

His first attempt to gain sexual 'experience' had been thwarted, probably by two things. Apart from the comical 'bag of chips', his innate capacity for real relationship with everyone he met did not allow him to commodify this woman, he could not see her simply as a 'call girl'; instead he had ended up talking for hours, something that never was any bother to him. Also something of the old conditioning reasserted itself. He left her feeling that 'grace had mastered instinct', repression and indoctrination had triumphed once again. However on his return from a trip to Greece that same summer, a journey he would compare to 'a kind of pilgrimage', he did finally overcome the inhibitions, he did contact her again and this time freed himself from at least some element of troubled and repressive inwardness. Back in Dublin later in the year, he had the confidence to respond to the overtures of Lydia Carlyle. It is perhaps best to let him tell the story as he told it in one of his post-*Nostos* talks. In the talk he had been elaborating on the consequences of the second law of thermodynamics, and agonising about human insignificance in the universe, when, eyes dancing with humour and mischief, he continued:

But of course like, instincts are instincts aren't they? And it's hard to subvert them isn't it? And I'm one day standing in the main hall in UCD and there's a few of us there, being, I suppose, existentially anxious, the kind of thing that you'd be at that age, our emotions slightly bleeding, when Lydia Carlyle comes out of a lecture and she begins to tell us that she is endlessly weary of French irregular verbs. And she's standing there talking to us, and she talks quite a bit about irregular French verbs, but I'm picking up this word irregular. And I'm thinking irregularity, and maybe of the joys of irregularity as well as the difficulties of irregularity, and maybe Lydia means more than she's saying here.

Then she picks an apple out of her bag and being bold, and in a sense almost wanting to say that I'm a bad girl, she just takes a bite out of her apple and then, in front of everyone, invites me to have a bite of the apple. Well, I think what anyone would think in that situation; this is an old, old scenario after all. But I also know Lydia and I know that she's not going to be won easily. Inviting her to see *Wild Strawberries* in the Plaza Cinema below in the Quays isn't exactly going to win her heart. She's going to take some real poetry or something, something fairly big like, so my initial way of maintaining her interest in me is that I basically disappear for three or four days and I don't let her catch any sight of me at all.

I make myself hard to get in a way, but then I show up and I tell her that I did Greek in Listowel like, and there are some mighty irregular verbs in Greek and I decline the verb 'horao', 'to see', and I leave it at that. Now she knows that I know about irregularity too. A day or two later, meeting her near the Parthenon pillars in the portico of UCD I tell her that the word 'parthenos' was one of the first words I learned in Greek, and that it means virgin, and that the Parthenon is a temple to the virgin Athena. Now the way I'm talking, it looks like irregularity might be getting somewhere, because she looks at me kinda wonderfully and she says,

'And are you, are you parthenos?'

'Well, maybe not,' I say

'Who is she?' she asks

And I tell her that it was a call girl in London, and I then talk about the Burren in Clare and the gorgeous paradisal flowers to be found in the limestone grykes there. And this is the way I'm trying to woo Lydia, hoping that we might go home and be irregular with each other ... and in a couple of days we do go home together and we are wonderfully joyfully regular with one another. There is, of course, nothing irregular at all.[18]

And so, after that gloriously stage-managed and pedantic courtship, he wants to write love poetry. And he searches for images with which to express joy and love and beauty, which the drastically engineered city cannot provide and the only image modern science can provide is to tell him that his girlfriend is merely 'transformed groceries'.[19] But he knows that there is a mysterious beauty in a hawk on the Dublin mountains and in heather on the Wicklow hills and in sunlight catching the bronze of a deer in the Phoenix Park. And while this perception of beauty cannot prove a whole lot, for a while he is delighted with the power of the sexual instinct to overcome the modern scientific view of who we are and what the universe is. Just as he had sensed some sort of 'mirum' or wonder in the depths below the psyche, he again senses some underlying 'mirum' in the world that science teaches is heading for annihilation. His poem becomes a prayer.

Since I cannot be a canal, find me acceptable as a wild river. Since I cannot be a Euclidean bush, find me acceptable as a wild whitethorn. Since I cannot be the kind of Christian who is willing to be nailed, ego and instinct to the cross, please, I beseech you, find me acceptable as the kind of Christian who, after a night in bed with her is able to say to Lydia Carlyle:

But I could tell Death

I have loved you and so

I am deeper than scythes ... (*Nostos*, pp. 43–44)

4

'A KILLED DRAGON ISN'T A DEAD DRAGON'

Greece; a big decision; anodos; keeping faith with bogdeal; the life of the world; Divine Ground; 'us and them'.

That summer spent working in Wall's ice-cream factory in London proved a turning point in many ways. It was the summer before he met Lydia Carlyle, it was the summer he spent in search of 'experience', and it was the summer of his trip to Greece.

> Towards the end of July I had lunch with Babs, my sister in London. She worked as an air-hostess with British United Airways. Looking at the books I had bought that morning, all of them books about ancient civilizations, she told me she could get me a cheap flight to somewhere within easy reach of one or another of them. I had no problems choosing which one, and that evening she phoned me to tell me that she had booked a return flight, open at both ends, to Athens, with a stop-over in Rome on the way back. (*Nostos*, p. 60)

The trip to Greece was not intended as a holiday. It might safely be said that John Moriarty never took a holiday in anything like the usual sense of that word. He spent his entire life on a quest to understand himself and the world in which he lived. Years later he told Andy O'Mahony 'I came from the bogs, I became a glutton for punishment like, I ravened through libraries, because I was hungry, not because I wanted to become an encyclopedia, but I was hungry to name myself, to speak myself to myself, and old myths and symbols, legends and stories were doing that for me, so I went through libraries seeking vocabulary, basically.'[1] His use of the word 'ravened' is well chosen. He was ravenous for knowledge, for ideas, for stories, and it is the nature of this kind of hunger that it can never be replete. 'The more I learn,' said Einstein, 'the more I realise how much I don't know.' Quite simply, John was always searching, always analysing, always dramatising, always in conversation with those he met on his journey who might furnish him with a new insight. It was insight more than knowledge that he sought, and in that search he never gave his head a holiday.

He made the trip to Greece on his own, with very little money, a sleeping bag and 'languageless' as far as modern Greek is concerned. He did have an initial sense of being knowledgeable about Greek history, art and culture. He had not cycled the road to Listowel for nothing! He admits 'I was a bit cocksure of myself, I thought I was well learned in the Greek culture' and he intended to 'judge the Greek achievement ... stand before statues ... say this or that about temples I visited. All the while imagining myself being overheard and admired by my friends ...' It did not turn out quite like that. On his very first morning, having arrived at 3:00 a.m. and sleeping for a while on a park bench, he awoke to his first view of the Parthenon, high in the distance, and utterly magnificent. All of the reproductions in the all of the books had not prepared him for the experience of it. He describes it as a blow, a shock. He had never expected it to stop him in his tracks. 'It shook a kind of secular impiety out of me ... it evoked a feeling of reverence in me ... I had come here in a lordly mood but now if I was anything I was a pilgrim, paying tribute.' (*Nostos*, pp. 61,64)

Awe at the beauty of it, reverence at the holiness of it, humility at the scale of it, 'I was beginning to have a sense of real divine presence, of holy height, and I wasn't ready for it. I needed to put something, a wall, between me and it, and so when, farther along the white street, I found a cafe had just opened, I went in. I was the first customer of the day and it suited me to sit in a corner with a cup of Turkish coffee and think things through.'[2] Here he realised that what he faced was a pinnacle of human achievement, a temple made by men to honour their goddess, Athena, and to John it represented all that is god-like in human beings. He imagined a conversation that another God might have had with Adam and Eve.

'I have done as much in six days as it was right and good that I should do. Yours is the seventh day, a day in which, imitating me, you can, if you will, do something splendid.' Like so many other peoples the ancient Greeks took up the challenge and even if we only had one surviving piece of sculpture to go by, that single draped figure from the east pediment of the Parthenon, even if we only had her, we would have to conclude that they had succeeded miraculously. (*Nostos*, p. 67)

Awareness of the glory of this achievement also had another effect. It rattled his confidence; he was from a world of turf and bogdeal that was light years from the marble of the Parthenon, and he had an impulse to turn around and go home. 'Coming as I do from the bogs of North Kerry, maybe I haven't eyes for Athens, shouldn't I stop thinking rather grandly of myself as an heir to ancient Mediterranean culture?'[3] And yet something else in him was suggesting that bogdeal and marble were not entirely incompatible, that the depths represented by the bogdeal and the heights represented by the marble, were only superficially opposites. Cutting turf in the bog had become his image for delving into all that we are in the deepest and oldest part of our nature, that aspect of ourselves that was 'below history'. Here in Greece he realised that in looking at 'all that we inwardly are' he had been inclined to overlook the tremendous capacity for greatness inherent in us. His encounters with Sir Charles Darwin and Sir James Jeans had undermined all optimism about the human species. The Parthenon challenged him to look again.

Already, while living on the Rathmines Road, he had experienced what he had called his *kathodos*, his journey into his own underworld. Now, in climbing the Acropolis towards the Parthenon, he felt he was in some way undergoing the opposite experience, what the Greeks called *anodos*, a journey or ascension upwards towards a possible enlightenment. He had read of the processions held in honour of Athena, now, as he approached the Parthenon, he imagined that he was walking in a procession of one. His purpose was to do reverence and give thanks. In the end, as though they were alive and could hear him, he directly addressed the Caryatids of the Erechtheion.[4] 'However ruined your world,' I said, 'and however weary you might be, I beseech you, please do continue to support the vision.' The vision he pleads for is a vision of a world where reverence and grace are paramount, where *kathodos* and *anodos* are the one road, where the divine potential that exists in human beings can flourish, and can integrate and possibly even absorb the more destructive impulses.

Even as he was climbing, and in spite of his prayer, he was aware that he was climbing among ruins. He knew that the glory of ancient Greece had collapsed because of wars between the city states, he knew that this divine temple had, in the seventeenth century, been used to store gunpowder and had been seriously damaged by cannonball fire, he knew that all the great ancient civilizations had ultimately been annihilated, but in his *anodos* he had rediscovered at least a sense of possibility. 'It was a question' he said, 'about our capacity to evolve.' Was there a way that Western humanity could escape the fate of our predecessors? Are we destined forever to aspire to greatness only to end by annihilating all that we achieve? Could we, he would later ask, learn to walk beautifully on the earth? For now, he could only struggle with the questions and the contradictions. And naturally, the Greek myths were never far from his mind. In the course of this adventure, which had now turned into a kind of pilgrimage, he decided to let the myths guide his journey.

He would travel, either walking or hitching, through the mountains of Nemea, he would visit Mycenae, he would cross the sea to Crete, all the time examining the stories associated with those places that he found not only fascinating but relevant. *Iphigenia at Aulis*, by the tragedian Euripides, tells a story of murder, rape, blood sacrifice and a doomed family, and even while studying it in St. Michael's, he had linked it to the killing of pig and hen in the yard at home. Now, making his way to Mycenae, where the story of Iphigenia is situated, he thought again about the murderous impulses that it dramatised, impulses that can overwhelm even the sanest person. 'All that has to happen is that a war should break out and I can pull a balaclava down over my face and turn myself into something worse than a reptile. I can go out and kill people. Look at what has happened in Europe during our century. We can do things that animals won't do at all.'[5]

He thought of Oedipus, whose story represents total ignorance of who we are and what we are capable of; of Actaeon whose pride caused his downfall; of Orestes and his capacity for vengeance; of Hippolytus who denied his own nature; of Medousa who turned the wonder of the world to stone; of the lust of Pasiphae; of the savagery of the imprisoned Minotaur; these he rehearsed on his very real journey to Crete, finding in them the mirrors of passions he recognised in himself. 'The road to the Labyrinth isn't measured in miles, it is measured in myths, every myth an *anagnorisis,* a discovery, of how much I have in common with Actaeon, with Oedipus, with Hippolytus, with Orestes, with Medousa and, very likely at the end of the road, with the Minotaur.' It was a difficult and unsettling journey and it presented a huge challenge.

In the first place it was a physical challenge. With very little money he was living on his wits, often helping himself to fruit from the farms he was passing. He was sleeping under the stars and the elements were not always kind:

> That night I was wakened by an onslaught of insurgent, savage thunder ... the universe had turned on itself. It was fracturing itself ... It snarled and fractured ... And then the rain. No. The water. Sheets of water ... In less than a minute I was wet to the skin. Getting out of the sodden sleeping-bag, I walked downhill a little way and sat on a rock ... Dawn was a long time coming. It was a long time too until there was enough heat in the sun to steam me dry. (*Nostos*, p. 87)

That was one extreme. He also suffered from the sun.

> Coming as I did from the northern temperate zone, I had only ever experienced encouragement and kindness in the sun. Here in Greece it was different. By mid-day the land was sun-savaged, and everywhere, snarling from every surface

was the tyranny of light ... Recovering from sunstroke and not having eaten for three days, I came by a mule track to a house in dazed country. I heard her before I saw her, an old woman coming round the gable of her house leading a donkey ... Her clothes, long-hanging and coarse, looked like hand-me-downs from the days before myths opened their half-animal, half-human eyes on the world ... In awkward sign language I asked her for something to eat. Coming back, deeply bent through her door, she gave me a side of bread and a slab of goat's cheese. (*Nostos*, 91, 131)

These extremes of weather and circumstances were reflected by the extremes he was struggling with in his head, how to reconcile the heights of the Parthenon with the depths of Mycenae, and this proved another and altogether greater challenge. Can we live with and as Minotaur without causing terrible damage to ourselves and others? More and more on this journey he was gaining awareness of the dangers of repression. He had seen it in the story of the Minotaur, instincts repressed turned savage; he saw it in the story of Perseus, who in order to defeat the sea-monster must become beast himself; it was absolutely clear in the story of Cadmus, the founder of Thebes. In order to build his city Cadmus had to kill the dragon, but as John was to repeat again and again in his writings 'a killed dragon isn't a dead dragon',[6] that which is brutally repressed, be it mythical monster, natural instinct or perceived enemy, it always will and always does, come back to haunt us.

It was not only the Greeks who slew their monsters; he thought of the familiar Roman Catholic statue of 'Mary, the new and victorious Eve, standing on the head of the Serpent'. He visualised what he now saw as the only possible outcome: 'As Mary laid her heel on it, crushing the Serpent's head, his tail grew into a new head, arrogant, and angry beyond anything I could ever have imagined.' It was absolutely clear to him that repression was counter-productive.

More than anything else now, I wanted to go back and stand in the river at home. This was the river that had carried the four bad eggs out of our land. It was the river we fished for eels in. Herakles had killed the lion ... Mary had crushed the Serpent. As a boy of seven, an Archangel Michael in my own eyes, I had taken on the eel and one day in delighted triumph, I held him up, wriggling but dying, on a table fork. Standing again on that exact spot, I wanted to acknowledge that fifteen years down the road I saw things differently. (*Nostos*, pp. 74–5)

As a boy of seven killing eels he had imagined he was killing the bad luck brought by landing on a snake when he played a game of Snakes and Ladders, he was defeating the enemy by impaling it on a table fork; he was Hercules, he was St. George, he was Michael the Archangel, he was a hero killing dragons. Now, at twenty two, he knew that all attempts to kill the beast, to kill the dragon, to kill the eel, were counter-productive – all such images of serpents, dragons, monsters to be killed, represent the things that we perceive as threatening – sometimes they are our own powerful passions, sometimes they are an external enemy, whatever the perceived threat, attempting to repress and destroy is not only brutal but brutalising to oneself.

If he was learning anything from the Greek myths it was the need to acknowledge and suffer all of what it means to be human. If there is no god then there is no devil, there is no external evil force that can be fought and defeated. The humanity that can produce the Parthenon also includes the capacity for warfare and for blood sacrifice. He wanted somehow to reconcile these extremes without a consequent and damaging repression. He was passionately hopeful that there was nothing in human nature that was not redeemable, 'I couldn't accept that something in me is unredeemable. I couldn't accept that something of me must suffer eternal exclusion.'[7] Surely, he felt, we could use our Parthenon capacities to better manage our Minotaur, our Serpent.

Greece was proving to be very hard work, but certain things were being resolved. Throughout this very difficult section of *Nostos*, the section where as he said himself, most readers simply gave up, he also seems to have been grappling with a major personal decision. This trip to Greece happened only a few weeks after he had made the first phone call to the London call girl, and so as he made his pilgrim's progress from Athens to Crete, he was still 'parthenos', still a virgin. And he seems to have considered remaining so, opting for a celibate life and devoting himself to the pursuit of some kind of spiritual or intellectual enlightenment. This would explain the sense of elation he had felt weeks earlier after his failed attempt at gaining 'experience'; as he headed home that London evening he had concluded that 'grace had mastered instinct'. Later in his journey he even imagines himself replying to Jameen Kissane 'No, Jameen, you have got it wrong, it isn't my instincts that will make a man of me, it is spirit that will make a man of me.'[8] It would also explain the constant questions. Sitting in a cafe under the Acropolis he says he was struggling to make a decision, to stay with the spiritual quest or to stay with his humanity. Staying with his humanity would involve allowing his sexuality, taking his heel from the head of at least one serpent, and as he put it, 'letting nature happen to me'.

It was a mighty struggle of spirit versus instinct, soul versus body, and it was mirrored in the landscape, in the weather, in the history and in the myths of this ancient civilisation. He was in a sense having a tremendous internal argument as he wandered through the Greek countryside. It was as if the puritanical conditioning of church and school was battling it out with the earthiness of farmyard and homeplace. And it was not alone the voice of puritanical Catholicism that he had to contend with. He remembered lines from Shakespeare's *King Lear* 'But to the girdle do the gods inherit, The rest is all the fiends.' In Lear's tormented vision, sex and procreation belong to the world of the devil, it is only from the waist upwards that men and women are 'good'. John seems to have had great difficulty in shaking off this sense of inhibition and prohibition, while at the same time being aware that in this, as in all other aspects of human nature, prohibition and repression cause things to fester and become poisonous. As he explored the Greek countryside everywhere he was conscious of fertility, of an earth that bore fruit, of soil that had been ploughed and seeded, of other Greek myths that confirmed the sacredness, bounty and generosity of the soil, of wholeness in the world of nature that was only possible by a journey into the darkness of the earth. Life he saw had to be embraced in its totality, there could be no renouncing or rejecting of any part of his own nature. He made up his mind that as soon as he returned to London he would make the call, whatever would happen he would embrace the crookedness of his humanity. And there was also another straightness that he was resisting. The 'straightness' of modern thinking that he encountered in the academic world, where older worlds with their myths and stories and their wisdom were no longer seen as relevant.

> For reasons of pure psychic need my life couldn't be a progress from the world of *The Golden Bough*[9] to the world of *The Origin of Species* it couldn't be a progress from the bogdeal of North Kerry to the Pentelic marble of the Parthenon.
>
> I had no choice. I could never walk away from bogdeal. I must always keep faith with bogdeal. I must always be able to sit in the silence under history. I must always be able to go back to a house in which a hatching hen took precedence over the noise of the metallurgical ages. (*Nostos*, p. 70).

'It couldn't be a progress *from*', he could not live the life that the modern world seemed to require, a life of relentless progress where the world of his childhood was seen as backward and primitive. A world where being 'civilised' meant being 'citified', meant pretence and denial of 'all that we inwardly are', meant 'psychic topiary'. Much of his later life was spent in opposition to a concept of progress that demanded exclusion and abandonment. After five weeks and a few more myths, he had made a decision. He would resist exclusion, he would resist repression, he would keep faith with bogdeal and with instinct.

Greece had given him an answer but it had also given him a new question. 'Can we devise a culture that will enable us to flourish from the roots of who we are?'[10] Throughout his walkabout he had now and again remembered a pregnant Jamaican girl with whom he had worked earlier in the summer. He wondered if it might be possible to inaugurate a world that would be good for her and for her baby. What story, what understanding of the universe, could create a world that would shelter them in all of their being? Of one thing he was sure, there would be no going forward unless we were first to go back. 'If only we would suffer our questions and crises with the same sincerity that the Greeks suffered theirs, I thought ... If only we could suffer whatever it is Auschwitz is saying about us.'[11] The Greeks, because they were not afraid to face themselves 'opened the road to a new kind of redemption, the redemption of winning through to fierce clarity about the terror, and pity, and the truly dreadful wonder of being who we are.'[12] That would have to be the first step in any attempt to make a better world.

In John's view, to date all of our attempts at revolution have failed. The aspirations of the eighteenth century Age of Enlightenment, the great age of science and reason, had failed. The French Revolution had failed. The Russian Revolution had failed. Tragically, they had all begun with idealism, with a vision of a better and fairer social order.

> And they bring in a Statue of Reason to Notre Dame, and they believe that it is by reason and science and music and education and the arts that we will perfect ourselves ... ..but what the people in the eighteenth century forgot was the animal in us and the beast in us. The people in the eighteenth century believed that if there were animal instincts in us anyway that they could be reformed to the extent that they would no longer be animal or beastly. They believed in the perfectability of the human. A century or so later we are up to our highest aspirations, but within sight of the steeples of Europe ... there are people made anonymous in the mud of Flanders. And then a few decades later, there are trains in the night travelling through Europe and in these trains, cattle trains mostly, there are the Jews of Europe, and they are being carted away to concentration camps where they will be gassed and incinerated. And that is where the belief in reason, I think, precipitated us into.[13]

The heroes of the French Revolution overthrew the *Ancien Regime* of monarchy, of feudalism and of church. What they ignored was the inner individual 'ancien regime' which is not amenable to reason and will. It frequently erupts and hampers efforts at living a perfect life. To make a better world for the Jamaican girl and her baby, any new revolution must firstly involve a journey to the Labyrinth, otherwise all we will ever achieve is yet another journey to 'stake, guillotine and gulag'.[14] And on that journey to the Labyrinth John believed that we will need more than reason and idealism to keep us safe. 'If only', he found himself thinking, 'if only we had a religion that could guide us through it.' (*Nostos*, p. 126)

So what did he bring back from this soul-searching, self-led pilgrimage in Greece? He would no longer be 'parthenos', on return to London he would make the telephone call and from there on he would attempt to integrate and manage all of instinctive life in him. He would not forget the wonder of the Parthenon and the human capacity for splendid achievement that it represents. However he saw that the Greeks could not offer an alternative religion but in their myths, in their capacity to recognise the totality and terror and wonder of our humanity, they give us a healthy way of seeing and accepting ourselves. He admits that a kind of 'secular impiety' had been knocked out of him and he came back in search of a vision of a better world for 'the girl who, great with child, sat day after day by the mouth of a machine, in a row of machines, in Wall's ice cream factory'.[15] He would spend the rest of his life seeking a vision of all that might still remain sacred, of all that might still shelter us, in a machine dominated secular world. He would 'keep faith with bogdeal'.

Back in Dublin for the next academic year, having experienced the Parthenon, he was more than ever soul-shocked by the city.

> Another day, walking up Nassau Street, I thought of all the work that went into putting all of these stones one on top of another, that went into putting all of these bricks one on top another, that went into fitting out all these offices and shops, that went into installing all these telephones, laying down all these roads, devising all these traffic rules, and I couldn't, no, I couldn't put my shoulder to this modern commercial wheel, and this was particularly so when I thought that in neither wall of it nor walk of it did I find either image or metaphor for what I saw in Lydia when I was in love with her ...
>
> A city is justified, in its very existence is justified, only when it sings its own song to the human soul. It is justified only when it sings that song pictorially, sculpturally, architecturally, when it sings it ritually and theatrically, when it sings it by cradle and coffin, when it sings it in a hermit's cave and during carnival, when it sings it in folksong and symphony. (*Nostos*, pp. 137, 139)

He thought of what Yeats had said, that there is only one history and that is the soul's. Every impulse, every action, every creation, is an expression of soul and wherever he looked all he could see was telling him that the modern soul is in big trouble. It was time to complete his Greek journey. It was time to go home to Moyvane.

Three days before Christmas I caught a bus to the Red Cow[16] and from there I hitch-hiked home to North Kerry. Outside Loughil, walking along by the Shannon, which was being carried back to Limerick by the incoming tide, a ramshackle car, a Morris Minor, drew up beside me. What I first noticed when I got in were the cold, perished hands at the wheel. Hands become stiff and awkward in their joints. Even as I talked to him, inevitably about the bad weather, my eyes kept coming back to them ... an old bachelor farmer if ever there was one, he was down now, he told me, to nine cows.

'How, with your hands as they are, do you milk nine cows?' I asked him.

'Whatever life is in me I get from the paps of cows ... And do you know the grandest thing in the world? The grandest thing in the world is when you are teaching a calf to drink milk from a bucket. You must know what it is like yourself. You're Mororty, aren't you? I'd know you anywhere I met you from your mother. Ye had cows, so you must know what I'm talking about when you put your first two fingers into a calf's mouth and he curls his tongue round them, holding them tight and sucking on them, drawing on them, like they were one of his mother's paps. That's when the life of the world comes into you, comes out into you from somewhere inside you, you drawing his mouth down into the milk, sinking your hand into it, so that he gets a taste of it.' (*Nostos*, p. 148)

'That's when the life of the world comes into you, comes out into you from somewhere inside you,' – the life of the world emanating from the core of one's being – a sense of this was being restored to John on his journey home by an old man who could still find shelter in the world. Moyvane itself however did not present such a sheltering aspect.

There are wuthering places, I thought. Places in which people and bushes and cattle are weathered, are withered, and this is one of them. All these fields, I could see, had been reclaimed from beneath the great raised bogs, only islands of which now remained. And a sense I had is that this land, rushy and wet, didn't want to be claimed, didn't want to be coerced into human intention and purpose ... and the best thing therefore to do with it would be to say a Requiem Mass on it, for it, and then, letting nature have its way with it, let a new raised bog grow over it.

As bog, with patches of bog myrtle, bog cotton and bog asphodel – as bog, with patches of sphagnum moss red and green – as bog, with patches of heather and sedge and dwarf gorse in it – as bog, with wild duck and curlew and snipe nesting in it and calling in it – as bog this place I was born in and grew up in would remember Paradise, and it would give us images and metaphors for how we feel when we are in love. (*Nostos*, p. 149)

This image of beauty in an unclaimed bog was his answer to the Parthenon. Beauty in the heights of Greece and beauty in the depths of a Moyvane bog, whatever damage was being done to the world happened somewhere in between, in that place where the world is at the mercy of 'human intention and purpose', when that intention and purpose has lost sight of soul. And even within that 'wuthering world' of 'the blowing wind and the wet rain' an old man's soul could be nourished by a suckling calf. There might still be hope.

Later that evening, after his mother and father had gone to bed, he sat alone by the kitchen fire.

With the sound, a slightly gulping sound, of its turf-yellow flaming, the fire drew attention to a blessed silence in the house ... And sitting in it, I knew, without argument I knew, that this world isn't the whole story. In its rivers and in its moths and in its stars, our world, I knew, isn't separate from the whole story, is everywhere pervaded by the whole story, and however restless it might be, it is eternally at rest within the whole story, and the whole story is good. It is God.

It is God as Ground.

It is God as Divine Ground.

It is the God who, while not being a Ground, grounds everything ...

The moment passed. But I didn't with its passing come back into exile. Not for hours. Not till long after the fire had too little vigour to flame. (*Nostos*, pp. 152–3)

He was back for a little while in the old world where things can be known 'without argument'. Back to the world of 'night knowing, a knowing not narrowed by ... intellect' which he had insisted on defending in his discussions with fellow students in UCD. For a few hours, in the half light of the kitchen, he knew that our world of rivers and moths and stars and restlessness isn't the whole story, he sensed that there is a divine ground to all being, and he sensed that the divine ground is God. This was not the God of the Bible, not the God who walked out when Darwin walked in, but a deep mystical sense of something good and eternal that is beyond comprehension by the faculties of reason and logic. This was a night-time glimpse of something 'other' and understandably, by the next day, he was 'back into exile', his head again wrestling with the compelling theories of science and philosophy.

He was at home in Moyvane and it was Christmas Eve. He went out to Mikie Fitz's haggard to gather sticks for the fire. He listened to the crows as they settled down to roost with their 'great flourishes of talk, like you would hear among farmers striking bargains at the October horse-fair in Listowel'; he listened as a vixen called and a dog fox answered, and knew he was listening to the master male warning off all others; and then he saw the little robin 'settled down already for the night on a dead branch of a briar-covered bush'. And he remembered being five and the desolation he had felt on recognising that it was an ordinary night in the cowstall. Now seventeen years later he felt he could articulate what had happened to him on that night.

Standing in the door of the stall and seeing for the moment only what wasn't there, the word 'we' fell asunder into 'us-and-them'. From that night on, the new word 'us-and-them' was a wound, open and gaping, that ran the whole length of our yard, separating animals and humans, and it was from the far, even far-off side of it that we now brought milk and eggs to our house.

Ours was a yard of two wounds: a wound heart-deep to a pig and a wound heart deep to the word 'we'.

What I was sure of tonight is that both wounds ended up as wounds in my mind and their bleeding there was fantastical not physical. (*Nostos*, p. 160)

Only days earlier he had spoken with the old farmer who knew exactly what 'we' feeling meant, who found 'the life of the world' coming in to him as he nurtured his calves; he remembered the 'we' feeling of the Hard Man who nurtured the baby hares he had rescued on Clounmacon bog; he had the example of his mother who would not allow the noise of hammering to disturb a hatching hen. And all of this made him yearn for a world where 'we' feeling would take precedence over bleeding wounds, and he yearned for a religion that would take care of all of these contradictions. He imagined it. A new Nativity Play, where the new Jesus would take on a new Passion – all of the desolation John had so far encountered in his life. Scientists and philosophers would be the new Magi bringing their tremendous theories to be suffered and integrated, and the Minotaur, half man and half bull, having been rescued by Ariadne, would be the first sacristan in the new church. This would be a church that could incorporate both Parthenon and bog…

It was only a dream, and fortunately for his sanity, he could always hear his mother's voice and what she might say to him, 'no remedy much in imagining things'. But perhaps, in the mystical experience of God as Divine Ground, and the vision of a new Passion, the seeds of a remedy were already sown.

'SOMETHING RIGHT ROYAL IN US ALL'

*London; this Titanic wheel; hypnotism; the man from Porlock; teaching; philosophy
in Leeds; Gorgocogito; Marilyn; a mabinog; 'no bloodless myth'; Canada.*

After Christmas he returned from Moyvane to Dublin and to his final exams, which were scheduled for the end of summer. In spite of achieving a 'Double First' – first class honours in both Philosophy and Logic – his attitude towards the academic world had not changed since in first year he had disengaged from it and was going his own way. He did not attend his graduation and Phyllis, his youngest sister, remembers the carelessness with which, months later, he opened the envelope from UCD and tossed the degree parchment that it contained into the loft. What he described as his 'very expensive European education' had left him unimpressed. It had also left him without any plans for the future, and because the exams came at the end of summer, he had not found summer-work and was consequently almost penniless. The options were few. He would not go back to Moyvane this time, the turf was long cut and drawn home, and anyway he had no answers to give his mother in terms of career prospects. He was well aware of her expectations. Succinct and direct as ever Brenda summed it up 'Sure all she wanted was for him to come home in a Morris Minor and be driving her to Mass.' Since there was never any chance at all of that happening, and since he simply did not like Dublin, he again headed for London, this time with only three Irish half-crowns in his pocket and no job lined up.

Luck was on his side for a little while. On his very first day there, walking down Oxford Street, he met an acquaintance from Dublin who owed him five pounds and with that returned to him he could survive for a few weeks. Afterwards he wondered 'why in God's name I hadn't asked him to put me up. It must be, I concluded, that the only thing on my mind at the time was food, so it hadn't even occurred to me to think of shelter.' It was an unfortunate oversight he would realise in the small and not so warm hours of the following morning, sitting on a bench in St. James's Park. He was in London, he was cold, he was sleeping rough and he had no plans. Three weeks later he was still walking the streets and the parks by night, and by day sleeping at a desk upstairs in a library near Leicester Square Underground Station. And what was going on in his head? He already knew that there was something in him that could not automatically conform. A few years before the Beatles arrived on the scene he had been wearing his hair long, 'long hair in opposition to an identifying university scarf, I even found it difficult to be identified as the boyfriend of a girl I was in love with. From the day I arrived in University that was my hirsute plea, don't conscript me into the everyday world, don't fence me in.'[1] This he recognised as core of his being. 'If I had a deepest need in relation to people in society it was that – don't fence me in.' Now, here in London he was not fenced in, but neither was he free.

> Anyway, it didn't look like my prospects would improve. What defined me now in relation to the built-up world all around me was simple refusal. In the way that someone would conscientiously object to being conscripted into an army so did I now object to being conscripted into this thing called the workforce, not because I didn't want to work for a living, but because the sheer shock of what was all around me so bewildered me into staring incomprehension and, in consequence, so disabled me, that I couldn't even think of putting my shoulder to this Titanic wheel. (*Nostos*, pp. 163–4)

'I couldn't even think of putting my shoulder to this Titanic wheel.' While in Greece he had thought about the human capacity to subdue and conquer the environment, and he saw how that conquering had been gloriously successful; *homo sapiens sapiens* was now the dominant species on the planet, but at enormous cost. The Greek myths had it that Prometheus, one of the gods known as Titans, had stolen fire and given it as a gift to human beings, who were thus enabled to forge metal and ultimately become enormously powerful. Titanically, and in John's thinking, blindly and disastrously powerful, forging the tools of domination and the weapons of war. This theft from the heavens John saw as an evolutionary disaster. Its consequences in the modern city he was now enduring appalled him. Noise, pollution, hustle and ugliness. 'Inhaling this Hell let loose, inhaling it with my eyes and ears as well as with my mouth, I could only conclude that in our energies and in our works, that we were the Titans.' All he could see was modern human beings, 'in our millions, whole populations dazed, we are dumbfoundedly co-operating with our conscription into the modern world.'[2] Modern humanity had been conscripted and hypnotised en masse. He remembered:

A famous hypnotist came to Listowel in the nineteen-fifties. Mostly, people didn't know what a hypnotist was or what he could do ... His wholly unsuspecting victims he hypnotized into doing all sorts of daft things. In the audience there was disbelief, amazement and laughter. Above all laughter. Uproarious laughter. In the end he hypnotized them into thinking they were milking cows, so there they were sitting on illusionary stools squeezing illusionary paps. Criminally he didn't bring them completely back to their senses at the end of the show so that when they came out into the streets, one of them, and then contagiously all of them, imagined that the parked cars were cows and they squatted down beside them milking them.

Is that us I wondered? All of us hypnotized? All of us milking cars?...

Oxford Street in London, Church Street in Listowel.

As far as I could see the difference between them was that in Oxford Street there was no one who was laughing, no one in other words who wasn't hypnotized. (*Nostos*, pp. 164–5)

Human beings hypnotized into compliance with a way of living in the world that is utterly destructive to the natural environment and deeply damaging to themselves; and almost everyone completely unaware of their part in an illusion. An illusion of modernity, of progress and of improvement that John saw as essentially flawed. For the moment, walking the London streets, he was both resisting conscription and undergoing a fundamental crisis, a crisis that had begun in his initial collision with the 'engineered' and soulless Dublin that had horrified him only a few years previously. Now he could not see how he would participate in this exploitative culture, what he called 'our Pequod culture', referring to the whaling ship that is at the centre of *Moby Dick*. This is the story of Ahab, captain of the Pequod, and of his obsessive pursuit of the great white whale; harpoon-bearing man pitted against a powerful force of nature. It ends in disaster for Ahab and his crew, and this became John's image for the ultimate fate of the human species. Having, with ever more sophisticated technologies, taken up arms against the natural world, and being entirely blind to the consequences, he foresaw only shipwreck for the planet. Years later, in the Introduction to *Nostos* he would write about the Earth:

that sunlit wonder has been voyaging for four thousand, six hundred million years, and what a sadness it would be if, for want of refounding ourselves psychically and culturally, we became the iceberg into which it crashed. (*Nostos*, p. vii)

Even as he perceived all around him an unthinking compliance with a state of affairs that seemed headed for ecological disaster he had not forgotten the lesson of the Parthenon. 'Human beings are tremendous', tremendous in their capacity to think, to feel, and in their capacity to 'do something splendid'. It was this contradiction that he now found most bewildering, how could people, so capable of greatness, not see that this industrialised modern way of life was both diminishing and destructive? Was he the only one disabled by it? What was the source of the hypnosis? What, in all of these people, had happened to the capacity for greatness? What had happened to soul? He had already come up with ideas that could provide at least a partial explanation – what he had called the 'psychic topiary' of a modern education; the failure of traditional religion to tackle the challenge presented by modern science; and the mistaken assumption that human beings, and consequently society, are perfectable. Now, during these weeks of personal crisis, he recognised another contributory factor.

He was reading a biography of Samuel Taylor Coleridge and was particularly struck by an account of the composition of his great unfinished poem *Kubla Khan*. Coleridge, in a trance-like state, had been composing his poem when there was a knock on his door. It was a man from nearby Porlock who had some business that he wished to transact. It took about an hour. When Coleridge returned to his desk, all of his vision for the poem had dissolved. Business had interrupted the creative process, business had interfered with the work of soul, busy-ness had destroyed vision. John concluded that the person on business from Porlock is a full-time lodger in all of our lives, constantly distracting us from any connection with our deeper selves. We spend our lives hypnotized into thinking that day-to-day concerns are of ultimate importance and utterly blind to all that is of real significance. Consequently, we might as well be 'milking cars'.

This type of thinking was not doing him any good nor was it solving the problem of his own day-to-day survival. He was beginning to feel sorry for himself and the colder October nights were taking their toll.

> I was living on a shilling and a penny ha'penny a day, a sum of money that was burnt, was branded into my mind, for with it I could go into the little delicatessen cum restaurant next door to the library and buy as much bread and cheese as would break my hunger three times a day. (*Nostos*, p. 165)

Libraries and museums could provide daytime shelter and intellectual distraction from his immediate circumstances, but by early November he was down to his last ten shillings. The full reality hit him one day on Charing Cross Road. He was counting his money to see how much he had left when a sixpenny piece slipped through his fingers and rolled away from him. A frail old lady who had been rummaging in her handbag bent to pick it up, assuming it to be hers.

My first impulse was to go up to her and say, 'You won't credit this, but the sixpence you picked up, it is actually mine, so can I please have it back?' I didn't because, small though the incident was, it seemed like an intervention by fate or, at the very least, it seemed as if there was a message of some sort in it for me. Anyway there was something inordinately wrong with my life now that circumstances meant that a sixpenny piece counted for so inordinately much. It was half of tomorrow's grub and that the last I could afford, that I saw disappearing into the old lady's bag. My reaction, as though my life was threatened, saddened me. And of all the humiliations, small and not so small, that I'd met with since I found myself walking the streets on that first night there was none that had so conclusively shown me as this one did that I was down-'n-out. The next move was that I would beg, that I would be a bum. But that was unthinkable. Hard though it was to do so, I admitted that night that my bluff had been called. (*Nostos*, p. 172)

He was left with no choice but to conform and for a few days he wandered around trying to figure out a way of looking presentable enough to find a job. As so often in John's life, help was at hand. Making his way to the British Museum one afternoon he ran into Una McCullough, a girl he had known in UCD, and her obvious alarm at how he looked led him to explain that he had been sleeping rough for the previous two months. She insisted that he accept her offer of accommodation, and a few hours and two hot baths later he was dressed in clothes that she and her flatmate had provided and was sitting down to his first hot meal in over two months. The existential crisis over for the moment he acknowledged that he would have to find work. By early December he was teaching English in a Catholic boarding school for boys in North Staffordshire, in an atmosphere so stultifyingly polite that he described it as 'a comedy of manners' with no 'reek of the human' whatsoever.[3]

There was no way that John Moriarty from Moyvane was going to survive for long in that environment but the end came sooner than he expected. Towards the end of the second term he received a letter from two boys who, a week earlier, had walked out the front gate of the school and simply gone home. As soon as he received their letter John, in typical unorthodox Moriarty style, had replied to them saying that he completely understood their action. A parent got hold of this letter and, furious that he would support such wayward behaviour, and suspicious that he might have triggered it, complained to the headmaster. Not surprisingly, he was dismissed. However the dismissal was fortuitous. He had recently met with Professor James Cameron, head of the Philosophy Department in Leeds University, who had asked if he was interested in reading for a postgraduate degree. The only problem that John had with the proposal was the fact that he could not afford the fees and so, as an alternative, Professor Cameron had suggested a job tutoring first-year students. He was now free to accept the offer.

Random opportunities would always play a significant role in John's life. He was neither ambitious nor career-oriented, he did not have a practical bone in his body, everyday comforts and personal possessions (apart from books) were irrelevant to him and planning for the future was an altogether alien concept. His life was directed by chance encounters; people he met who were captivated not only by the depth of his thinking and the independence of his ideas, but by the magnetism of a personality totally free from clichéd posturing and absolutely sincere in his passion for knowledge and ideas. Professor Cameron, himself unconventional in many ways, was building his department and took a chance on this maverick Irishman. John plunged himself into the world of seminars and tutorials, and once again he was confronted with that aspect of philosophy that caused him so much trouble. It was the philosophy of what he called 'two-hundred-watt clarities', and 'stainless-steel' thinking,[4] the world of 'philosophical brand names – Descartes, Locke, Hume, Wittgenstein, Ayer', all of whom, great as they were, he took issue with because of their conviction that understanding of the world could be accessed by reason alone. This is rationalism, a logical mathematical approach to philososphical thinking which John maintained had led to 'the modern consensus or conspiracy about reality'.[5] He coined a word for this, 'Gorgocogito'[6]– thinking which categorises, analyses, dissects, formulises – and which discounts insight, wonder and revelation. These latter were the categories of knowing that John believed to be deeper than thought but just as valid and far more enriching. As a partial response to this narrowness of vision that he found all around him, and in spite of their bewilderment, he told his students wonder tales.

A Cotswold shepherd had herded his sheep to high summer grazing ground. One day, having nothing else to do, he sat on a hill knitting a scarf for himself. Soon he was distracted by two hares standing on their hind legs and putting their nostrils together. The better to see them, he shifted his body sideways a little, but that meant that his ball of thread rolled from his lap and off down out of sight between two bushes. Going to retrieve it, he found that it had disappeared through an opening into the hill. Seeing it now for the first time in a hill he knew so well, this opening intrigued him. Curious, he entered it, and after going down a long and winding passage, he found himself in a great hall. At the far end of it there was a bier and lying on it, in all his majesty, was King Arthur. Beside the bier there was a great oak table and on it there was a horn and a sword. Taking the sword, the shepherd struck the table, struck a great blow on it. With that, King Arthur, raised himself up a little and, turning his head towards the startled shepherd, he said, 'If only you had blown the horn I would have awaked and come back as their king among my people. But now, for how long no-one knows, the opportunity has been lost.' Saying no more, he sank back into ageless sleep. Picking up his ball of thread, the shepherd came back out and, however much and often he afterwards searched for it, he never again found the opening. (*Nostos*, p. 177)

Whatever first year philosophy students might make of that story, John told it because of what he saw in it:

The sleep of what is best, of what is most creative and most imaginative in a people.
Genius asleep.
The Genius through which a people would become a great people, that Genius asleep.
Arthur asleep.
The King and Queen in us asleep.
Royalty of feeling and of thought asleep. Sovereignty, like that which resides in a standing stone, asleep.
And no one knowing where the opening is.
And no Cotswold shepherd sitting on a hill, knitting a winter scarf for himself. (*Nostos*, p. 178)

Retelling it in another place he would say 'No matter how much it has faded from the surface of our lives, there is something right royal in us all.' And he would quote Nietzsche 'Perhaps there is a realm of wisdom from which the logician is exiled.'[7] This was the wisdom of folktale, of myth, of poetry, of drama, of all great art; a wisdom that could be grasped with the imagination and with the heart and with the senses; a wisdom that could cultivate and enrich soul; a wisdom dismissed by both philosophy and science because it was not arrived at by the rigorous intellectual methods of deduction and reasoning. This was to become an important focus of John Moriarty's life, a struggle to make the case for what William James called 'immediate luminousness'[8] a different way of knowing, which might allow us to 'devise a new culture' and help us to live with more reverence on the earth. He recognised something of that 'luminous insight' in Wordsworth's *Ode on the Intimations of Immortality*:

Our birth is but a sleep and a forgetting:
The Soul that rises with us, our life's Star,
Hath had elsewhere its setting
And cometh from afar ...
Not in entire forgetfulness,
And not in utter nakedness,
But trailing clouds of glory do we come
From God who is our home ...
At length the Man perceives it die away,
And fade into the light of common day.

He had a deep appreciation of the central vision of this poem – the vision that there is within us something that is part of us but also more than us, more than the sum of our rational, biological, neurological parts, that comes to us from, and connects us to, something indefinable but far greater and more mysterious, something that elsewhere he calls 'the universal mind'[9] and that this poem calls God. This vision was at once uplifting and disheartening, offering as it does a glimpse of 'something right royal' in us that sadly fades 'into the light of common day'.

What else but the biography of the person from Porlock is this stanza? The biography of the person almost all of us have become?
 If only we would build something of the forgotten vision into our houses, into our hospitals, into our prisons, into our churches, into every wall and every walk of every city ...
 If only ...
 If only ...
 If only, wagering as Pascal did, we gave ourselves a chance.
 If only, wagering as Pascal did, we ran the risk of who we are, of whence we are, in Wordsworth's sense. (*Nostos*, 170–1)

Pascal, Blaise Pascal, the seventeenth century French mathematician, physicist and philosopher, when grappling with the existence of God, had argued that since God can neither be proved nor disproved then it is wise to make one's best bet, and live accordingly. To Pascal it was self-evident. If God exists one has all to gain, if he does not, then one has lost nothing (perhaps some finite pleasures but that would be a small stake given the possibility of infinite reward!). When recommending that we wager as Pascal did, John was not thinking in terms either of the biblical God or of eternal reward. John's wager would offer a return in the here-and-now. His fervent wish was that we would live in accordance with the belief that there is something 'other', call it sacred or divine or transcendent, that permeates the entire cosmos. If we were to live with a sense of reverence for the wonder and miracle of the world, then we would surely 'build something of the forgotten vision into our houses, into our hospitals, into our prisons, into our churches, into every wall and every walk of every city.' Living with a sense of the sacred we might build a better world. There would be a very real return for such a wager.

Finding something of Wordsworth's vision, that soul of the universe, in myths and folk-tales, he would continue to tell stories. His ideas found few takers in the seminar room of the Philosophy Department, even though he did have the support of Professor Cameron and of his supervisor, Roger White. Nonetheless, and in spite of feeling somewhat the outsider, he was happy in Leeds because 'a lovely lovely thing happened to me there. I met Marilyn Valalyk there.'[10] The circumstances of their first meeting did not bode at all well. He was living in what can only be called a 'squat'.

I was only just in bed one night when I heard footfalls on the stone steps and then on the flagstones outside my basement door.

'Are you there John?' a voice called. 'It's Jane.'

Jane was a student who worked part-time in a cafe across the road from the university.

'Come in,' I called back.

Since the door had no lock, she only had to turn the knob and in she came.

'The light switch is on your left, on the wall,' I said.

Shedding light on where I lived, a condemned house in a district due for demolition, wasn't something I could be proud of, but the light came on, and my discomfiture deepened to embarrassment when I saw that she had someone with her, a girl who, in her bearing and dress could only look Dadaistically out of place in a grotty little underworld like this ...

I defensively and instantly relapsed into the old strategy of creating a smoke screen of interesting but fascinating talk so that this, and not the poverty of my circumstances, is what the girl who had introduced herself as Marilyn, would see, would only see.

What a bummer, I thought to myself. If only I had the good luck to not be in bed, I'd have some chance. But Jesus, she was lovely. I couldn't look at her and not try to impress her. So, the initial exchanges over, off I went into the Celtic hazel wood at twilight, it being my hope that they would follow me. It was dawn when we came back out.

As she walked through the door before Jane, she didn't look back.

So what the hell, I thought, lying on a bed that looked more grubby than ever now – what the hell was the point of puberty, of all its promise, if it continues to end, as it did just now, in girls walking away? (*Nostos*, p. 174–5)

However, his Celtic twilight smokescreen had the desired effect because within a few nights they were back in his room and he and Marilyn were singing songs together, she taught him the Welsh *Night-visiting Song* and he taught her *Carraig Donn*. Grottiness and grubbiness were being overshadowed by music and romance. Within a few months he was exploring the high moorlands of North Wales with her and discovering the ancient wonder-tales of *The Mabinogion*.[11] As a gift for Marilyn, in order to tell them to her, he had begun to learn the stories as a *mabinog* would and so he became entranced with the world of Ceridwen and Taliesen; of Pwyll, Prince of Dyfed; of Glyn Cuch, Glyn Cree and Glyn Dhu; people and places that he believed revealed a mood of the human mind, the 'once-upon-a-time' time of the mind, wherein wonders, great wonders, are possible, and where 'the worldly way of experiencing the world isn't the whole story'. In this mood there is vision of an 'Otherworld' which is in effect a way of being, a way of seeing, in this world, and which with our mechanical reliance on logic and reasoning we have all but destroyed. Talking about this in seminar he suggested 'that there was maybe an ancient Welsh way as well as an ancient Greek way to wisdom.' For the sake of the world we live in, he was saying, we need to live with a belief that there is always an 'Otherworldly' way of being to which a part of us already belongs. That must be our wager.

He also found something of this wonder-world in the literature of modern Wales. He was reading Dylan Thomas and the poem *Fern Hill* resonated hugely with him.

> And then to awake, and the farm, like a wanderer white
> With the dew, come back, the cock on his shoulder: it was all
> Shining, it was Adam and maiden,
> The sky gathered again
> And the sun grew round that very day.
> So it must have been after the birth of the simple light
> In the first spinning place, the spellbound horses walking warm
> Out of the whinnying green stable
> On to the fields of praise.

A mood of the world captured in poetry, a glimpse of Paradise at the heart of the universe, resistant maybe to analysis or interpretation but conveying its own truth, what Keats called 'the truth of the imagination', and what John would see as part of 'an alternative kind of intelligence' that we needed to grow back into. However, thinking about the world in its wonder-mood, arguing against the reductive nature of modern philosophy, becoming a mabinog for Marilyn and immersing himself in ancient tales, this was not the whole story of Leeds. As always, there was a contradictory process going on. In total contrast to the mood of *Fern Hill* was a poem called *Genesis* by the poet Geoffrey Hill who was then a lecturer in the English Department at the University. This poem does not celebrate 'fields of praise', but offers a bleak unrelenting vision of the savagery at the heart of the natural world. In such a world, Hill writes *'There is no bloodless myth will hold.'*

> At first reading it stunned me this line did:
>   'There is no bloodless myth will hold'
>   And yet it comforted me, if only because it enabled me to think again of the slaughtered pig ... hanging from a cross-beam in our kitchen, if only because it enabled me to think again of the bowl of cock's blood on our dresser.
>   The question was, did it enable me to think of them with redemptive confidence? (*Nostos*, pp. 189–90)

There was nothing of Paradise in it and the poem posed far more questions than it answered for him. It forced him to think about what he called 'the sleight of hand at the heart of civilization ... with our attempt to sheathe Jack Scanlon's[12] knife in the glitter and sheen of our silver service.' It forced him to think again about why he had walked away from Christianity. Yes, it had been Darwin and Professor Ramsay's sums, but somehow also, it was because of revulsion at the bloodiness that was at the heart of the Christian story and its sacramental re-enactment at Mass. He remembered the hymn that was sung during Holy Hour at the church in Newtown:

> Deep in thy wounds Lord,
> Hide and shelter me,
> So shall I never,
> Never part from thee.

He had walked away from blood sacrifice. Now in the light of the 'immediate luminousness 'of a line of poetry maybe it was time to re-examine and try to interpret, or perhaps re-interpret Christianity. In Greece, thinking about the Jamaican girl and her baby, he had posed a question. What story, what understanding of the universe, could create a world that would shelter them in all of their being? It was with a deep sense of irony that he realised that he might have to revisit the

Christian story. It was an irony, and an undertaking, that would preoccupy him for
years to come. Meanwhile, there were the preoccupations of the everyday world to
be getting on with. He was very much in love with Marilyn.

> But now, here we were Marilyn and myself, singers one night in a Saxon hall,
> but now, this evening, climbing a hill in Wales, bringing hay to her pony ...
>> To touch hands up here was to know our loss when we come too soon to sex.
>> The tenderness of hands,
>> of hands that have touched an animal's nostrils,
>> that was a wonder,
>> a moment as long as it took a pony to eat an enticing fistful of hay
>> between a
>> man and a woman, that too was a wonder.
>> Walking back down the hill, I held up my hand behind Marilyn's head.
>> 'My banner over you is love,' I said. (*Nostos*, p. 182)

It was now 1965 and the end of term was approaching. He had only part-time
hours at the University and even those were precarious as he was not signed up for
any post-graduate course. He planned to return to London for the summer to take
up a job as a night-watchman but future prospects were again uncertain. Another
chance encounter came into play. A Canadian student, Margaret Smith, introduced him to her mother Marion. Marion Smith was a professor in the English
Department at the University of Manitoba, she was on a lecture tour in England,
and she was now spending a few days with her daughter. They chatted for a while,
eventually adjourning to the pub, and three hours later Marion suggested that
he apply for a position as a lecturer in the English Department in Manitoba. In
spite of his misgivings – on the grounds of minimal credentials and his training
in philosophy rather than English – she continued to encourage him, and with a
sense of having nothing to lose, he did so. To his surprise, within six weeks he was
offered a position. References from Dublin and Leeds and an informal interview
in a pub had yet again changed the course of his life. He would take the position,
but Marilyn was on his mind.

> This past summer we hadn't seen each other as often as we would have liked
> to. She was in Wales and I was in London, and in the end, after a long and
> bruising struggle, I hadn't asked her to come to Canada with me. To have done
> so would have meant that I was asking her to marry me, and I wasn't able for
> marriage, not now and maybe never, and the reason for this was as old as I was.
> I had spent the first eighteen years of my life inside of a marriage, the marriage

of my father and mother, and I was carrying the damage of it in the deepest places of who I was. My oldest memory was of a fight, was of being wakened by it, and the killing thing in all of this was that my father was a good man, a very good man, an exceptional man, and my mother was a good woman, a very good woman, an exceptional woman, but you only had to put them together and there was trouble, sullen, silent trouble or loud, very loud trouble. Marriage for us was a blessing only when the Irish Sea flowed between the partners to it. By the time I was four I had decided that I wouldn't get married. I would live the way Jameen Kissane did and the way Dan Scanlon did. I'd have a few cows and a horse, above all I'd have a horse, and that way things would be as quiet as they were in Jameen's house, as they were in Dan's house. One evening when a fight was at its highest I went out and walked down through the haggart to McGrath's. Passing their kitchen window I heard them saying the rosary, and the contrast between the roaring in our house and the praying in a neighbour's house was saddening and shocking. And yet, even if I had the choice, I would choose my mother to be my mother and I would choose my father to be my father, only for God's sake don't have them within fighting distance of one another ...

My father was a good man, my mother was a good woman, marriage was the culprit.

The culprit once I wouldn't give it the chance to be the culprit again.

Like an electricity pole, marriage for me had the lightning sign, the danger sign, the sign saying KEEP AWAY on it ...

Also, there were needs in me that were bigger and, in the demands they made upon me and in the direction they were giving to my life, they were more totalitarian than my need for company and intimacy. They were needs that required solitude, more of it than I could ever legitimately expect to find within marriage.

In the end, I could only plead guilty to being the kind of man I was, and then go and make the best of it.

So, no, Marilyn. I didn't ask you to come to Canada with me, I didn't ask you to marry me, but you must have known that I wasn't just a wild-oats man, from beginning to end you must have known that my banner over you was love. (*Nostos*, pp. 200–1)

6

'FOXWOMAN WAS MY STATUE OF LIBERTY'

The voyage; conquerors and exterminators; dolphins; Who made the world?; the genius of the universe; 'we-feeling'; posh; a Cree Indian; a medicine hat; Lascaux, the primal blind trespass.

John's voyage to Canada proved 'a rough crossing'. A hurricane from below the Bermudas was blowing itself out in the North Atlantic but in a sense, wild and uncomfortable though that was, it suited him. His mood was a mixture of sadness at leaving Marilyn and doubt about the direction his life had now taken. Still very much in the eye of his own personal storm, still 'man overboard' from the Christian story, still seeking an acceptable 'sheltering mythology', he had immersed himself in reading the history of the 'New World' and as the ship battled the elements, he wrestled with the savageries and atrocities of the voyages of discovery and of all the blood-filled conquests that had ensued. The story of Pizzaro's army, looting the tombs and palaces of the Incas, and the savagery as 'they axed and axed and axed' plagued him.

> By going ashore into the New World, was I participating?... Was I inheriting the guilt of it?... Was I setting out, rifle in hand, on the Oregon Trail?... Was I forcing people who were here before me onto their Trail of Tears...
>
> What did it mean being a passenger in this ship?...
>
> As an Irishman, I had always thought of myself as one of the conquered. But now what? Had I now joined the conquerors?... Had I joined General Sheridan, the Irishman who said that the only good Indian is a dead Indian? Had I joined Custer? Had I joined Buffalo Bill Coady in his war of extermination on the Prairies? Had I joined General Rossas in his war of extermination on the Pampas? (*Nostos*, p. 204)

As John was very well aware, wars of extermination were no new phenom-
enon. He had read enough history to be able to list them off, going right back
to the battles, both real and mythological, fought in all of the great civilizations.
So-called civilization was more often than not the result of one people conquering
another. But now, another thought struck him. He remembered what Darwin had
found on the beach at Punta Alta, evidence of animals conquering the territory of
other animals! When in the geological ages the land masses of North and South
America were connected by land-bridge, the carnivorous sabre-toothed tigers from
the north had made fast work of the native herbivores. The ships that sailed from
Europe millennia later, manned by explorers and adventurers, were no less destructive and no less sabre-toothed. Conquest, domination and extermination, this was
the fate of the native peoples that they encountered:

> I was moving onto ground that had been cleared by predatory conquest. A tipi
> might once have stood where my bed would be. And the ground where I would
> stand explicating a poem by Keats or Blake? Did a medicine man once dance
> there? Did he suck a woman's sickness out of her there? And the songs, the
> medicine songs he sang there? Did Thunderbird give them to him?... Had this
> medicine man been compelled to move away so that I could move in? And how
> mad would it be to think that I could stand in his place?... What medicine was
> I coming with? Was there medicine in the texts that I would be dealing with?
>   And if there was, could I release it?
>   Was there medicine in *King Lear*?
>   Was there medicine in the *Immortality Ode*?
>   Was there medicine in the *Heart of Darkness*?
>   Could we say of all of these texts that there was in them the medicine of
> insight?... the medicine of great vision, greatly articulated? (*Nostos*, p. 205)

He might have been sailing to the New World but all of the old concerns were
travelling with him and he was no nearer to the 'medicine of insight' than the
occasional glimpses he received in the depths of his own psyche and in wonder
tales, poetry and myth. The culture of the America he was sailing towards had been
made in the image and likeness of the world he was sailing from, it was European in
its inheritance, and had its origins in ancient Greece and Rome. This journey did
not offer an escape. He was still walking and suffering the road to the Labyrinth,
the labyrinth of the human past, the labyrinth of the human mind. And he was still
searching for a sheltering story, one that would help him to inhabit that labyrinth
and move forward from it into 'a healed future'. With all that was going on in his
head, and the confinement necessitated by the ongoing storm, there was no doubt

that it was a rough crossing. On one particular day, seeking a reprieve, he defied the safety warnings.

> I opened a storm door and went out on deck. Momentarily, the screaming fury of the wind took my breath away but, seeing a pride of dolphins plunging along in what seemed sheer delight beside us, I struggled forward and then downward by metal steps onto the lower deck. Finding my way to the very bows, I bent over and greeted them. (*Nostos*, p. 199)

Dolphins, creatures perfectly adapted to their environment and doing no damage to it. He thought of a story he had once heard of the Greek god Dionysus who, captured and shackled by Etruscan pirates, had overcome them and transformed them into dolphins. In the process the pirate ship had become a dolphin-shaped sail boat, its mast entwined by a fruit-laden grapevine, with the transformed pirates swimming alongside as delighted attendants. For John it depicted nothing less than a miracle: this story of ultimate harmony between god, man and nature John sees as an alternative origin story for human beings. Instead of seeing ourselves as fighting pirates at war with our god and with our world (and exiled from our Eden), we might imagine ourselves going the way of Dionysus and his dolphins, in harmony with and adapted to the world of nature and at ease with our god. 'There are two ways', John argues, 'of relating to the world. One is to shape it to suit us. That is the way of Prometheus. The other is to allow it to shape us to suit it. This is the way of the dolphin.'[1] As he would say time and again, human beings have already gone the way of Prometheus, disastrously so in terms of our effect on the natural environment. We have become technological Titans and the effects are everywhere, visible in our cities but even more pernicious in our rain forests, our ice-caps and our atmosphere. He had already made his diagnosis. 'In our behaviour now we are AIDS virus to the earth. We are doing to the earth exactly what the AIDS virus does to the human body: we are breaking down its immune system.' (*Dreamtime*, p. 174)

Time and time again John would return to this theme of ecological disaster. How, he would wonder, did we get to this place of utter disregard and disrespect for our environment? And he found what he believed to be at least a contributory factor in the story, the origin story, which is at the heart of the Judaeo-Christian Bible. He believed that our western European culture went wrong right at the first chapter of the Bible, where God gave man the divine mandate 'to rule over the earth and to subdue it and have dominion over the fish of the sea, and the birds of the air.'[2]

In his talks years later he would remind his audience of the catechism questions at school. 'Who made the world?' and a forest of hands going up, and the answer 'God made the world'. And then came the second question 'Why did God make the world?' and another forest of hands, and the answer parroted out, 'God made the world for man's use and benefit.' This biblical origin story gave human beings a world made for *use and benefit*, with a mandate to conquer and subdue. It was an origin very different to what he saw in the story of Dionysus and the dolphins, and it was with a deep sense of regret that 'I could only ask what, now that we have made our choices, are our chances? What, now that we have made the wrong choice, are our chances?'

Without a doubt, a rough crossing. But never without a story and a sense of optimism, he was inventing or re-imagining an answer. Again it was a wonder story, a story, he says, told in yurts in the Old World, told in tipis in the New World ...

Once upon a time there was a hunter who lived far off by himself in a part of the bush that was lonely even for owls and difficult for bears. Every morning at first light he would leave his hut and go off on a great round checking his snares and nets and traps, and looking for signs of animal movement in the night. Coming home one day, three trapped mink hanging from his belt, he saw smoke rising from his chimney. This was strange. In a world in which he never saw any human footprints but his own, it was very strange. All of his senses alert, he pushed open the door and now he saw that as well as a great fire on the hearth there was a steaming hot meal on the table. Signs of who might have done this there were none. Not on the floor, not on the walls, not on the wolf pelts that served him for bed clothes. Clearly the meal could only be intended for him, so hanging up his bow and arrows and taking off the three mink, he sat down and he ate it.

Next morning at first light he was on his way. That evening, careful to stay downwind from a grizzly bear just out of hibernation, he turned for home, and again from a long way off, he saw smoke from his chimney. Pushing open the door, he saw a steaming hot meal on the table. On the third morning, his curiosity having got the better of him, he turned off his track and sitting concealed in a clump of bushes he kept his house in view. It wasn't long till he saw a fox trotting all the way to his door and pushing it open. Soon there was smoke, and so, instead of continuing on his round, he retraced his steps, closing the distance with all the patient, silent and invisible stealth of a great hunter. Entering the darkness of his hut as noiselessly as his shadow would, he saw a woman bent over his fire, coaxing it into flame. Detecting it by its smell, he saw a fox pelt hanging from a peg at the back of his door.

Seeing him when she rose from her work, the woman said, I am your wife now. I will keep house for you. And if your hunting ever fails I will go with you into the bush, I will only need to sit on the ground and close my yellow eyes and then I will see where the animals are.

It was a new life for the hunter.

Every morning he had dry well-mended clothes to put on.

Every evening, his belt laden or light, he'd see smoke in the distance.

Towards the beginning of spring, he complained of the smell of fox in the house.

Saying nothing, she carried on.

By the time the last grey victory of geese had gone north, he was saying that he couldn't stand it.

One evening, his vexation intense, he sat as far off from her as he could.

Still saying nothing, she went to the door, she took down the fox pelt, she draped it over her shoulders and, turning back into a fox, she trotted away, never once looking back, into the bush. (*Nostos*, p. 202)

This evocative little story, one of the six stories that John had told his philosophy students in Leeds, became seminal to his thinking and imagery.

There are times when I want that to be my $E=mc^2$, it is near to the genius of the universe ... We live in a world of terrible fixed species and Berlin walls between all the species. This old story suggests that all our personalities, all our natures, are masks in a way ... I love this sense that the species, far from being fixed, they are interchangeable ... my person, my empirical personhood, is really a mask assumed for the moment by the one great spirit. There is one universal, great spirit and it wears many masks and the masks are interchangeable. Is that a terrifying vision of the universe or is it a beautiful vision of the universe? I don't know. I only know that when I hear that story about the mysterious housekeeper as it is sometimes called, about the fox who is fox but is also woman, I find it a pity that the poor man wasn't able for his animal nature even though he was a hunter.[3]

For a little while the hunter, the human in the story, is able to live in reciprocal harmony with the animal, accepting and in harmony with the miracle that she represents. For a while 'it was a new life'. But he was not able for it, the smell of fox became too much for him and he became afraid. He repressed his inner nature, he closed himself off from animal or instinctive wisdom and he reverted to a smaller safer life. This, according to John, has been the Western European way, a deliberate rejection of instinctive power and knowledge, a rejection of 'we-feeling'. On the other hand, the fox-woman is what we fundamentally are – far, far more than we know, or can ever know any more, in our worlds that are dominated by two-hundred-watt light bulbs, rational arguments and scientific proofs. She represents the world of nature and instinctive life, the world of spirit, of miracles and synchronicities and connectedness, all the strangeness and mystery of the universe; because we have turned our backs on her, she has taken her magical fox pelt with all of its transformative properties, and trotted away from us, back into the bush.

'How infinitely sad,' John would say, 'to see the animals giving up on us.' Effectively, he was saying, how infinitely sad to see us giving up on ourselves. He was reading some of the origin stories of the Native American peoples and he had come across Old Man, the Being who had made the world and who, having completed his creation, retired from view but left the following advice:

> Now if you are overcome you may go to sleep and get power. Something will come to you in your dream, and that will help you. Whatever those animals are who come to you in your sleep tell you to do, do it. If you want help, are alone and travelling, and cry aloud for aid, your prayer will be answered – perhaps by the eagles or by the buffalo or by the bears. Whatever animal answers your prayer, you must listen. (*Nostos*, p. 203)

How infinitely different that was from the story told in the Old Testament, where Yahweh told Noah

> 'And the fear of you and the dread of you shall be upon every beast of the earth, and upon every fowl of the air, upon all that moveth upon the earth, and upon all the fishes of the sea; into your hand they are delivered.'[4]

Two creation myths, – one suffused with 'we-feeling', the other starkly proclaiming 'us-and-them'. John had no illusions about which myth had survived and had conquered, with what he believed to be disastrous consequences for all of humanity. The *Mayflower* carrying the Pilgrim Fathers to Plymouth Rock had brought with it all of the assumptions of European culture; Old Man and his people had little chance against it. But in deference to the beauty of the message, and in need of a prayer to come ashore with, John turned to Old Man.

> That prayer to all the animals who were here before me, that prayer even to the extinct animals of Punta Alta, that was my Plymouth Rock, and standing on it the Foxwoman was my Statue of Liberty. (*Nostos*, p. 205)

With Foxwoman as a re-imagined Statue of Liberty then it might one day happen that 'coming home, the Mental Traveller looks up and sees smoke rising from his chimney. After incarnations of seeking he has found the place and state of mind to set out from.'[5]

§2

As was usual with him, he arrived in Winnipeg having done very little forward planning. He booked into the Montcalm Hotel on the Pembina Highway and was taking it from there. Chance encounters would again play their part. Two days after arrival, on his way to search for more permanent accommodation, he was standing at a bus stop when a passing motorist, possibly recognising a fish out of water, stopped and offered him a lift. He accepted, admitting that he didn't actually know where he was going. As luck would have it, the driver, Tom Durhout, was working at the University of Manitoba, and offered to help in the search for a suitable place. 'Hospitality as candid as this I had never previously encountered. In Canada, however, I would soon find out, it wasn't exceptional.' With Tom's help he found an apartment far grander than anything he had previously occupied.

> I was delighted with myself. Me having a place with a separate kitchen! A kitchen with an electric cooker and a fridge in it! A kitchen with cupboards and wall cabinets in it! A kitchen with a long work-top and a stainless-steel sink in it! And then the living-room, with a posh Chesterfield that opened out into a posh bed, and the wide window giving onto a tree-lined street with well-kept green swards on either side of it!
>
> Overnight I had come up in the world. (*Nostos*, p. 206)

'Posh'. This was indeed a new life for John Moriarty. It was 1965, he was twenty seven and he finally had a regular income and a regular job. Back in Moyvane, Mary Moriarty was pleased but sceptical, he might have gone up in the world, but would it last? She wondered what Canadians would make of 'the cut of him'. And there was some initial reaction in the first few weeks. There was some jeering from groups of students on campus and on another occasion, curious as to why he had been refused service in a restaurant, a colleague enlightened him. 'It's the price you must be willing to pay for being the first person west of the Great Lakes with long hair.' These were only small incidents, in general he settled in altogether more happily than he had expected.

> Already by the end of my first week teaching I was experiencing the move from
> philosophy to literature as a liberation, and this sense of having walked free was
> daily reinvigorated by contact with other lecturers in the department, as indeed
> it was by contact with lecturers from other departments whom I would meet in
> the senior common room of University College. (*Nostos*, p. 208)

He had found a place where it was not unacceptable to talk about Mary
Hegarty and Mary Ann Danny O' and this sense of having walked free into a
larger world, was also reflected in the immensities of landscape and weather that he
everywhere encountered. Only a few weeks into the term he was invited to spend
the Thanksgiving weekend at a cottage on an island in the Lake of the Woods.

> The bone-bright chill of winter already in the air, this was seriously savage
> country. To survive here, trees had closed their leaves into needles and there
> they were, spruce trees everywhere, down to the water's edge on every shore.
> This country didn't make excuses for itself. Standing in it, I felt I was an exotic
> from a gentler place and I knew that if I were to attempt to live here, in the
> bush, I would sooner or later have to do what the bears had done, I would have
> to close my life down to shelter, reproduction and food. (*Nostos*, p. 209)

The final stage of the journey to the cottage involved a short boat trip. Waiting
for them when they arrived at the jetty was a Cree Indian, who would ferry them
over to the island. This was John's first encounter with a Native American and it
had an impact. The Indian was dressed in tatty brown shoes, baggy blue jeans, a
red sweater over a white vest and a faded, frayed anorak. Sitting in his boat John
attempted to make contact, even eye contact, but he was ignored. Nothing John
did would entice this Cree Indian to engage with him. 'As though I didn't exist,
he was looking at the horizon beyond me.' Imagining that in his face he could
see 'all the sullen hurt' of oppression and dispossession John was conscious of his
own position; he was Paleface, he was heir to the conquest of this land, and he
was guilty. As a Western European, both as a consequence of and on behalf of his
culture, he was feeling guilty – guilty of being a European. This did not sit easily
with him. Talking about it later in the evening to his host, Doris, she laughingly
suggested that he had been fighting the Indian Wars all over again.

> 'Yes,' I replied, 'but this time the Indian won. With his deliberately heedless
> eyes he pushed me back off the continent.'
>   'So where does this leave you?'
>   'It leaves me where I am, here in Canada. But it also leaves me trying to

come ashore. It leaves me trying to come ashore in a way that will induce him, or maybe compel him, to welcome me.' (*Nostos*, p. 215)

'Trying to come ashore.' A phrase that could describe the previous ten years of his life. Since, at age seventeen, he had read Darwin, he had been 'man overboard'. All attempts to come ashore since then had simply reinforced this sense of himself. But by now he was convinced that he was not alone; western culture, western humanity was overboard with him, and in precipitous trouble. In trouble in its religions, in its history, in its philosophies and consequently in its future. These were the topics that flowed back and forth during dinner that evening, the most controversial being John's contention that the western European way of being in the world was in trouble since its very beginnings in ancient Mesopotamia and very much in need of healing. His suggestion that it might be in need of a Native American medicine man his hosts found both perplexing and startling. On the journey to the Lake of the Wood earlier in the day they had passed signposts for towns with fascinating names ... Yellow Knife, Moose Jaw and Medicine Hat and John's imagination had immediately taken flight:

Living in any one of them, I might one day walk free from the ideological tyranny of Jerusalem, Athens and Rome.

And if, looking at my hand in a dream, I saw that yellow knife in it, what would I do with it? Would I cut my moorings to Classical- Christian culture with it?

And the medicine hat? (*Nostos*, p. 212)

The medicine hat, could a native American medicine man offer healing to all who were suffering from the illness of the modern age – from the soul-sickness at the heart of modern European culture? A medicine hat for western European culture? For a culture that in John's thinking was exemplified by repression, domination and 'cogito'. No doubt Doris and Marion must have had questions about the sanity of this intriguing Irishman and his preposterous suggestions. Similar to the reaction it had met with in Leeds, it was the concept of 'Gorgocogito' that met with most resistance. It again appeared like madness ... here was someone who insisted that the medicine man, the native American shaman, had something to teach the modern scientist. Here was someone who dared to say that the entire scientific community, Einstein, Darwin, Newton, all the greats included, was neither seeing nor telling 'the whole story' and that consequently their science was 'Simple Simon science' looking to catch a whale but fishing only in 'the empirical water of his mother's empirical pail'[6] This argument with empiricism[7] was the central argument of John Moriarty's life, he could never, would never accept that the only truth was that which could be proved scientifically by what he called our 'QED mentality' ... he would forever argue that the world, the cosmos, is stranger, more marvellous, more wonderful and inherently more miraculous than we, given our western European conditioning, can even imagine. In his view to have turned a scientific back on native wisdom was not progress but regression.

Here in Canada he was not only immersing himself in native American lore he was also avidly reading the work of Joseph Campbell, in whose fascinating research and commentary on the mythologies of the world he found much that echoed his own intuitions about ultimate truth. Campbell's expression, 'the bondage of reason'[8] precisely encapsulated Moriarty's sense of the inadequacy of any explanation of the world which relies solely on that which can be proven scientifically. Campbell again:

'Then it must be conceded that ... whenever a myth has been taken literally its sense has been perverted; but also, reciprocally, that *whenever it has been dismissed as mere priestly fraud or sign of inferior intelligence, truth has slipped out the other door.*'[9]

It was Moriarty's contention that ever since the great Age of Enlightenment, for all of its extraordinary achievements and discoveries, truth had indeed 'slipped out the other door', leading to a modern culture that for all its apparent freedoms and creature comforts is in serious danger of annihilating itself. Thus the need for a medicine hat 'for everyone who suffers from the illness of the age to wear.' A medicine hat that he felt in sore need of himself, 'maybe unknown to myself', he would later write, 'maybe I came to Canada in search of the medicine hat that would heal me of our European covenant with cogito, cogito being a jealous god who will have no other gods before it.' (*Nostos*, p. 227)

Towards to the end of that first evening with Doris and Marion, John referred to the Manitou, the Sacred Powers of the land, and asked them both, perhaps mischievously, if they had ever had any contact with them. His question was met with disbelief and a warning about any attempt 'to go bush' in this seriously savage Arctic landscape, where in winter temperatures could reach forty below zero, intensified by winds of forty-miles-an-hour. Sitting there with them, in this highly refined and civilised atmosphere, drinking claret from a delicate crystal glass and basking in the warmth of a blazing fire, he attempted to imagine the polar wilderness.

It could be I thought that somewhere in the Arctic just now, maybe, a glacier is calving an iceberg. I tried to hear the first tremendous crack, and then the crash, the sound of mountain ice falling down into the sea.

That sound.

And the sound of a cork coming free from a bottle of claret.

The iceberg. And the breakable elegance I was holding between forefinger and thumb.

How infinitely fragile, if not also evanescent, civilization seemed ... (*Nostos*, p. 217)

Enormous glaciers that 'calve' icebergs in contrast to the civilised elegance of a glass of claret; he was struck by the almost ridiculous incongruity, such power versus such insignificance, the wilful blindness of a civilization to the destructive power that surrounds and threatens it and the indifference of that power to the existence of human beings. To illustrate his point further he thought of another contrast, an image of the Greek pastoral poet Theocritus, playing a lyrical air on his reed pipe, and an Assiniboine medicine man playing his own death song on a pipe made, not from reed, but from the thigh-bone of an eagle. The two pipes are extremely significant, one represents the refinement of the ancient Greek world and thus also the refinement of modern civilisation, from which so much that is real is excluded; the eagle pipe of the Assiniboine medicine man is used in direct contrast to this artificial refinement – he sings of and therefore accepts his own death, his entire being is intertwined with the eagle that he has killed and eaten, to whom he is consequently beholden and whose bones now provide his sacred music. There is no barrier here between man and nature; his civilization, his sacred ritual, acknowledges all that he is and all that he must deal with. It is a ritual, and consequently, a civilization of inclusion. John again thought of Old Man and his creation story with his advice that animal wisdom is available to human beings, but 'you must listen'.

Advice such as this might well have been given and heard in the deepest caverns of Les Trois Freres and Lascaux, but a lot has happened in that world since. At its simplest, the walled city has happened, and Greek philosophy and Hebrew theology have happened and that accounts for the fact that in our yard at home is a wound with the cowstall on one side and the dwelling-house on the other.

Old Man and his world and his final advice fell into that wound. All the great painted caves of our Paleolithic intelligence fell into it. But maybe at the bottom of it somewhere some old Pleistocene shaman is still playing the thigh-bone tunes. (*Nostos*, pp. 217–18)

In fact the very wound itself was graphically depicted in one of those great painted caves. The Lascaux cave paintings, dating back almost 20,000 years, became a central symbol in Moriarty's work. One painting in particular depicts a bison bull that has been spear- wounded through the genitals by the only human figure depicted in the entire cave complex. This incident Moriarty refers to as mankind's 'primal blind trespass', as 'the big ecumenical calamity.'[10] It becomes his image for 'our long war with the world as we first found it', his image for man killing other creatures for his own 'use and benefit', killing them not only individually, but destroying their generative power, power that Old Man tells us could help us if we would only respect and recognise it. If we must kill animals, then we should recognise and in some sacred way acknowledge our debt to them. Maybe in that way we could learn to live sustainably with them, and reconnect with the spirit that we share with them. It was a long evening in the cottage in the Lake of the Woods.

> It was well into the small hours, the fire was newly fervent, and tired though I was, I still couldn't think of going to bed.
>
> To give credence to a train of thought, I went to the door and opened it, and yes, sure enough, it was into a great absence I was looking. Some years ago now I had somewhere read that the bedrock that outcrops across so much of lowland Canada is all that is left of a range or ranges of mountains as extensive and possibly as tall as the Alps. Stone by stone and particle by particle, peaks that had no name, neither Matterhorn nor Mount McKinley, had been broken down and carried away, and here I was standing on a lake-mirrored root or rudiment of them.
>
> Will someone one day stand on a rudiment of the Himalayas?
>
> Will someone one day stand on a rudiment of Mount Everest?
>
> Will someone one day stand late at night in a cottage door and look out into a great absence? Into an absence of waterfalls and gorges? Into an absence of ammonites and yogis? Into an absence of peytoias and prayer wheels? ...
>
> Or will it be all over for humanity by then? Will there be no one who will come to spend a Thanksgiving weekend on a rudiment of the Matterhorn, on a rudiment of Mount McKinley?
>
> Thoughts such as these shipwrecked Ishmael ... and there it was that Saturn's grey chaos rolled over him and so far we haven't imagined a *nostos*, for him. (*Nostos*, p. 218)

Ishmael, a central character in Moby Dick, is overwhelmed by the apparent indifference of a hostile universe, and all the science and philosophy of the world since the Renaissance, Reformation and Enlightenment, have not found a *nostos*, a sheltering homecoming for him, there is nothing for him but existential despair. Standing at the door of this cottage and looking out into this vast absence John could find no rational argument that might offer comfort. And yet ...

And yet, in spite of an initial, half-frightened concession – even now looking into the absence ... something about the light at the heart of a cowslip in the Hill Meadow at home, and something about the feel, first of five eggs, and then of five chicks, in a wren's nest – memories much more vivid than present sernsations, suggested that the universe we live in is not as palsied as Ishmael believed it was.

In the end, arguments to the contrary being so persuasive, Blake's four lines were an act of faith.

> The Atoms of Democritus
> And Newton's Particles of light
> Are sands upon the Red sea shore
> Where Israel's tents do shine so bright.[11]

By now, as I recited them, I knew that as well as being an act of faith they were an act of defiance. (*Nostos*, 218)

Obviously, the existential trouble has not eased. He has not found any solid answers for the 'palsied universe' that Ishmael battles with in Moby Dick; the universe is still ultimately as Sir James Jeans diagnosed 'a great absence'; Matthew Arnold's 'sea of faith' has retreated even further here on the vast naked Canadian Shield shingle; and the 'mis-evolved' or 'over-evolved 'human being has walled out, has obliterated, his own animal past, and with it all animal wisdom and healing powers. John Moriarty's rational brain could neither deny nor answer any of this and yet the vivid memory of the five- year-old boy who felt something instinctively wrong in the absence of Christmas in the cow-shed, who shared his father's sense of 'we-feeling' with the animals, who saw Paradise at the heart of a cowslip, made him defiant. He would find the medicine in the medicine hat, he would take as his guide the Assiniboine medicine man with his pipe made from the thigh bone of an eagle, he would provide a *nostos*, a homecoming, for Ishmael, he would keep faith with that deep feeling that told him that there was more to the universe than science could ever fathom, he would find 'a sheltering mythology'. The 'act of faith' that John makes is an act of faith in his own instinctive sense of things. Mary Moriarty could at least be proud of his defiance.

7

'BE NOT AFRAID OF THE UNIVERSE'

Snow; 'play with ideas'; the key to the mystery; a green house on the ice-cap; the Blackfoot Buffalo dance; Tsetsekia; 'be not afraid of the universe'; ill with the great illness; repression of soul.

The well-known phrase from Socrates that the unexamined life is not worth living can have had few greater exemplars than John Moriarty. It was second nature to him to interrogate and indeed internally dramatise his every experience and in this sense the newness and vastness of Canada provided enormous intellectual excitement. In the first place the weather provided opportunities for reflection.

Aware of a hush in the world, I looked out and it was snowing. All over delighted, I went to the window. Down out of the grey it was coming, and how, I wondered could miracles so white come down out of something so grey. I had heard that the Inuit had several different names for different kinds of snow. What their name for this particular kind was I didn't know. I only knew that I hadn't seen snow like it before. In over the roofs it came, little eddies and swirls of wind windrowing it down the street ...

So often in Ireland snow was a disappointment, feeling wet to the face and the hands and melting as soon as it touched the ground. ... Here, looking at them landing on a shrub, I could well believe that snowflakes had a perfect crystalline structure, perfect as the gold filigree on the Ardagh chalice, and yet like human fingerprints no two snowflakes were the same. Falling in their billions all over North Dakota and Manitoba, falling on Prairie farmhouses and falling farther north into the lonely bush, falling there on to the fur of fox and wolf and mink, in their billions falling all around us, and no two of them the same. And the universe makes galaxies and makes them in numbers as great as it makes snowflakes ... (*Nostos*, pp. 222–8)

The sacred geometry inherent at the heart of a snowflake; the infinite patterning, and yet the infinite variety in all the vastness of the universe; the inability of our conditioned minds to recognise such wonders; the need to cleanse our way of looking at the world; these were the issues posed by a simple fall of snow. The 'perfect crystalline structure' of a snowflake leads to a renewal of his confident and somewhat startling challenge to both Newton and Einstein

> Here in my street tonight, here among icons and snowflakes, I have news for you Isaac, I have news for you Albert: the truth about things is miraculous. (*Nostos*, p. 229)

Naturally, such an exhibition of his mother's bravado did not last for long, there were too many counter arguments to balance this moment of optimistic vision. It would only take a change in the weather.

> That weekend the temperatures dropped to twenty below zero. By Monday morning it was clear that the Arctic ice-cap had come into the city. Wherever they struck it, the rays of the sun came back like flick-knives off the frozen snow
> ...
> Coming back into it at dusk that evening, my street felt like a verification, never again to be gainsayed, of the second law of thermodynamics.
>   Once inside my own door I went and took down his book to see again what Sir James Jeans had said about it ... I wanted to encounter the thing in his exact words:
>   'the universe is indifferent and even hostile to every form of human life.'
>   ... here in my street, a December sun having set, it felt like the truth. (*Nostos*, p. 234)

And so the perpetual see-saw continued, the voice of the small boy in the Hill Meadow sometimes triumphantly in the ascendant but more often than not the savageries of a Winnipeg winter annihilating the hopeful vision and he would fear that he was 'losing the fight with Medousa', succumbing to the world of the rational mind that did not allow for miracle, that turned everything to stone. However, the compulsion to be true to the hopeful vision, to listen to the voice of his past and the voice of his instinct, the compulsion to 'find th'answer', had a vice-like grip on him and would never be completely silent. If nothing else, he was stubborn.

In this respect the academic environment in Canada suited him far better than that left behind in Leeds. In the University of Manitoba he had taken on a new discipline. Instead of teaching philosophy he was teaching literature, and he enjoyed it. Art in general, he would claim, and poetry in particular, 'is more hospitable to the truth and mystery of things than is the clarity of Descartes.'[1] Intuitive insights into the nature of things, the world of the creative imagination, the world of magical stories, the openness to 'otherness', it was in these realms that he was most at home. On route to Canada he had wondered 'what medicine hat was I coming with?' and had hoped to find 'the medicine of insight' in the texts that he would teach. Frequently he did just that:

> Sit, Jessica: look, how the floor of heaven
> Is thick inlaid with patines of bright gold:
> There's not the smallest orb which thou behold'st
> But in his motion like an angel sings,
> Still quiring to the young-eyed cherubins;
> Such harmony is in immortal souls;
> But, whilst this muddy vesture of decay
> Doth grossly close it in, we cannot hear it.[2]

This vision of the harmony that is 'in immortal souls' would be the 'medicine hat for Medusa', and in his more optimistic moments he would feel 'as if J. B. S. Haldane and William James had been walking either side of me, Haldane whispering that the universe is queerer than we can even imagine and James whispering that there should be no premature closing of our account with reality.'[3] These two quotations became central to John's thinking, both advising against the danger of any certainty about the nature of the world, both advising openness of mind.

His aim in teaching was to bring this sense of openness, of 'play with ideas' to his students – 'playfulness of mind, that, more than anything else was what I needed to put on show for my first year students. Some of them were song-writers yet when it came to writing an essay they turned Bolshevik heavy and deadly'. It frightened him to see the lack of critical thinking displayed in their work. He wanted intellectual honesty and on one occasion in order to provoke independent thought he introduced them to a poem by the Irish poet Thomas Kinsella and admitted that he had no idea what it meant. Their assignment was to write a personal response to the poem. Returning the work, he put the bundle of essays on his desk, and said 'D'ye see the height of this? ... Bullshit from top to bottom. I haven't the remotest clue what that poem is about and every one of you pretended to understand it. Why the pretence? If you don't know or understand something have the confidence to say so!'[4] He encouraged them to challenge and to question, to think critically and independently, and in his lectures he modelled this type of thinking for them. One of those students, Brian MacKinnion, recalls 'the adventure of first year English' in which John 'stretched our minds and souls'; watching him 'we got a sense of what a great mind was capable of.'[5] Above all, they were to challenge 'the modern consensus about reality,' to see the wonder in the world around them and to be aware of the urgent need for transformation in the modern scientific worldview.

> And some of my students, whose less-than-enlightening essays I had read, were already intent on careers in science and technology. At the end of one such essay I concluded that we should seriously think of doing with $E=mc^2$ what our forebears did with Excalibur. (*Nostos*, p. 221)

At the request of the dying King Arthur, Excalibur was thrown back into the lake from which it had emerged, thus ending both Arthur's reign and the power of his sword. Moriarty imagines a similar fate for the science that underpins the modern world – a science that he believes has been misused and abused because the wisdom to manage its enormous power has been blatantly lacking. This was a theme to which he would return again and again, and he would tell the famous Sufi story of a man who comes home late at night and in the darkness drops the key to his front door. There is a street lamp near his house and he begins to search the ground by the light of this lamp. A neighbour approaches and helps in the search. On their hands and knees carefully scratching around in the earth the neighbour finally asks the man exactly where he thinks he dropped his key. 'Somewhere over there beneath the tree', is the man's reply. Dumbfounded the neighbour wonders why they are not looking over there. 'Because over there there is no light', comes the bewildering response.

John would tell this story to illustrate the central problem that he identified at the heart of the modern scientific world view. 'All the while', he would say, 'the key to the mystery is in the dark corner', but minds trapped in the belief that the only way of knowing the world is through 'the very narrow circle of intellectual sensory light' may well be missing the greater part of the story. Science, he would repeatedly say, 'is not the whole story'. Again and again he would insist that he had no argument with the scientific discoveries in themselves:

> I am simply saying, when we come away from seeking and searching, when you come away from your lab, when you come away from the lab of your mind and your eye, and you let the world come to you, it comes to you in very strange and wonderful ways, it comes to you in ways that you know that what Haldane says, that the universe is queerer than we can even imagine, is in some sense true. So

if the universe is as Haldane says it is then folk tale and folk story are as much places of revelation about the universe as mathematics can be.

I'm just saying that maybe there are other ways of talking about the universe than the mathematical way, which has been the way of the last three or four centuries ... there are all kinds of other ways of being in the world than the modern scientific way. I think for all its successes the modern scientific way is a limitation.[6]

However these ideas were received, there is no doubt that he embraced his teaching with enthusiasm, enjoying the status of a young, handsome and certainly exotic lecturer in this land of snow and ice. In an interview years later he told Maurice O'Keeffe 'Jesus, I loved it. I would go into a lecture room every day the way Jack O'Shea would break out into Croke Park. Do you remember the full scope and *scaoil amach* of him? Where's the ball, Gimme the ball ... I was that excited by ideas. Ideas to me were passions. I loved it. I flourished. It suited me down to the ground.'[7] He was radical, he was challenging and he was popular. There were parties and, while still writing regularly to Marilyn, there was at least one girlfriend, who made quite an impression. She drove a Mustang and wore a mink coat – it was the mink coat that fascinated him

'Jesus', I said, 'your coat, a shaman would love it. Shaking it he'd shake thunder out of it, he'd make rain.'

While John was undoubtedly unconventional, this woman of the Mustang and the mink was anarchic, and mesmerised as he was by her, after a few wonderfully passionate days he was afraid that she would move in.

Coming into my street that evening, I was delighted and yet uneasy to see Clara's sports car parked outside my apartment.

Had she already moved in? I wondered, because if she had, that could be trouble. I needed solitude. I needed silence. I needed a room like the one I had in Rathmines in Dublin. In that little room I used to switch off the light and let the deeper levels of my psyche be in séance with me. Without solitude and silence and lights switched off for some couple of hours every day, or night, I wouldn't be particularly pleasant to live with. (*Nostos*, p. 231)

He need not have worried, the relationship ended almost as soon as it began in a flurry of angry energy.

Screaming, she called me a bastard, and then, leaving only the shimmering of her coat in my room as she did so, she pulled the door shut with such violence behind her that the whole building shuddered. (*Nostos*, p. 231)

On this occasion the issue was resolved for him without too much heartache but, as has already been seen with Marilyn, this battle of conflicting impulses – the need for intimate relationship and the opposing, irreconcilable need for solitude, silence and space would haunt him throughout his life. That was not the only conflict bothering him. Successful as was his teaching, and enjoying it as he was, something felt wrong. He was living in an alien inhospitable landscape and his knowledge of it was confined to those aspects of it that had been 'tamed' by the white man. Yes, he was experiencing the extremes of weather, but on a day in January, after a walk in the snow- covered Prairies, he realised that

> I didn't know this land. I certainly didn't know it in a way that a Cree hunter or an Assiniboine shaman would know it. I had heard it in a couple of places where it spoke out loud. I hadn't heard its whisper. And yet, here I was, seeking to make contact with it, but all I could so far see is that I was all out of place ...
> Next day, a student who was giving me a lift home suggested a detour to the conservatory in the town park. (*Nostos*, p. 237)

This tropical greenhouse in a land of snow and ice felt completely out of place, and it struck him that the English Department at the university was very similar, 'a greenhouse on the icecap' where he was teaching literature much of which had little or no connection to the place in which he was living and attempting to learn from and understand. Here was yet another disillusioning; he had hoped that in teaching English literature he might find, and possibly impart, the 'medicine of insight', but now it occurred to him that this literature, however profound its revelations, was not adequate for the enormities and extremes of Canada. He wanted to see and experience the New World in the way that it existed outside this 'European greenhouse' and he now attempted to do so by immersing himself in the native stories, where he hoped to gain insight into the worldview of those who could truly be said to have lived in this land.

A story that resonated powerfully with him, which he often retold, was the story of how the Blackfoot Indians explained the origin of their buffalo dance. In order to kill these tremendous animals the Blackfoot had devised a ritual whereby a shaman, having prayed and fasted, would don a buffalo robe and mask and, approaching a herd, would seek to arouse their curiosity. This achieved he would lead them towards a precipice, near which the rest of the tribe were in hiding. Ultimately the trick was to panic the buffalo into thundering forward and pouring over the edge of the precipice.

> Cows and calves and bulls would pour over it, down down down into the corral

below. Their backs broken, there they would lie, waiting to be slaughtered ... that's how the Blackfoot would secure meat and hides and so much else besides for the winter. (*Nostos*, p. 238)

But once upon a time, so the story goes, the decoy failed. Again and again the herds avoided the trap and there was famine among the Blackfoot. Their salvation was achieved by the mysterious action of an adolescent girl. One morning, when she went to fetch water, she saw a distant herd of buffalo and, following some instinctive urge, she called out

'If you will come and be food for the people I will marry the chief bull among you.' To her astonishment, it happened. Hardly had she made her offer than the whole herd had broken off from their grazing and were thundering across the Prairies and this time, breaking neither to the right nor left, they poured over the precipice into the corral below.' (*Nostos*, p. 238)

A bargain had been made with the buffalo, and the rest of the story concerns the manner in which the bargain was kept. The girl surrenders herself to the chief bull but eventually, recognising her suffering, the bull agrees to let her go back to her people, and gives her 'the greatest gift that we have, our song and our dance' to take back with her. In the story she in turn takes back an understanding of buffalo suffering, and it is with this understanding that ever after, the Blackfoot dance the buffalo dance in acknowledgement of their debt to and dependence on this great beast. 'That's how it happened, that's how the Blackfoot came up out of an old way into a new way of being in the world.' John found many levels of meaning in this story but that which struck him most profoundly was the sense of contract between man and beast.

Thinking of the Blackfoot story, I would think of the night I crossed the yard at home. It was Christmas Eve and how ruined I was when I saw that it was an ordinary night in the cowstall. That night the word 'we' fell asunder into the word 'us-and-them'. But now I had found the remedy. The song and dance the buffalo had given us was the remedy. Danced on our yard it would heal the wound that had opened between us and our animals, between us and all that wasn't us. It would turn 'us-and-them' into 'we', a word of stupendous moral and spiritual implication, a monosyllable which, all on its own, could be our constitution, reconstituting us in relation to all things. (*Nostos*, p. 242)

The sense of excitement is palpable, he has found the remedy for the disaster that he sees engulfing the planet – not of course a literal buffalo dance 'on our yard' (Mary Moriarty would have made short shrift of that!) but in that deceptively little word 'we', 'we-feeling', a shared earth, not an earth dominated by one species imbued with a divine biblical right to 'lord and master' over all the rest. The Blackfoot origin myth he saw as entirely ecumenical, in contrast was the Judeo-Christian myth, which gave the world to man for his 'use and benefit' regardless of the impact on other creatures or the environment itself. This tribe of Blackfoot Indians had developed a better way of being in the world, and European conquerors and settlers with their 'superior' European mind-set had all but wiped them out. For the rest of his life, a central part of John's mission was his effort to convey the understanding that this 'better way of being in the world', if ever it could be achieved, was now the only hope for a planet otherwise doomed to ecological disaster and consequent cultural breakdown.[8]

To John's mythologically accustomed eyes there was even further contrast and significance. He wondered about this Blackfoot girl. 'And who is she? I wondered. Who is this girl who went out onto the Prairies and later that night went out into them again, this time as bride to the Bull?' Naturally, he thought of the Greek story of Pasiphae, also bride to a bull, whose story had a very different outcome. The Blackfoot girl came back to her tribe having come to accommodation with the bull, with the beast that lives both within and without. A story of inclusion and integration. On the other hand Pasiphae's encounter with the bull led to the birth of the Minotaur, half-man, half-beast, who, in her shame Pasiphae had hidden in the labyrinth and whose anger could only be appeased and controlled by human sacrifice. A story of exclusion and repression.

> Typically in Europe, we slay the Dragon, we slay the Bull; contrariwise, the Blackfoot won the good will of the Bull and, wisely, they then went on to ritually institute that good will not just at, but as, the beginning of their culture. (*Nostos*, p. 243)

Here among the Blackfoot he believed that he had found an answer to the terrible questions that had been bothering him in Greece – how we could use our Parthenon capacities to better manage our Minotaur instincts? How could we help Mary to take her foot from off the head of the serpent? The Blackfoot had ritualised these powerful frightening instincts in their buffalo story and buffalo dance and so had acknowledged and included them.

He found further ritual enactment of this type of inclusion in an account of a ceremony of the Kwakiutal, a native people who lived on the southern Pacific coasts of British Columbia and Vancouver Island. The ceremony was called the

Red Cedar-bark cycle or, in their language, Tsetsekia. In it, trying to come to grips with everything that is terrible in the world and in the human psyche, they gather around the fire in their communal log house, and in the depths of a dark winter night, they open the door to the Great Iakim. He is their dragon, their monster, the one they most fear, and they welcome him in. Singing, drumming and ritually dancing they sing:

'The Great Iakim will rise from below. He makes the sea boil, the Great Iakim, And we are afraid.'

It is their intention to let him emerge, to let him be luridly illuminated in the flames of their firelight, and by so doing to try to come to terms with him. How different from the ways of the dragon slayers of European culture, different from the buried Minotaur, different from all efforts to eliminate and suppress that which we fear or do not understand. As John would say again and again, a killed dragon is not a dead dragon, a suppressed instinct will not remain forever repressed, an enemy killed does not go away. Inclusion, integration, understanding these were the lessons he was learning from so-called 'primitive' cultures.

> Tsetsekia surely is the remedy.
> I imagined all of Europe's dragon slayers sitting in the log-house.
> Watching, they live their fear of the Great Iakim. They live their fear of all
> that is in the sea's entrall, of all that is in their mind's entrall.
> And that is their healing, theirs and ours. (*Nostos*, p. 267)

Years later, he would elaborate on this: 'Conceding, for the moment, that the great Indian ceremonies had no direct or immediate influence on the fertility of the animal herds and the earth, could it not be however that these same ceremonies were not without favourable influence in another direction, in helping us to confront, enact and, as a consequence, cope with our Andromeda[9] dread of ourselves. In the course of these ceremonies, in other words, they became Andromedas to the Great Bull Buffalo, which, as from nowhere, can appear bellowing havoc, and murder and rape at us out of our inwardness.'[10]

'Our Andromeda dread of ourselves', our knowledge that the Great Bull Buffalo resides within us all, that animal nature in us makes us capable of terrible atrocities, but such is our dread of this aspect of ourselves that we refuse to confront it. Culturally and individually we hide it, we bury it, we deny it, and then ultimately and always tragically, it erupts into our daily lives and in bewilderment we suffer the consequences of our Guernicas, our Srebrenicas, our Afghanistans, our Syrias, our Bloody Sundays, our Auschwitz. The Beast that we believe secured and under control in the Labyrinth bellowing on our streets. In Tsetsekia, and in the Blackfoot

Buffalo-bride, story John saw a cultural effort to come to an understanding of the frightening forces that threaten human beings. He saw in Native American ceremonies and stories an effort at assimilation that he believed conspicuously lacking in the origin stories inherited in Europe.

He found other origin stories that were equally inclusive of and respectful to the natural world. The Cherokee story of how fire came to the people, as a gift of coal from the Thunders to the little spider Kanana'ski Amai'yehi, rather than a weapon stolen by Prometheus; and then there was the Inuit story of preparing for the hunt. The tribal shaman would go on a great journey to liaise with Takanakapsaluk, the mother of all of the sea-beasts, and he would win her good will by combing her hair with a comb made of walrus ivory. Not until this journey had been undertaken could the hunt begin. Once undertaken, the hunters make their way to the seal's breathing holes, 'And when one of them harpoons a seal he calls out to the others and they come and together they haul him out onto the ice. Speaking to him, they thank him for having offered himself as food for the people. Ritually, they open his side and cutting out his liver they eat raw morsels of it, and speaking again to the seal, speaking to its spirit, they tell it to go to where we assume new bodies and come back.'[11] Reading these stories gave John a sense that here were people on good terms with the totality of their own nature and the world in which they lived. They evoked a fervent response in him.

If only time was reversible.

If only history was reversible.

If only we could speak those stories, the Cherokee and the Inuit story, into and at the beginnings of our western way.

If only we had the good fortune to come culturally forward from them and with them ... There are peoples who locate themselves in sacred space. In the morning they pray to the Sacred Powers in the West, to the Sacred Powers in the North, to the Sacred Powers in the East, to the sacred Powers in the South, to the Sacred Powers in the heavens above and to the Sacred Powers in the Earth beneath their feet. It has been claimed that since sacred space and its directions are forever unchanging, it is likely that people who live in it will on the whole be much more psychically stable than people who live in the endless and often useless progressions and regressions of history.

If only we had waited till the Thunders sent fire down to us.

If only, even now, some sacred one among us would go down ... and comb Takanakapsaluk's hair. (*Nostos*, p. 252)

Here was a heartfelt plea for sacred ritual that might provide a more enlightened way of being in the world, a way that would help to acknowledge, accept and integrate all of animal nature, both the animal capacities in human beings and the humanity in animals. In his enthusiasm for new ritual he fancifully envisaged re-dedicating the University of Manitoba, re-dedicating it as the keeper of the coal and the comb, with a new banner depicting the great shaman setting out with his walrus-ivory comb to the floor of the ocean, and little Kanane'shi Amai'yehi coming home with the coal. Fortunately, he kept that idea to himself. It was quite enough to have his sister Madeleine, on hearing his more fanciful notions, declare 'shur, he must be mad'.

Mad or otherwise he was developing an alternative vision even though he was well aware that native American culture was not at all homogenous. There was evidence of savagery, of cannibalism, and environmental recklessness in some tribes. He knew, for instance, that in certain areas they were guilty of extensive over-stocking of horses resulting in the near extinction of the native bison, but among certain tribes, in particular those of the far north, he found evidence of a culture that he believed, had it been allowed to develop, would have provided a healthier spiritual as well as environmental foundation for humanity.

Again on the spiritual front he would cite reports of encounters with living shamans. In the work of Joseph Campbell he read accounts of Aua, of Igjugarjuk, and of Najagneq, Eskimo shamans whose extraordinary lives were recounted by the famous explorer Knud Rasmussen. In the case of Najagneq:

'When Dr. Rasmussen asked him if he believed in any of all the powers he spoke of, he answered: "Yes, a power that we call Sila, one that cannot be explained in so many words. A strong spirit, the upholder of the universe, of the weather, in fact all life on earth – so mighty that his speech to man comes not through ordinary words, but through storms, snowfall, rain showers, the tempests of the sea, through all the forces that man fears, or through sunshine, calm seas or small, innocent, playing children who understand nothing. When times are good, Sila has nothing to say to mankind. He has disappeared into his infinite nothingness and remains away as long as people do not abuse life but have respect for their daily food. No one has ever seen Sila. His place of sojourn is so mysterious that he is with us and infinitely far away at the same time."[12]

This sense of a power in and beyond the universe, Sila, resonated strongly with him. In his own optimistic moments Sila was what he referred to as 'Divine Ground', the glory that he had sensed at the heart of the cowslip, and here that vision was echoed in words from an ancient past, a tribal past, words that he believed would have been understood by the Paleolithic hunters in the caves in Lascaux. Even more heartening was the observation, again to Dr. Rasmussen from Najagneq, that the voice of Sila is gentle, like a woman, 'a voice so fine and gentle that even children cannot become afraid. What it says is: *sila ersinarsinivdluge,* 'be not afraid of the universe.'[13]

Sila ersinarsinivdluge, 'be not afraid of the universe.' What an answer that insight might be to all those who suffer from our 'western way of understanding things', what an answer to Newton's 'nothing but'[14] universe, what an answer to Shakespeare, who in King Lear provides the extraordinarily bleak view of man as 'a bare forked animal'. Naked and unaccommodated, without a sheltering story that could protect him, Shakespeare's line 'Poor Tom's a-cold' is to Moriarty the plight of modern man, and it contrasts sharply with 'an old Eskimo shaman' who could say 'be not afraid of the universe'. It prompted the question:

> How come that he wasn't naked under his clothes? How come that, sitting there by the light and fire of the seal-oil lamp, how come that sitting in his snow house, he wasn't cosmologically cold? How come that, sitting in his snow house, he was at home?
>
> What furs, invisible to us, was he wearing?
>
> What psychological, cosmological furs, growing like good dreams from within, was he dressed in? (*Dreamtime*, pp. 175–6)

'Psychological, cosmological furs, growing like good dreams from within'. How comforting that sounds, and how badly needed those furs are. As John saw it, in the so-called 'first' world where actual furs, creature comforts, are in abundance, there is an inner and more devastating deprivation. There is what he diagnosed as 'repression, exclusion of soul', and as usual, to illustrate he had a story.

In Africa, two or more centuries ago, a white man had accumulated a great store of precious, merchadisable goods. If only he could get them to Europe his fortune would be made. To further this purpose, he hired the best African porters he could find and one morning, having eaten, they assumed their burdens and set out, hoping to rendezvous with a ship that would be lying off the coast at the full of the third next moon. They weren't only strong men these men he had hired. They were happy men. And, singing their ancestral songs as they walked, they were brave men. They didn't turn back, or so much as look back, at the borders of their tribal lands. Even in a seemingly endless savannah they were, happily, for going on. By the full of the second moon the white man was sure they would make it to the coast in time. Then one morning a strange thing happened. Strange, that is, to the white man. Sitting there, not eating, their eyes closed, the porters, to a man, sank into a trance. By midday that day, the man who must at all costs make his fortune, was bullish. By midday three days later, he was totally at a loss. In the end, every ruse and remedy he could think of having failed, he sat beside one of them and, his bearing and tone altogether more accommodating, he asked him, Will you please tell me what is happening? Slowly, over hours the porter came back from his trance. Yes, he said, I will tell you. During the past two and a half moons we have moved so far, so fast, that now trance deep in ourselves yet awake, we must sit here and wait for our souls to catch up.[15]

This was his diagnosis: 'In Europe during the past three centuries, we too have moved too far too fast. It is time, I believe, to do as the Africans did, to sit down and wait for our souls to catch up. Among the first peoples of the world, loss of soul is thought of as the great illness. Only the most powerful shamans can deal with it. ... The question is, are we ill with the great illness?'[16] As has already been seen his answer was yes, and his quest was to find soul-medicine, a medicine hat, that would provide some protection from the existential cold. The Eskimo shamans provided some hope, there might be a vision of the universe which could counteract existential fear. There might, after all, be a medicine hat for Medousa.

8

'THE TRUTH ABOUT THINGS IS MIRACULOUS'

Pilgrimage to the Kwaikutl; the Northern Lights; 'a spring of love'; a silent river, a roaring river; Narada; the summer of love; Mexico; the snake in the rope; 'that art thou'; a bum trip; only let things be ordinary.

It was now the summer of 1966 and John had the unprecedented luxury of months of paid vacation before him. There were plans to spend some time with Marilyn in Montreal but prior to that he had another journey in mind. He was headed for the Rockies and for the western coast.

> My reason for going west was to let the Kwaikutl have their say, their Tsetsekia say, in my soul, and to this end I had it in mind, over a week or so, to walk the wild Pacific coasts they once lived on. (*Nostos*, p. 262)

The Kwaikutl ceremony of welcoming in the 'Great Iakim' had taken powerful hold of his imagination, and in deference to it he was making a pilgrimage. The pilgrimage had a spectacular start. In the back seat of a car, travelling west along the TransCanada Highway, he was alarmed by an extraordinary light and, startled, asked if they were on fire. No, he was told, it's the Northern Lights, it's the world that's on fire. They stopped and he stepped out of the car, 'not onto the earth, but into the galaxy, the galaxy opening and closing its curtains of fire and light, curtains of amber light, curtains of fox-coloured light' into what he could only call 'celestial fire'.[1] It was as if the universe was allowing a glimpse of itself, into the heavens dancing, dancing outside any attempts to classify or explain them.

> Tonight in Saskatchewan the naked eye sees what the conceptualising eye cannot see. It sees and it knows that the heavens are dancing outside our astronomies, it sees and it knows that the cosmos is dancing outside our cosmologies.

Never till tonight did I see that the universe is much more a thing of fire than it is a thing of earth air or water. ... (*Nostos*, p. 261)

This glorious spectacle could only, and should only, inspire awe.

How tremendous the universe is I thought.

Tremendous in the little water-walking spider who comes home with a cultural alternative to Western Titanism.

Tremendous in the Arctic Shaman who leaves his body and sets out on the trail to the floor of the ocean, to the floor of the psyche.

Tremendous in the girl who, having learned it from the buffalo, enacts we-awareness among us.

Tremendous in auroras that turn a car travelling west to the Rockies into a chariot of fire. (*Nostos*, p. 261)

A day or two later he was on Vancouver Island 'climbing a Kwaikutl beach onto Kwaikutl land', paying personal homage to a people who, in his view, had a better estimate of the 'tremendousness' of Nature and of the human condition, and a better way of handling it, than that offered by the European past. Very much aware of his status as a Paleface, his gesture in coming ashore on their land was an attempt to inherit their world-view and, even at this late stage in history, pay it due respect. It was an individual, personal re-imagining of an alternative past. He was again in 'If only' territory; if only the 'conquistadors' had played fair, if only the Pilgrim Fathers had been willing to learn, if only we could go back and heal and come forward again, this time bringing with us acceptance, acknowledgement and forgiveness. In this respect he thought of Coleridge and his Ancient Mariner.

The well known story at the heart of the poem, of an ill-fated mariner who shoots and kills the auspicious albatross, becomes for John a powerful image of the devastation that ensues when man sins against nature. The ship is becalmed, as if under some terrible spell, the ocean rots, and 'slimy things did crawl with legs/upon the slimy sea'. The spell is only broken when the mariner changes his outlook. Trapped mid-ocean, surrounded by the corpses of his shipmates, somehow he learns to pray, and when he does, before his eyes, the 'slimy things' are transformed:

O happy living things! no tongue
Their beauty might declare:
A spring of love gushed from my heart,

> And I blessed them unaware:
> Sure my kind saint took pity on me,
> And I blessed them unaware.
>
> The self-same moment I could pray;
> And from my neck so free
> The Albatross fell off, and sank
> Like lead into the sea.

For John, the weight of the dead albatross, a powerful image for man's disconnection from the natural world, hangs around the neck of western European culture, but the poem does offer some hope of healing, 'a spring of love gushed from my heart/and I blessed them unaware'. 'A spring of love'. What else is this but we-feeling? What else but another way of welcoming in the Great Iakim? What else but another and better way of being in the world that does not involve repression and exclusion?

With all of these connections going through his head on a cold and misty beach on Vancouver island, he was physically a long way from Moyvane, but still in a sense cycling the road to Listowel, still with a sense in his heart of 'the bog sadness in the world', still trying to find a way to heal it. Perhaps his entire life was in some way an unconventional pilgrimage, but happily there was also a more normal life going on, where he was enjoying new friendships, exploring a new country and negotiating the intricacies of relationship. Marilyn had agreed to spend the summer with him in Montreal and they spent a lovely time together. Unfortunately it was bitter-sweet, Marilyn had a return ticket, Canada was not for her and John did not see a future for himself in England. Nor could he overcome the old reluctance to compromise his freedom and space for the intimacy of a shared life; this time the parting was final.

The new academic year began for him with a change of address. He moved into the upper floors of an old house on Assiniboine Avenue, a street which took its name from a nearby river, prompting new reflections and new connections. Again inspired by the work of Joseph Campbell, he was reading the Hindu and Buddhist philosophies, and this Assiniboine River became a central image for the insight he found in them.

> Flowing through land traditionally occupied by the Assiniboine people, it is a silent river. It was hard to imagine how it could exist and yet draw so little attention to itself. For me that was its mystery.
>
> Along its course, from source to sea, the Colorado River drops by as many

as ten thousand feet. That means that along some of its reaches it is a loud river, a roaring river. (*Nostos*, p. 271)

A silent river. A roaring river. John would use these contrasting images to illustrate a central concept from Oriental philosophy, the concept of 'the ever-living life in all lives, which appears to be many but is really one.'[2] The 'ever-living life in all lives', that is like the silent river, flowing, always flowing in the background but largely unnoticed and unseen. It flows in all lives as their life-source, but it is also life itself. That source 'appears to be many', in other words it manifests itself as individual personalities, as plants, as animals, as mountains, as the loud roaring Colorado, as 'the ten thousand things' that the Taoists speak of, it never tires of manifesting, but it is always also itself, silent and flowing. 'Abundance flows from abundance, yet abundance remains' is how the Upanishads[3] express it. It is God, it is Tao, it is Brahman, it is Sila, it is Divine Ground. It is the source and it is eternal.

Once again he found a story to illustrate the point. He told of Narada, a saint-like man who lived, according to Hindu tradition, in the holy long-ago. His whole life was devoted to the great god Vishnu, and such was his devotion, that one day Vishnu appeared to him and offered to grant him any boon that he might desire. Narada immediately asked to know the secret of Vishnu's 'maya', his unique power. Vishnu reluctantly agreed and he and Narada set off on a journey. They walked for a long, long time, through the forest and beyond it until they reached a terrible red-hot desert. Eventually, appearing to suffer greatly from heat and thirst, Vishnu said he could go no farther. In the distance Narada could see a shimmering greener world, and with the last of his strength, promised to go and return with water for Vishnu. It was a longer journey than he had anticipated but he reached his goal and found a village offering shade and water. He knocked on the first door he came to and it was opened by a beautiful young woman. Instantly enchanted, he altogether forgot why he had come; forgot his quest, forgot his lord, Vishnu. He walked into the house as if he had just returned from working in the fields, and the family accepted him as if that were the case. He stayed and worked with them and when the year's work was done he asked for the hand of the daughter in marriage. It was granted, and in time Narada became the father of three children and head of the household. So the family prospered and were healthy and happy, until one year the monsoons came early and violently and their village was engulfed by water. Seeking to escape Narada attempted to lead his wife and children to higher ground but they were violently swept away by the torrential floods. No-one was saved. Narada came to consciousness in a red desert. He heard footfalls behind him, and then a voice: did you bring the water? You've been gone for almost an hour.[4]

So the story went. The world in the way that Narada had experienced it in his village life was certainly real, but also a manifestation of a deeper reality that for the most part remains completely hidden from the 'busyness' of daily existence. The earthly manifestations of this deeper reality, the farms, the families, the plants and animals, are eventually swept away, but the reality itself remains. The creative power, call it Vishnu, or whatever name a particular culture gives to it, is unchanging and unending. It is 'the ever-living life in all lives which appears to be many, but is really one'. And it is to that that all life ultimately returns.

This as a possible understanding of the way of things became one of the strands in John's thinking, the possibility of a power in the universe that is both Manifest in all of the terrors and glories that can be witnessed and experienced (life as Narada lived it in the village), but is also silently Unmanifest (Vishnu eternally in the background), a power that is beyond limited rational minds, beyond the circle of sensory intellectual light, that can only be understood, if understood is the correct word at all, through alternative ways of seeing, alternative ways of knowing. He would spend his entire life in search of these alternatives.

As usual, he brought the ideas with which he was 'playing' into his lectures. His intention was to provoke thought, to challenge habitual ways of seeing and understanding, to shake things up. On occasion the result was disturbing.

> In any one year, almost inevitably, there would be a Mennonite or a Hutterite[5] boy or girl from rural Manitoba in one of my classes. For them every word of the Bible was the word of God ... After a lecture one day, a Hutterite girl came to me and told me that she wished to transfer to the class of another professor who was teaching the same course. Afterwards, a friend of hers told me that she had left for the reason that she had seen the devil in my eyes. (*Nostos*, p. 321)

Her name was Abigail, and her reaction shocked him, not because of the fundamentalism that it reflected, but because of the responsibility he felt for her as a student and the dilemma that posed for him. She still lived in the shelter of the biblical mythology that had once, in a slightly different form, sheltered him. How would she fare if she crashed, in her thinking, into the modern world? This is where his teaching, should she listen, could lead her. And how would she fare if she didn't? Would she continue to see the devil in anything that did not fit with her inherited world view? He wondered how she could be both enlightened and protected. Would Hindu stories, Indian stories, Greek myths, make any sense to her? In a way it was the old question, the question of providing an understanding of the world that could provide comfort, 'the psychological furs' of the old Eskimo shaman, without involving indoctrination, exclusion or condemnation.

While Abigail represented a religious view of the world that is narrow in the extreme, a visit to San Francisco in the summer of 1967 provided an extreme of the more secular kind. He had rented an apartment and intended to spend the summer there but his first impressions were baffling to say the least. On arrival, alone, a bit exhausted and very hungry, he headed onto Market Street.

> Going into a restaurant, I walked up the aisle between two rows of tables, all of them occupied, to the food counter. Coming back with a salad, I sat by myself at a table that had just become vacant. Conscious that I was in America for the first time, I tried to seem self-assured, a private man going about his private business. As soon as I felt composed, I looked around and I noticed something very odd. It was all women who were in the place. Thinking that in coming in here I had blundered, I felt very uncomfortable. But then, that woman over there, the one arranging her tresses down over her breasts, she doesn't sound very feminine, nor indeed does she look very feminine. Careful not to gawk, I looked further afield, and then it dawned on me, I am among men, the difference between me and them being that they are all in drag and I am not. (*Nostos*, p. 278)

He was both fascinated and disturbed. All he saw, in this haven of free expression and free love, was confusion everywhere. As he became familiar with the district of Haight-Ashbury, the heart of hippie counterculture in San Francisco, radical and alternative though he was, he was not impressed by 'the summer of love'.

> It was all the streets of revolutionary Paris in the seventeen-nineties rolled into one. It was all the revolutionary streets of St. Petersburg and Moscow in nineteen-seventeen rolled into one ... And the call was, come West, come to Haight- Ashbury, come to the LSD party, come and shake off all oppressions, all the oppressions of all old worlds –

He recognised the dream, here were people attempting to find a better way of being in the world, but he also saw that

> Visually it looked like a circus the animals had walked out on, leaving the artistes and the acrobats introvertedly amazed ... No exception, Lucy in the Sky with Diamonds had a dark side. (*Nostos*, p. 279)

Drugs and confusion and all the while Bob Dylan prophetically singing:

> Oh, what did you see, my blue-eyed son
> Oh, what did you see, my darling young one? ...

I saw guns and sharp swords in the hands of young children
And it's a hard, and it's a hard, it's a hard, it's a hard
And it's a hard rain's a-gonna fall

A bleak vision set alongside the naive optimism of 'flower-power', and in the midst of it all, a sad reminder of Abigail. 'One day,' he writes, 'while walking back from the revolution, I saw and heard a teenage boy coming toward me. Tapping and shaking a timbrel, he was singing in a language which, from the skull cap he was wearing, I guessed must be Hebrew.' When asked the reason for the celebration the beaming reply was that it was because Moshe Dayan had beaten the Arabs! It was June 1967 and the Six-Day War in Israel had just ended with the capture of east Jerusalem. Was this where all religions led? War and fundamentalism on the one hand, and on the other, the Haight-Ashbury effort to escape from all religious restrictions, only to result in a 'circus' without centre, purpose or direction, simply individuals left to their own devices, well intentioned but damaged and vulnerable? There was no soul-medicine to be found here and he was tired of it all.

Sitting on a bench in Union Square I was when it occurred to me that this city wasn't nearly so exciting as people made it out to be. A half an hour later, walking the streets more or less aimlessly, I caught sight of a TWA office. I went in and asked the girl at the desk if they had a plane going anywhere interesting in the next couple of hours. She mentioned New York, Singapore, Cairo. No, no, no. She mentioned Mexico City and I instantly said yes, that's where I'll go. (*Nostos*, p. 282)

On arrival he rented a chalet in the suburbs of the city and was then disconcerted to find that as part of his contract a woman would be coming in for a couple of hours every day to keep the place clean. 'Can't I pay her to stay at home?' he argued, but the estate agent was having none of it, and so he had to acquiesce to a new image of himself, 'an Irish peasant having an Aztec mother for a maid.' It was amusing to think about what his mother would make of that, but it was also uncomfortable and he tried to alleviate his awkwardness.

Knowing that it wouldn't do anything for the hurt of the ages or for my feelings, I made her a coffee.
    She was surprised. And I sensed she didn't think well of me for it.
    At a loss, I having no Spanish and she having no English, I sat down.
    Sitting there, aware of her coming and going, I thought about her people.
(*Nostos*, p. 284)

If however, in coming to Mexico, he wanted relief from dark thoughts, Aztecs and their history did not provide it. A history of savagery on all sides was what he encountered, savagery in accounts of the conquest of their territory by Spanish explorers, but savagery also in the accounts of the pre-conquest Aztec religious ceremonies that included human sacrifice on an enormous scale. As ever he was unable to protect himself from the horror of it. Typically he did not flinch from the grisly details and did not distance himself from the perpetrators of gruesome ceremonies and practices. He read the eyewitness account of Bernal Diaz, chronicler of the Spanish conquest.

> How horrified to the point of vomiting something of his essential humanity he was when he would hear the awful drum announcing a new round of sacrifices. Among the hearts being offered were the hearts of those of his own men who had been taken alive.

He read of how the Aztecs had treated the daughter of a neighbouring ruler given to them as a royal bride. On his first official visit to them after her marriage the father was met by the Aztec high priest dressed in his daughter's skin. Descriptions such as these had 'a violent effect' on him. He could never reconcile himself to the human capacity for barbarism, nor did he resort to the protection of 'us and them', he did not delude himself that these were incidents from a heathen past – he thought of Auschwitz – and he did not delude himself that it was 'other people' who did these things.

> Having imagined it as often as I already had, I didn't now need to actively imagine the scene, the sacrificial stone and the sacrificial drum, the summit shrines with their gods looking on, so much of the place black with gore, and the gore itself reddened with veins of fresh human blood.
>
> Having held the basin to the gushing, spurting throat of a pig on our yard at home was no preparation for this.
>
> When Cortez declared his horror to him, Moctezuma replied that in his view it was altogether less horrifying to sacrifice a human being to a god and then eat him than it was to sacrifice the god himself and eat him.
>
> Becoming acquainted with each other in Tenochtitlan, Christians from *Auto Da Fe*[6] Spain were horrified by Aztecs and Aztecs were horrified by Christians. (*Nostos*, p. 295)

Obviously savagery and barbarism are part of the entire human inheritance, both 'heathen' and 'christian'. Cortez was 'rolling the scenery of one stage play away and replacing it with the no less fantastic scenery of another.'[7] Nietzsche's observation "I have discovered for myself that the old human and animal world, indeed the entire pre-history and past of all sentient beings, works on, loves on, hates on, thinks on, in me" was never far from his thoughts, and here in Mexico he saw it all again, institutionalized in an empire and a religion. In all instances the atrocities are normalized and justified.

He recognised that the Great Pyramid of Tenochtitlan 'was the ritual centre of a universal order of maize fields, volcanoes and stars that must be sustained and maintained with excavated, hot human hearts';[8] Aztecs believed that this horrendous ritual was the only way to maintain world order, their gods were brutal gods who demanded blood. Coatlicue, the Earth Goddess, whose statue he saw on display in the national Anthropological Museum, is an accumulation of terrors. Her head, 'is composed of two fanged snake heads facing each other ... she wears a necklace of severed hands and excavated hearts ... she wears a skirt of coiled interlaced serpents. She has jaguar's feet'.[9] The most awful part of this for him was that she was what he called 'mind-born', some human brain had invented her as a representation of 'the sustaining Powers of the world', she was a projection of some human mind. She was one culture's answer to the age old quest for an understanding of the world, a particularly frightening projection that dominated and controlled an entire empire, an entire culture and gave rise to ritualized savagery. This he saw as the power and the danger of the human mind. Again he had a Hindu parable to illustrate.

> There is a man walking home at evening. Having worked all day in the rice fields, he is weary and thinks only of coming back into the cool of his house. Suddenly, he sees a snake coiled and ready to strike on the side of the road. His weariness instantly at an end, he leaps sideways away, away again, and again away. Opening his eyes, he sees that the very inert thing on the side of the road is a coil of rope that has fallen from his neighbour's cart. (*Nostos*, p. 288)

How many times, he would ask, in the history of human beings, have cultures been deluded by the projection of a snake onto a rope? The man believed it was a snake, and he jumped and he jumped and he jumped. To what extent are we all jumping in response to a projection that has us in its grip? Is that what is happening? To the little Jewish boy singing for Moshe Dayan? To Abigail changing her class because she saw the devil in John's eyes? To the hippies in Haight Ashbury believing that flower power and psychedelic drugs could deliver a better world? To those educated by western European science who believe that human reason has all the answers? Is that what happened to the Aztecs? To the Christian crusaders and conquistadors? To the Arab /Muslim conquerors of the early middle ages? To the

French revolutionaries, the Russian revolutionaries, the Nazis? All jumping to the snake projected onto the rope and all totally unable, because so totally conditioned, to open their eyes?

> The snake in the rope.
> The cow in the car.
> The Hindu diagnosis of what ails us suggests that we are all milking cars, as though they were cows in Church street in Listowel. (*Nostos*, p. 302)

This was the diagnosis, human beings shuttered by their culture, and the solution that Hinduism offers is radical. In order to achieve spiritual enlightenment it is first necessary to extinguish all thought processes, to stop the 'eternal chattering' that the mind indulges in, to allow one's inner silence to prevail, to enter, through prayer and meditation, the inner darkness that the great eastern masters say is not darkness at all but is where 'moksha', liberation, awakening, can ultimately be achieved. It is in that place of darkness that one will find the god beyond all gods, the divine source behind all life, the One. At that point the ultimate realisation is 'Tat tvam asi',[10] that art thou, that is what you are, that is what a Christian is, a Hindu, a Buddhist, a Muslim, a Jew, a cat, a dog, a blade of grass, all one and all equal. If that vision is accepted, then the only way to live will be in accordance with that, there will be no more projection, and thus no more 'red rituals'.

As a possible understanding of divinity this resonated with him, but could it provide the 'sheltering mythology' that would protect humanity from the savageries of its own nature? Could living in accordance with this vision prevent the atrocities, both human and environmental, which have blighted, and continue to blight, human history? In other words, can we be safely guided by any creed or philosophy that does not openly incorporate all that we phylogenetically are, all that we are savagely capable of, that does not welcome in the Great Iakim? The danger that he suspected in the Hindu/Buddhist approach was the old danger. Is trying to extinguish mind another form of repression, of exclusion? Is there a danger, that on the way to the summit of enlightenment, the old powerful energies will, because unacknowledged in the ritual, re-emerge with all their primitive force. He felt it was a very real danger and he thought again of the line from the Geoffrey Hill poem 'There is no bloodless myth will hold', and he was back again in familiar territory, fighting the old battle with bloody rituals which on the one hand he so utterly rejected, and on the other, he could fully understand.

This power and the danger of the human mind, of the human psyche, and the need to be aware of and manage it, would concern him for the rest of his life. It confronted him in a different form a few days later when

Walking along Reforma one evening two young Americans came towards me. Clearly they had put a lot of effort into looking hip, even trashy, all of their so hurtable souls hanging from their ragged sleeves. They asked me if I knew of a cheap place to stay. 'You'd be welcome to stay for nothing in my place.' I told them. (*Nostos*, p. 310)

Glad of the hospitality they repaid it with what they described as 'pure Acapulco Gold, the best grass in all Mexico'. They rolled two joints of it for John, and reckless to the last, he smoked both. The 'trip' began with the ornate wrought-iron fire grate, unweaving itself and surrounding him, turning into an extraordinary hymn of praise to a God of the greatest glory, a hymn that was harshly interrupted by the students eating at the table ... suddenly the sound of the scraping of their knives and forks became unendurable and to escape from it he went out onto the lawn.

And as I walked in it headstones, headstones, headstones, hundreds of head-stones kept springing up all around me ... Suddenly they vanished and then it was fish – fish, fish, fish, – fish most wonderful, coral-reef fish – everywhere fish – swimming around me. I looked at the moon but I couldn't take its bright-ness. I sheltered my eyes with my arm. A dog barked and that too, that sound, that too had come out of its long pretence to be ordinary, and I thought, good God, I must tell my students never to take this stuff. Never, never, don't ever take it. The word 'never' was never so real.

It went on.
It went on.
It went on.
Only let things be ordinary, God.
Only let things be ordinary.
Awake they weren't. Asleep they weren't. (*Nostos*, p. 310)

It took more than twenty four hours for his mind to settle and in that time he found himself longing for Coleridge's man on business from Porlock to come and knock at his door, all he wanted was ordinariness, he wanted no vision of 'a damsel with a dulcimer', no matter what great poem it might inspire! The experience was unsettling to say the least but it gave an insight into the capacity of the mind to hallucinate an alternative reality. He was astonished at how real the headstones had seemed, how real the fish had seemed. 'As real', he reflected, 'but of course only as real, as the snake we sometimes project onto a rope.'

In the course of what he referred to as his 'bum trip' he had prayed, 'Only let things be ordinary, God. Only let things be ordinary'. If any phrase could capture the essence of John Moriarty's life, it must be this. His fundamental question was always, what is behind all of the projections, all of the illusions? What remains in the rope when and if we banish the snake? Are the Hindu Brahmins right when they assure us that it is 'moksha' or are we caught between a world of dangerous projection on the one hand and the utter dejection and emptiness of Matthew Arnold's 'naked shingle' on the other? The one answer that he always seemed to come back to was, look at the rope, the ordinary rope. And when he looked, he saw nothing ordinary at all – nothing ordinary about the auroras of fire in a Saskatchewan sunset, in the sacred geometry of a snowflake, in the beauty at the heart of a cowslip in the Hill Meadow. Ordinary miraculous things, a universe in which a caterpillar could metamorphose into a butterfly, in which a yellow butter-cup could come up out of black soil, tremendous manifestations of life, perhaps the miracle of the ordinary rope is the first miracle that must be acknowledged. That day in Mexico at the Pyramid of the Sun, when he had suffered all of its horrors, he had become aware of something else

> A Mexican family, a man, a woman and their little girl sitting among their baskets at the foot of the pyramid of the Sun. Colourful in their homespuns, the father and mother were eating. The little girl was playing and so red was her dress that beside her the great pyramid itself was wholly insignificant. Compared to the immense, solid ascendancy of the pyramid in whose shadow she played, she was tiny, and yet, looking at her I felt to have caught sight of her was all that was needed to open all doors into all worlds. 'Sight of her alone, if it was cherished', would open all doors into all worlds in a way maybe that the rituals of Teotihuacan, Tula and Tenochtitlan would not. (*Nostos*, p. 304)

'Sight of her alone, if it was cherished.' Cherish is the significant word, it is equiva-lent to the Ancient Mariner's 'spring of love', for the 'happy living things', cherish that, cherish the ordinary, cherish the sight of this ordinary little girl, the rest will follow. It was a thought that made him feel 'we are and we can be more evolved than our brain-stems', because we have the capacity to cherish if we would only let that capacity guide us. Unobserved ordinary life going about its daily business, and his reaction to it, had restored some small sense of hope for humanity. Surely, after a difficult but colourful struggle with Mexican history, there was some form of soul medicine in that.

9

'WHO WILL TAKE UPON HIMSELF THE BURDEN OF LIGHTING THE WORLD?'

The danger of the human mind; 'crying for a vision'; Morri Mostow; to eat the bitter herbs of history; 'a terrible Holy Book'; France; Mona Lisa walking back; the Tao; Rose window, Chartres Cathedral; 'one immortal wonder'.

It had been an eventful, difficult summer and he was glad to be back, living again on the bank of the Assiniboine, his silent river, bringing back to his classes new stories, fresh thinking, and a friendly warning about the dangers of hallucinogenic drugs. Ordinary life was a relief but Mexico was not easily shaken off. Principally it had confronted him with the struggle between two powerful, bloody and antagonistic mythologies, Christian and Aztec, each convinced of its owns god-given rightness, each incomprehensible to the other, each completely justified in its own atrocities, and each in the grip of a god-vision, god-projection that was as far from real godliness as it was possible to be. At the same time was a growing awareness that the peace and detachment inherent in Hinduism might not be sufficient for 'all that we phylogenitically are'. Also the Aztec sacrificing stone and the terrifying image of Coatlicue, the bloodthirsty earth goddess, had a profound personal resonance, which he wrote about in a piece he later called 'Aztec Sun'.

In the Anthropology Museum in Mexico City is the great Calendar Stone. Sun stone I prefer to call it, because at the heart of it is a dreadful sun, a sun which isn't a shining, a sun that dazzles us with heavy horror not with light, the sun as a brutal human head with an obsidian knife in its mouth ...

At this time in my life I had learned to live, however unsurely, with certain facts about myself and the world. Teeth, I'd already told myself, had beaten ideas to a place in my head. Canines and molars had roots in me before tenderness had. Often and often I'd seen the frightened glamour of butcher shop-windows in Ireland. As a child I had looked at and prayed at the fourteen stations of the Christian cross, scenes of lividly explicit violence in which a strangely feminine young man was turned into bleeding meat. And with the congregation I sang

> Blood of my saviour
> Sanctify my breast
> Body of Christ
> Be thou my saving guest.
>
> Deep in thy wounds, Lord,
> Hide and shelter me,
> So shall I never,
> Never part from thee.

Devotionally I was accustomed to violence. Surely therefore I was ready for the sun stone, ready for ancient Mexico ... But I wasn't. (*Turtle was Gone a Long Time*, vol. 1, p. 141)

Devotionally accustomed to violence as he was he could not keep the institution-alised but actual violence at arm's length. This was human savagery and he was implicated. 'In that obsidian knife I saw my own mind.' Louder than any Hindu parable, the sun stone was saying 'Tat tvam asi', that is really what you are, and in spite of all the glories of nature and the achievements of man that he would occa-sionally set against it, in spite of the Hindu concept of 'moksha' or enlightenment, the dominant feeling that he returned to Canada with was one of defeat. Vision of a greater destiny and a deeper glory defeated by what man appears instinctively to be.

An Aztec creation myth had intrigued him. In the beginning, so the Aztecs believed, before there was either night or day in the world, the gods came together in Teotihuacan. They talked among themselves and their pressing question was 'Who will take upon himself the burden of lighting the world?' Ultimately, so the story went, two gods volunteered to sacrifice themselves and they did so by walking into the heat of a burning cosmic fire, one god then becoming the sun and the other the moon. In order to keep these deities shining on them the Aztecs devised the bloody spectacle that Cortez encountered, and so human sacrifice was the unfortunate tragic outcome of their visionary question. For John that was both the pity and the danger. A vision for a better world, for 'light' in the world 'is often as deluded as it is enlightened. Standing in Auschwitz, we know that it is often as wicked as it is blessed. And the fact that it was blessed to begin with that doesn't mean that it will continue blessed. For every St. Francis who lives by a vision there is, across a small water, a Torquemada[1] who lives by it also.' (*Nostos*, p. 320)

And so after Mexico he was grappling, as always, not only with the danger of the human mind and of human instinct, but also of human vision, an Aztec vision gone wrong, a Christian vision also gone wrong.

Perhaps it was the burning issue of his life, this question of lighting the world. Years previously, while working in Wall's ice-cream factory he had wished for a 'sheltering story' for the Jamaican girl and her unborn baby, and, painstakingly, he was still searching. So far in his quest, neither science nor philosophy, for all of their emphasis on 'truth' and 'reality', had provided a framework that might guide, shelter and protect human beings and their environment. Of art and literature he had concluded that 'there is a power the arts do not have in their giving.'[2] Religions had equally fallen short; environmentally and spiritually the planet was 'bereft', with individuals for the most part mesmerised by the 'busyness' and distractions of an economically driven and corrupted world. Up to now, all that he could set against all of this was his own rare glimpses of a greater reality and what he had learned from native North Americans of 'the need to be in league with the world and not at war with it'. Their stories and customs 'testified to a humanity that had a just estimation of itself and of things. As well they testified to a humanity that lived in a right relationship to itself and to things.'[3]

A feature of Native American practice that really astonished him was the practice of 'crying for a vision'. It was a very individual ritual in which the seeker of vision would first undergo 'inipi', a purifying sweat, intended 'to drive out all weakness and confusion of mind and body' and allow him to 'breathe in the power of the earth itself, of the whole earth'. That done he must now go off into the wilderness

So far into it must he go that he no longer sees the smoke from the campfires of his people. Here is where we find our bush soul. Our soul outside of society. The soul that mountains and rivers and rocks and stars give us. The soul evoked in us in and by the tremendous solitudes of nature. (*Nostos*, p. 318)

In that solitude he must go down into a vision pit and in his nakedness, covered only by a star blanket, he will cry for a vision. After days, as he weakens, he tires and he sleeps. And in his sleep he may dream of some animal or spirit who will come to him offering help, help for him and for his people. On return to his tribe, the wise ones, the elders, will help to interpret the dream, whether or not to trust it, and will discern if anything can be learned from it by which to live.

The significance of this for John was the willingness of the vision seeker to humble himself before the powers of nature, to put himself at their mercy, and to look for their power. This was 'native adaptation' as opposed to Biblical domination and he could only wish that the Pilgrim Fathers had 'sailed round the Horn and come ashore, swordless and seeking to learn'[4] from the peoples who were there before them. There was a further significance that was not lost on him. The vision quest was first and foremost the task of the individual, a personal lived experience, completed under the guidance of the community but always allowing for the possibility of unique insight. It was not an authoritative imposition from on high. No doubt the Pilgrim Fathers could have learned much! And perhaps this native American vision, which had in John's view a 'just estimation' of the place of the human being in the world, was the only way forward for humanity. Could we, he wondered, teach ourselves backwards into, and forwards from, better beginnings, to and from a vision that would not, this time, fail us? It was a tall order.

In the meantime there were more mundane things on his mind. The weather was a constant challenge. By January, Winnipeg was a 'refigerated city, colder, much colder than the freezer in my fridge, with a thin, stripping, forty mile an hour polar wind blowing through it ... and on days such as these it wasn't exactly a delight to see your bus pulling away while you were still a hundred yards off.' The freezing wind was one thing, the snow was yet another – 'mixed with car pollution, piled up by snow ploughs and turning to ice on both sides of every street, it was a threat to eye and mind'.[5] He was aching for a reprieve from what he termed 'the cosmically criminal cold, the cosmically criminal light'; to counteract this colour deprivation he bought books on art, regardless of size or cost once they provided good reproductions, and he spent hours 'soaking, osmosing' their riches. But nothing worked. What he wanted, and he knew it, was mountains, fields, woods, even bogland, once there was green, maybe even all forty shades of it; he was becoming restless.

Life however was not all sense deprivation. He had fallen in love again. Morri Mostow was her name and the romance began with a few chance glances as they passed one another on the college corridors. Eventually, one Friday, 'the prospect of another waiting weekend ahead of me, I contrived to walk where I anticipated she might walk' and with the ice broken, he asked her out. She was 'a challenge and a delight to be with' and as winter moved into spring the relationship blossomed. 'Six weeks later, when trees were a haze of green intimations and when great victories of wild geese were flying north to the tundra, she was driving me to celebrate Passover with her family in her uncle's house.'

This invitation had been problematic. He had long ago left behind the concept of God that the Jewish Passover celebrates, that of a powerful God, who with 'great terribleness' punished the enemies of his chosen people and brought them out of Egypt to a land of milk and honey. 'What was so terrible about this night of course was that to be able for it at all I had to be able for atrocity from on high' to be able for a god who not only sanctioned but aided human atrocities. Taking down his King James Bible he read the relevant verses; to Moses God promised a plague that would kill the firstborn of all the land of Egypt, the firstborn children 'even unto the firstborn of the maidservant that is behind the mill' and God said 'that there shall be a great cry throughout the land.' Then on their way through the wilderness to the Promised Land the children of Israel warred with the Midianites and they did to them as the Lord prompted Moses to command:

'Now therefore kill every male among the little ones, and kill every woman that hath known man by lying with him. But all the women children, that have not known a man by lying with him, keep alive for yourselves.'[6]

That particular passage led John to reflect that maybe 'there was a greater cry than the Egyptian cry, the cry of a Midianite Anne Frank', the name he deliberately chose to symbolize the 'women children' who had been let live in order to be 'used' for their pleasure by the conquering Israelites. How was he to participate in a celebration that had such atrocity at its core and such a god? Recognising that while he hadn't made it to a world of any greater or better gods surely, he thought, surely there was no going back to the old ones. He had to remind himself that it is human beings who create their gods, usually in their own image and likeness, and for their own purposes. Maybe therefore during this feast of Passover he could privately acknowledge what it is to be human and 'whatever else, I must stay with human beings as we are'. He was reminded of the warning words of the French philosopher Michel de Montaigne. 'Man is neither angel nor brute, and the unfortunate thing is that he who would act the angel acts the brute.' With this in mind, or as he put it, 'the distress of the two Anne Franks, the Midianite and the Jewish, in my bones, I got up one evening and dressed and I went with Morri to celebrate Passover with her family.'[7]

His biblical preparation for the evening, and the evening itself, was revelatory. He participated fully and on being offered the unleavened bread and the bitter herbs, he ate them, 'in sacramental solidarity with suffering Egyptians and suffering Jews ... with all Anne Franks, Egyptian, Jewish, Midianite ... in solidarity I ate them'. Eating the bitter herbs of history, of humanity, was an image for him of facing up to the totality of human nature, and was at the core of his own philosophy of inclusion and integration. On this evening he began to realise that it was perhaps possible to do that from within his own Holy Book. 'The sacred reading at an end, we came to table and, throughout all that long and gracious Paschal supper, I was reconciled, in conflict, with what I had long ago concluded I could never be reconciled to, a terrible Holy Book.' He thought of advice he had one time come across, 'the story of the young man who went to the East, to Kyoto, seeking wisdom. He stayed for ten years studying under a great Zen Master. At the airport, saying goodbye to him, the Master gave him a present. Settled in his seat, waiting for take-off, he opened it. It was a very beautiful, leather-bound Bible. The message was clear: seek for enlightenment in your own tradition.'[8] The irony was not lost on John, the celebration of the Jewish Passover had led him to a new insight, a new question. Was it somehow possible to re-imagine or re-interpret his biblical inheritance, the Christian story, in a way that might be relevant and sheltering for modern man? It was to become the question that guided the rest of his life.

For all of its philosophical difficulties, the evening ended beautifully. When supper was over, Morri drove him home and they spent the rest of the night together. Odd as it might seem even this most natural conclusion to their evening took on a biblical significance. He explains:

Ever since I walked the road to the Labyrinth my bed had a lot in common with Job's couch:
'when I say my bed shall comfort me, my couch shall ease my complaint, then thou scarest me with visions and terrifiest me through dreams'
Morri with me though, we interwove the *Book of Job* with the *Song of Songs*.
(*Nostos*, p. 329)

The Song of Songs, the Song of Solomon, a celebration of intimate union and probably the most beautiful passage in the Old Testament, wherein the Shulamite girl speaks of the love she feels in her soul for her shepherd and of how her lover reciprocates:

'I am the rose of Sharon, and the lily of the valleys. As the lily among thorns, so is my love among the daughters. As the apple tree among the trees of the wood, so is my beloved among the sons. I sat down under his shadow with great delight, and his fruit was sweet to my taste. He brought me to the banqueting house, and his banner over me was love.'[9]

Verses from the Song form part of Passover and so they were in his mind, beautifully and hopefully in his mind, as testimony not only to what he experienced with Morri, but also to the human capacity for love. At a most instinctive level, and in the place of primal passion, there is not only animal nature, there is love. The answer to pain, suffering and brutality had to lie somewhere in that great capacity, and again he was back to the Ancient Mariner who loved what he most feared:

'A spring of love gushed from my heart
And I blessed them unaware.'

He realised that this hope might be foolishly optimistic but he needed the hope, needed to believe that within man might lie the power to heal, to heal all the way back to misguided origin stories that authorised killing and persecution, exclusion and repression, as valid responses to that which is feared or misunderstood. Human tenderness, the tenderness of the Hard Man towards the baby hares, just might be less fragile than it sometimes seemed.

John's relationship with Morri continued through the rest of that academic year and into the summer of 1968. He had decided to spend the vacation period in London, she was travelling in Europe and in July they took a trip to Greece together. This time Greece was a holiday, it was enjoyable and for the most part he managed to avoid the intensity of his earlier visit, but unfortunately there was an intensity of a different sort. After one particularly uncomfortable night sleeping outdoors, they had their first big fight. By the end of their holiday it was clear that the relationship was in trouble; Morri returned to Canada and John to London, where he made plans for a change of direction. He contacted Sidney Warhaft, his head of department, to say that he was thinking of taking a year off. Warhaft was reluctant, sensing that he might lose him altogether, and offered to negotiate a year on half pay in return for a guarantee that he would come back to Canada, at least for a couple of years. It was a deal.

He decided to spend the year in Paris; he was already familiar with the language. However, he had not done any preparatory work in the sense of making connections, he had not enrolled in any extra-mural courses, he was simply doing as he had always done, relying, probably unconsciously, on the power of his personality to open doors. Equally 'three Prairie winters' had made him intolerant of what he called 'civic self-admiration' and the bohemian student culture of Paris in the 60's left him as unimpressed as had the hippies in Haight-Ashbury. In a sense he was a fish out of water. Naturally, he immersed himself in French art and literature and typically his observations were original and entertaining. 'The acclaimed novels', he commented, 'they struck me as being good, but good only in the way superior gossip is good.'[10] As always he was looking for 'soul medicine' and he found nothing of that in them.

He structured his stay in Paris with visits to museums and art galleries. He had plenty time to spend absorbing the myriad treasures in the vastness of the Louvre, so much so that it was only after weeks of visiting that he overcame 'a half-disdainful reluctance' and eventually stood before the Mona Lisa. As he said,

> Beaten paths, even the beaten path to *Mona*, I tended to resist, but this morning, in late autumn, I had the XV1–century Italian room to myself and so, knowing well where she was, I turned and crossed the room and stood before her. After about an hour but it could be a century, it could be an age, I was half dumbfoundedly putting a question to her: how come that Italians can do without you? ... how come they haven't come north over the Alps to bring you home? (*Nostos*, p. 338)

What struck him, not immediately, but when it did most forcibly, is the beauty that this almost too familiar icon represents. He saw mystery in far more than her smile. It was the mystery of human beauty. It was also the mystery of creativity, in which lies the mystery of human beings and of human consciousness. Of course it was the old dilemma, clearly identified years before at the Parthenon in Greece, when he recognised that in man there are not only depths of savagery but also heights of creative glory. Standing in front of the Mona Lisa, the necessity for the expression of this creative capacity was profoundly obvious.

> There is a something without which we cannot survive. Whatever it is, that something, if we lose it, or if it is taken from us, we go into a decline and it won't be long at all till we have ceased to be as a people ...
>
> Whatever it is, that something, we have lost it. But we mostly don't know or won't acknowledge we have lost it. And so, not knowing what ails us, we have turned annihilatingly on each other and, still not knowing, we will again. (*Nostos*, p. 338)

The cultivation of the creative spirit is what we have lost, the cultivation of soul. Beauty is an expression of spirit and that is why we must put things of great beauty at the heart of our culture, and that is also why, figuratively at least, the Italians must cross the Alps and reclaim Mona. He thought of the final lines from Keats' Ode on a Grecian Urn:

> "Beauty is truth, truth beauty,–
> that is all Ye know on earth, and all ye need to know."

Apparently simple but profoundly difficult; he was reminded of the inscription that he had read over the door of the Anthropology Museum in Mexico: 'Civilizations pass but man has always within him the glory of those who struggled to bring him into being.'[11] That must be our task, he decided, and again it is an individual struggle, 'the task of bringing ourselves into being, into rich, cultivated, cultured being.'[12] So Mona is really an enormous challenge for each and every individual but, on another level, he had a challenge for her:

> Thinking of all this, as much to shield myself against Mona as anything else, I abstractedly took my eyes off her, and now, with growing surprise, I saw the background which, in reproduction, I'd never taken particular notice of. Within minutes I was talking to her and still that night I was talking to her, telling her that, yes, you are beautiful, as outlandishly beautiful and as wonderful as everyone says you are, but I hope that I won't hurt your feelings if I tell you that, marvellous and all as you are, you are blocking my view, so if you wouldn't mind, would you please move aside and then I'll have unobstructed vision of the world behind you. (*Nostos*, p. 339)

The fantasy continued:

> You could stand out here with me and the two of us then could look at the world. For centuries now you've had your back to the world. Twould do you good I'm sure to turn round and look at it. To walk back into it. Back into the mountains. Back to where thunder is. And wonder. And water. Water in streams. Water in rough rivers. Water in gorges. Water in waterfalls. I imagine you walking back. Growing smaller and smaller ... You are walking into the mountains. Into Tao. In the mouth of the final valley you look back and I know what your smile means: the human head blocks the view. It was never meant to fill the whole frame. (*Turtle was Gone a Long Time*, vol. 1, p. 122)

So Mona, as well as representing beauty and creativity, also represents another aspect of man; man who turns his back on the natural world, man who dominates and exploits the earth, with no recognition of the damage that he does or the wonder that he neglects, man without a 'just estimation' of his place in the world. To put Mona in what he saw as her proper perspective John made reference to another painting, one that had long captivated him, which came from the eastern tradition. *Early Spring* by Kuo Hsi is a Chinese landscape painting completed in the year 1072. Primarily it is a panorama of mountains, clouds, trees, streams, canyons, all morphing, one into the other, all indicative of ever-moving, ever-changing tumultuous life. On the most obvious level a landscape, but then subtly, almost imperceptible, there in the midst of this natural tumult, the human presence, no more than 'a little wisp crossing the causeway'[13] and again, perfectly situated, barely noticeable, a monastery. Into this setting he directs Mona, she is to walk back into this natural world where she will become 'a little match-stick woman introvertedly crossing that slightly humped, three-eyed bridge on the right, or, perhaps, a basket of stuffs hanging from the crook of her arm, maybe we'll find her, still match-stick size, walking home along that winding road on the left.' (*Nostos*, p. 339)

To paraphrase a beautiful passage from *Dreamtime* which he called 'Mona, our Moses',[14] addressing her he says, 'it is time to return, Mona, it is time to return, and it is who you must lead us back into a just estimation of ourselves. It is only then, inspired by the spirit of the Tao, and living in harmony with the way of the world, that we will not damage the earth.' Jokingly he would later say about his time in France 'Jesus, like, I spent a lot of my time talking about the Tao to a picture!' but the fanciful aspect of this dialogue aside, he saw in Taoism a way of living in the world that resonated for him. He had read Arthur Waley's *The Way and its Power*, and had become interested in the *Tao Te Ching* which outlines this particular Chinese philosophy. According to Waley, *te* means a latent power, a 'virtue' inherent in something, and *tao* means 'the way the universe works'; "ultimately, something very like God, in the more abstract and philosophical sense of that term."[15] Like God, but very unlike the God of the Bible. Not lord, master and creator, not a mathematician with a compass, not a craftsman,[16] not the image of a very powerful human being, but a potential, creative cosmic spirit that is working through and manifesting itself in all things, that is immanent in all things but is also in No-thing, and so is transcendent.

> Great Tao is like a boat that drifts;
> It can go this way; it can go that.
> The ten thousand creatures owe their existence to it and it does not
> 　disown them.
> Yet having produced them, it does not take possession of them.
> Tao though it covers the ten thousand things like a garment
> Makes no claim to be master over them
> Therefore it may be called Lowly.
> The ten thousand creatures obey it,
> Therefore it is called the Great.[17]

In this tradition the ten thousand creatures 'obey' the Tao only in the sense that they exist in harmony with it. To exist in such harmony the individual must listen within, not to all those internal hypnotised voices that echo the desires and demands of the external world – for reputation, for riches, for rank – but to the smaller, intuitive, instinctive voice which is still alive and well in animals who know, instinctively from birth how to live, and in times of threat how to survive.

This is the voice of the Tao, the inner potential or *li* which exists in everything and which is there to emerge and flourish if only it is unobstructed. The task for each individual is to seek to be 'unobstructed'.

> The practice of Tao consists of subtracting day by day,
> Subtracting and yet again subtracting
> Till one has reached inactivity.
> But by this very inactivity
> Everything else can be activated.[18]

And that brings us back to Mona! To subtract the enormity of the human head and the human ego, to allow the organic creative spirit, that is already inherent in every human being, to emerge and find its proper expression in the world. That might be a way 'of bringing ourselves into being, into rich, cultivated, cultured being', and of entering into 'Early Spring'. Interestingly it also brings us back to the Ancient Mariner, where he says:

> Sure my kind saint took pity on me,
> And I blessed them unaware.

The poet, Samuel Taylor Coleridge, was not a conventionally religious man. In his use of the word 'saint' he did not mean any external, sanctified individual, instead his 'saint' was a prompting that came from within, a prompting that the mariner found when everything else had been stripped away, had been 'subtracted', and this prompting was good and it was holy; it was what ancient Chinese sages called Tao, and working from it, from that small intuitive voice, the mariner had 'blessed them unaware'. Having been in a place of utter hopeless annihilation, a living death on 'a painted ocean', behind and beyond that terrible reality he had found his 'kind saint', and he re-emerged from that living nightmare with a different perspective. As it was put by another of the Taoist sages:

> First there is a mountain,
> Then there is no mountain,
> Then again there is a mountain.

What happens is that we see the mountain differently. If John Moriarty, in his life and in his writing, was about anything, it was surely this. Driven by an intuitive sense that the modern Western European worldview is seriously misguided, leading humanity into economic and ecological catastrophe, he was intent on changing that view, on finding a perspective from which to live that would both nourish the individual and benefit the whole. What he knew for certain was that it was not the external world that needed to change; the opening quotation of his first published book *Dreamtime* came from the Roman lyric poet Horace, *Animum debes mutare, non caelum*, you should change your state of mind, not the sky. Up to this point in his life the effort to change his own state of mind was the single greatest challenge, to recover from 'gorgocogito' and to see the world with 'cleansed eyes'.

Apart from his conversations with Mona the year in France provided one further powerful experience. It was a visit to the twelfth-century Cathedral of Our Lady of Chartres which again he approached with a certain degree of reluctance. He was aware that the view of God and man that this Cathedral represented he had long ago rejected. It was the view, depicted in a sculpture of the Last Judgment on the arch over the entrance, of man as a fallen sinful being and of a god who will come on the Last Day and condemn all sinners to hell. It was the view that Michelangelo had so painstakingly represented on the ceiling of Sistine Chapel, a vision so frightening that it had driven him to include on it, in contrition for his sins, an agonised self-portrait imposed on an image of his own flayed skin. This *De Profundus* self-portrait is the epitome of the Christianity of sin and punishment, of the biblical advice 'if thine eye offend thee, pluck it out', and 'that, when I was eighteen or so, I translated: if your sexual instincts are a source of sin in you pluck them out and cast them from you ... That was moral surgery and I didn't heed it'. The 'moral surgery' required by that type of Christianity he felt he had left behind. However, the old conditioning was not too far away.

> It had been a long time since I was in a church, but so native to me was everything it stood for that I didn't have to dig very deeply to uncover the old threshold reverence. The shadow of the Last Day upon me, and that a Judgment Day, I made the sign of the cross upon myself, and went in. Walking slowly, I walked up the aisle. ... because my eyes were drawn up, I looked up, and to get a sense of the ribbed roof along its entire length I turned around and I saw it.
>
> And five minutes later, fifteen minutes later ... I was still trying to credit the west rose ... It had taken my breath away. It had taken my breath away and given me breath not of this world to breathe with. It had given me eyes not of this life to see with. (*Nostos*, p. 345)

The sun shining behind it, the west rose window was glorious, overwhelming in its sparkling 'auroras' of deep, deep greens and purples and yellows and blues, all the colours of a rainbow, pulsing, dancing in a hymn of joy. It was the Hallelujah Chorus emanating from stone, and he was dumbfounded. It sang he maintained of 'one immortal wonder'. He believed that the twelfth century stone masons had somehow exposed the heart of all matter, and that cutting and carving the stone they had released its very essence; in that essence, in the richness of light pouring through the cut stone, he believed he saw the living spirit of the universe. It was what no microscope or telescope could ever see. It was what he would ever afterwards maintain was at the heart of each and every atom, but it would only ever be seen with a visionary, or indeed even a mystical, eye. He maintained that the very geometry of the window exposes what is hidden at the heart of 'the thing we so blindly think of as matter'. 'All the Copenhagen physicists had to do was come here and look up at the atom, at its *quanta* in self-revelation ... Also, there is in this rose window an instruction for those physicists who sleep-walkingly assume that to know things in their causes is to know them as they inwardly and essentially are.'

This was challenging stuff, he was throwing down the gauntlet to scientists everywhere. He was questioning all of those with their scientific methodologies, with their reducing, their dissecting, their analysing, their empiricism, are they sure that there is not something that they are missing? Could it not be that the thing is greater than the sum of its parts? Is it not possible that the universe is alive in ways that they cannot see? Is it possible that Wordsworth was right when he said

> Sweet is the lore which Nature brings.
> Our meddling intellect
> Mis-shapes the beauteous form of things:–
> We murder to dissect.[19]

Again and again he would think of William James. 'There must be no premature closing of our account with reality.' For all the doors that science opens, maybe it had prematurely closed at least one, the door into Chartres Cathedral. He was calling on scientists to look again, to 'change your state of mind, not the sky'; he was calling on all western Europeans to walk with him and with Mona into Early Spring, to listen to the instinctive voice of the Tao and to bring into full being all the beauty that is at the heart of life; to listen to the Ancient Mariner, to the American Indian; to eat the bitter herbs of history and by so doing, and by bringing the Song of Songs to bear on them, there may be a better way to light the world. In many ways France had been good for him.

10

'I MUST PLANT MYSELF IN WILD SOIL'

Earthrise; a Year One Reed; movement local/movement essential; a road trip; the
Ghost Dance; the Grand Canyon; a new holy book; Bright Angel Trail; staggering;
spiritual puberty; don't fence me in.

It was September 1969 and he was back in Winnipeg. All was more or less as it had
been a year previously, he had found a new apartment and he was still commuting
to the University via the Pembina Highway. The year he had been away was the
year of the American moon landing and it was on an advertising billboard along
that route that he first caught sight of 'Earthrise', the amazing photograph of the
earth taken from space, and he was stunned. Stunned by the sheer beauty of the
image, but also struck by the freshness, the oneness of what he called 'that shining
jewel'; it had to be the old world, but it looked so new, so pristine and in a sense
so vulnerable. As ever, his reaction was mixed; how amazing it looked, yet how
much damage had been inflicted on it and how much more could it withstand?
His imagination took flight; in spite of the fact that it was 'some billions of years
old' could this become a 'New World' in the best sense; now that we had this
'miraculous' image could we somehow make one last voyage of discovery and find
a new way of living on it and with it?

This revelation of earthrise demanded a new vision and in order to achieve it
he imagined human beings going the native American way, sweating out all the
old metaphors, all the old corrupted modes of understanding and finding what
the poet Wallace Stevens called 'a new intelligence' to go with the new wonder
that had been revealed. There must be a Year One Reed,[1] a new beginning, for the
whole earth and all the peoples on it, not just for all of those conquered peoples
but almost more important, for the Conquerors. The first task will be to sweat
out all concepts of human domination, of domination over nature as well as
domination over one another, and the second will be to sweat out all 'economic

seeing', and all scientific seeing which reduces all that man is to molecules of DNA.

Seeing the earth as a whole, as a single entity, one home that all creatures share, inspired another imaginary banner. 'If only for a day, I thought one morning, maybe we should lower all our national flags and send up a single planetary flag, a flag displaying a single reed.'[2] It would at least be a commitment to a new beginning.He did not see any such new beginning in the moon landing itself. Apart from the wonderful photograph, the extraordinary achievement left him unimpressed. The 'giant leap for mankind' he saw as 'a very small step indeed'. Probably even destructive, reinforcing our misguided sense of ourselves as masters of the planet, a planet on which we were already inflicting incredible ecological damage. The journey we really need to make, he would say, is not a journey to the moon but a journey to the Earth we were born into.[3] That achieved it is only then we will have taken a 'giant step'.

The moon landing prompted a further reflection. It was an 'insignificant step' because it involved only 'movement local', from which he distinguished 'movement essential', an idea he had found in the writings of the sixteenth century philosopher Sir Francis Bacon.[4] 'Movement local' means going from one place to another, from Ireland to Canada, from the earth to the moon, or from one position to another, from nurse to matron, from a junior operator to C.E.O.

> Other than in external circumstances, no significant change has occurred ...
> However ... movement essential is transformative ... it is movement from being
> a caterpillar to being a butterfly, movement, as Buddhists would understand it,
> from being deluded to being enlightened; movement, as Christians understand
> it, from being a sinner to being a saint.
>
> In the modern world, almost universally now, we give ourselves to
> movement local. Ours is a movement local culture. But, even though it carries
> us supersonically from London to New York, Concorde isn't a cocoon. The
> person who climbs up into it in London is in everything except address the
> same person who climbs down from it in New York.
>
> By the time we have reached our early twenties many of us have gone rigid.
> Changes of course will continue to occur in our lives. The chances are that we
> will get married, that we will become parents. We might become managing
> directors or professors of psychology. But all these changes are changes in
> circumstances only. ... More often than not all these movements local are
> symptoms of the extent to which we are fugitives from our own inwardness.
> Fugitives from the vast possibilities of transformative growing. ... And this is
> frightening. We flee from it. But we still need to be somebody. To be a big noise

even. So we substitute chauffeur-driven movement local for movement essential. At the end of it all, however, is the terrible chance that we will only have been a big noise. In a noise world. (*Turtle was Gone a Long Time*, vol. 1, pp. ix–x, 102)

Movement local, which means that we are 'fugitives from our own inwardness' he saw as incredibly damaging, going so far as to say that 'Macbeth spoke the epitaph of this way of life: it is a tale told by an idiot, full of sound and fury, signifying nothing.' A shocking indictment of modern life and an interesting take on the moon landing! Movement essential is what is needed and that, as already seen, means a sweat lodge for the western European mindset, which must involve each individual on his own transformative journey. He was not joking and at the end of that year's teaching, in the interests of personal movement essential, and 'needing to be alone for a few weeks' he rented a cottage on the Shetland islands. He spent five weeks there, meditating three times a day, reading and walking, re-examining the biblical myth and also the man, Jesus, at the heart of Christianity, and wondering about the path his own life had taken. How much of it was movement local or how much movement essential? What was happening to him in Canada? Seriously questioning his way of life he moved from the Shetlands to London and spent the rest of the summer there.

Of all the cities I had lived in, I liked London best ... but now, and particularly towards the end, I found I had little desire and less talent for civic living. Also I sensed that I had lost my way. In the plane on the way back to Winnipeg, I argued with myself as to whether I would quit or stay at the end of the coming academic year.

I still hadn't decided one way or the other, when coming up to the Christmas holidays, two students, David James and Lloyd Girman, approached me in the lobby of University College. 'A proposal', David said. 'We have a transit van and not much money. You have no transit van and, we suppose, a fair share of money. What we were thinking is this: if we pooled resources, we could go on a four- or five-thousand mile journey through the States, spending most of the time in the mountains of the Southwest.'

'Count me in,' I said. (*Nostos*, p. 355)

Driving through the various states, snow a constant impediment, his thoughts were guided by the landscape and the various encounters in roadside restaurants. In North Dakota, heart of the Prairies breadbasket, he wondered if the group of wheat farmers at the counter knew the Ojibwa story of the coming of corn to the world. Through that story were they aware of the sacredness that is in all things?

Did they ritually re-enact it? Watching them as they guzzled their rare buffalo steaks with the eggs 'easy-over' he decided not to run the risk of asking them. 'They were', he decided, 'what they appear to be, men like ourselves, destitute men living in destitute times.' To set against this modern destitution, he was still engaged with the culture of the Native American Indians. In *The Oregon Trail* he found Parkman's account of an old Indian man: 'I saw him seated alone, immovable as a statue among the rocks and trees. His face was turned upward and his eyes seemed riveted on a pine tree springing from a cleft in the precipice above. The crest of the pine was swaying to and fro in the wind, and its long limbs waved slowly up and down, as if the tree had life. Looking for a while at the old man, I was satisfied that he was engaged in an act of worship, or prayer, or communion of some kind with a supernatural being.'[5] Whatever was happening there it was not 'movement local' and it was not 'destitute'.

Continuing on their 'movement local' journey they drove through Minnesota and south to the state of Iowa, an experience of a different kind of destitution. Here, he noted, it was as if all difference had been ploughed out of the land and he could only say 'Iowa was absence'; all he found to comment on was the bland sameness of the many local radio stations telling him 'that you couldn't be in a better place or in better company, for not only do we have the latest news coming to you every hour on the hour, from here as from nowhere else, you will hear the latest songs..and so, as I always say, and say it again now, stay tuned.' Destitution. And more destitution in the songs that were 'spun', Paul McCartney singing about 'all the broken-hearted people living in the world', Joni Mitchell singing about 'life's illusions' and Kris Kristofferson claiming that 'freedom's just another word for nothing left to lose', bleak themes but the tunes were nice. Through Iowa, Nebraska and into Colorado when they could manage to persuade Lloyd to 'tune out' from the endless optimism of the local stations, they sang their own songs. Whenever the road got boring or when night came down and there was nothing to see 'we would sing every song we knew and then we would fall back on a single line of a John Lennon song that had become our mantra –All we are saying is, all we are saying is, give peace a chance.'

On the long, winding climb into Colorado, the Rockies atmospherically looming, we saw two hitch-hikers ahead of us on the hard shoulder. They turned out to be Apaches, old and spectral, he wearing an uneasy combina-tion of Native and Paleface clothes, his white hair, all of it, flowing back into a perfect plait that ran all the way down to the middle of his back, she in skirt and shawl, her white hair, no rib out of place, flowing back into a loosely bundled up plait. (*Nostos*, p. 368)

At their own insistence the Indians sat on the floor space, among the luggage, in the back of the van, with the three young white men sitting in their usual seats up front. Just as he had felt with Anna, the Aztec cleaning woman in Mexico, John was uncomfortable. The burden of history and racial guilt, that baggage of conquest, was weighing heavily. He wondered what this dignified couple were thinking. Given how old they looked he concluded that they must have been born into 'desperate times'. 1890 was the year that particularly weighed on him, he knew the story. By that year almost all of the remaining native tribes were in reservations, including the Apache chief Geronimo and the great Sioux warrior Sitting Bull. Conditions in the reservations were dreadful, starvation was widespread and disease was rife. Given that nothing else was possible to them it became a time to dream. There were many shaman dreamers but the one who proved most powerful was Wovovka, a member of the Paiute tribe.

> Just before dawn on New Year's Day, 1889, far out in remote Nevada, the 34–year-old Wovovka fell ill. In his delirium he dreamed he visited the Great Spirit in heaven. There, he was told that a time was coming when the buffalo would once again fill the plains and dead tribesmen would be restored to their families. If the Indians refrained from violence, and if they were virtuous and performed the proper ritual dance – the Ghost Dance – they could hasten the coming of the new world, which would cover the old, and push the White men into the sea.
>
> > The whole world is coming,
> > A nation is coming.
> > The Eagle has brought the message to the tribe.
> > Over the whole earth they are coming;
> > The buffalo are coming, the buffalo are coming,
> > The Crow has brought the message to the tribe.[6]

While some tribes remained sceptical the Ghost Dance took hold. All across the reservations they danced; born of desperation it became a religious frenzy; from tribe to tribe it was adopted and magnified, the dancers wore "ghost shirts" painted with magical tribal symbols that they believed would protect them from the white man's bullets. It became so widespread and so frantic that the authorities, fearing an uprising, took action. Troops were ordered to the Sioux reservations and in a horribly mismanaged encounter, Sitting Bull, who had supported the Ghost Dance only because he believed that it would give succour to his people, was shot through the head. What ensued was the tragic massacre at Wounded Knee, its aftermath simply and hauntingly described by Black Elk, a Sioux eye-witness:

"It was a good winter day when all this happened. The sun was shining. But after the soldiers marched away from their dirty work, a heavy snow began to fall. The wind came up in the night. There was a big blizzard and it grew very cold. The snow drifted deep in the crooked gulch, and it was one long grave of butchered women and children and babies, who had never done any harm and were only trying to run away."[7]

The innocent fervent hope with which it all began made the final catastrophe all the more heart-breaking; for John, the Apache passengers squatting silently in the back of the rickety Ford transit made it very real. He was again eating the bitter herbs of history and experiencing for himself the sense of powerlessness that had originally inspired the native tribes in their desperate dance. Could there be any possible healing for a world which, over and over again, repeated the same terrible mistakes? At their destination as he watched the old couple walking away 'it occurred to me that we must take up where they left off.' Years later in his talks he would return to what struck him that day:

> We have to undertake a Ghost Dance ourselves: ghost dance our ways of seeing things out of our eyes, ghost dance them out of our hands, ghost dance what Wordsworth calls 'the light of common day out of our eyes', ghost dance what Traherne calls 'the dirty economic devices of the world', the philosophical assumptions and axioms, ghost dance in a sense the Medusa mindset, the modern European mindset, out of our eyes so that we can again see that the corn is 'orient and immortal wheat', so that we can walk, ourselves enfranchised on an enfranchised earth.[8]

A modern ghost dance, he fully realised, could only be achieved through movement essential, a challenge to each individual to embark on their own transformative journey, to face their own demons, to face the demons of their personal past as well as their cultural historical past and to 'dance' it all into an integrated whole. 'It is always in the single individual,' he wrote, 'that humanity comes to its feet.' Having come to one's feet as an individual one might then find a better way of 'standing on the great and sacred earth'. He could see that his entire adult life had in some way been a solitary attempt at such a dance, and the process was both difficult and frightening. Growing ever stronger in him was the suspicion that he could not do it on his own; suppose, he thought, that one could bring all of 'the darkest impulses', the deepest personal secrets as well as the difficult herbs of history, into full consciousness, what, within one's own conscious state, is going to help to heal them? It was not a question that he could answer, but an answer was intruding itself. 'The thought that we needed divine assistance with our lives and that Christians might therefore be right – that, against that, I closed my mind.'[9] But the thought was there, was it really possible to expect the single individual, no matter how self-aware that person might become, to bring about human improvement?

> I'd wonder, over how much of my mind, over how much of my life, do I have control? ... Both in my own life and in the lives of others I was all too acutely aware of the ease with which unconscious life can sweep consciously decided life away. (*Nostos*, p. 371)

He had been aware for years that repression and exclusion have not worked for humanity – 'a killed dragon is not a dead dragon' – he was now faced with the real challenge of integration, when and if the individual acknowledges all that he 'phylogenitically' is, what happens then? The only answer that he could fall back on, and again it was not an answer based on logic and reason, but he was convinced of its truth nonetheless, integration of all that one is will allow access to a greater vision of what he called the 'diamond dimension' of the universe. It was the blazing 'mineral-green lucence' he had seen in the sky a few evenings previously in western Nebraska; it was 'those blizzards of cosmic fire and light' that had startled him in Saskatchewan; it was the pulsing rainbow of light he had seen in the rose window in Chartres Cathedral; it was the diamond brightness of a winter day in Manitoba when the universe appears to expose the radiance that it truly is. These were glimpses of a greater glory that prompted him to say, 'And when you meet them you tell your friends who are physicists that the vibrations they study are hosannas', revealed in 'the eternally praising brightness you'd walk in walking to work on a winter's morning in Winnipeg.' There is, he would claim, a hosanna at the heart of the atom. The vision of that hosanna, a vision of a radiant and harmonious power that is eternally manifesting, that vision built into a culture, that would bring healing; to live in accordance with that hosanna might enable all of humanity to 'come to its feet'. A modern 'ghost dance' to roll back 'all the nonsense and ignorance that has accumulated sensually and cerebrally'[10] in us, might make that vision possible.

> 'Thinking of all of this in a motel a mountainous mile high in the Rockies, it occurred to me that the Diamond Sutra[11] we have need of, we haven't yet written.' (*Nostos*, p. 372)

This 'Diamond Sutra', wherever it is to come from, might form part of a new holy book, and again on a flight of fancy, he imagined the first chapter of such a book. He remembered the biblical story of Jacob's dream. On a difficult journey through a harsh landscape Jacob lay down to sleep using stones of the place for his pillow. He dreamed of a ladder which ascended to heaven and of a prophecy from God concerning his people. The lines that resonated for John were:

'And Jacob awaked out of his sleep, and he said, surely the Lord is in this place, and I knew it not. And he was afraid, and said, how dreadful is this place! This is none other but the house of God and this is the gate of heaven.'[12]

This would be the theme of the first chapter of the new holy book. To begin with it would call on the individual to awake out of sleep, not out of 'dream sleep', but out of the sleep of everyday seeing and hearing and knowing. That awakening, once achieved, will be an awakening to the realization that 'this is the house of God', right here on this earth, is where it is possible to see and know God, a god that is the universe in its 'diamond dimension'. The imagined new book 'will tell us that God doesn't need to come down upon a mountain, for the mountain itself is the revelation. We will only have to look at it and we will know how we should live.'[13] And if we don't know, the rest of the envisioned book will direct us. Such a book would provide for the individual what the elders of the tribe provided for the young brave who returned from his vision quest – guidance and shelter.

All such deep and fanciful thoughts aside, the journey continued. So far in the space of less than a week they had travelled through six states and in Santa Fe, New Mexico they planned the rest of the journey. 'In the end, all three of us agreeing, we took the road I hoped from the beginning we would take, the road west into Arizona, the road west to the Grand Canyon.' As ever there were more thought-provoking experiences along the way, a Navajo reservation that was 'as sad as sad can be', and a colourful encounter in a gas-station cafe with a trio of 'wannabe' cowboys who accused them of being hippies and sent them on their way with the classic line 'That highway out there leads out of here and you are going to be on it right soon'. Once the initial threat had subsided they delighted in being 'run out of town'! Eventually, 'our van at full geriatric throttle, we climbed by a winding way to the carpark on Kaibab Plateau, on the edge of the Grand Canyon.'

Skimming through a booklet about the mighty chasm he quickly absorbed the geological facts. Its length – two hundred and eighty miles, its width – varying from four to eighteen miles, its depth – on average one vertical mile, that very depth exposing thirteen different rock formations, with the deepest dating back almost two billion years. It had him fascinated, a journey down into it would be a 'look into the infinity of time past';[14] its fossils revealing the very process of evolution, back almost to the very beginning of life itself. Here were geological depths almost too vast to contemplate, and here as well were human depths equally vast; human life emerged from the creatures that were fossilised in these rocks, some-where within the human psyche the instincts that guided these creatures must still survive. As he began his trek down into it, down into the side canyon intriguingly called Bright Angel Canyon, he had much on his mind.

> Nietzsche on my mind: 'I have discovered for myself that the old human and animal life, indeed the entire prehistory and past of all sentient being, works on, loves on, hates on, thinks on in me.' And Hopkins on my mind: 'O the mind, mind has mountains, cliffs of fall Frightful, sheer, no-man-fathomed. Hold them cheap May who ne'er hung there ...' (*Nostos*, p. 386)

He was now descending into the very depths of all life. Physically the trail was icy and treacherous. Where the descent was steepest he felt as if he were tight-rope walking and, the worn cleats on his boots a further hazard, it was unnerving. Concentrating solely on the steep descent, he wondered why he had not invoked Bright Angel before setting a risky foot on his trail! Physically risky and psychologi-cally troubling, in the midst of the tremendous beauty of the Canyon, and in spite of all thoughts of diamond dimensions, the old despair and sense of destitution settled on him again.

> Down, down, down we went. ... Down to where we were cousins and contem-poraries of the first suggestions of biological life. And then, rounding a cliff we heard it, the roar of the Colorado River. Down into that roar we went, and before we knew what was what we were walking over it, by a suspension bridge, to the more open and accommodating far side.
> And this was it.
> This was the floor of the Grand Canyon. (*Nostos*, p. 389)

He felt the vastness, the insignificance, the nothingness of all human and animal ages press down upon him. He thought of how in *Moby Dick* Captain Ahab had 'staggered' under the weight of such a vision, of how Nietzsche had staggered, of how Kepler and Pascal had staggered, of how Matthew Arnold had staggered, of how he had himself staggered years previously in the yard at home in Moyvane. And he wondered who or what might stay such staggering:

> Will you do it, Bright Angel?
> Will you, I beseech you, Bright Angel?
> Putting your hand to his shoulders, will you stay Ahab in his staggering?
> (*Nostos*, p. 389)

Here, while he was once again agonising as to who would have the burden of lighting the world, David, who had accompanied him, was involved in the practical details. Night was falling and they had not organised beforehand to stay at Phantom Ranch, the only accommodation on the floor of the Canyon, indeed the only accommodation below the rim, and it was completely full. Too dangerous now to attempt the return trek, David had been lucky enough to meet a Park Ranger who had given him a can of sausage and a blanket. This meagre fare did not help John's mood nor did the difficulty of sharing a single horse-blanket bring much comfort. It was a very long night. The 'diamond dimension' of the universe as elusive as ever, he was in rational philosophical mode, 'staggering' under the apparent meaningless of human existence that had terrified so many great minds – the prospect of human annihilation and anonymity almost too much to bear. A few lines from the poetry of Emily Bronte were the only lifeline:

> Though earth and moon were gone,
> And suns and universes ceased to be,
> And Thou wert left alone,
> Every Existence would exist in thee.
>
> There is not room for Death,
> Nor atom that his might could render void:
> Thou – Thou art Being and Breath,
> And what Thou art may never be destroyed.[15]

Emily insisting that 'Thou', the ground of all Being and Breath, in which all share, can 'never be destroyed'. It was flimsy, it required an act of faith rather than intellect, but it had the ring of some deeper truth, of some Divine Ground of all being, and for the moment, as a 'stay', it provided some comfort. He was very glad to see the light of morning. Of the journey up out of the Canyon he later wrote:

Descending by Bright Angel Trail,[16] we had gone down to the floor of the Grand Canyon together. We came up through the several Palaeozoic seafloors the next day, but I didn't know looking back down into it, that it had already claimed me for the whole rest of my life. (*What the Curlew Said*, p. 203.)

The Grand Canyon was the turning point of the road trip. They had spent Christmas on the road and the intention now was to return to Winnipeg for the New Year celebrations. The homeward journey took them through Utah, Idaho and Montana, and it was snow and ice all the way. By now, they were tired and tempers were becoming slightly frayed.

It was late one evening when we turned into a motel in southern Montana. Quite by chance I discovered that we hadn't as much money as I thought we had. Having picked up a hitch-hiker we were now four, but having to keep money for petrol we only had as much as would pay for three, and at this late hour in a bank holiday season there was no way we could get money transferred from the Bank of Montreal in Winnipeg. We decided we would present ourselves as three and then when the coast was clear we would smuggle in whichever one of us stayed behind incognito in the van. Within ten minutes the janitor had spotted the deception. He came to complain. Instantly indignant and intolerant, and in no mood to have dealings with this little Scrooge, I picked up my stuff and charged out. Stunned it must be by the violence of my reaction, David and Lloyd and the hitch-hiker followed my lead, and off we went, leaving what we had paid him to the janitor. And now without sleep or food or money we must drive all the way north to Miles City where we would drop off the hitch-hiker, across North Dakota, and north again to Wiinipeg.

There were times when I thought they would turf me out and leave me to fend for myself. They didn't. But the mood didn't improve when, fitful at best, the heating finally gave out.

And then, of all places, on a Polar reach of road in North Dakota, we got a puncture. Our tools wholly inadequate, and having no gloves, it took us the best part of an hour to change the wheel.

It was getting dark on New Year's Eve when we made it home to Winnipeg. (*Nostos*, pp. 394–5)

It was the eve of 1971, he would be thirty three in February and he was no nearer to a decision as to his future. At one point during their journey 'breathing the earth browns and the earth reds, all of them vivid, all of them vibrating, in arid New Mexico', he felt that he needed to get back in touch with 'red earth' in himself, 'else, I'll become what I am already becoming, an intellectual.' Against that intellectual future he had set two images, one of the old Indian 'engaged in an act of worship' and the other of Jacob, a man of simple faith who could say 'this is none other but the house of God and this is the gate of heaven.' Something at the very core of his being responded to these two men. Here on this earth they were in communion with a greater spirit – they were walking in Paradise in the here and now. There was an inner compulsion to explore that vision. By the time he was back in Winnipeg he believed he had found a compromise, he would teach for the academic year and then 'either build or rent a cabin in the American South-west and spend my summers there.' It may have been the ideal solution, giving him the space he needed for the spiritual journey, but perhaps it would have been too easy.

A little over three months later, on the Wednesday of Holy Week, I came home from work and sat down ...

Out of nowhere all the old arguments for quitting came back.

Now again I could see her. Eleven or twelve years ago it was, in the library of University College Dublin ... she was a mathematician and the figures and symbols were just pouring onto the page, down the page like a river finding its way they flowed, over onto the next page, then suddenly, she stopped. I surmised that things weren't working out, and yes, back she went to the previous page, running her eye down along it. Twelve or fourteen lines down she found the error and drawing a line through everything after that she started again.

It wasn't so much that I had made a mistake. If I continued as I was, I'd end up as a mistake, I'd be a mistake. Identified with the mistake, would I then be able to draw a line down through it and start again? ...

I had for a long time felt I had come forward on too narrow a front. Keep going, and I would surely end up as an intellectual, a walking, talking paradigm of the psychic topiary[17] I had always resisted and feared.

I looked at a potted plant.

I was like that. Having met the limiting, containing plastic, my roots had nowhere to go but back into the old, exhausted, sour soil.

I must haul myself out of the life I am living. I must plant myself in wild soil. But no. Not in the wild soil of New Mexico or Arizona. Or in Montana for that matter.

Three months before, travelling through the tremendous world where the Missouri has its headwaters, it struck me that I must seek my bush soul, my soul outside of society, my soul outside of civilization with all its restrictions and Lady Windermere fans, my soul reunited with the terror and wonder of the natural world. And that, I clearly saw, meant returning to Ireland.

Yes. I'd quit.

But then, as it always did in the past when I thought about quitting, the opposite argument came at me: how would I live?

As on every previous occasion, I countered it with an assurance from Jesus: 'Seek ye first the kingdom of God and all things else shall be added unto you.'

Could it be true? I asked myself. Is this thing that Jesus said as true of the universe, is it as true of the earth and the stars, as the laws of gravity are?

In the end it must be an act of faith. (*Nostos*, pp. 395–396)

And in a sense that is what it was, it was a belief that his 'kind saint' was directing him and he had to follow. His roots were elsewhere, they were in a soil that might have been little more than bog, but it was nearer to reality than all of the refinements and artificiality that he encountered in the sophisticated academic environment, which he had already identified as a 'greenhouse' on the tundra. This might have offered an easy life but it was not the stuff of ordinary reality. He could not go with that, and he had also long ago recognised another need:

> Give me land, lots of land,
> Don't fence me in

If I had a deepest need in relation to people in society it was that – don't fence me in. (*Nostos*, p. 566)

This rebellion against conformity and constraint, combined with both courage and recklessness, was a powerful impetus. Friends and colleagues argued vehemently with him, but then new reasons would emerge. He told one friend that 'puberty has caught up with me'. There was simply no answer to that.

There is a sexual puberty and, however shyly or hesitantly at first, most of us learn to go with it. As well as this sexual puberty, however, but altogether more demanding than it, there is another kind of puberty – for the moment I am refusing to call it spiritual puberty – but whatever it is, or will turn out to be, I am yielding to its claims. I am going with it ... It is a question of recognising our deepest yearning – forget about our desires, our desires only serve to muffle and hide our deepest yearning from us – and, having recognised our deepest yearning, we then go on and so set ourselves up that we can live from it and with it ...

For a breathless moment in Iowa I sensed or something greater than me sensed that our deepest yearning doesn't have who we individually and empirically are in mind. (*Nostos*, p. 397)

He was going with his 'deepest yearning', with what he later called a spiritual hunger, and therefore arguments were useless. To entice him to stay he was offered tenure and was shocked to think that his decision had been seen as a bargaining ploy; it was pointed out that were he to re-apply in a year or two he might be turned down on the basis of qualifications – he did not intend to re-apply; as to how he would live, he would be paid until the end of August and that would keep him until Christmas, after that he didn't know! It was only then he discovered that he had been paying into a pension fund and by cashing it in he had what he considered a bonanza.

That evening the comptroller gave me a cheque for just over three thousand dollars, and now, all going well, I knew I wouldn't have to worry about a roof over my head or bread on the table for the next three years.

Five weeks later Lilian Mostow drove me to the airport.

'So now that you are leaving it, what has Canada meant to you?' she asked.

'I've already answered that for myself,' I said 'and it's simple. Like so many others I came to the New World thinking of a future. That it gave me. But as well it gave me a past, alternative to our European past, to go home with.' (*Nostos*, p. 399)

It gave him Native American adaptation and reverence which included Tsetsekia, 'we-feeling' and 'the coal and the comb'. It reinforced his vision of 'the hosanna at the heart of the atom'; it gave him both the Grand Canyon and Bright Angel; it began a journey into what he would later call Canyon Christianity; it gave him the beginnings of a new understanding of Jesus. It had been an altogether enriching experience but in order for the 'movement essential' voyage to continue he realised that he had to leave. Like his father before him, after a few years in the New World, he was going home.

11

'TO SHIP OARS AND GIVE THE WORLD A CHANCE'

Inisbofin; Uvavnuk; Christian Taoists; the yoga of horror; silver branch perception; a swan's nest; the lobster-pot and the Grail; Gethsemane; Otherworld seeing.

During the six years in Canada John had been in regular correspondence with and had occasionally visited his family in Moyvane. Now that he had indicated that he was coming home for good, there was a mixed reaction. Mary would be glad to see him, but, what was he up to? She knew that Chris had sourced a cottage for him on the island of Inisbofin, nine miles out from the coast of Galway, and she was alarmed. Was it just for the summer and, if so, what did he intend to do then? Would he get a job in a university in Ireland? What plans had he? Answers were not forthcoming. He was on an entirely different journey and 'plans' were the last thing on his mind. In fact he was thinking about Uvavnuk, an Eskimo medicine woman whom he had read about in Canada, and whose song had come back to him on the journey to Inisbofin.

In Galway today I had a long wait for the bus that would take me out to the Atlantic coast, so I took to the streets, letting them take me where they would. Coming to a bridge over the Corrib River, I looked over the parapet. There was the big rushing river itself and running parallel to it there was what I took to be an engineered, stone-embanked side-channel of it. Growing in this side-channel were drifts of weeds, each of them flowing in perfect adaptation to the flowing, lucid water. In their shapes they were beautiful, in their textures they were beautiful, in their night-green colours they were beautiful. But they were beautiful above all because they made sense.

'The great sea has set me in motion,
Set me adrift,
Moving me as a weed moves in the river.

137

The arch of the sky and mightiness of storms
Have moved the spirit within me,
Till I am carried away,
Trembling with joy.' (*Nostos*, p. 401)

On his boat journey out to the island, Uvavnuk's song was still on his mind and this line of thinking continued. He knew little about Inisbofin other than the fact that it was populated, that its name meant the Island of the White Cow, and that it contained the ruins of an early Christian monastery originally built by St. Colman. On the boat journey out from Cleggan pier John thought about the monks who must, one long ago day, have made the same journey.

> Following an old Christian custom, it is likely they would at one stage have shipped oars, and then, wherever the currents took them, that's where they would settle.
> To ship oars.
> To surrender to something bigger and wiser than we are.
> I thought about it. (*Nostos*, 399)

Those monks, he wondered, who were willing to 'ship oars' and to become 'plankton in a sea of faith', out of what depths of their minds were they living? They were going with the 'way' of the world, 'as a weed moves in the river', they were Christians but they were also, in John's words, 'Taoists relying on Tao.' And maybe they were right. 'Maybe there are dimensions of our own minds and of the world that we can only enter when we have shipped oars, when we have shipped self-will, when we have shipped all consciously conceived, all consciously pursued purposes?' There was only one way to find out. 'And every cell that has something to do with consciousness in me, maybe it should simply ship oars and give the world a chance. In reckless surrender to it, maybe the world would do better by me and for me than I've done for myself.' He was going the way of the Tao and Mary Moriarty was hoping for plans!

> Early Christian monks and Eskimo medicine woman
> Shipped oars and fluent reeds in a river.
> Maybe that's what the Beautiful is. The Beautiful is that which is most adapted to how things are. (*Nostos*, p. 402)

Naturally the thought did not stop there. 'Judged by such a standard, of course, Western humanity is hideous. Hideous because evolution has come to so rigid an end in us.' It has come to an end in us because as a species we have ceased to adapt to the world in which we live; in effect, we have turned evolution on its head. Using titanic technologies, we have attempted to force the world to adapt to us, with, as he would say time and again 'disastrous consequences' for ourselves and the planet. In an effort to go ashore on Inisbofin in a more hopeful frame of mind he concluded:

> Maybe Uvavnuk's song will sing us out of our dead-end rigidities. Maybe it will sing us into more hopeful evolutionary shape ... Maybe we are still in with an evolutionary chance. (*Nostos*, p. 402)

He had 'shipped oars' in order to find his 'bush soul', in the almost desperate hope that in so doing he would also find some insight that would reassure him that 'we are in with an evolutionary chance'; in the hope also that he might better formulate his instinctive perception that there is more to the universe than science and maths can comprehend. From the outset it was obvious that it would not be an easy journey. It was a typical Irish summer on the island

> I woke to whining, to a house wind-whining and wind-complaining at every one of its sash windows, and at its two doors ... I rolled out and looked at the all-too forlorn consequences of my decision to quit. It didn't help when I went to the window and saw how out of sorts and surly the Atlantic was. Coming back I forced myself to look up at the only picture in the room. It depicted the Sacred Heart of Christ. Christ himself had long hair, he had pink cheeks ... and so delicate were his hands that you could safely conclude that they had never even touched a carpenter's hammer. He was feminine ... And his heart wasn't where you'd expect it to be. It was outside his ribs ... It was girdled all round by a spiky squeeze of thorns. It had a deep open spear wound. Drops of blood rained down from it. And it was on fire ...
>
> We had such a picture at home. Under it, burning night and day, was a small red-globed Sacred Heart lamp. Within the picture itself, just under the heart, there were two lines, and the names of our whole family were written on them: James, Mary, Madeleine, Chris, Barbara, John, Brenda and Phyllis.
> We were dedicated, all of us, to the Sacred Heart.
> It was terrible.
> As terrible as anything I had seen in Mexico. (*Nostos*, p. 402–3)

Terrible because of what it exposed, a spear wounded bleeding icon that represented pain and suffering more than it represented salvation and love. At the heart of the Christian message was the terrible story depicted in this picture and also depicted in the suffering of the fourteen Stations of the Cross.

> I had turned away from it, but then, in a very short time I had replaced it with Michelangelo's *de profundis* self-portrait, hanging at half-mast above the Colosseum, hanging at half-mast above Auschwitz.

What he saw in the holy picture, and in the newly imagined flag with its *de profundis* self-portrait, was what Aldous Huxley called the 'yoga of horror', – 'the yoga of finally confronting all that is terrible, unmendably terrible maybe, in ourselves and in our world.'[1] This is the 'yoga' that Job, helpless and bereft, had to undergo when his religious beliefs proved hollow; this is the 'yoga' of the road to the Labyrinth and to the Canyon, where the presence of animal, even bestial, nature at the core of human nature must be acknowledged; this is the yoga of recognising that life feeds on death, of recognising the full significance of Jack Scanlon's pig-killing knife 'in our yard at home', of his mother harvesting the blood of a cock whose throat she has just cut. 'In our house, illuminated as it was by a little lamp, the Sacred Heart picture made sense ... It was simple: where things are terrible, a terrible pharmacy is called for.' (*Nostos*, p. 404)

There was much on Inisbofin to remind him of just how terrible things can be. Stories from Cromwellian times were still being told. On the journey into the island Paddy Halloran, the boat-man, told him the story of Bishop's Rock.

> In the sixteen-forties, or in the sixteen-fifties maybe, the Catholic archbishop of Tuam was on the run from Cromwell's soldiery. Apprehending him here in Bofin, they chained him to a rock at low tide, and then, standing guard where I was standing now perhaps, they waited till the tide returned and drowned him. (*Nostos*, p. 405)

This fanatical, merciless, precise hatred had its roots in some unacknowledged and unconscious depth of human nature. And there was more:

> An officer in Cromwell's army reconnoitred Connemara, that wonderful, wild part of the world west of Galway City that I had come through yesterday. In his report back to his seniors he declared that in it there wasn't a tree tall enough to hang a man from, or water deep enough to drown him in, nor soil to bury him.
> And Connemara of course was as beautiful then as it is now.
> No, he most certainly wasn't the kind of man who would ship oars. He most certainly wasn't the kind of man to who would allow himself to be inspired by

a reed flowing in a river. And yet, all too often, he is the kind of man who is out there driving history. (*Nostos*, p. 405)

Here he was revisiting very familiar territory, but going back into all of this, alone, and without the external focus of university life, might have been unwise. There had been times, even in Canada, when he had experienced a sense of the fragility of his own mind. 'Here now, all over again, it terrified me to think that my mind might one day open up in ways that I couldn't handle.'[2] It was why he would so often repeat the warning he found in Moby Dick,

Ishmael warned us:
'Consider all this; and then turn to this green, gentle, and most docile earth; consider them both, the sea and the land; and do you not find a strange analogy to something in yourself? For us this appalling ocean surrounds the verdant land, so in the soul of man there lies an insular Tahiti, full of peace and joy but encompassed by all the horrors of the half known life. God keep thee! Push not off from that isle, thou canst never return.' (*Nostos*, p. 336)

'Push not off.' He was aware of the risk that he had taken, aware that a journey from the 'docile earth' of everyday thinking and experience into 'the appalling ocean' of the 'half known life' in the depths of the psyche might exact a high price. However, as he would often admit, there was enough ego and self-will in him to ignore Ishmael's warning. Whatever was in him, forever driving him to 'push off' from safer shores, it was a compulsion that he could not withstand. Here on Inisbofin it was very easy to respond to the imagery of that passage in Moby Dick. Walking to the very western end of the island and looking out across the Atlantic Ocean he knew that, according to medieval geographers, he had come to the western end of the world. The end of the known world. Out there it was a world of threat and terror, of Leviathan, of Behemoth, of everything in the natural world 'too great for the eye of man'.[3] The sea was 'an alien immensity'. And because of all that it suggested to him, 'there was a lament in me. It was the same lament that I felt on the floor of the Grand Canyon.' A lament for what the sea represents – both the unknown depths of the psyche and the enormous destructive capacity of nature itself; of what the Canyon represents – that self same ancient destructive capacity in each human being. In a sense the sea and the canyon are one and the same, both representing the frightening totality of what man is and the extent of his individual insignificance.

Hearing a solitariness in the sound of my footsteps as I walked back along the road, I sensed a kind if fatality. It was as if ... never being able to anticipate when or where, I must go down, all the way back down to the Grand Canyon ... Night falling... it terrified me to think that the Grand Canyon had become my permanent address. Anywhere else I might live, including Lacey's cottage here in the island of the White Cow, was but a place of temporary rest, of temporary convalescence.

What I had to sustain me was Emily's 'mahavakya'.[4]

> Though earth and moon were gone,
> And suns and universes ceased to be,
> And Thou wert left alone,
> Every existence would exist in thee. (*Nostos*, p. 410)

There was a sense of sadness on him during these early days on the island. As usual, he was writing and walking, reading, reflecting and meditating, but he sometimes found himself looking seawards to Canada and thinking of the friends that were there. Fortunately he was getting to know the local people and on one evening he overcame what he called 'a shrivelling shyness' and he went into a pub. People were singing and there was a hush for each performance, one haunting song after another seeming to proclaim the spirit of the place. What struck him particularly was the sense of yearning that came across in the singing, a yearning that each singer was pouring into his or her song, and it occurred to him that in music is the expression of a dimension of internal life which is normally repressed. There is, he thought, in human beings an 'infinite yearning', and this yearning can be heard in music and in song. A yearning, in every human being, that belongs to, and longs for, the creative genius of the world. Invited to join in he sang *Wild Mountain Thyme* and a new song for them, *The Night Visiting Song* that he had learned from Marilyn. He wished that she could be there to sing it for them. As he had recognised as a very young man cycling and singing his way through the boggy landscape on his way to school, the sadness of the world could be expressed in song.

Other more ancient music was also on his mind. He had spent the previous weeks reading Irish myths and folktales, he had become familiar with the island story of a rock that every seven years turned into an old woman driving a white cow, he had considered the derision with which science would treat this story, and yet he said, a universe in which a caterpillar turns into a butterfly 'is a very queer universe indeed'. A universe in which strange things can happen, he claimed, can never be fully accounted for by the philosophical, mathematical and mythical categories by which we seek to comprehend it. Ironically our very explanations blind us to the *draíocht,* the magical strangeness, that is everywhere manifesting but is hidden from the 'single vision'[5] which is the curse of modern science. He was enthralled by the early Irish story *Imram Bran*, The Voyage of Bran: One day, while walking in the neighbourhood of his royal ringfort the mighty chieftain Bran Mac Feabhail heard music so wonderful that he knew it could not have come from this world.

> Looking behind him he saw a single silver branch and to his great surprise it was out of this branch, no one holding it, no one carrying it, that this otherworldly music was coming. Unable for such sweetness, he swooned away. Coming to himself, he went indoors. In the night, sensing a brightness even with his closed eyes, he looked up and there on the floor before him was an otherworld woman. In strains as sweet, if not sweeter again than the branch, she sang fifty quatrains to him, telling him that both she and the branch came from an island far away in the ocean. Having described the wonders of the island, she invited him to come and see it and experience it for himself, and then she was gone, and the branch was gone. (*Nostos*, p. 414)

Naturally, he being a hero and it being a wonder tale, Bran set off in search of the otherworld island. Out over the waves went three groups of nine men. When they were two days journey out they saw coming towards them the God of the Sea, Manannán Mac Lir, not in a boat as one would expect, but riding in a four horse chariot. And he too is singing, a song that tells Bran that what looks like a forbidding sea is in reality *Mag Meall*, a Plain of Delights, a plain that Bran, with his eyes for only the everyday world, cannot see.

This is a story, a myth, obviously not intended to be taken literally. It is however pointing to what might be called an 'otherworld sense', a way of seeing this world in a different way – not as the world of matter that is envisaged by reductive science, but a world of wonder and miracle and unknowable 'otherness' that can only be glimpsed occasionally. It is a sense that there is something both within and without every individual that the light and the eyes of common day keep eclipsed, that everyday thinking keeps hidden. It is the music of the silver branch, it is spirit. To be known it must be cultivated. It demands a journey out over the waves. What the story implies is the need to listen for the voice of the spirit within, to give it its say, and the reward will be what John calls 'silver branch perception', a vision of *Mag Meall*, the Plain of Delights, the diamond dimension of the universe, the hosanna at the heart of the atom. William Blake put it well:

> To see a World in a Grain of Sand
> And a Heaven in a Wild Flower
> Hold Infinity in the palm of your hand
> And Eternity in an hour.[6]

It is only by discounting the conclusions of science, conclusions that suggest the 'immense hopelessness' of an alien and inhospitable 'nothing but' universe, that such vision can be achieved. It is a vision that requires an act of faith.

> I was willing to believe that if only I could see it through Manannán's eyes
> I would see that every limp frond of seaweed on the shore is a silver branch
> singing behind us, leaving us with no choice but to muster three companies of
> nine and put out to sea. (*Nostos*, p. 416)

'I was willing to believe'; the willingness, the capacity, to believe was both fleeting and temporary, but it was for the most part strong enough to sustain him against the onslaught of 'the yoga of horror' with which he was all too familiar. This sense of a divided self and a divided world is ever-present. 'As I had every night since I came here, I slept between worlds, between seaweed and hay, between the putrid smells of a shore littered with little festerings coming through my front windows and the honeyed smells of three small meadows coming through my back windows.'[7] Putrid festerings and honeyed meadows, was it possible to find a cosmology, a 'sheltering story' that would accomodate both the vision of Mannanán and the worldview of science?

Within a few weeks on the island he was no longer a stranger. He might have been a rather odd figure, this solitary academic, but neighbours soon realised that his feet were solidly on the earth. He could be called on if help was needed.

> On his way from the sea one evening, Stephen Lavelle called to tell me that
> just above the head of the bay they had seen what looked like a swan stuck in a
> sheepwire fence. It might be as much as half an hour before he could attend to
> her himself, so he wondered if I'd go instead.
>
> It was indeed a pathetic sight, her four cygnets bobbing below in the waves
> and she herself totally stuck in the opening they had so easily walked through.
>
> What surprised me about her was how light she was. After the long hatch
> she felt as little substantial as a paper bagful of her own feathers.
>
> It was good to see them swimming away, the four cygnets like four gold-
> green pin-cushions full of little whisperings, and she herself, so alarmed, so
> white, her wings raised, her head raised, and nothing but their collective safety
> on her mind. (*Nostos*, p. 420)

It was a very fine evening and as he walked back towards his cottage he passed the dried out marshland where her nest was. On impulse, he lay down on what had been her spot. He thought of her fragility, of the fragility of her four little chicks, of the wide expanse of unknowable sea that they had to face, and yet they were able for it. What a contrast that was to the state he found himself in. All of the distress and sadness that he had made such efforts to counteract flooded over him and he lay there for a long time, thinking that he needed re-hatching, that he needed rebirth. It was all too easy to lose faith in the silver branch. Could he somehow be re-born into that vision? Lying there for quite a long time he remembered the lines from *Fern Hill*:

> And then to awake, and the farm, like a wanderer white
> With the dew, come back, the cock on his shoulder: it was all
> Shining, it was Adam and maiden,
> The sky gathered again
> And the sun grew round that very day.
> So it must have been after the birth of the simple light
> In the first spinning place, the spellbound horses walking warm
> Out of the whinnying green stable
> On to the fields of praise.

'The fields of praise' are not fields that can be measured, ploughed or bought and sold, they belong to a different dimension of reality and they have their source in a different kind of vision, the kind of vision that has been all but destroyed by reductive thinking. What he longed for, lying there where the swan had nested, was a *Fern Hill* cosmogony, an explanation of the origin of the universe that would include the miracle of spirit.

A few days later another experience of the natural world had a profound effect. He had been invited to join Stephen Lavelle on a day's lobster-fishing. In the glorious early-morning sunshine as the boat left the shore the competitive savagery of the seagulls screaming and swooping for leftover bait led him to observe that it was easy to imagine the dinosaurs that they are descended from. That was only the start of it. Bait now at the ready, they began to haul in the lobster pots. The contents of the very first pot were forever scored on his memory. 'In it was a black, brown-black conger eel, a pink crayfish, a slate-blue lobster, two crabs making intimidating bubbles at their small foaming mouths, and a sea-slug, the colour of three very distinct, very glamorous poisons.'[8] Firstly, the conger eel was swiftly decapitated and hauled from the pot, its head still attached by a filament of skin. Thrown on the floor of the boat it continued, in involuntary spasms, to snap at the empty air. He was reminded of the kitchen floor at home and the bleeding head of 'a gloriously combed and wattled Rhode Island Red cock.' Next out of the pot was the slate-blue lobster, destined to turn a hectic red colour in the process of being boiled alive in some faraway restaurant. Then came the crabs, whose claws were removed with a deft twist, and the useless torsos thrown back into the sea. This was savage havoc and it continued until all eighty pots were hauled, cleared, baited and re-sowed.

All day he witnessed an even more vivid version of the 'yoga of horror' than that on display in the Sacred Heart picture on his bedroom wall. Between the seagulls and the lobster pot, nature 'red in tooth and claw' was on display and there was nothing to mediate it.

> Two revelations:
> Manannán's Sea
> and
> The sea of the lobster-pot
> The weak choice would be to credit one and not the other. The heroic choice would be to credit both.
> The lobster-pot
> and
> The Grail
> Eliot is right:
> Humankind cannot bear very much reality. (*Nostos*, p. 427)

By 'Grail' he is here referring to the Holy Grail, the blessed vessel used by Jesus during the Last Supper which is said to have been brought to Britain for safe-keeping and hidden in the castle of the Fisher King. In the stories of King Arthur's court this mythical grail is the ultimate goal of every knight's quest, a quest which in modern times has been interpreted as the quest for soul, a unique journey which each individual is challenged to undertake in order to 'find himself', to find and develop his personal spiritual potential. In the waste land of the modern world there are few who rise to that challenge. In John's analysis, the world of the Grail is the world of 'silver branch perception'; the world of the lobster-pot is the world of meaningless suffering, brutality and ultimate annihilation, the world of nihilism, of 'Naught'. It is all too easy to credit the latter, to adopt the scientific mindset and see only the lobster-pot; on the other hand it is far too simplistic to credit only the 'silver branch' which of itself might offer refuge but not an answer. 'The heroic choice' he says, 'is to credit both'; in other words 'that the world of scream-ing, feeding seagulls is the world of the singing silver branch', that the lobster-pot belongs on 'the fields of praise'.

'The great man has room in him for all things'. It was a line from the Tao Te Ching, and John wondered if that great man has room in him 'for unsentimental self-knowledge.' Is he willing to know, able to know, that his hand, holding his book of wisdom, is structurally similar to the fin of a shark? Hands that compose, that write, that paint, those hands that create civilizations, 'all of them structurally homologous to conscienceless savagery.' The willingness to know this, to know consciously what he is and what he is capable of is the great man's 'Gethsemane' experience. The Christian story was regaining its hold on his imagination and this time he was not inclined to turn his back on it. He was beginning to explore it in a new light. Christ's suffering on Holy Thursday night became a powerful symbol. According to the gospel of St. John,

'And Jesus went forth with his disciples over a torrent called the Kedron. And they came to a place which was named Gethsemane: and he saith unto his disciples, sit ye here, while I shall pray. And he taketh with him Peter, James and John, and began to be sore amazed and to be very heavy.'[9]

Jesus in Gethsemane, 'sore amazed', became central to the development of all of John's later thinking. He imagines that Jesus is 'sore amazed by what he knows',[10] Jesus knows the depths of man and of nature, he knows the lobster-pot; Jesus is 'Grand Canyon deep in the world's karma', and he suffers it all. On behalf of all of humanity, in Gethsemane he suffers what man phylogenetically is, he incorporates it and it is only by so doing that he can ultimately redeem and transcend it. What John found fascinating is that the word 'gethsemane' means the oil press or olive-press, all that one is becomes pressed into being in Gethsemane. Years later he would write 'Jesus is our hero of integration',[11] Jesus has pioneered a way to face the 'yoga of horror'; interestingly he had asked his disciples to watch with him but not one of them had the strength to stay awake. As John was beginning to see it, the task for humanity is perhaps to stay awake with Jesus on this step of the journey. In Gethsemane Jesus is 'the great man who has room in him for all things'. In a sense to experience Gethsemane is to experience a Christian Tsetsekia. These were enormous thoughts for a day spent lobster-fishing on Inisbofin. However there was a sense in which the entire day had been a profound and all-embracing religious experience. As they returned to the island, the evening sun was glorious, so glorious that

This evening now in the west of Ireland, even to think that we are exiled from Paradise would have been a sin against how the world looked. And there was something more. Appearances this evening weren't deceptive. I was somehow sure of it. As the world looked, so it essentially and metaphysically was.

More even than the night in Saskatchewan when the Ford car I was travelling in blazed with auroral fire, I this evening had a tremendous singing sense of the universe. As if its ultimate particles weren't particles at all, as if they

were crimson hosannas, it sang in every rock, in lobster and in lobster-pot it
sang, and I remembered and I accepted the invitation to sing with angels and
archangels that comes to us out of the all too resonantly red heart of the Mass.
Sanctus Sanctus Sanctus. (*Nostos*, p. 430)

Hosanna in the highest; a holy hosanna was what he intuited, singing at the heart
of the universe.

Continuing the next day in a similar mood he visited the ruins of St. Colman's
Abbey on the eastern side of the island. He was still thinking about the Christian
story. Standing there in what would have been the nave of the ruined church he
thought about all that it represented, all that he had been baptised into. According
to St. Paul's account of it he had been baptised into the life and death of Jesus.

Baptised into death, and that on the third morning after I was born. I must
catch sight of it: a baby, newly born, baptised into one of the more terrible
deaths that we have record of:
  'And they bring him unto the place Golgotha, which is, being interpreted,
the place of a skull'.[12]
  A baby baptised into such a death!
  Could anything be so shocking?
  And yet religion is almost always shocking. (*Nostos*, p. 432)

But shocking as it is, perhaps religion is necessary in order to mediate for us all
that we so shockingly are. He remembered it again, the thought that had struck
him when contemplating the lurid picture of the Sacred Heart – 'where things
are terrible, a terrible pharmacy is called for.' Perhaps, he thought, if we could
properly inhabit our baptism, to include recognition of human suffering and of the
capacity to inflict suffering, then maybe we could better inhabit our lives and our
earth, maybe Christianity, re-imagined, could provide that kind of pharmacy. In
the course of the baptismal ceremony the officiating priest anoints the child's senses
and uses the Aramaic word *Ephpheta*, meaning *Be Opened*. It made him wonder,
'Opened to what extent though?' Is it to be opened only to Gethsemane, to all
that is terrible both within and without, and into the death and dark of Calvary,
of Golgotha, which means 'the place of the skull'?[13] Is Christ's cry of dereliction
the end of the story for humanity or is there also within the sacrament of baptism,
and therefore within Christianity, the potential for a greater opening out? He
imagined the sixth century monks filing into this abbey on a cold and dark January
morning, their breaths condensing as they chanted their psalms and listened to
the gospels, what vision sustained them? What vision illuminated the pages of the

Book of Kells? How, in all the discomfort and deprivation of their lives did these extraordinary men get beyond a Gethsemane vision of life? He could understand and accept 'the red heart of the Mass' because it is obvious in all of nature and in all of human history, but was there a way to understand and accept the miracle of transformation, hope and redemption that was also at the heart of it?

In answer he had only the fleeting glimpses of the numinous in the natural world, he had his own intuitive sense, he had the inspirational words of various philosophers, poets and story-tellers, and he had the process of creativity itself. From what or from where does creative genius emerge? In response he would tell about the composition of the beautiful Irish air *Port na bPúcaí*, the tune of the Fairies. An old fiddler had left a neighbour's house to cross three fields to go home, but he didn't reach home that night. It was days later before he returned, and on being questioned as to his whereabouts he took out the fiddle and played a new tune,

> a tune never till that moment heard in our world.
>
> 'That's where I've been,' he says. 'I've been where that kind of music comes and goes. No one playing it, it will come to you out of a wood, or, you not expecting it, it will come to you over the grouse moors.' (*Nostos*, p. 431)

'It will come to you', and it seems to come from somewhere else, and in 'Once-upon-a-time' time that is what is called the 'Otherworld', but the old fiddle player knew differently. The Otherworld, he told his wife is 'another way of seeing this world, it's another way of being in it. The otherness isn't in the world. It is in our seeing.' The tune had come from somewhere inside himself, not from his familiar self, but from another dimension of himself that sometimes awakens. The creative genius of the world is within.To have lost this way of seeing the world John saw as nothing less than total 'impoverishment of heart and mind'. To be open to the possibility of 'otherworld' thinking and seeing is profoundly important. The extraordinary thing is that in the rational empirical world apparently otherworld miracles happen all the time and are totally taken for granted.

> When in our world the temperature drops below freezing point, very surprising things happen. Water, even where it is fluent or turbulent, turns to ice. Instead of rain we get snow. In damp houses frost flowers bloom on the window panes. The moisture in our breath condenses in the air before us.
>
> But, as there is a freezing point in the world, so is there a miracling point. People, usually people who meditate and pray, come unexpectedly into it. In the end they live from it, and they don't even need to perform miracles, miracles happen in their presence.

A universe in which a caterpillar becomes a butterfly might itself one day spin a cocoon, leaving us having to think again about our dogmas, religious and scientific.

The Silver Branch

and

A cloak hanging on a sunbeam[14]

Surely, whoever reckons with the universe, must reckon with these. A cosmology that doesn't reckon with these is reckoning with something much less than the whole story. The whole story requires new eyes, new mind, new intelligence. It requires new lives. (*Nostos*, p. 435)

Could a re-imagined Christianity provide any or all of these? And if it could, would we then be in 'with an evolutionary chance'? Could silver-branch perception provide a better way of being in the world? He had shipped oars in order to find out.

12

'WHAT ELSE CAN ONE BE BUT
AN INTELLECTUAL OUTLAW'

Amergin; the scald crow; the hare's nest; the Fall; baptism in a trout stream; the world
of the senses; a new home; Jimmy and Mary; the heron and the brown trout.

In September 1971, John decided to relocate to the mainland. He wanted trees
and rivers and lakes, a wider landscape in which to spend the winter. True to form,
the nine mile boat journey provided more scope for imaginative reflection. On
his *imram* to Inisboffin three months previously he had been preoccupied with
Uvavnuk, going the way of the reed in the river, shipping oars. On his journey back
to the mainland it was Amergin he had on his mind. Amergin Ghlúngheal, poet
and seer was a leader of the Milesians, the last of the mythical invaders of Ireland,
and so the immediate ancestors of the Irish people. Legend has it that Amergin
ultimately outwitted the native Tuatha Dé Danann and came ashore 'over nine
waves' singing his incantation, now known as the Song of Amergin:

> I am a wind in the sea
> I am a sea-wave upon the land
> I am a sound of the sea
> I am a stag of seven fights
> I am a hawk on a cliff
> I am a teardrop of the sun ...

Imagine, John thought, imagine that Amergin's vision of himself had come
ashore with him and had evolved into an inclusive and sheltering cosmology that
had 'room in it for all things', what a coming ashore that might have been. That,
however, had not been the eventual outcome, the Milesians being weapon-wielding

151

conquerors, but was it a dream that might yet be realised? So far, his sense of it was that the Amergin vision had come to nothing; that as yet 'we are all nine waves away from the world'; still awaiting the next great evolutionary step for humanity, 'the day someone is willing to be carried in over those last nine waves in a swan's nest' and sets foot, not on the moon, but on the earth, this time willing to be ecumenical with all that it is and all that we are. 'That, surely', he said, 'would be a giant step for humanity.' (*Nostos*, p. 441)

Imagining himself developing Amergin's original vision he thought about what that would mean; it had already brought him away from the academic world; would it involve still further 'subtraction'? What changes would it now take to integrate and live from the insight 'I am a hawk on a cliff', could it be possible to live in harmony with such primal energy? However those questions would be answered, there were other more practical matters to be taken care of. For four pounds a week he rented a house in Dohulla, a townland close to the village of Ballyconneely, between the towns of Roundstone and Clifden. He also bought a 'big old-fashioned Raleigh bike', as blue and as shining as the one that he remembered 'resting against the bin at home all those years ago'.

> With the first such bike I had cycled through the bogs, through them and away from them, to Athens, Jerusalem and Rome. With this one I would cycle into the bog, and that I did every day for weeks. In most cases of course the little bog roads would bring me to the edge of the bog and then I'd drop the bike and I would set off walking. (*Nostos*, p. 442)

The mood of these early weeks, of this journey back into the bog, he described as 'a kind of exhilarating anguish'. Exhilarating both in the sense of freedom, of a world without fences, and in the simple beauty all around him. The mirroring lakes, everywhere receptive to the world that they so beautifully reflected, the low hills and distant mountains, and the beauty that was under his feet. 'I only had to look at the tussock of deer grass or the patch of red sphagnum I was setting my foot on, or I only had to lie down on a ridge of high heather, and then I knew that here, if anywhere, is where I'd find my bush soul.' And yet there was an underlying anguish. It was the old story.

> One day weary from walking I lay down, flat-out, on a wave worn bed of granite at the edge of a lake. In no time at all, and seemingly from nowhere, a scald-crow circled, calling raucously. I knew what he was thinking, thinking with an empty craw, with an empty gut, mouth-wateringly, he was thinking that I might be carrion ...

He knew what the crow was capable of doing to a ewe that, in the throes of giving birth, is at her most exposed and helpless; that crow will descend on her and pluck out her eyes and eat them; that crow was now expectantly watching him, ready to gobble eyes that had seen the Parthenon, had seen the auroras of Chartres, had read *Romeo and Juliet*, and he thought

So this was it.

This was my bush soul. My bush soul was being raucously overshadowed by the nihilism of nature.

And the meaningless lap lap lap lap lap laplaplap of it.

Disappointing the bird, I got up and walked away. (*Nostos*, pp. 442–3)

He was distraught and nauseated by the power and immediacy of the image that the circling crow had evoked in him; it was the lobster-pot all over again. So, this was it, the bush soul, what shelter could he possibly find within it? He walked, almost unseeingly, away from the lake and crossed into high heather. Suddenly a hare sprang away from her resting place just ahead of him and, before he knew what he was doing, he sank down onto the ground and laid his head, face down, into the warm form.

It was a perfect, sheltering fit and as I lay there, breathing in the rich warmth and the rich musk, I asked it to be two things: I asked it to be a poultice sucking out all that was damaging and limiting in my European way of seeing and knowing things and, that done, I asked it to be a cocoon bringing a new and blessed mind, a mind of nature, to life in me ...

Cycling home along the coast that evening ... what left me wondering was that I had so suddenly crossed from an apprehension of nihilism in nature to an apprehension of healing in nature ...

It was desperation, I concluded. The desperation of someone who had lived for so long in the no-man's-land between a world lost and a world not yet found. (*Nostos*, p. 443)

The desperation of living in a no-man's-land between 'a world lost and a world not yet found.' He was still on the existential see-saw; sometimes weighed down by the visions of nihil, of bleak nothingness as the lot of all living things, which he had again experienced here at the side of the lake. This same sense of nihil that he had already encountered in the 'nothing but' world of Newtonian science; in the Christian story, where the passionate suffering and integration of Gethsemane was followed by the darkness, dereliction and emptiness of Good Friday; in the

Buddhist tradition with its absolute annihilation of self into the emptiness of nirvana; and in the Hindu tradition with Vishnu's revelation of world-illusion to Narada. Balancing the see-saw at other times, this nihilism was outweighed by a more healing vision of a paradisal world and a conviction that the trouble lay with the limitations of human perception, with the 'single vision' of the modern mind-set that looks for the key to the house only in that corner where the light shines. For that reason, his head achingly immersed in the hare's form, he had prayed that it would suck out 'all that was damaging and limiting in my European way of seeing and knowing things'.

Years previously he had written a poem called *Paradise Lost* in which he declared that Paradise is lost to human beings because

> That it might see us,
> Understand,
> We solved the earth.
>
> That it might see us,
> Show its hand,
> We blitz the rock
> With metaphors,
> We blitz the land.

Modern attempts to 'solve the earth' have led to an incredible impoverishment. In an effort to scientifically explain the universe, there has been a 'blitz', a blitz with language, a blitz with formulae, and all alternative ways of seeing and knowing have been annihilated. The eye of science is the eye of the Cyclops, it is the eye of Medusa, it is the eye of Balor of the Evil Eye, the *Súil Mildagach* which has blinded the eye of 'silver branch perception'. It is also the bad tongue, the *Nemtenga*, the reductionist language that has 'blitzed the land'.

> Our collective eye is a Balor's eye, poisoned and poisoning, reducing everything
> in sight to commodity. And as is the collective eye, so is the collective soul ...
> we have reduced our originally stupendous planet to economic size. (*Invoking
> Ireland*, pp. 8, 10)

Soul has been poisoned. He wondered if this might not be the 'Fall' that humanity has really undergone. According to the Bible Adam and Eve were exiled from Paradise, as if it were an actual place, and descended into this lower mortal world, a world situated between the heights of a heaven that they had lost and the depths of hell, a further fall which awaited them should they again transgress. This is the biblical myth but perhaps, in dismissing the myth, a deeper truth is also dismissed. Maybe the Fall does not, in any real way, involve actual hierarchical worlds.

> But what if we were to understand the Fall, not as a wandering downwards into ever darker and more impoverished realms, but as a calamity that happened to us as perceivers. In other words, we didn't move from where we were, but we did lose our capacity to see our surroundings for the Paradise they then were and still are. (*Nostos*, p. 446)

In a poem by William Blake, referring to the Fall,[1] John had come across the imagery of 'opacity' and 'contraction'. These he thought appropriate terms to describe the modern European way of being in the world. Human beings, in closing themselves off from paradisal vision have reached the limits of opacity and contraction. By closing off the possibility of miracle and wonder we have 'contracted', become smaller beings and our souls have shrivelled away; we no longer see glory, our vision is clouded, opaque, we are blind to translucence and transcendence. Opacity and contraction are the marks of death. They are the Fall. The world that the modern European inhabits is a world dominated by 'Clenched fist, clenched heart, clenched eyes, clenched imagination, clenched life.'[2] However, just as the diagnosis had come from Blake, so too did a possible cure: 'If the doors of perception were cleansed everything would appear to man as it is, Infinite. For man has closed himself up, till he sees all things thro' narrow chinks of his cavern.'[3] And so, resting his agonised head in the hare's form John also prayed that the form would be 'a cocoon bringing a new and blessed mind, a mind of nature, to life in me.' He longed for a 'cleansing' of his faculties, a return to a 'pristine' state of seeing and hearing and understanding, convinced that he would then achieve a clearer vision of what he intuited to be a 'pristine' world.

> One day, reborn in my oldest and deepest instinctive and mental depths, I would be able for the splendour and terror and danger and wonder of a world everywhere and in everything eruptively Divine. (*Dreamtime*, p. 33)

What did he need to do to achieve that rebirth into 'silver branch perception' of a world 'everywhere and in everything eruptively divine'? 'Standing by this mirroring lake, I felt corrupted and polluted. Corrupted and polluted by culture. My eyes were museums.' His mind was a museum, and in it were labyrinths of rooms devoted to all of the different cultures he had ever studied and internalised – Greek, Roman and Judeo/Christian rooms; Egyptian, Babylonian, Sumerian rooms; Renaissance rooms, Aztec rooms, Plains Indian rooms; Celtic rooms. Science, history, philosophies, mythologies and at the end of it all, he was what Nietzsche had called 'a mythless man', 'grubbing around' in the hope of finding some ultimate myth 'that would explain me to me'. Here in a bog in Ballyconneely 'I had collided with what I had become, and I felt the anguish of having to start all over again.'[4]

> I imagined it.
>
> I would be the mosaic-maker of my own mind, and pristine sensations of the pristine world would be the 'tesserae'.[5] Taking my time with it, I would look at a patch of red sphagnum. Picking it from one of the wizened bushes behind me, I would taste a haw. Growing on the next rock I'd pass, I would touch a little tussock of sable moss. Without picking it, I would smell a stem of bell heather. And then, sitting by a turf fire at home, I'd listen to a curlew calling below on the shore. Starting again with sensations such as these, I'd remake my own mind. (*Nostos*, p. 450)

He was beginning his own personal 'ghost dance'. He wanted to roll back all that he had ever learned from the day he had correctly translated a Greek sentence in St. Michael's in Listowel; roll it all away and 'remake his own mind'. To begin with, and in keeping with his lifelong love of ritually enacting important ideas, he initiated his 'ghost dance' with a baptism. A baptism 'out' of everything he had ever learned about the world. On his way back across the bog, he came to a stream that runs into Loch Fada. 'I knelt down and immersed my head three times, baptizing myself out of culture, baptizing myself out of Christianity. To complete the baptism, I knew I would have to come back a second time and a third time to do the same thing.'[6] Exactly why he did not know, it had been an impulsive and instinctive gesture; he simply trusted that his psyche was prompting him and that at some level it knew what it was doing. There was 'a kind of a fright' on him and a sense that he had crossed some boundary, but, hair dripping wet and conscious of the state he was in, he was also oddly amused. He had often referred to his 'very expensive European education', and now almost casually, he had set about washing it all away. This could never be admitted to at home in Moyvane!

This extraordinary personal and impulsive mini-ritual, to baptise himself out of everything he had ever learned about the world, to shake all off all conditioned ways of seeing and knowing, had emerged from the tendency that had always been in him, 'to think outside the permissions and prohibitions of my culture.'[7] He was only too familiar with the foundation stones of that culture, and it can be said that the very word 'stone' is key to his dismissal of it. Every fibre of his being resisted the science that insists that the world of matter is the only reality; here in Connemara, a wonderful 'immaculate' world of stone and water, he was convinced that the Owenglin River, as it 'tumbled, poured and collapsed' its way over rocky outcrops, was more than the sum of its parts.

> To look at, it was a delight of water, as if in every molecule of it that one atom of oxygen and those two atoms of hydrogen were still amazed by the strange, miraculous new thing they turned into when they came together. (*Nostos*, p. 451)

Science might reduce the Owenglin down to 'nothing but' atoms and molecules, but could that really explain what it becomes? And the mountains, and the lakes that mirrored those mountains, 'all seemed to say that there is a mood, a world mood, in which things aren't things, in which actions aren't actions, and that means that when we get up and go out into the world we should leave our nouns and our verbs at home.' Our nouns and our verbs, our namings and our doings, only serve to reduce, to corrupt and to pollute. He went a step further, not only is matter not the whole story, he made the intriguing claim that 'matter is mind in hibernation', a proposition that remained central to his mature vision. What did he mean by it? It appears to be what William James called a 'moment of luminosity' but it may also have been inspired by the Hindu concept that consciousness or 'aliveness' is what underpins everything in the universe. In this way of looking at it the universe emanates from an underlying conscious aliveness which is eternally manifesting itself, and thus all things, even stones, share in that consciousness; however in apparently inanimate things, consciousness or mind is 'hibernating'. Very obviously, such a claim completely contradicts current scientific thinking, which, while it cannot explain 'the hard problem of consciousness'[8] still insists that it is produced biologically/chemically when an organism reaches a particular stage of maturity. Therefore science describes consciousness as a derivative of the complex human brain, while being in no way able to explain how that can possibly happen.

For as long as human history, and back into the realms of prehistory, human societies have attempted to understand their origins. It can be argued that all of the various explanations they have come up with belong at some point on the spectrum outlined in the above paragraph. At one end of that spectrum is the belief in a pre-existing creative living power, the religious and mythical depiction of which varies dramatically from time to time and from place to place, and at the other end is the scientific materialism of Big Bang and Big Crunch. Here in Connemara John had arrived at the rather terrifying, but also uplifting, conclusion that the world is inexplicably more marvellous and more miraculous than any cosmologies anywhere on that spectrum can comprehend, is in fact more marvellous than the human mind can understand. In the presence of lakes and mountains

> there are days when we have to down tools, down ways of seeing, down ways of knowing, down cultural and habitual ways of being. There were days in Connemara, and this was one of them, when I would look at the mountains around me and think, how unworldly the world is. On such days worldliness wouldn't be in the world, it would be in my way of seeing it and knowing it, and then I would be in trouble. ..
>
> ... and what else could you do but kneel on the bank of a trout stream and immerse your head, your eyes and your mind, three times, and again three times, and again three times, baptising yourself out of Europe, out of Africa, out of Asia, out of the Americas native and modern, out of Australia aboriginal and modern, out of, out of, out of, out of all the myths and metaphors through which we have sought an accommodation with ourselves and with the world we live in. (*Nostos*, pp. 456–7)

No cosmology that he had ever come across would suffice, but there was one absolute conviction that he had expressed in a poem written in Canada called *The Second Law of Thermodynamics*. In it he expresses a core belief – 'that aliveness is chiefly what characterises the universe, and it isn't with a dead-and-alive aliveness that it is alive, it is alive with the aliveness of a hovering hawk, it is alive with the aliveness of a striped and leaping tiger, it is alive, in its rocks and in its mountains it is alive with prophetic and visionary aliveness, and no matter how many times we compel it to marry our cosmologies, it was, it is, and it always will be, a maiden.'[9] In other words we will never be able to fully explain it and following from that conviction came the impassioned declaration that 'the nothing-but universe is a modern lie'.[10] 'We should', he concluded, 'put the sender's name and address on the envelope of any cosmology that we send out into the universe. For one thing is sure, it will not recognise itself in what we say about it ... so our cosmologies will be sent back saying *not known at this address, please try your own minds*.'[11]

He was back again to what he had recognised in Mexico, it is your own projections that you are imposing on the universe. Return to sender! Ever since he had read Darwin all those years ago he had felt that there was 'nowhere *inside* his head to lay his head', and he had spent years searching for some sheltering place, some satisfying answer. Now, while recognising that this quest had provided some enormous insights, he could clearly see that there really was nowhere inside his head, where that shelter would be found. Hence the swan's nest, the hare's nest, and the baptismal pool in the trout stream. But there was to be no easy resting place there either. On the day after his 'baptism' he followed the course of the Owenglin River up into the mountains and came to a waterfall. Here he would continue the process of emptying his mind and allowing his senses to experience the world. Closing his eyes, he set about getting to know the cascade through hearing, attending to all the voices, loud and not so loud, of the waterfall. He listened to the strangeness, and 'in the end there was no me', almost as if the strangeness was listening to itself; this continued for a long while until the sense of selfhood returned and he opened his eyes. He then set out to get to know what was in front of him through the sense of sight ... 'and how utterly different from each other were experiences of hearing and seeing.'

> That long lovely pouring there in the cascade – I well remembered what it sounded like to hearing, but now, experienced in seeing, what an altogether different reality it was.
>
> Returning to hearing and then coming back to seeing many times over, I gave myself all the time I needed to live the difference.
>
> This sense that there is one world, I thought, is pure illusion. There are in fact as many worlds as there are ways of perceiving ...
>
> Six days after each other I came back. (*Nostos*, p. 453)

'There are as many worlds as there are ways of perceiving.' It was a profound experience of the mystery of the natural world, but it came at a cost.

> On what turned out to be the last day for now that I would do this, I opened my eyes and like someone who had been born blind but had suddenly without warning been given the sense of sight ... I was frightened not just by the unaccountable strangeness of hearing and seeing, my very existence, that too unaccountable – unaccountable in that I existed and in how I existed – it frightened me.
>
> Knowing that I had been shaken in a place deeper than my everyday sense of myself, I got up and turned for home.
>
> The swan's nest, the hare's form and the baptismal pool in the trout stream.
>
> No, even at the cost of never acquiring my bush soul, I wouldn't now be going back for those final immersions. (*Nostos*, pp. 453–4)

'A place deeper than my everyday sense of myself', a place where that everyday sense of self does not exist, that is the internal void that waking awareness eclipses, which when experienced, can feel dark and empty and threatening. With that sense of fright upon him he set out for home, but that was not the end of it. He underwent a similar epiphany a few weeks later but this time with a different outcome. He was cycling along, above the shingle shore of Lough Inagh, delighting in how the lake mirrored the Maamturks and the Twelve Bens, and he thought of how the mountains, reflected in the lake, were both themselves and not themselves, and he wondered how it would be to exist like that, 'to let the intentionless, limpid lake do my reflecting for me.'

But why settle for this? I thought.

Why not let the intentionless lake speculate me into intentionlessness? Or, more challenging still, why not let the egoless lake speculate me into egolessness? (*Nostos*, p. 457)

This state of being empty of oneself, of being egoless, he recognised as the state the Buddha had achieved after he had won enlightenment; it was also, in a more terrible form, the dereliction of Christ on Good Friday. The Buddha spoke of how the rafters of his house had been broken; similarly the self of Jesus was broken on the cross of Golgotha. John was forced to wonder whether the price one had to pay on the spiritual journey was the death of the self, and if so, did he have the nerve for it? It was at this point, while cycling homeward, that nature seemed to provide at least a partial answer.

Emerging from the Ballinahinch Woods, the road followed the course, it followed the turn and rush of a lovely river. (*Nostos*, p. 458)

The river was a delight in itself, a delight of salmon pools and tumbling water, alive in its flowing and in its sparkling sensuous being, it had an identity, a self, it was the Owenmore; and yet it was rushing carelessly towards its own extinction in the ocean. But what in effect would be extinguished? He remembered the Mundaka Upanishad:

As rivers leaving name and form behind them
    flow into their home in the ocean
so does the Knower, from name and form released,
    go to that Divine Person who is beyond the beyond. (*Nostos*, p. 460)

Changed, perhaps not ended? Who could know? He wasn't sure he was either ready or able for this Oriental diagnosis but

In the end it was simple. Cycling along beside it, I felt that this river would be sensuous soul to someone who came here having no soul at all, and for that reason I decided that I'd rent the nearest available cottage to it.

Around the next turn I found myself looking, beyond the trunks of two big elms, at the black gable-end door of that cottage.

A cottage among trees.

A cottage by an estuary.

A cottage across a narrow road from a great pool in which river and ocean meet, in which sweet water from among the mountains and salt water from beyond the headlands become a single surprise mirroring a little island overhung on its near side by a spreading oak. (*Nostos*, p. 458)

In no time at all he had negotiated with Lynne, the owner, and in spite of 'an incipient dilapidation' and a 'damp feel' to it, he agreed to take it, principally because of its location under Derrada Hill and on the estuary where the Owenmore entered the sea, but also because it had a great open fireplace. The cottage was one of three, part of a converted stable, across the yard from the main house, which Lynne ran as a guest house, a house which gave him the sense of being 'solid and strong, there was in it a sense of friendship with the earth, of earth and house being at peace with each other.'[12] He moved into his cottage on December twenty-first, 1971, the shortest day of the year. It was an altogether fortuitous move. The friendship with the earth that he had sensed in the house was what he experienced from the very outset. Through Lynne and her neighbours and friends he entered a new community and during the very troubling years yet to come this was the place that he said sheltered him, sheltered him in his more difficult depths.

It was now Christmas time and he went home to Moyvane to be with his parents.

It was dark when I got off the bus in Tarbert, but I had been hitching only for a few minutes when Mick Carmody came along in his Morris Minor car and he gave me a lift to the crossroads. He'd have taken me all the way but I wanted to walk the ascending side-road, that last three-quarters of a mile, in the dark.

I didn't only know this road in the soles of my feet. I knew it in the barefoot soles of every lobe of my mind, both conscious and unconscious. I knew it in the barefoot soles of old childhood disappointments and longings. I had come to know it driving our cows from the stall to the Cross Meadow, from the Bridge Field or the Middle Field or the West Field to the stall, from the stall to the Hill Meadow. With a horse called Peg, Chris and myself drew the wyands of hay up the road ... Glad of its sheltering hedges, I got to know it cycling every morning to St. Michael's in Listowel.

Taking me on a long peregrination through ancient Mediterranean lands, the purpose of my education was to help me escape from this road. (*Nostos*, p. 462)

An education that he now believed had led him only to the 'naked shingles' of Dover Beach; an education that he had recently attempted to escape by baptising himself out of it in a trout stream; the irony was not lost on him, and now he was about to face his mother. He had not seen her since he had come home from Canada but he knew that she was both puzzled by him and worried about him. Chris came home regularly 'and every time she would ask him had he seen me and how was I, and Chris would tell her that I was fine, in ten different ways, giving all the enviable reasons he'd tell her that I was fine, but at the end of it all she'd simply sit back and announce, 'I don't care what you say I still think he's a pity.'[13] As he walked in the small gate and crossed the yard he wondered what reception was in store for him now. The first thing that met him was Jimmy's gracious and warm welcome, 'Thank you for coming to see us at Christmas John', and then his mother's eye, as she looked him up and down trying to assess how he was getting on in the world. Change was what struck him most forcibly. It was a grief to him to see that they were getting old and that Mary was getting forgetful.

Did you close the door on the hens, Jimmy?
Did you close the door on the hens, Jimmy?
Did you close the door on the hens, Jimmy?

Three times she had asked it, and it saddened him. But they were happier together now, and 'they were still carrying on with things, with cows and calves and pigs and hens ... and their thirty two acres of bad, rushy land, they still hadn't tired of it, and clearly they had prospered, in their hearts and in their minds and in their lives they had prospered.'[14] Naturally it was not long before she asked him. What had he done in Canada? Why did he give up a good job with good prospects and a pension? Sure wasn't he a professor in a University, what more could he want? And what had taken him to Connemara? All he could do was to reassure her that it had been his own choice to give up the job and tell her that he had enough money to live on. Needless to say he did not mention his bush soul!

What also saddened him was the change in the house itself. 'Coming home', he said, 'was like living the last three centuries of European history in a couple of hours.'

The old great fireplace with its great chimney breast was gone, replaced by a modern stove. The double-wick paraffin lamp on the wall was gone, replaced by a naked hundred-watt bulb hanging from the ceiling. The old board table was gone, replaced by a smaller formica-topped thing declaring its antibiotic brightness courtesy of the hundred-watt bulb. The old brown bin the bike used to be parked against was gone, replaced by modern chipboard units. The loft was gone. The thatch was gone replaced by slates. The sparrows were gone. Jameen Kissane was dead. When my father got up to go out and give the cows their last feed of hay he didn't take down his lantern and light it. On his way out he switched on a yard light. Ours was now a modern house. It was no longer hospitable to all that we are. Things had no shadows. Water came from a tap not from the well with a whitethorn growing over it and hart's tongue ferns growing around it and black water-beetles swimming down to the bottom of it. All that, and the floor was covered in shining linoleum. (*Nostos*, p. 469)

The house 'was no longer hospitable to all that we are.' It was no longer a house in which one could 'go down below history', a house in which 'light and dark were gypsy partners in a gypsy dance', a house in which there were 'dimensions and moods of our minds' that were beyond the reach of everyday experience, a house in which *draíocht* and wonder was alive and well; that world with all of its riches was gone, replaced by linoleum, a hundred watt-bulb and a formica table. Labour-saving no doubt, but otherwise an enormous impoverishment. What this new kitchen brought home to him, so forcefully, was that it was a physical symbol of the modern myth, the myth of progress, that has made us what we now are 'a burden and a plague and a poison to ourselves, a burden and a plague and a poison to the earth and the stars.'[15] And what flabbergasted him was that, after all the horrors of the last three centuries,

Even now, after all that has happened, there are people who still believe in progress, who still believe that earthly life can be all ladders and no snakes, all ascents and no descents. (*Nostos*, p. 464)

Later that evening, after Jimmy and Mary had gone to bed, he sat there thinking about the house and the family in which he had grown up.

The life that gives rise to stripes in a tiger, to antlers in a stag, to fur in a rabbit, the life that came up with the instinct to nurture its young in mammals, that comes to flower in the hawthorn, to venom in the snake and to sanctity in the saint, the genius of life for unhindered primary life, that genius was in my mother. A farmer in her yard, and in her house a fire-maker, a bread-maker, and a neighbour to everyone who came to her gate and her door, she was a wonder.

And if, in the pelting night, King Lear came into her yard, came through her door, she'd look after him but she'd knock sense into him, particularly if she sensed that he was staging his sufferings, displaying them for all to see ...

It was shocking to see that she was slowing up.

My father was different, a born thinker. Looking at him sometimes sitting over at the end of a small table, you'd think that he had found his way to the heart of a mountain, Mount Brandon, the mountain he was born under, and it was there, in there in the silence at the heart of that mountain that he was thinking. He was thinking with the mountain ...

I remembered him going to the door and standing there at ease. Looking out into the wild night I could hear him saying, *mar go bhfuil mo threabhann is mo fhuirse déanta is mo thread agam ón síon*, for the ploughing I've had to do, I've done it, and the harrowing I've had to do, I've done it, and the bad night doesn't worry me for my cattle are housed. ...

Mrs. McGrath came in one day. 'How are you Missus?' he asked. 'And how's all your care?'

In that word 'care', in that sense of things and of animals and of people, that's where you'd find him, my father.

And after she gave birth to Josephine, her last child, Mrs. McGrath wasn't at all well for a few weeks. My mother took in the new-born baby, and one evening while she was milking the cows I was looking after her. In spite of my best efforts to pacify her with her bottle and with baby talk and with gentle rocking, she was crying when my mother came back in. She dropped her bucket and coming to the cradle she took over saying, as she lifted her up, ''Tis hatching she needs,' and sitting down by the fire, that's what she did, in the way that a mouse, all soft fur and tits, would, in the way that a hen, all spread feathers and wings would, she hatched Josephine.

'How's all your care?'

''Tis hatching she needs.' (*Nostos*, pp. 471–2)

That is what his home had given him, the humanity of 'care and hatching', this capacity for thinking with the mountain, and this 'genius' for primary life, along with a rich treasury of folk stories and a culture rooted in an ancient past. Side by side with it, and yet in opposition to it, it had also given him Darwin and a modern European education. Apparently contradictory worlds and yet:

Superstition and science most people would say. But then, when you think about it, isn't science itself burdened by the biggest of all superstitions, the belief that the universe is explainable as a system of material causes giving rise to material effects? ... In strict conscience, what else can one be but an intellectual outlaw? (*Nostos*, p. 479)

Was it any wonder that he had baptised his head out of the whole lot of it. But where to now? There was another memory.

Sometimes, coming down from the cows maybe, coming very quietly, I would look over the parapet of the bridge and I'd see a heron. A strange, ghostly bird he was, and how tall he could stand, standing from the tips of his yellow legs to the tips of his yellow bill ...

Always, always, meeting a heron had a strange effect on me. Even physically I would feel different. It was as if, just by seeing him, I became him. I became his silence, I became his solitude, I became his distance, the almost holy distance he kept from the human world.

We hated being alone, but he didn't mind it at all. He didn't even need to have a dog with him the way my father did ...

Standing tall and alone, or, his head pulled back like a snail's into the shell of his shoulders, the heron was silent and, drawing his sense of himself from within, always from within, he never once needed to see his own face in the water.

Meeting a heron is like meeting all the shy sequestered parts of ourselves. It is like meeting all the parts of our own soul that the economic world has no use for and is afraid of.

And there was the day that I imitated my father. Lying face down on the bank of the river, I put my hand in under it and this time it happened. I felt a brown trout, and going about it as he said I should, I finally closed my hand on him and hauled him out, and looking at the colour of his flanks and at the stars along his flanks, so tiny and so lovely, more lovely than the insides of cowslips in the Hill Meadow, it was like the Gates of Paradise had opened, and I was afraid, and I put him back, but once reopened maybe they never again closed, not so formidably as Christian doctrine demanded.

The heron and the brown trout. (*Nostos*, p. 466)

He remembered the night when he was seventeen that he had read the fateful passages in *The Origin of Species*, he remembered the blown scrap of paper that he had followed across the yard and that he had, in one way or another, been following all of his life since then. It struck him that by 'baptising' himself on the mountain, he had finally abandoned that scrap of paper, the paper on which all cosmologies are written, the bit of paper that represents all intellectual attempts to 'find dh'answer'; but he also recognised that he had not abandoned the other more intuitive vision, that sense of an ancient, infinitely rich darkness which lies beyond the reach of rational minds, and which is somehow connected to the hints of Paradise afforded by the silent self-possession of a heron, the stars on the flanks of a brown trout and the beauty at the heart of a cowslip in the Hill Meadow. The quest would continue.

The next few days were spent reconnecting with family and friends, glad to make the acquaintance of his little niece Amanda who came 'to light six candles in Granny's six windows for Christmas' and to see his sisters Phyllis and Madeleine now looking after their own families; Phyllis, who had inherited the fun of her mother's wit, Madeleine with her mother's capacity to cut one down to size, and both of them with both Mary and Jimmy's sense of 'care'. 'Madeleine's fire meets you at her door. And it is a short walk to her table.'[16] He would return to Connemara with that sense of family warmth.

13

'WHAT CHANCE HAVE WE, WHEN THAT'S WHERE WE THINK WE LIVE?'

Care; an external soul; the eternal flux; an Easter awakening; the perennial philoso-phy; the intelligence of instinct; Martin Halloran; working at the Castle; the mystical journey; the shattering on the mountain; the dark night of the soul.

During the journey back to Connemara, first hitching to Limerick and from there travelling by bus to Galway, that sense of warmth and care remained with him. For the previous few days everywhere he turned there had been memories and recollections; one in particular preoccupied him.

> After school one evening, when I was five or six years old, my mother sent me back up to the village for sugar and soap. Seeing me from the door of Brosnan's pub Mikie Welsh, the postman, waved a letter at me. It had something big and soft in it. As soon as she felt it, my mother knew what it was, a nipple for Pyhllis's bottle, and she was delighted, because this was during the war, and over the past few months not a nipple was to be found in Bally, Tarbert, Newtown or Listowel. (*Nostos*, p. 472)

At that time Jimmy was working in England and had posted home a rubber teat for the baby's bottle. How strange, John now thought, care for our own kind coming out of the London blitz, coming out of war, one ordinary man looking after his child. To honour the gesture and the hope, however small, that it represented John re-imagined Picasso's *Guernica* and added his own detail, that envelope opened and showing its contents in a conspicuous place at the heart of the painting. For John the Guernica painting was the iconic symbol of the twentieth century, a fragmented agonised war-torn world, brutal and bull dominated, the outcome of so-called 'progress' and 'enlightenment'. Epoch after epoch, century after century, this was endgame. Care and compassion shattered. This was the world John Moriarty desperately wanted to heal and in Jimmy's small gesture he saw what might be the seed of a new humanity, a humanity that would put 'care' before progress and profit and that might consequently integrate and learn from its mistakes. Undoubtedly naive, but impassioned and idealistic, he needed to find 'a sheltering mythology' that was big enough to allow that innate human sense of care to flourish. Only then would further evolution be possible.

His father was also on his mind for another reason; he remembered the conversation he had had with him years previously when Jimmy casually remarked that he had 'come to th'end of thinkin' and I shtill haven't found th'answers'. The irony of it was not lost on him now. What else had the baptism in the trout stream signified if not just that? He too was at 'th'end of thinkin', aware only of what he called 'the vertigo of alternatives' that his education and travels had presented to him; there was simply no coherence and nowhere within any one philosophy or creed where he could 'lay his head'. The new understanding that he believed so vital was not going to emerge from the old arguments.

It was New Years Eve 1971 when he returned to Connemara from Moyvane. On that same day last year, with the mighty road trip concluded, he had returned to his apartment, to his job, and to his friends and there had been a party to welcome in the New Year. This year he would be alone, but there were no regrets. His mental image of himself in his office in Winnipeg was of being in touch only with manufactured things, with desks and blackboards and functional spaces. He had walked away from the 'pot-bound grow-bag' of so-called civilization, from city life, from a world that he believed had lost its way, and he did not want to return. That evening he lit a log fire and settled down to enjoy 'the constant heat and the fitful light' while listening to the wind in the elms outside. He was reading of Cúroí MacDaire, one of the great pre-Christian gods of the Irish, of whom it was said that he had an external soul. His soul lived in a salmon in a stream that ran beneath his cashel and it was said that if one could kill the salmon then one would kill Cúroí. This of course triggered further reflection.

> But what about us? I wondered. Isn't there a sense in which we too have an external soul? Don't we have something of our soul in bushes? Don't we have something of our soul in mountains? And isn't it true that if we damage a river we damage ourselves? And wouldn't that account for the very poor shape that Western humanity is in right now? (*Nostos*, p. 480)

Lines from *The Death of Fionavar* by Eva Gore Booth seemed to capture his mood. "She has broken her faith with the wind and the sea, she is false to the sun." Fionavar represents Western humanity which has also 'broken faith'; 'we too have assumed we can cut our connection with rock and bush and get away with it. We too have assumed that we can shake off our bush souls'[1] and go on to cover the earth in concrete! Kill a river, he thought, and we kill ourselves.

> I listened for a long, long time to the wind in the elms and coming near midnight I walked up the road and crossed a footbridge onto an island in the river. Going round behind a fisherman's hut, I sat on a spur of rock which with other rocks further out sent the river rippling away either side of me. It was there, listening to all the river's sounds, listening to them for Fionavar, that I crossed from 1971 to 1972. (*Nostos*, p. 481)

It was his requiem for modern humanity, a requiem for a species that had taken a sword to the world and its creatures without counting the cost and which, like Captain Ahab in his relentless quest of the white whale, could not see that the attempt to defeat the great beast would lead to his own annihilation.

In spite of the sombre thoughts and sombre requiem he did have a sense of a new beginning; the next day the weather was cold and bright and he made the most of it. Climbing Ben Lettery he was struck by the wonder of it all.

> And that today is what the world looked like, like wonder coming continuously out into the open, coming out as mountains, coming out as woods, coming out as rivers and herons flying home, coming out as bogs and otters, as lakes, as otter paths between lakes, coming out as stars, coming out as hearing and seeing, as the taste of a blackberry and the smell of heather.
>
> Coming out in the way that our minds are always coming out, out into sensations and thoughts, into sadness and hope and fear and forgiveness. In dreams in the night coming out. And what is happening in our minds is happening in rocks. It is happening in mountains. (*Nostos*, p. 483)

Life eternally emerging in an eternally changing wonder, where what on one day is one thing is tomorrow another, where 'thing' is not the correct word, every individual thing is in a state of becoming, from what it was to what it is to what it will be, and he remembered Heraclitus who said, one can never step twice into the same river, and Hopkins who said that *Nature is a Heraclitean fire* with at its heart the 'immortal diamond'[2] of life that is eternal. Kuo Hsi's painting of *Early Spring* was with him again, clouds that become mountains, mountains that become clouds, an eastern way of seeing and accepting a world in constant flux, a world in which eternity is not static. That eternal flux is what he saw everywhere and for the next months, climbing, walking, cycling, he lived a richly sensuous life.

> A fear I had when I thought about quitting in Canada was how would I get on without the company, without the very presence and shape, of a woman. So far it wasn't an issue. And the reason wasn't far to seek. I was living a richly and a splendidly sensuous life. Sensuous not just in my five senses. Sensuous in my mountain-climbing muscles. Sensuous in my bog-crossing, river-crossing, wood-sitting and wood-recumbent bones. Sensuous in my mind. In a mind as sensuous as my senses. Sensuous in my waking and in my sleeping..
>
> And I was wild ...
>
> And as well as being wild in my senses I was philosophically wild ...
>
> Philosophically in Connemara, what else could I do but climb up out of Europe and say a Hindu hello to the clouds and the stars and the earth. (*Nostos*, p. 489)

Experiencing the world in this way he believed that his senses were the channels through which soul could awaken, soul in him was responding to soul in Nature and was experiencing something of its own splendour and wonder. How 'eternally unexplainable' it all was.

> And what a poverty of mind and heart it is to have explanations for everything.
>
> What a poverty of mind and heart it is to never stand before things in their eternal unexplainableness.
>
> How corrupted by a mind that needs to explain things are the eyes with which we see things! (*Nostos*, p. 492)

How arrogant human beings are, he thought, in their attempts to solve the earth. He thought of the words that came to Moses from out of the burning bush, 'put off thy shoes from off thy feet, for the place on which thou standst is holy ground.' Be humble is what this advised. It was becoming clear to him that all ground is holy ground and every bush is a burning bush, burning with the fire of eternal life, but to see this he must not only 'put off my shoes from off my feet, but from off my mind and heart.'[3] In Connemara, living beside the Owenmore River and under the shelter of Derrada Hill, those shoes were off and it was only now that he could fully appreciate a story told about Maidhc File:[4]

And there was an evening in the Dingle Peninsula when a stranger stopped to talk to a local man on the road outside Dunquin: It was a breathlessly silent evening. The ocean was silent. The mountains were silent. The fields were silent. The sheep and cattle were silent. And people were silent. The only sound was the sound of a stream coming down the near side of Eagle Mountain. The stranger remarked on it. The local man listened a long while to the sound, then said, *tá sé ag glaoch orainn isteach sa tsíoraíocht as a bhfuil sé féin ag teacht*, it is calling us into the eternity out of which it is itself flowing. (*Nostos*, p. 487)

Was that what the Owenmore was doing for him? Awakening him to an eternity that was here in front of his eyes? He knew the ancient Irish belief that all of Ireland's rivers had their source in an Otherworld Well, sometimes called Connla's Well, and he knew that at the core of this myth was the belief that life owes its existence to an Elsewhere, an Otherworld, the world that Manannán inhabits, the world that Bran Mac Feabhail glimpsed as the *Mag Meall*, the Plain of Delights, the world that 'silver branch perception' gives access to. Again he thought of the old fiddle player who said that the Otherworld is not an 'elsewhere' but another way of seeing this world that comes to us from within. He knew and loved Yeats's poem *The Song of Wandering Aengus*:

> I went out to the hazel wood,
> Because a fire was in my head,
> And cut and peeled a hazel wand,
> And hooked a berry to a thread;
> And when white moths were on the wing,
> And moth-like stars were flickering out,
> I dropped the berry in a stream
> And caught a little silver trout.
>
> When I laid it on the floor,
> I went to blow the fire a-flame,
> But something rustled on the floor,
> And someone called me by my name:
> It had become a glimmering girl,
> With apple blossom in her hair
> Who called me by my name and ran
> And faded through the brightening air.
>
> Though I am old with wandering
> Through hollow lands and hilly lands,
> I will find out where she has gone,

> And kiss her lips and take her hands;
> And walk among long dappled grass,
> And pluck till time and tides are done,
> The silver apples of the moon,
> The golden apples of the sun.[5]

This was Yeats' insisting on another dimension of reality. Now John wanted to meet that old and wandering Aengus and tell him that that dimension, that Otherworld, is not that far away from us at all. He wanted to advise him to go back to his house that has a hazel wood at the back of it and a trout stream below it; it is there that he will find his 'Trout Girl', his transformative miracle, because 'it is to where we are that she calls us'. A miracle is taking place in the world that we see every day.

> Stop your wandering Aengus.
>   Since the day we were born, and from long before the day we were born, the ordinary world has been calling us.
>   It is still calling us
>   *Tá sé ag glaoch orainn.*
>   *Tá sé ag glaoch orainn.*
>   *Tá sé ag glaoch orainn.*

Calling us back to the ordinary world, to our ordinary selves, calling to us to recognise the spirit that is within, the personal 'otherworld' well that is for the most part buried beneath the 'busyness' and distractions of what he called 'our conscription into the modern world'. The 'stones and grit'[6] of the world block the well, to clear them is the greatest challenge. Thinking these thoughts brought another revelation, another insight into and interpretation of, the Christian story:

> There is of course a Christian way of putting all this. There are two Easters.
> There is an Easter in which we awaken to the extraordinary. There is an Easter
> in which we awaken to the ordinary. Of these two, the second is by far the more
> blessed. (*Nostos*, p. 487)

'An Easter in which we awaken to the ordinary.' It struck him that Easter, in that it is about 'resurrection', happens first when one awakens to the wonder of the ordinary world. The buried spirit must be resurrected before any other 'awakening' is possible and that spirit can only be resurrected in the here-and-now. Again he was grasping at something he intuited, a spirit at work in ourselves and in the world to which we have rendered ourselves blind. To express this vision he was using the language of Christianity, probably for two reasons: because as he said, it was 'mother tongue' to him, it was the tradition in which he was reared, and also, in deference to the Zen master who advised that truth, if it is to be found at all, is to be found in one's own tradition.

Insight or truth is to be found in one's own tradition quite simply because it is in all religious traditions. In short, at the heart of all religions is one supreme insight, a 'philosophia perennis', a perennial philosophy which finds that, regardless of what outer form it takes, there is 'a divine Reality substantial to the world of things and lives and minds.'[7] This divine reality, this 'holy ground' has been experienced and described by mystics, saints, shamans and even ordinary individuals in all traditions – traditions that are independent of one another, separated not alone geographically but by aeons of time. The challenge in describing and comprehending what can only be described as mystical insight is the inadequacy of language on the one hand, and the danger of the over-familiarity with religious language on the other. What John now recognised is that, in line with this perennial philosophy, there is a 'Good Friday' and an 'Easter Sunday' in all religious traditions. On Good Friday the individual who is on a soul quest will experience the death of his ego, his personal self, his worldly concerns and then recognise his own nothingness. This can be terrifying. On Easter Sunday he recognises that there is a deeper self, an essence that exists in him and is also part of something far greater, that one can call soul. To 'grow' this soul, this god within, to find this 'Otherworld' well, is the 'movement essential' journey.

During these months in Connemara he was adding bits and pieces to the 'new holy book' that he believed was needed. With Moses still on his mind, he imagined just one commandment, more invitation than commandment: 'Be as little different from the world as you possibly can be'. Be a Taoist, be St. Colman, be Uvavnuk, 'ship oars', become, as he had advised Mona Lisa, a little 'matchstick man or woman'. Listen within. Everywhere he turned now he could see the natural world operating in this way. The Owenmore is a salmon river, the spawning beds made him conscious not alone of 'the fantastic will to reproduction and the fantastic cost' but the incredible instinct that guided the salmon home; the same instinct that led the elvers all the way from the Sargasso sea to 'the remotest and farthest bogholes of Ireland', all guided on the final leg of the journey by the individual smell of their own river. And then there were the birds:

> What a wonder of instinctive life it was. Flying in victories over my house, the
> wild geese had gone back to the tundras of Canada. And that noisy squabble
> of terns perched on that rock in the estuary – sure of their route in what looks
> like a trackless world, they have come all the way from Patagonia. The little

sedge-warbler has come from Africa. Swallows have come from Africa ... and finding their way by the stars, the stormy petrels have come in off the open ocean and are hatching their eggs in their old ancestral burrows ...

And what a sadness in us it is that we refuse to accord the dignity of intelligence to instinct, whereas instinct is life so intelligently sure of what it wants that it doesn't have to bother its head about alternatives, about a vertigo of alternatives.

And there is genius in the universe, genius that doesn't need to have recourse to deductive intelligence. And if only we would give the genius of the universe a chance. (*Nostos*, p. 507)

That is what he was attempting to do and there were times when he realised that this could be dangerous. It meant hours spent meditating in solitary places in an attempt to overcome the all too powerful grip of the ego sense of self. It meant silencing his mind, allowing that inner darkness, that inner otherness, that instinct, to have its way.

But that doesn't mean that silence is good enough. If the silence is my silence, if it is me being silent, then it isn't good enough. Only being out of the way is good enough. But then, aware of the threat, my whole life would close like a fist into and around its identity and, the danger survived, I would come home. (*Nostos*, p. 489)

There was a 'threat', a fear that he would go too far, a fear that he might not be able to regain his hold on himself, a fear of losing his identity, a fear of letting go. Fortunately, there was a home to go to, a place where he felt sheltered, and where there was a grounded life to hold him. He was becoming part of Lynne's world, her friends were becoming his friends, the animals in her yard were his animals.

I would sometimes open my gable-end door and there would be five or six horses, one of them a beautiful Palomino, in the yard. There was a sheepdog, always fussily anxious to be friendly. Her name was Ceeva. And there were two cats ... Both of them soon learned that I was a soft touch. They also learned that I stayed up late into the night and that I always kept a good fire on, and so, when Lynne put them out in the night, instead of going to bed in the hay, they'd come straight across the yard and call at my door ...

Living where I now lived, with horses sometimes in the yard, and cats calling nightly at my door I felt that I was an Aengus who had made it, I had come home. (*Nostos*, pp. 485–8)

He had come home to neighbourliness and community and one neighbour in particular became very important. That was Martin Halloran, a local bachelor, of great character and colour, who visited and connected a relatively disparate group of people, all of whom became John's friends. Martin, accompanied by his dog Rover, would arrive to John's house at nightfall on most evenings. He would announce his arrival as he approached the door, 'Is that 'hoor' of a Kerryman at home?' and the entertainment would proceed from there.

> Martin was like an old song that you'd hear at a fair ... Whereas some people could live by the Sunday sermon, Martin must live by the song. The Christ that Martin knew had turned water into wine and wine was for drinking, and for Martin it worked. Since he could remember, there was no tomorrow that hadn't looked after itself. But that was by no means the whole story. Martin coming into my house was Christian Piety itself coming into it. But as well as that, all of pre-Christian Ireland also came in with him. Hallowe'en came in with him. May Eve came in with him. Living on in him, the dead of Tuaim Beola graveyard came in with him. (*Nostos*, p. 512)

And very often what went out with him was John himself, because Martin would be anxious to go to the Castle for a drink and would eventually prevail on John to accompany him. The drink and the company and the singing of songs was what Martin loved. John recounts one occasion, when on leaving the Castle after closing time Martin's enthusiasm for the girl who had sung the final song of the evening was such that it led him to exclaim that he was prepared 'to shtand naked in the shnow lishenin' to her'. John would then be prevailed on to sing him another verse of 'her song' in order to shorten the road home. On one such journey his concern for John's immortal soul was the topic of conversation. Martin, with a few drinks in him, was "proud a' God an' his Holy Mother" but he was very bothered about John. "John, you ha' me kilt, You're a fine man John, an a grand man, and a great friend, but you ha' me kilt, not believin' in God, man or the divil. Why do I never see you at the Holy Mass below in Roundshtone?"[8] There was no acceptable answer, as far as Martin was concerned, John was "on the wrong road!" It was not simply John's immortal soul that he worried about. In conversation with Bridie Prendergast, later repeated to John, he had asked 'John is a grand man and he's a fine man and he's a good neighbour, but Bridie, what do you think Bridie, do you think is there a little bit of a want in him?'

> Martin shared his world with other beings, mostly invisible and, whatever else, he mustn't provoke them, and in all situations, no matter how big the cost in

inconvenience to himself, he must take them into account. However great his need, he wouldn't just choose the most suitable site and build a house on it. First he would consult the invisible world and this he would do by erecting three stones at the very centre of the proposed foundation. If they were knocked in the morning, that would be that; unhesitatingly he'd move and try again elsewhere. Never would it occur to Martin to build his house on a fairy path. Apart from anything else there would be no sleep in such a house. All night long the fairies would be trouping through and, given the sacrilege, it isn't blessing they'd be leaving behind.

No, Martin couldn't be a capitalist. He couldn't just look at the world and it as an economic opportunity, that and no more ...

Opening it one night in my house, an ordnance survey map of Connemara made little sense to Martin. Mostly it was what wasn't in it that he had an eye for. Refolding it, he handed it back to me saying, "What chance have we, when that's where we think we live?"

An awful lot of what I had forgotten, and an awful lot of what I had yet to learn came in my door every evening with Martin. (*Nostos*, pp. 514–15)

Those years, 1972 and 1973, were years of great change and learning; he felt that he was coming home to the earth. He was happy in that he felt he was 'growing in pure wonder'. Naturally all of the old existential concerns were still bothering him: the 'dolorous stroke' of a species that had taken a 'harpoon' to the world; the sense of being 'Grand Canyon deep' in the world's karma; the disenchantment and disillusionment that science has inflicted; the blind faith in relentless progress; the suffering and pain that is the lot of so many people; 'the human head that can be as terrifying as a hauled lobster pot';[9] but in spite of all of these he could say 'I somehow no longer so despaired of our chances as I formerly did'. More and more he was convinced that one must follow the path of Bright Angel Trail down into the Grand Canyon, which is also the path of Jesus in Gethsemane, and having acknowledged and accepted 'the hauled lobster-pot' of all that one is, it is then that one can begin the 'Easter' ascent of the Trail; an ascent first of all to a true humanity, and perhaps then, given that 'there is something more serious about us than the immensities of our humanity',[10] after that to a realisation of divinity. He did acknowledge that, in pure evolutionary terms, he couldn't quite see where Bright Angel Trail might lead: 'Try as I might I couldn't see out over the rim', but there was no doubt that here in Connemara, immersing himself in the 'otherworld-liness' of Nature, he had found that there is 'a genius in the universe', 'a miracling point in the universe', 'if only, if only we would give it a chance.'[11] Some lines in a story he had written capture this mood:

Clear days bring the mountain down to my doorstep, calm nights give the rivers their say, the wind puts it hand to my shoulder some evenings and then I don't think, I just leave what I'm doing and I go the soul's way. (*Nostos*, p. 491)

Beautiful as that is 'the soul's way' does not pay the bills and by early 1974 he was faced with a more practical problem.

Early in March I got a letter from the manager of the Bank of Ireland in Clifden. As luck or as providence would have it, three evenings later Michael Vahey, the farm manager at Ballinahinch Castle Hotel drew up outside my gate. He needed my help. A bus-load of French tourists had arrived out of season at the hotel. Staff or no staff, the manageress couldn't find it in her heart to turn them away. Someone had said that I spoke French. Would I come up and help them settle in?

Afterwards I had a drink in the bar with Michael. As I was leaving by the front door I heard someone calling me. It was Annie Joyce, the cook. All unexpectedly, she said, there were guests in the house tonight. Would I be an angel and give her a hand in the kitchen?

We got on great, and when we had finished and I was leaving she smiled at me saying, can I expect you at eight in the morning?

Without looking for it, I had a job. I washed and peeled and sliced the potatoes. I washed and peeled and sliced the carrots. I prepared the other vegetables. I brought meat from the downstairs cold-room. I washed the pots and pans. Moving up to the stillroom, I washed dishes and the cutlery from the dining-room. I scrubbed the tiled floors. And then I'd sit and have a cup of tea and a chat with Annie.

Glad to have a man around the place at this time of year, Miss Anne Egan, the manageress, wondered if I would move in. I could have room fourteen.

Room fourteen overlooked the river, a long, sumptuous reach of it all the way to Lowry's Bridge, which was just out of view. (*Nostos*, p. 517)

It was another change of address but he was still living by the Owenmore, still happy to let this lovely river be soul for him, here where 'ordinary sensory seeing is soul'. He was also meditating and during the past months the meditation 'was bigger than I was and I was going its way.' Often, during the breaks from hotel work he would sit for hours by a waterfall called Poll Odhrán, 'looking at the pouring flow of water' and even with his eyes open it would feel like meditation.

One day, a day of soft rain, rain-drops glistening in the high heather, I sank to

> where there is no ego and now, instead of saying 'I hear' I found myself saying,
> 'Hearing is taking place, hearing is happening ... and instead of saying 'I see'
> I found myself saying 'Seeing is happening, seeing is,' and I said it to myself,
> 'There's a rare state of mind that makes the head obsolete.' ... I was back the
> next day and all of this I experienced all over again and at dusk it happened. I
> crossed, or no, I was let into other ground. In it bliss would be a distraction and
> a vulgarity. Utterly bewondered, I said, 'So this is it!' (*Nostos*, p. 518)

He could only describe it as a 'moment of blessed hospitality in a blessed elsewhere'.
As he said, he felt he was 'let into other ground', 'bliss' was too small a word, and
in this state his thinking head was 'obsolete'.

> Now there was something I knew. In the best sense of the words, it is secondar-
> ily and derivatively that the Divine is a God.
>   Prior to being God the Divine is Divine Ground. (*Nostos*, p. 519)

Here he describes a 'knowing' that is beyond reason, something that he had
intuited all of his life, what in earlier years he had called a 'night knowing', the
small boy's sense of something sacred at the heart of a cowslip, the 'diamond dimension' of the universe, for a few moments here by Poll Odhrán he felt he had been
'let through'. This can only be described as a mystical experience and needs to be
understood in that context. In her classic book on the subject Evelyn Underhill
writes that mysticism is probably 'one of the most abused words in the English
language'[12] Mysticism, she says, has nothing to do with either magic or the occult
but deals with truths about the universe that cannot be expressed in precise words;
she explains it as 'the science or art of the spiritual life'. It is not exclusive to any
one tradition or creed. 'All mystics, said Saint Martin, speak the same language and
come from the same country. As against that fact, the place which they happen to
occupy in the kingdom of this world matters little.'[13] What is most extraordinary
is the fact that regardless of the tradition or the historical era to which mystics
may belong, their aims and their conclusions have been substantially the same.
Keeping this in mind, their experiences should not be lightly dismissed, regardless
that what they describe cannot be proven empirically and may be said to lie outside
the boundaries of what is generally called 'sense'.

What typifies the life of the individual who eventually undertakes the mystical
journey is firstly an intense reflective engagement with the world around them, and
secondly, an innate, intuitive conviction that there is, behind, below, beyond or
within, what is experienced as 'ordinary reality', another dimension of that reality,
a deeper 'truth', something absolute and eternal, and this vision, often only very

fleeting to begin with, gives rise to a hunger for a deeper knowledge of that reality. The craving for this knowledge becomes the driving force of the person's life, it goes beyond mere intellectual speculation, and becomes the process of their entire life. There is no doubt that, without as yet being aware of it, John Moriarty's journey to find his 'bush soul' was in fact a mystical journey, and the moment of 'blessedness' at the waterfall was a significant stage in it. John's insight that 'prior to being God, the Divine is Divine Ground.'[14] is the mystical concept that is at the heart of the 'perennial philosophy' – there is a 'divine ground' of all being, and here in this 'moment of blessed hospitality' John appears to have moved from a mere knowledge of it to an experience of it.

The moment had been fleeting but enough to make him hunger for a deeper experience, and every day after hours spent working in the Castle, he cycled up to Imleach dhá Rua and, positioning himself in the crotch of a great beech tree, he would close his eyes and meditate. His aim was to experience something of the void that must have existed before senses and mind developed, 'I would travel back in time, back behind the evolutionary origin of hearing and seeing' and, attempting to enter that emptiness, which he was now convinced was 'divine ground', he would stay until darkness fell.

> This went on for weeks. Once I seriously asked myself, what, if having gone out into that void, I couldn't get back, what if the return door closed against me? Forever? And ever?
>
> The thought of it terrified me, but I persisted. (*Nostos*, p. 519)

One day in a change from his usual routine and in a mood that he described as 'perturbed' he cycled instead up to Lough Inagh and then continued the climb on foot. The going was rough but he kept climbing until something he saw stopped him short. Washed down by a flood and deposited on bare bedrock of the river was 'the skinned, pink-fleshed foreleg of a lamb. What gave it its terrible, lurid pathos was the fact that it was left there in the shape of a Christian genuflection.' Looking at it with a sense of shuddering pity he was reminded of something Paddy Joyce, one of the local sheep farmers, had told him. He had been up on this side of the mountain to track down some stray sheep and 'he came upon a berried holly bush and hung up right in the middle of it was the whitened skeleton of a goat.' The goat, in search of food, had clearly become entangled and, unable to get back down, had been left hanging there until it starved. The juxtaposition of these two stark images shocked him.

The lamb and the goat.

The genuflection and the hanging.

The genuflection on a Gethsemane rock, the hanging from a Calvary tree.

It was like some awful retelling of the Christian story. (*Nostos*, pp. 519–20)

For some reason what struck John most forcibly was that the Christian story, in its Gethsemane and Good Friday form, is a gruesome reflection of the natural world.

> Dispirited, I turned to come back down, and then it happened. I was ruined.
> Ruined beyond remedy and repair, I felt. The universe had vanished from round
> about me. I saw a last fading flicker of it and then I was in an infinite void.
> And the terrible anguish was, not only was the world I had hitherto relied on
> for my sense of myself an illusion, it was a deception. In terms of the Hindu
> parable, the snake had vanished but I could not sense the rope. And I felt very
> badly done by. The way I had lived for the past three years, curling up in the
> swan's nest, healing my head in the hare's form, baptizing myself out of culture,
> seeking to walk the world with a barefoot heart and a barefoot brain – I felt
> that all of this was a genuine search for the truth, not a merely speakable truth,
> but a truth I would surrender to, a truth I would live, that would live me, not
> just for myself, but for others as well. And now, in an instant, it had all ended
> in ruination. The world in and through which I had been a self, that was an
> illusion, it had vanished, leaving that infinitely isolated self in peril of disintegra-
> tion. (*Nostos*, p. 520)

'Trembling and bewildered', he did not know what had happened to him and by no act of mind or will could he stop it. For some reason, the image he had conjured of the lamb and the goat had catapulted him into crisis and his entire worldview had collapsed.

> In less than an hour I felt like Narada, the voice of a god behind me saying, 'You
> have been gone for almost an hour, meaning thirty or three hundred incarna-
> tions. Did you bring the water?' And that was a hopeful way of putting it.
> (*Nostos*, p. 542)

Trying to keep some grip on reality, on his way home he called to his neighbours the Prendergasts and told them that something terrible had happened to him in the mountains. They did their best but could offer no comfort. Once back in his own home he was grasping at straws to understand this sense of utter despair and nothingness. Ever since reading Darwin he had suffered what he called 'the deso-lations of the age' but he had coped, he had refused to accept the 'nothing but' universe and had relied on his intuitive sense of a deeper reality to sustain and motivate him. Now that sense had been shattered.

> I didn't know that I could cope now. It is one thing to find oneself engulfed in an infinite universe that has neither centre nor circumference, it is something else altogether for that universe to disappear, to vanish like a mirage, leaving you in the void. (*Nostos*, p. 521)

In his distress, and quite inexplicably, he found himself praying. 'I fell instantly and instinctively back into Christianity'. Identifying what he had experienced as similar to the dereliction of Christ on Good Friday, 'It was to Christ and it was to the God that Christ called out to in dereliction – it was to both of them that I now called.' He was surprised at himself. He recognised that up to now, even though he had kept in touch with Christianity, he had been 'playing' with it, in the way that he had played with other myths, finding correspondences, using its language and imagery to explain certain ideas, identifying a universal journey in the story of Jesus, re-imagining a myth. It had been an intellectual exercise; suddenly it had taken on a profound significance, he was living the symbolism of the myth, perhaps the myth was living him.

> But now the myth had shown its hand ... And I wasn't big enough. And I didn't know any prayer that was big enough, none except Christ himself, none except Christ sore-amazed in Gethsemane, none except Christ looking down into his own empty skull on Golgotha. The skull is empty and the Son of Man has nowhere to lay his head, nowhere outside it, nowhere inside it.
>
> Christianity was true, is true, not because Jesus is God – he might well be the one true God incarnate – but it isn't because of that that Christianity is true. Christianity is true because in Gethsemane and on Golgotha Jesus lived a truth about us and our world, he lived it into shocking visibility, he lived it and it lived him. He walked into the olive press, the mind press, that brings everything out into the open. It brings all that we phylogenetically are out into the open ...
>
> In Gethsemane Jesus must have looked like Coatlicue ...
>
> He looked down into the skull.
>
> I had learned a lot in a few hours. Only this wasn't learning.
>
> This was simple seeing. In the mountain today I had been shattered into seeing. And it wasn't with my eyes I saw it. It was with whatever was left of me that I saw it.
>
> Surprised, almost managing a smile of embarrassment, I was a Christian. Not a 'Christian again'. I was a Christian for the first time.

The dumbfounding question and yearning was, could the God that Christ cried out to, could he do what all the King's horses and all the king's men couldn't do, could he put world and self together again. Could he, would he, say, let there be light? (*Nostos*, p. 522)

'A Christian for the first time', something he understood now that he had overlooked before; he had already recognised Jesus as a man living the enormity of the human condition in Gethsemane, he had recognised the darkness and suffering of Good Friday, but Jesus had 'looked into the skull' and found it empty, there was nothing there, and he was derelict and 'forsaken'. Jesus died with a cry of abandonment on his lips. For John this dereliction was as awful as the Crucifixion. The story of Jesus as a dis-illusioned human being, a Narada, he fully identified with now. And who was that God that Christ had called out to and could that God, if found, be of any help now? If there was no answer to that question then there was nothing. 'Otherwise Golgotha. Otherwise a last awful looking down, or worse, an endless looking down, into my own empty skull.'[15] Like Jesus he had been stripped of his vision of Divine Ground, that sense that had motivated and driven his relentless search for answers for his entire life.

Somehow, in spite of an anguished night, he showed up for work the next day and continued with the work of scraping and sanding and painting in preparation for the summer season in the Castle. To a certain extent he was at a loss to know what was happening to him.

It was my anguish and my killing regret that, sitting in that beech tree in Imleach dhá Rua, I had pushed at boundaries I shouldn't have pushed at. What I feared might happen had happened. Only it wasn't so much that there was a door closed against me preventing my return to the ordinary world. In a terrible sense there was nothing to return to. What was so awful was that, while there was no snake, I couldn't sense the rope. And I wondered if it was from here that Christ cried out in dereliction.

How strange! Christianity making sense to me!…

And Christ a companion. Christ the only thing in sight – Christ in Gethsemane and on Golgotha, the Christ whose passion carried him that far, that Christ the only thing in sight that could speak hope to me.

Night after night I mined the Bible for words. (*Nostos*, p. 524)

And he found the words, words in the Book of Job and in the Psalms that described his 'dereliction', words of 'deep calling unto deep' and words also that brought a promise of some comfort. 'They that go down to the sea in ships, that do business in great waters, they see the works of the Lord, and his wonders in the deep.'[16] These, and words like them, he said, kept him from going under. Others, those psalmists whose experiences were recorded in the Bible, had experienced what he experienced. He recognised that he had suffered a complete 'dis-illusion-ing' and 'nightly it shook me and shuddered me, leaving me only barely able to hold on, leaving me only barely able to be the person I used to be.' His great fear was that he had 'ship-wrecked' himself into what he called 'the nihilist's naught' – into absolute nothingness and meaninglessness. He desperately needed a life-raft that would vouch for the sanity of what had happened to him, maybe even the normality of it. Whatever it was that had happened, he found himself praying.

> Now, every evening after work, I walked up and down along the river, until nightfall up and down from Ted's place to Dervikrune Bridge, and I prayed, prayed, prayed and there was more of me more intensely involved in that praying than ever there could be in the most sensuous, the most passionate love-making. Prayer of the kind I was now experiencing – and that's how it was, I sometimes felt I had turned into prayer – that kind of prayer, it emerges from depths our instincts have no access to.
>
> At home in North Kerry, when I was young, we couldn't afford gates into our fields. So, when we wanted to fence in or fence out cattle we cut some bushes, usually whitethorn, and we blocked the gaps with them. And that now was my prayer:
>
> Let me not be a bush in the gap between us, God.
> Let me not be a bush in the gap between us, God.
> Let me not be a bush in the gap between us, God. (*Nostos*, p. 528)

This was a prayer from the depths of his being, a soul crying out against aban-donment and despair, a soul that had lost its sense of 'Divine Ground'. It was in this state that he picked up a book that he said had followed him for years, it had been with him in Dublin, in London and in Canada, but he had found it indistinct and had put it to one side. Now, as if by providence, he picked it up again, and a few pages in he felt it had come to his rescue. It was the *Ascent of Mount Carmel* by St. John of the Cross. It was by no means an immediate rescue; its demands, he said, were cruel. Instead of sending a raft to the struggling soul, it encourages the soul to blindly surrender to the abyss of faith. On the road to God, the road to Divine Ground beyond any God, John of the Cross advises the traveller that if he wishes to be sure of the road he travels on he must close his eyes and walk in the dark. Neither senses nor intellect will take him any further on this journey. The faculties with which he would seek God, these were what eclipsed God. This is what the darkness of Golgotha demands, the total emptying of the self, the 'bush in the gap' must be annihilated if the god is to be resurrected in you, if there is to be an Easter Sunday of spiritual awakening. For now however, for John, it is Golgotha; he has entered 'the dark night of the soul' and all previous 'illumination', all 'silver branch perception', is shattered.

Somehow he felt that John of the Cross might make sense, perhaps he had to surrender to this terrible darkness, perhaps the only way out is through. Even though he felt he was clutching at straws, he sensed that there might be something alright in what was happening to him. A saying he had heard from Jimmy, *Bíonn sceamh ar gach sceach siar*, there is a leaning, a leaning with the wind, in every bush that grows in the west, that helped; maybe he must learn to lean with this wind now, must 'ship oars' all over again. He began ordering books, the works of the Christian and Muslim mystics, and so began the next phase of the journey.

14

'A NEW CHRISTIANITY?'

Caterpillars and butterflies; Triduum Sacrum; Eileen; a cry of dereliction; the cowrie shells; destructive impulses; a dream; in need of help; a Carmelite Priory.

The years following the 'shattering' on the mountain were years of grief-filled growing. In spite of the reassurance found in the writings of St. John of the Cross and in the mystical tradition in general, the reassurance that is clearly stated in the Chandogya Upanishad: 'Where nothing else is seen, nothing else is heard, nothing else is thought about, there is the Divine Plenitude', for the most part he experienced only the dreadful 'nothing'. The experience had left him 'looking into his own empty skull', it was Golgotha, and 'it did feel like nihil'.[1] His prayers to the God that Christ called out to on Calvary were an act of faith. On good days that faith was reinforced by what he saw as the 'miracling point' in nature.

> If, after three years in Connemara, someone were to question me about my understanding of the universe, I wouldn't say $E=mc^2$, I would point instead to metamorphosis in insects ...
>
> What happens inside a cocoon?
>
> If nature can handle the destruction and reconstruction of a caterpillar into a butterfly, why shouldn't I surrender and trust that it can handle what is happening to me? (*Nostos*, p. 533)

He imagined a butterfly, perched on a great cabbage, talking to an audience of caterpillars. The butterfly brings good news. Opening her glorious wings before them, she tells them that they can become butterflies too, but, far from being delighted the caterpillars are horrified.

The thought of ceasing to be who and what they were, that was outrageous, that was mad. In their anger, they turned on her and killed her, and then they crawled away, each one, back to the bitter leaf they had been eating. (*Nostos*, p. 533)

They had rejected the hope, the promise, of metamorphosis, of reconstruction in favour of the 'clenched' single vision of their caterpillar world. He saw the same choice facing human beings, incorporated in the message of the *Triduum Sacrum*. These are the three holy days of Gethsemane, Golgotha and Easter and they could provide a framework for what John saw as the essential human journey if there is to be 'further and final evolution' for the human species. Gethsemane is the individual journey to the floor of the Grand Canyon, there to experience and suffer all that one phylogenetically is; Golgotha involves death, the death, not necessarily of the physical self but of the individual identity, the ego, the sense of oneself as a separate personality, a realisation of the 'nothingness' of personal identity and worldly concerns, a process of self-loss; Easter is resurrection, a realisation of one's spiritual identity, a recognition of Divine Ground, of unity of being with the divine source and with all that is. This, he would say, is the process begun when Jesus crossed the Kedron in Gethsemane, this is 'our transtorrentem destiny' proper to everyone, open to everyone, and for the most part, refused by everyone. It is a mystical understanding of the Passion, and is a demanding but necessary journey, its greatest difficulty at the core of the Golgotha experience – nothingness, emptiness, how to live in that abyss and keep faith with the promise of metamorphosis, of an Easter morning? In spite of all that he was reading and all that he was praying, there was profound suffering. He was still caught in 'a no-man's-nothing between a world lost and a God not found'; the destruction part of the process he was familiar with on a nightly basis, reconstruction, for the moment, was only a faint hope. He had to live through the abyss.

It was the summer of 1975, he had finished painting the staff quarters in the Castle yard and had moved into one of the rooms there. Guests were arriving, and also the summer staff, a mixture of locals and students who had been taken on for the busy season. One of these students, Eileen, an art student from Limerick, made a profound impression on him. A fleeting glimpse of her crossing a corridor a few paces away from him was the first thing to stop him in his tracks, she was extremely beautiful but he was instantly convinced that there was something more than beauty at work here. There was a sense of recognition. 'That's her', was his immediate reaction, and this mystified him. 'How could I recognise someone I had never met?', and yet the overwhelming feeling was that, at some level of himself, he had always known her.

There was never a time when I didn't know her. What had happened was that I had lapsed into a coarser world of coarser concerns and somehow, over years, over incarnations, I had forgotten, and oh! For God's sake! Do we know who we are at all? Are we so hidden from ourselves that we only rarely catch glimpses of who we are? And is our hiddeness from ourselves a blessing? One little glimpse of who we immortally are, of who we are in the hazelwood.

That was it! I had it!

Who we sociologically are

And who we are in the hazelwood. (*Nostos*, p. 535)

He was back again to *The Song of Wandering Aenghus* with a new insight. Mostly he thought, we exist in a world of ordinary concerns, living ordinary lives as carpenters, accountants or prime ministers, these being our sociological identities. However, for the most part hidden from us, we also exist at another level, we have a 'hazel-wood name', and sometimes, something or someone calls us by that name and we are 'released from the spell of the common world, no, from the spell of the common way of seeing the world'. From the first moment he set eyes on her that is what Eileen did for John.

The first time I saw her that's what happened, a corridor leading in from the yard in Ballinahinch Castle Hotel became the path to the very strange Elsewhere that isn't other than where we are ...

After work one night, their work finished too, a few people joined me behind the counter in the still room. She was among them.

Her beauty was something much more than good looks. So suffused with soul were her good looks, they seemed, entirely, to be a manifestation of soul. They were her soul's song of itself. And any world she had shown up in couldn't be just a place to make a living in. (*Nostos*, p. 536)

In a sense, as well as his reading of the mystics, Eileen's beauty was calling him back from the abyss of 'the nihilist's naught', she was a reminder of 'the blessed Elsewhere' that he had been so sure of only a few weeks previously but had so dramatically lost to the image of bare bones on a mountain; if beauty such as this could emerge in the human world, then it had to have its source in an 'Otherworld well'; just as the Mona Lisa was testimony to the creative genius of a human being, Eileen was testimony to the creative genius in the world. In this sense his encounter with her was a joy, but from the very outset there was pain.

In relation to her I had an almost infinite sense of hands off, of instinct off, of everything except lost longing off. And even the lost longing must not show itself. If it did it would be violation. (*Nostos*, p. 536)

He was afraid. All of the old arguments that had prevented commitment and marriage were as real as ever and now it was even more complicated, and so he kept his distance. However, living and working in such close proximity, the inevitable happened.

> Quite without contrivance one evening I found myself walking towards her in the empty yard. Infinitely, as it was at first, my attitude towards her was hands off and in a way that gave me courage not only to greet her but to stop and talk to her. In so far as I could I was all poetry to her, but that wasn't my fault, and it wasn't seduction, Jesus! No! It wasn't seduction, she'd evoke as much in a stone. And yet I was of course showing myself in as good a light as I could. Listening to me it would be hard for her not to conclude that I was a lovely man, all kindness, not a single economic thought clouding my eyes or my soul.
>   Don't fall for it, Girl.
>   Don't fall for it, I thought. There is more to me, an awful lot more than I'm letting you see. And as well as who I am, I wanted to say, I don't know if it will ever recover from what happened me recently under the mountain. I knew I shouldn't. I shouldn't be talking like this, a month ago, maybe. A month ago, yes. But not now. I didn't know if I would ever again come ashore, if I would ever again come together around a new centre. What happened to me under the mountain was like an earthquake, there were after-shocks.
>   In spite of appearances, in spite of being out and about and doing my work, I was only barely making it from day to day, yet here I was now, so charmed by her continuing, delighted presence, so charmed by her continuing delighted eyes, that it was next to impossible for me to walk away, it was next to impossible for me not to try to charm her in return. (*Nostos*, p. 539)

They spent the remainder of that evening in animated conversation, he having invited her into his living quarters, she fascinated with the books everywhere, a copy of the Middle English *Tale of the Sankgreal* lying open on the floor. She asked him to read from it and in reading it to her the magic of it was reawakened in him. It is the story of the Grail quest and he explained that the Holy Grail was not a thing. It was a way of seeing things – a way of seeing a bush at the ocean side of a bog road, the way of seeing that had been wrested from him so recently. Her presence uplifted him at least temporarily from the darkest of places and by the time she left that evening he realised that he was in love. For a few weeks their time-off was spent together; they walked and cycled many of the routes with which he was so familiar. But he hadn't yet let her know that he was 'only barely making it', and also that he sensed there was worse to come. His greatest fear was that the devastation he was undergoing might have nothing at all to do with the process identified by John of the Cross as 'the dark night of the soul'; to put it simply, he was afraid that he was going mad.

Whatever was happening to him, it was not compatible, not now and possibly not ever, with an intimate relationship and in order to protect them both he nego-tiated some weeks leave and returned to Lynne's. The only cottage available was dilapidated but in spite of Lynne's protests he insisted that it wasn't luxury he had in mind, just somewhere to keep the rain out and a bed on which to sleep. After more than a year in Ballinahinch Castle he was once again back living where the Owenmore enters the sea, but watching the river now, as he suffered his own spiritual and emotional turmoil, he found it almost unbearable:

And now, after all that, the Owenmore leaving name and form behind.
    The Owenmore leaving all that it is in pool and ford and fall behind.
    The Owenmore leaving all that it has mirrored and still might mirror
behind.
    The Owenmore leaving all that it mirrors in all its tributaries behind.
    The Owenmore leaving a world of particulars behind and losing its identity
in the great waste of the ocean. (*Nostos*, p. 547)

'The great waste of the ocean', the void, the abyss, the Buddha's 'udana', goat bones on a mountain, Christ's cry of dereliction, Golgotha, the skull at the foot of the cross, ultimately only the final cruelty of emptiness. Lines from a poem by Sylvia Plath haunted him:

My bones hold a stillness, the far
Fields melt my heart.

They threaten
To let me through to a heaven
Starless and fatherless, a dark water.[2]

In the way that Sylvia feared it might, the world which until then had founded and grounded me had 'let me through' and in spite of what the mystics say, there were days and nights when the nothingness felt like 'nihil', and it was therefore to my own projections that I was praying, and yet it was as if there was something in me, something deeper than mind in me, and it knew, if only as blindly as could be, it knew that there is a God, so I prayed and prayed.

Give me grace, God. (*Nostos*, p. 548)

'But', he goes on to say, 'God was not within shouting distance.' The voice that had comforted him years previously on the floor of the Grand Canyon, when he had staggered under the weight of the world's karma, those lines from Emily Bronte:

> Though earth and moon were gone,
> And suns and universes ceased to be,
> And Thou wert left alone,
> Every existence would exist in thee.
>
> There is not room for Death,
> Nor atom that his might could render void:
> Thou – Thou art Being and Breath,
> And what Thou art may never be destroyed.

These were now but a thin small voice, and were no match for Sylvia's cry of godless dereliction. This was modern dereliction, Sylvia did not even have a god to plead with, and almost every day and night now he felt as bad as Sylvia did. Unless the mystics, and his own mystical intuition, were correct, he was praying only to his own projections. The empty skull at the foot of the cross seemed final destination. Only a childhood memory offered an alternative, more hopeful, image.

> On the mantelpiece in our parlour at home there were two cowrie shells, wedding gifts that had come with my mother and father from depressed America.
>
> It was Madeleine who first put one of them to my ear. To begin with I couldn't hear a thing. Then she moved it and there it was. 'It's the sound of the ocean they came from,' she said. (*Nostos*, p. 556)

At first there was nothing, but then he heard it, the sound of the ocean they came from! 'The cowrie shell and the skull', was there some eternal ocean to which there is an ultimate return, or is it silence and emptiness? Surely, he reasoned, what has happened in the modern West is the transformation of the shell into the empty skull, leaving modern man 'in the dark water'. If the Christian story can bring us as far as the empty skull, can it bring us a step farther? Can it send some ship, some raft of rescue, from an eternal ocean? There was some inexplicable part of him that simply could not walk away. He had recognised that, at its core, Christianity has integrated dereliction and he realised that, one way or another, he would spend the rest of his life 'attempting to tell the Christian story. Even if Christianity ceased from the earth and no Christian was left, I must still attempt to tell it.'[3]

Because he was required to return to Ballinahinch before the end of the summer season, before the casual staff had departed, there was no escaping his destiny with Eileen. It was again a joy to be with her, and to experience what she did for his long-suffering spirit. 'A sense of who I am in the hazel wood, that she re-awakened in me'; and for her he was fascinating, attentive and handsome, even if a bit dishevelled!

> I wasn't worried at all about what might look like some obvious disparities between us. I was thirty-six, she was nineteen. I had lived my young life, she hadn't. I had had my time in the high street, she hadn't. Not only did I not worry about this, I was hardly aware of it. What I was aware of was how I felt for her, and I trusted that. And also, I didn't forget that my feelings for her gave me no rights in relation to her, gave me no claim to her ... (*Nostos*, p. 566)

That they would become a couple and that love would blossom between them was inevitable.[4] Unfortunately September was on the doorstep and Eileen had to return home. There were promises of letters and visits but his reprieve was over. After they had said goodbye,

> As I climbed the stairs to my room overlooking the river I knew I couldn't hold out any longer, and I sensed that I was in for it. I was. (*Nostos*, p. 572)

If the aftermath of the shattering on the mountain was spiritual and intellectual devastation, then this was an emotional psychic apocalypse. For the duration of the wonderful weeks with Eileen he had been aware of trouble brewing but he had managed to keep it at bay. Now it overwhelmed him. It was as if a flood of dark energies had been unleashed. In dreams and in dreadful nightmares, images of sexual transgression, of murderous impulses, of wounds and woundings, flooded his sleeping mind. Then, waking, every morning dead on twenty to four, the fears for his sanity would start again. Someone he knew had been diagnosed as suffering from schizophrenia, that possibility terrified him. Again and again, in dream and nightmare, he would find himself in the yard at home, listening to the squeals of a dying pig, looking at the cock's wattled head on the floor and its blood in a bowl on the dresser. Somehow in his dreams sexual urges and violent urges, both already categorized in his mind as part of what humankind has repressed, became mixed up and almost one and the same. In his nightmares it seemed that the phallus had somehow assimilated the knife; that the sexual impulse was destructive. In some way it now seemed that he had sexually suffered those killings. He wondered what karmic energy had been unleashed in him and what would become of him. These were not thought processes which he could control.

> Night after night now I was whelmed and overwhelmed by tempests of suffering, and what I couldn't understand is that I got up every morning and went down to work, and I did work, and only Bridgie Joyce noticed. One day, with what sounded like a hearty laugh, she said, full in my hearing, 'John have nerves.' (*Nostos*, p. 573)

What made it all even worse was his inability to analyse it himself. He sensed that it had to do with what he called 'wounding potency', the capacity to do harm, the capacity to dominate, to control and to kill that has so blighted human evolution. In the cave painting in Lascaux, the shaman who has speared the bison bull through the genitals is lying on the ground and he is ithyphallic, his penis is erect and pointed. It is as if spear and phallus have become one, the actual spear has grossly damaged the animal; the erect phallus ensures the transmission, generation after generation, of that cataclysmically damaging capacity. That capacity, in its personal dimension, was ravaging him now. All the darkest impulses in the human psyche seemed to have awakened in him, it was no longer a matter of knowing of their existence, they were now a nightly experience; his dreams were of blood and killing, he was regularly 'nightmared into slaughter house and butcher's shop', there was the 'karmic inheritance' of generations and he was terrified. He did not know where it might lead.

> I was afraid.
> There were awful impulses simmering in me and maybe when I was off guard in the night they'd take over and I'd somnambulate to murder.
> The only blessing I asked for was that I would be the only victim.
> I thought about suicide. I imagined modes and means. In comparison with possible alternatives, it was the best kind of news that my parents could get, that I had stepped too close to a precipice on Ben Bawn. But looked at from the depths I was in now, suicide wasn't the answer. However awful the process of dying, death itself was a little transition, I'd arrive with all my trouble, magnified now in the bigger light.
> I saw three great doors in front of me: one into a monastery, one into a mental home and one into a high security prison.

It was in me to commit the unspeakable crime. And ask anyone and they'd say I was a decent enough sort of bloke, and if you asked me, if you asked me a few months ago, that's what I'd say too, I'd say I was a decent enough sort of bloke.

Where was it all coming from? (*Nostos*, p. 587)

He wondered if he was going through some form of purgatory. In his daylight working hours his rational mind was making an effort to process what was happening; he had had one dream that seemed to offer some hope. It was a dream, often recounted in later years, which involved a journey down Old Compton Street in London, firstly negotiating his way through a strip-tease club and then, streets later, an eighteenth century park, eventually to find himself in the African savannah. As he walks he is aware that he is carrying a four-pronged farm fork. With this he begins to dig and uncovers a granite stairway leading him down to an ancient sea. Here he is trapped. A sea monster arises from the depths and plunges towards him, furiously it plunges three times and he is convinced that he will be engulfed. Then there is a sudden change, a different light enters, and the monster has become 'a harmless little creature, swimming away about its business.'

This he saw as possible 'good news' from his psyche; perhaps there was nothing to be afraid of, perhaps, using the metaphorical farm fork, it is possible to work down into this psychic past, no sword in hand, exposing all of the repressed layers, allowing and acknowledging everything that is there, maybe eventually to come to a place where the psyche might be healed at its animal roots and become, not a monster, but 'a harmless little creature'. Then, confident that there is no more to fear, it might be possible 'to refound culture and civilization' from a place of 'alternative beginnings'. Could that be the next great step in evolution? And was that an outlandish thought? It was Gethsemane all over again – the farm fork might bring healing but it would involve personal suffering: an acknowledgement of individual as well as universal guilt and consequent moral responsibility. Was this somehow the medicine-hat that he had been seeking? Ultimately he realised that he could not handle what he was going through on his own; he would have to admit his suffering and vulnerability and find help. He remembered Professor Feithin O'Doherty, from the Philosophy Department in UCD, whom he knew did some counselling, and after three particularly cruel nights he decided to go and see him.

Difficult as it was, and avoiding for obvious reasons any mention of his colourful, mythological comparisons, he did manage to convey to Professor O'Doherty 'the full terror and peril' of what he was going through and asked his opinion on the advisability of seeing a psychiatrist. The answer was no, that might only complicate matters, 'and anyway, you are handling it,' he said.

Back on the bus, I was desolate, and bereft, no remedy anywhere in sight. Was I handling it or was it handling me? And into what further awfulness would it manhandle me? All I could do now was go home and consent to it. (*Nostos*, p. 592)

The bus turned into Morehampton Road and from out of the blue, or so it seemed, it struck him that there was a Carmelite Priory somewhere in the vicinity. He asked the conductor, and was told that it was near the next stop. Without further thought he was off the bus and within ten minutes was sitting in the Priory, talking to Father Celestine. The elderly friar, in his brown habit and looking blue with the cold, explained that he was hard of hearing, could John talk up, louder, much louder. John was feeling foolish.

Thinking the case was hopeless I kept going but only for reasons of good manners. As soon as it was polite to do so, I'd thank him and take my leave.

But it didn't happen that way. Having heard me out, he came to life and, with fervent good will, he talked to me, telling me that the man I needed to meet was in Oxford, Fr. Norbert is his name, and he has been through the fire, and there he was, this elderly, half-perished man, a survivor from medieval times, and he opening a door for me not into a mental home and not into a high security prison but into a friary.

Back in Connemara, I wrote to Fr. Norbert. Within the week I got a slightly austere but good letter back. It certainly held the door open. In response I wrote him a letter that went on and on, for as long as it took to tell him the whole story. (*Nostos*, p. 593)

This was at least a lifeline, but otherwise the trip to Dublin had not brought him any ease. By now he was convinced that repression was at the heart of what was going on. He felt that he was having a run-in with human nature; he was being menaced by 'poisoned energies', 'energies poisoned by years, by lifetimes of repression'; 'it was repression that had given them their snarl, their nightmaring malice'. Nature, he thought, never forgives; particularly repressed nature. And how much repressed animal nature is at the core of human beings? He already knew that when repressed it becomes bestial, it becomes the Minotaur, and given its opportunity, it will rampage. There was now a frighteningly new insight – he realised that the opportunity for terrible damage is often afforded when its opposite is in fact the original intention.

There was something I knew: open the door wide enough to let in God and you've opened it wide enough to let in the Great Malice or the Great Adversary; open the door wide enough to let in heaven and you've opened it wide enough to let in hell; open the door wide enough to let in the light and you've opened it wide enough to let in the dark. (*Nostos*, p. 594)

In other words, exposed to the heights one is more vulnerable to the depths. On a personal level his years of single-minded, passionate quest for a 'sheltering mythology', for a better way of being in the world, for his 'bush soul', for Divine Ground – had precipitated an awakening of dark energies that are latent but ever ready. 'I have discovered for myself', says Nietzsche, 'that the old animal and human world, indeed the entire prehistory and past of all sentient beings, works on, loves on, hates on, thinks on in me.' And this can be the case, not only for an individual, but for an entire society. How else could one explain the aftermath of revolutions that, aiming for reform and improvement, could lead to guillotine and gulag, how could the best become the worst, what is it that 'possesses' people and enables them to commit crimes far worse than anything seen in the natural world? A dream where these energies might become harmless seemed a very slim chance; overall it was with a sense of utter hopelessness that he again headed to Moyvane for Christmas.

Prior to departure, and in spite of everything, he thought about a Christmas present for Eileen. The song was on his mind – 'on the first day of Christmas my true love sent to me ...' and he wanted to emulate that imaginative gift-giver:

Thinking of Eileen I wanted to do what he did. No. Him I wanted to outdo. And so I went into the woods and I walked the bogs and I walked lake shores picking up every lovely thing that I came upon, a fir cone with an exquisite pattern of sprouting spores on it, a little tussock of moss, a hawk's feather, the turquoise shell of a heron's egg ...

In the end I selected twelve of the things I had found, and no, maybe none of them was so surprising as a partridge in a pear tree, and yet, I was sending her a walk in the Ballinahinch Woods, I was sending her the lichen soft sound of an Atlantic wind in a bog road bush, and, from the rainy end of the world, I was sending her a stone that left me wondering, how come I got it without having to fight or outwit a dragon, one of its eyes always open? How come that I only had to walk along the shore and pick it up?...

Reminders of where we are, although we don't know it, is what I was sending to Eileen.

A reminder every day for the twelve days of Christmas. (*Nostos*, p. 601)

A reminder of Divine Ground and of a happier frame of mind. Unfortunately it was not enough to sustain him and on the bus journey home the anguish overcame him.

> I had no answers. How could a psyche generate so many nightmares? ... How and why would something become all nine depths of hell to itself? ... And now I must go home and bring cheer and be cheer to my parents over Christmas. Less for my sake than for their sake I prayed and prayed that I'd make it. In the bus, somewhere between Newcastle West and Abbeyfeale, I turned to the window and wept ... An anguish and a sorrow as big as mountains was falling out of me. (*Nostos*, p. 602)

At home he did his best to conceal his trouble and thought that he had managed it, but there was to be no hiding. Both Mary and Jimmy were concerned, and this was eventually voiced by Jimmy.

> He opened the door and in a fatherly way, wholly characteristic of him, for I was still his son, he said, 'Don't push yourself to the point where your nerves will crack, John. What I came to tell you is that 'tis in you to have a strong mind, 'tis in you to weather it, whatever it is.' (*Nostos*, p. 602)

In him there was no such certainty but he was very moved by the care and concern. Back in Ballinahinch a few days later there was further reassurance, a reply from Fr. Norbert in Oxford; he had read John's letter five times and he extended an invitation to come to stay for a week or so, at his convenience. He did not delay, and by early February 1976 he was at the Carmelite Priory of Boar's Hill, six miles outside Oxford. His arrival coincided with suppertime and in the hushed corridors, as he was being guided to the refectory, 'a great wonder of comfort and relief came over me...I'm home, I thought, I'm home.'

The following week was spent in the rhythm of the Carmelite day, rising at quarter to six, for matins, Mass and silent meditation, then continuing into a day of work and ritual until Compline from eight to half past in the evening, and from thence to the silence of their cells. It was peaceful. He spent time reading, again Teresa of Avila and John of the Cross, their accounts of inner upheaval and afflictions 'enabling me, almost, to latch onto a hopeful diagnosis of what was happening to me.'[5] He also spoke at length with Fr. Norbert. He was listened to compassionately and was reassured on at least one front.

> I waited till the last day to come to my greatest fear.
>   'Is it madness?' I asked.

'No', he said.

'Why do you think so?'

He made a circle with his thumb and forefinger.

'In madness', he said, 'the circle is closed. The person is engulfed, is often deluded and isn't able to distinguish what is really profound from what is trivial. In your case the circle is open, he said, parting his fingers. You can walk round about your experiences and you make sense when you talk about them. Also, ours is a contemplative house. If it was madness we wouldn't have been able to go about things the way we do. Instead of being a disruption, even during the quiet of an hour-long meditation, the contrary has been the case.'

Before I left, I had a long talk with Fr Livinius, the prior. We agreed that I would come back in May for three or four months. (*Nostos*, p. 615)

Back in Ballinahinch the nightly struggle continued, along with an ever- deepening exploration of Christian mysticism. The message, from both the Rhineland mystics of the fourteenth century and the Spanish mystics of the sixteenth, was very clear. God can only be found in darkness and emptiness, in total self-loss. The personal implications were enormous. He was now burdened by a sense of contradiction inherent in the whole course of his life. Perhaps in all of his endeavours he had only been playing a game of his own invention; perhaps he would never find a place of shelter with which he could be intellectually satisfied. He was ready to accept the mystical message that in the quest for God, the intellect is of no use: 'As regards reaching God by their means, the workings of my mind were like the workings of my spleen, useless.'[6] Yes, he had known this before but it was even more startling now. St John of the Cross made it very clear: if one wishes to 'draw near unto God' then one 'must close his eyes and walk in the dark', it is a journey away from one's own 'senses and faculties'. All normal modes of experience are not only useless but a hindrance, and this meant that John's previous years in Connemara, attempting to know the world through senses other than his thought processes, were equally to no avail. At one level he had hit a wall, but at another he had come to a conclusion. He put it in two propositions:

1. The senses and faculties with which we would register the presence of God eclipse God.

2. In regard to registering the presence of God mind is the blind not the window.[7]

John uses the term 'metanoesis' for this process; literally it means 'going beyond knowing' suggesting that to know God it is necessary to go beyond all the faculties, and be willing to exist in the darkness of self-loss. The challenge is to accept this: that beyond our faculties, beyond our everyday knowing, in absolute darkness, there, and only there, is Divine Ground, is God. Not to accept this means absolute *nihil*, nothingness, it means that we say with Sylvia Plath and so many others, we are 'starless and fatherless', in a 'dark water'. This is the choice. Accept that there is a 'knowing beyond knowing' or accept despair. John could do neither. Still caught between a world lost and a God not found, now, he said, his only strategy was to have no strategy, other than surrender and trust. He was being challenged to 'ship oars' even more radically, the oars of his intellect and his senses. It was terrifying, but fearful and reluctant, he continued to pray. 'May I be as out of your way awake God as I am in dreamless sleep ... I'd have given anything to know I was in God's safekeeping. But no such knowledge was vouchsafed to me.'[8] He was glad when May came and, with the arrival of the summer staff, he was free to return to Oxford and the shelter and comfort that it offered.

> One thing I knew ... the rhythm of life there would enable me to walk more wisely than I had been doing on my own. To meditate in church with others for an hour was safer than to meditate alone and for hours in a beech in Imleach dhá Rua. (*Nostos*, p. 626)

The Priory offered him both routine and moderation. The former excesses of his isolated quest and questionings were avoided; it felt as if his tormented head was being 'held'. It also afforded opportunity to scrutinise traditional Christianity at first hand and, and in spite of his difficulty with what he called the 'red outrage' at the heart of the Mass, he was becoming reconciled even with that. 'A religion of blood and Beatitudes'[9] might be the only way forward in a world of blood and beatitudes, of depths and heights. Religion must be able for horror.

He became ever more convinced of the potential healing in the Christian story for the dereliction, for the spiritual wasteland, of the modern world. As John understood the *Triduum Sacrum*, Jesus was subversive not only in his parables, but in his passion. Perhaps, he thought, it is time to follow Jesus out of traditional Christianity, perhaps

> the Second Coming is a deeper understanding of the first coming. And so, just as some Jews followed you out of Judaism into Christianity, can it be that you are now inviting us to follow you out of a traditional Christianity into a new Christianity? (*Nostos*, p. 629)

And what would that new Christianity look like? It would have to go back to Old Man Coyote, to 'commonage consciousness', to the realisation that we share the world with other beings, and at a level in us that is not all that deep, that we share a world consciousness 'not fenced off from the consciousness of cheucau or fox, iguana or finch, not fenced off for that matter from rock and star.'[10] It is a Christianity that would have to go back, all the way to the pit in Lascaux, and heal the wound that it depicts. John believed that the Christian story, re-imagined and re-interpreted, had the potential to do all of this, and this in spite of the fact that, as he worked in the Priory gardens, he was looking down at the spires of Oxford, churches that had become sad empty monuments to a Christianity perhaps already dead. He was, however, an optimist. Perhaps Uvavnuk's song could be core of a new Christianity,

> The great sea has set me in motion,
> Set me adrift,
> Moving me as a weed moves in the river.
> The arch of the sky and mightiness of storms
> Have moved the spirit within me,
> Till I am carried away,
> Trembling with joy.
> Our crossover song. Singing it, we cross from domination to accom-
> modation, from being isolated to being with. (*Nostos*, pp. 643–4)

It was not a lot to help him given the enormity of what he was battling, but perhaps, here in the garden of the Priory, some small seed of hope was sown that he could take back with him to Connemara.

15

'THERE IS SURELY A PIECE OF DIVINITY IN US, SOMETHING THAT WAS BEFORE THE ELEMENTS AND OWES NO HOMAGE UNTO THE SUN'

Gardening; an Irish Upanishad; Amanda; illness; Lodge Park, County Kildare; a death in the family; a year at home.

He had been gardening for a number of hours each day at the Priory and had enjoyed working out of doors, but at the end of the summer his three month stay was up. Back in Connemara in early September 1976 he wanted to keep up the outdoor work and so decided not to return to his job at the Castle. He intended to go back to the first cottage under Derrada Hill and 'have a go at being a day-labourer', taking a chance on getting enough work to pay the rent. Eileen, who had never left his thoughts, had spent her summer working at the Castle and they met before she returned to college. It was a difficult meeting, not 'for want of love', but because of his sense of the impossibility of commitment, Fear, in his present condition, of the damage he might do her, that was his principal concern. Also he had a sense that he must allow the trouble he was afflicted by to work its way to some sort of resolution, that he must go with it and he did not know where it might lead. Having said goodbye they parted at Lowry's Bridge, walking away from one another, both of them mirrored by the same 'swooningly beautiful' Owenmore, he dared to hope, 'Soul to me when I had no soul at all, maybe the Owenmore would hold us till I got better.' (*Nostos*, p. 645)

Within a fortnight he had found work, gardening two days a week for five pounds a day for Dr. Hodges in Cashel and on the other days clearing and making a garden for Lynne behind the cottages. He recognised that this work was good for him as it gave him what he described as 'a break' from his own mind. Contending with the rock of Connemara was an entirely different kind of anguish and for the moment that's what he needed. It was also, he said, 'another way altogether

200

of getting to know the earth, working at it with spade and shovel and pick and digging fork and seven-pound sledgehammer and bushman's saw and axe.'[1] Rock that wouldn't yield to sledgehammer and wedge he would tackle with fire and water, eventually forcing the obdurate rock to split.

> Both here at Lynne's and in Dr Hodge's place, it was a winter of wrestling with rock and root. By March I had created my own patches of scree which I was now building into walls. It gave me a sense of the relentless slow labour that went into the making of Connemara's stone-walled, small fields. Almost every rood of ground had to be fought for, square by square, yard by yard. And then, every year after that, the thin soil had to be enriched with cow dung from the cowstall and with seaweed from the shore ...
>
> Cycling back along the estuary from Doctor Hodge's one evening, I looked across at Tuaim Beola graveyard and I wondered how many men knew Connemara in ruptured disks. How many of them, I wondered, knew Connemara in defeat, in a last patch not won, in a last wall not completed ...
>
> In April, after I had done the early planting in both gardens, I went to the bog and I cut turf for Martin Halloran and myself and, more than anything else that I did or said since I came to Derrada, it was this, the sight of me there on the bog working away on my own, that opened a door for me into the wider community. (*Nostos*, pp. 646–7)

That wider community was puzzled by him. One story had it was that he was 'an unfrocked priest' until a visiting friend from Canada – David James of Grand Canyon fame – told his story in the local shop. This only made matters worse, 'for now they had to explain how someone who had such a great job could have come so far down in the world.' There was, he said, 'always an air of scandal about me.' Nor did he say anything to counteract it. Scandal notwithstanding, he could cut turf skilfully, and that was enough.

> With that I was in. With that I was neighbour to all my neighbours on both sides of the river. I was neighbour to Ted Milne, to Lynne and Simon, to Josey Flaherty, to Joe and May Nee and their three young sons, to Petey and Julia and Mary Walsh, to Martin Halloran, to Annie Conneely, to Annie and Frank Flaherty, to Mickey Ward, to Mikie and Chris Conneely, to Lil Glynn and to Micheál, Kathleen, Mary Teresa and Noeleen McCahill.
>
> That it came naturally to me to walk across Tuaim Beola Bridge and to walk in along the estuary to the local graveyard and pray for the dead on November Day, that meant a lot to people.

> Within months, Martin Halloran having come with me to show me the place, I was digging a grave in that graveyard, and that was it, full acceptance among the living and the dead of Derrada West, Cluain Isle, Aill na Caillí, Tuaim Beola, Arkenry and Cushtrower. (*Nostos*, p. 647)

He was digging a grave in the shadow of a ruined monastery and imagined the monks chanting the Mass for the Dead. He knew the local story of this monastery, of monks who had been slaughtered by Cromwell's soldiers as they attempted to escape. He found himself praying:

> Eternal rest grant, O Lord, to the monks who were slain
> Eternal rest grant, O Lord, to the soldiers who slayed.

And then back to the grave he was presently digging. 'Eternal rest grant to Josey, O Lord: may perpetual light shine upon him, and upon all the dead of this grave-yard.'[2] These chants in his head were the great sounds of a Requiem Mass; in the distance he could hear the sound of the Owenmore, on its way to its own death in the ocean. It prompted his relentless question, a return to the 'great waste of the ocean' or a return to the 'eternal ocean' of the cowrie shell, to Divine Ground? The ancient Irish belief that the river of one's individual life has its source in an Otherworld well, Connla's Well, that resonated. At some profound level he could not accept James Joyce's terrifying destination for Anna Livia, the character in *Finnegans Wake* who represents the River Liffey. Joyce sends Anna out into the arms of her 'cold, mad, feary father' and her ending is 'old and old it's sad and old it's sad and weary'. Against this terrible modern diagnosis John sets the *Mundaka Upanishad*:

> As rivers leaving name and form behind them
> flow into their home in the ocean
> so does the Knower, from name and form released,
> go to that Divine Person who is beyond the beyond. (*Nostos*, p. 460)

Two radically opposed visions of final destination; how comforting the one, how terrible the other. Joyce's vision offered only caterpillar culture; the Upanishad offered the culture of the butterfly. And what a different world it might be if but-terfly culture were to take a firm hold:

> A culture that emerged around an understanding of ourselves as caterpillars and no more would be one thing, whereas a culture that emerged around an

understanding of ourselves as caterpillars who can become butterflies would, and must be, radically different. (*Nostos*, p. 621)

Butterfly culture would mean an acknowledgement that man, the rational animal, is also a spiritual being, one manifestation among many other manifestations, of the great creative spirit, the God, from which everything emanates and to which everything returns. Butterfly culture would give modern man the 'optimistic anthroplogy'[3] that he believed the planet so desperately needs. It would mean recognition of 'commonage consciousness', that this spirit is shared 'in common' with everything in the universe, and it would result in 'we-feeling', 'thou art that', a compassionate attitude towards the earth and all of its creatures, a full and total ecumenism, so that the planet eventually might become what he calls 'the Great Ecumene'.

For each individual this butterfly culture would be an enormous and enriching challenge; the challenge firstly to believe that: 'There is surely a piece of divinity in us, something that was before the Elements and owes no homage unto the Sun.'[4] That 'piece of divinity', that spark, that soul, is in everyone, but for the most part latent, perhaps recognised briefly in moments of great intensity, or in nature, or in the strange inexplicable synchronicities that can sometimes occur – the challenge is to grow that spark, to grow it and to grow it and to grow it, until it evolves into the butterfly that it surely is. It was John's view that for that growth to happen the soul needs both freedom and guidance, a loosely sheltering structure, a sheltering story, that can point the way and enable the journey, without being prescriptive or stultifying.

What was obvious to him is that a tremendous 'butterfly culture' has been in the safe-keeping of the Christian Church for two millennia, perhaps the great irony being that it has been kept too safe! That church, for many and varied reasons, has failed in its mission; initially it refused the modern journey, it silenced the voices within its own walls that might have saved it, it 'ran a tight ship. Too tight, maybe.'[5] And now, what it appears to offer is myth at the expense of meaning, rigidity at the expense of growth, security at the expense of adventure, and a consequent failure to provide 'a sheltering story' for the modern world. And yet, as John saw it, it has that capacity. His own journey had led him back to its central story and he saw the potential. He also saw that the story needs to be re-imagined. By nightfall he had finished digging the grave for Josey Flaherty. 'Leaving the pick and the crowbar to one side, I disposed the spade and the shovel in the form of a cross on the open grave.' That would have meaning for Josey. As would the Christian words that would send him forth on his journey:

Go forth upon thy journey out of this world, O Christian soul,
In the name of God, the Almighty Father, who created thee,

In the name of Jesus Christ, his son, who redeemeth thee ...
Depart, O Christian soul, out of this world.[6] (*Nostos*, p. 652)

How wonderful to be 'fit' in this way, and to have a ritual that is meaningful. Could there be rituals that would provide that kind of meaning in a secular world, for those for whom the traditional church is no longer relevant? What was needed to begin with was a new upanishad in a modern voice that might provide a basis from which to set out, and so:

> Hardly able to breathe a word of it to myself, out of a fear of transgression, I was writing an Irish upanishad ...
> An upanishad that would sensuously enact a journey beyond the senses.
> An upanishad that would thinkingly enact a journey beyond thought ...
> An upanishad in six stories ...
> In honour of Jesus and his parables, each story would emerge from a simple incident of daily life ...
>
> If I could bring it off, this upanishad would realise two proposals. It would enact the way of inclusion and integration as opposed to the way of exclusion and repression. And, concurrently with that, it would enact an exodus from metaphysics to metanoesis.[7] (*Nostos*, pp. 649–50)

This 'upanishad' of six stories became central to his vision of re-founding, of healing, modern culture and was the basis for many of the talks he would give in later years.[8] The stories are subtle, interconnected and wide-ranging but they contain one particular incident whose theme underpins them all. He tells of a visit home to Moyvane one particular Easter. It is Good Friday and he has been left to look after the house, there is a cow due to calve, and the rest of the family are going to church. Amanda, his four year old niece, keeps him company. Taking her with him to the stable to check on the Big Red he notices that the birthing has already started. The blister has burst, two little feet have emerged and these he points out to Amanda. She is puzzled, this is all wrong she tells him because 'Feet comin fursht is wrong. My head came fursht'. He is surprised at her knowledge, expecting that she would still be at the stage of storks and heads of cabbage, and so he asks her;

> 'And where did you come from?'
> 'From Mammy's tummy. And Mammy said twas sore.'
> 'From Mammy's tummy you came?'
> 'Yeh.'
> 'And Mammy, your Mammy, where did your Mammy come from?'

'From Granny's tummy.'
'And Granny, where did Granny come from?'

At that she was dumbfounded, in her experience there was no world before Granny; as he continued tending to cow and calf she continued thinking. He was aware of her intense struggle, 'figuring, figuring, figuring' and eventually 'she burst into jubilant life'

'I know it, I know it, I know it, I know where Granny came from'
'Tell me where Granny came from?'
'From her own tummy, I spose.' (*Turtle was Gone a Long Time*, vol. 1, p. 186)

From within the limits of her world Amanda came up with her answer. Naturally, as she grows and learns, that answer is 'vulnerable to further experience', but he wondered, is that not the case for everyone; her head is 'the quintessential human head', the head of his father over in the stalls *ag smaoineamh is ag macnamh dom féin*, it is the head of Aristotle, of Aquinas, of the Buddha, of Einstein, of Jesus ... 'the head of all these people trying to find the answer to the great mystery'; and all of their answers limited by their current knowledge and therefore 'vulnerable to further experience'. There can be no certainty, for the minute there is certainty there is no further growing. 'There is finally no answer on which you can lay your head, and that is the great condition ... all our statements, all our creeds, all our cosmologies, all our sacred books are vulnerable' and should be held to be so, otherwise dogmatism, fundamentalism and trouble. There must always be room for questions and for doubt. 'I can be a Christian and be doctrinally poor ... I don't think there are any of the Christian doctrines that I particularly would insist upon to myself and demand of myself that I believe them and yet in some sense I would consider myself a Christian.' On the cross, in his terrible dereliction, everything walked out on Jesus, all his questions and all his answers, and he felt 'forsaken'. Therefore, according to John, doubt is central to the Christian tradition and allows scope for questioning, for scepticism and for re-imagining. It is vital to 'play' with the myth, to recognise what parts of it belong to older traditions of gods and goddesses, and to find in it what is relevant now. For John, it is the story of Jesus, first and foremost as man, in his life and on the cross, which is of enormous significance.

In the first Christian centuries the big question was: Who is Jesus? Is he God? Is he man? Is he God and man? Is he God in man? Is he a consubstantial union of God in man in one person? A question of equal importance and urgency should be: What did he undergo? (*Nostos*, p. 533)

'What did he undergo?' It was in the Passion of Jesus that John found a metaphor that he believed has enormous relevance – Gethsemane, where by acknowledging primal animal energy everything can be integrated; Golgotha where there is a total loss of the ego-sense of self, where all intellectual knowing is over, where one enters 'the void'; and then, the garden of the Sepulchre, where spirit survives the death of all other faculties, where spirit enters Divine Ground. One does not need to die in a physical sense in order to undergo this transition, this resurrection. This is a metaphor for the soul's journey in this life as well as the next: firstly using all its faculties to recognise and accept its own nature, then recognising that it must let go of its own individual identity, its ego-self, into the darkness of self-loss, and finally, if the experience of the mystics is accepted, it is then and only then, that one will be 'let through' to the creative source, to God. This is the river, 'leaving name and form behind', flowing to its home in the ocean. This is the journey, and the Christian story provides a metaphor for that journey, but it also allows for the integration of many other metaphors from many other traditions; it leaves room for doubt, it leaves room for hope, it opens up love and compassion, it might provide the way through to 'further and final evolution' the evolution of the human spirit, it might even heal the world.

All of this as he was digging a grave for Josey Flaherty in Tuaim Beola Graveyard! The most powerful driving forces in his life were at work here – his passion to find 'th'answer' to the great mystery along with a fundamental belief that it is possible, even in the face of overwhelming odds, to bring about improvement in human culture. Regardless of his personal suffering, at some level these two passions were never extinguished; possibly in providing a focus for his mental energy they enabled him to process and heal the crisis he was experiencing. In writing his upanishad, his six parables, which he intended as a basis for a healing culture, he was firstly healing himself. In the meantime there was normal life to contend with: Lynne's hospitality provided stability; letters to and from Eileen brought both joy and heartbreak; visits from former students from Canada brought fun and intellectual excitement; and as always Martin Halloran brought laughter and community. Nonetheless the inner turmoil did not settle. He needed a more reflective space and the following January, 1977, he went back into the shelter of Carmelite living in Oxford, again taking on the role of gardener in return for inclusion in the community. This time he intended to remain for at least a year.

By November I had all but redeemed the garden. I was trenching the last square of it, digging it to a depth of fifteen inches or so and working cow manure into the subsoil. One day, where normally I would scarcely be aware that I was pushing it, I couldn't push the loaded barrow. I went in and I lay on the bed and within an hour I was a steaming jungle. I thought I might make it for vespers but not a chance. Three weeks later I looked in a small mirror and what I saw frightened me. A doctor I had gone to couldn't explain the recurring fever. Prescribing a seriously heavy dose of antibiotics, he talked, quite gratuitously about the unnaturalness of monastic life. The antibiotics didn't work. Fr Norbert eventually concluded that only contact with the soil of Ireland would heal me. Chris my brother met me at Dublin Airport and took me straight to his doctor who prescribed an even heavier dose of antibiotics.

Next day I travelled by train to Limerick where I met Eileen. We travelled together by bus to North Kerry so that my parents wouldn't be alone for Christmas. It was a mistake. The sight of me so alarmed them that there was little that they talked about for the next five or six days. In Limerick on the way back Eileen gave me everything she had, which was eighteen pounds. She suggested that she should come back to Connemara with me, but the thought of Eileen postponing her life in order to look after me was intolerable to me. All I could do was plead for time. (*Nostos*, pp. 654–5)

Back in his bedroom in the first cottage in Derrada West it took months to recover; a combination of physical weakness and mental anguish made him feel 'as if there was no substance or stuff in me any more';[9] he was suffering, the nightmares were as bad as ever, there were no prayers that he could pray and his books brought no comfort. It appeared as if the crisis he was undergoing was progressive; mentally and spiritually he had been shattered; emotionally he had been shattered; and now it was physical. All he could do was to submit and let the illness take its course. Friends and neighbours were the lifeline.

On her way up the hill to feed her cattle, Kathleen McCahill would come in with a jug of hot soup. Lynne and Veronica would come with soup. Mikie Conneely and Patsey Prendergast who were working in Ballinahinch left a trac-tor-trailer load of logs outside the elms. Bridie Prendergast would leave a loaf of homemade bread on my kitchen table. It was hard on them. All they knew was that I had gone to a monastery in Oxford and had come back on my last legs. I didn't talk to them about what was going on inwardly. (*Nostos*, p. 657)

It was six months before he had recovered sufficiently to work again, and instead of day-labouring he returned to the Castle, working in the gardens with Patsy Prendergast. It was at least easier than breaking stones! Eileen was also working there for the summer and her care and concern restored him but he was unable to resolve the sexual crisis that had erupted in him. He felt that he was losing her and also that he was ruining her life, yet he lacked the power to do anything about it. When she left to return to college that September nothing had been resolved between them. Also, and within a short space of time, life became complicated on another front; he had an enormous row with the manager of the Castle, and was again without a job or an income. He knew that heavy physical work would compromise his health, he would never even consider social welfare and he now needed a job that would give him both a home and an income. After a month or two, having answered an advert in *The Irish Times*,

> I was working in their eighteenth- century walled garden for Robert and Sarah Guinness at Lodge Park in Straffan in County Kildare. ...
>   To my great surprise I was given one of these wing houses to live in. The big room downstairs was almost of drawing room size. It had tall windows, and a fireplace big enough for a log fire. From my bedroom I looked down on the Liffey, on Joyce's Anna Livia Plurabelle, making her way, languidly here, to her feary father ... (*Nostos*, pp. 661–2)

This view of the river continued the old argument, 'the great waste of the ocean' versus an eternal Divine Ground, but somehow, here in Lodge Park, it came to a conclusion. Strange as it may sound, he began a conversation with Anna Livia.

> Going late that night to my bedroom window, I looked down at her shining in the moonlight, between dogwood bushes.
>   Greetings to you from a western river, Anna.
>   Greetings to you from the Owenmore, Anna.
>   I've a story to tell you Anna. (*Nostos*, p. 662)

And in his head he told Anna the story of Bran Mac Feabhail, of silver branch perception, of Manannán Mac Lir's message that there are visionary ways of seeing the world, that there is an Otherworld Well in which all of our rivers have their source, and that you, Anna, are going back, not to a 'cold, mad, feary father' but to *Mag Meall*, the Plain of Delights. Manannán is spirit Anna, your spirit, the spirit you have forgotten about Anna, sing his song Anna, because even if you are wrong, by singing it and by living from it, you will enrich the world through which you pass. And this is the message from our Celtic myths Anna, and it is also the message from our Christian myth. You have a spirit Anna, and its greatest symbol is Jesus, because he experienced that spirit in all its Gethsemane terror and in all its Easter glory. Sing the song of your spirit Anna; it is only in singing it that you will find it.

You must 'Go for broke Anna, wagering all that you are against a possible Nihil, the Nihil of the Nihilist.'[10]

In this way, in trying to argue Anna Livia out of her nihilism, his own battered spirit was definitely healing, and this in spite of the fact that the physical environment of Lodge Park was not in any way to his liking. It was far too civilized, all lawns and grandeur, ornamental and tidy, a pretence that nature is orderly and safe once all terror is locked out, beyond the gate, beyond the walls. Even the Blond Aquitane bull had lost his wildness and was pitiful. John was convinced that humanity needs to be saved from civilization such as this! 'A world made safe for humanity', he writes,' is a world in which humanity corrupts and dies.'[11]

The bull of course reminded him of Pasiphae and the Minotaur. He saw the irony. Convinced of the need to acknowledge and integrate the primal energies, he was instead living in a place that symbolised repression and exclusion. But it was restoring in him the energy and the enthusiasm to fight back. He remembered his 'pilgrimage' to Vancouver island to do homage to the Kwaikutl people and their ceremony of Tsetsekia, of welcoming in that of which they were most afraid; he remembered the shaman's journey to comb the hair of Takanakapsaluk, the mother of all of the sea-beasts; he remembered the Blackfoot girl who came to accommodation with the buffalo and brought their dance back to her people; he thought of four wonderful etchings by Picasso in which a young girl, with flowers or a dove in her arm is leading a blind Minotaur back into the world. These are the great healing stories and images, and now, he also has the image of Jesus in Gethsemane, Jesus on the floor of the grand canyon of the human psyche, accepting and integrating the dangerous and destructive energies that plague the human species. He could see a way forward, he needed not only an upanishad, but also a new ritual that would enable a 'twentieth century Enlightenment, the Enlightenment of recognising and integrating our inner *ancien regime*'.[12] The aborigine, he said, was fighting back.

In far better shape than he had been the previous year, he again headed home for Christmas. This time Jimmy was unwell, he was suffering from prostate cancer and 'he looked thin and wasted'; he thought that Mary had slowed up also but in spite of appearances they were in good form and the usual fun and cheer of the season was in the house. On the morning of his departure as he watched her tidying after the breakfast he wondered about her, this no-nonsense, capable and caring woman, 'I wondered if she had ever been hugged, hugged and sheltered in the deep places of her life.' Before he left he put his arms around her, 'this once mighty woman, and I held her for a long, long time.' (*Nostos*, p. 678)

Back in Lodge Park a few days later he had a dream that puzzled him. In it he was standing at the door of Nora Cronin's house in Moyvane. He was surprised to see that a new house had been built next door and he asked Nora about it. She pointed towards a hill in the east and said that an O'Brien woman from over there had recently moved in; the following night he dreamed again, this time he was walking with his mother in Kissane's meadow, walking towards a little stream; he could see the new church in the distance ahead of them, and as he looked behind him the neighbouring houses were sinking below the horizon. These dreams, he wrote, 'fascinated me into silent wonder for all of two days and more.' A few days later he had a call from Chris, it was bad news. His first thought was Jimmy, but no, it was Mary, she had died suddenly of a heart attack an hour previously.

> It was night when we arrived. One side of the road and the yard were full of cars. The house was full of people.
>
> In the room my father was sitting at the end of the bed. Trying to keep them warm, he had her feet in his hands.
>
> Seeing me come in, his anguish deepening, he came towards me.
>
> 'She came up into this room the morning you left,' he said, 'and she asked, "Why did John hug and hold me the way he did just before he left, Jimmy?" ...
>
> We were in the cemetery shouldering the coffin down towards the grave. Phyllis my sister was walking just ahead of me. 'Good God', she said, 'there will be talk on the other side tonight. Do you see who she is being buried beside, Nora Cronin.'
>
> Instantly I remembered and understood the dreams I'd had.
>
> The hill in the east that Nora had pointed to was Baragogeen, where my mother came from. Her maiden name was Mary O'Brien. In the second dream ... I had walked with her below the horizon of this world. (*Nostos*, pp. 678–9)

There's no doubt, in more ways than one, and most certainly in his dreaming, he was his mother's son.

> Watching my father looking down into the grave, John Barrett remarked that we might as well stay in our Sunday clothes because we'd have to come back to bury him in a couple of days.
>
> I stayed at home to look after him.
>
> His grief was passionate and outspoken, and having lived for so long in the expectation that he would go first, he was finding it difficult to adjust.
>
> 'Maybe there is a providence in it,' I suggested. 'Since praying comes so naturally to you maybe you were left behind to do just that, to pray for her.'
>
> From that moment he had a purpose and he took to it the way he'd take to saving a meadow of hay, he put everything that was in him into it. It was as if he had taken over where I had left off, just under the horizon of the world.

So as to be within nearer reach of him in the night I moved my bed up into the parlour. Anxious on his account, I'd wake every couple of hours and I'd hear him praying. These were dark January nights, and listening to him I'd feel he had rowed the house out into eternity.

From this distance, the big farmhouse kitchen intervening, I couldn't hear what his prayer was. Curious one night, I got out of bed and I went within a couple of feet of his room door. As I anticipated it wasn't the Our Father or the Hail Mary. It was in his own words that he was attempting to open and negotiate her way for her.

'May Jesus who died on the cross have no hard feelings against you, Mary.

May Jesus who died on the cross have no hard feelings against you, Mary.

May Jesus who died on the cross have no hard feelings against you, Mary.'
(*Nostos*, p. 679)

Jimmy's intuitive sense was that Mary's spirit must now journey into a great darkness and that it might need help. His prayer, using the only religious language he knew, was a mighty effort on his part to enable a peaceful passage for her. It bothered him that she had died so suddenly, he felt that she was still near him and he wanted to help her to leave. This upset John. It put him in mind of a poem *All Soul's Day* by D. H. Lawrence:

> Be careful then, and be gentle about death.
> For it is hard to die, it is difficult to go through
> the door, even when it opens.
> And the poor dead, when they have left the walled
> and silvery city of the now hopeless body
> where are they to go, Oh where are they to go?
>
> They linger in the shadow of the earth.
> The earth's long conical shadow is full of souls
> that cannot find the way across the sea of change.
> Be kind, Oh be kind to your dead
> and give them a little encouragement
> and help them to build their little ship of death.
> For the soul has a long journey after death
> to the sweet home of pure oblivion.
>
> Each needs a little ship, a little ship
> and the proper store of meal for the longest journey.

> Oh, from out your heart
> provide for your dead once more, equip them
> like departing mariners, lovingly.

What my father knew was that my mother was still in the house, and by way of prayer in the night he, in Lawrence's words, was building her ship of death for her. (*Nostos*, pp. 683–4)

Talking about this time in later years John would recall that he had 'this aching awful sense' that his mother was in trouble – in spiritual trouble – that somehow her spirit was struggling to stay in 'the shadow of the earth … not going on the journey.' He thought that this might have been because she was so suddenly 'crashed out' of her life and was totally unprepared. It took six months of mighty praying before Jimmy could say, 'She's gone now John. She's gone now.' In his own personal requiem for her, Jimmy had 'watched' with Mary to help her 'find the way across the sea of change'. He had sensed that her spirit was having difficulty and he had prayed her out into the darkness of eternity and had 'laid her soul to rest.'[13] For John, it felt as if he was living at the heart of the Kena Upanishad:

> There goes neither the eye nor speech nor the mind; we know it not; nor do we see how to teach one about it. Different it is from all that is known, and beyond the unknown it also is.

Mary was gone into that darkness that is beyond all knowing, but now for John, as well as for Jimmy, the 'oblivion' was oblivion of this life only; there was hope in the darkness, it was the hope of Divine Ground, of the river that has gone back to its source in the ocean, not to the 'cold, mad, feary father' but to the 'bliss of self loss' that the mystics write of, to what John of the Cross calls 'the night more lovely than the dawn'. Jimmy had prayed Mary home.

John spent the remainder of that year, 1980, looking after Jimmy and naturally, given the circumstances there was a great deal of reminiscing about Mary. He had a very particular memory of coming home from college.

> As I drew level with the house, whose gable-end was to the road, I caught sight of my mother coming across the yard. She had, obviously, been to the turf shed and to the fowl-house and now, heaped up in the hollow of her cross-over apron, she had turf and eggs, eight or ten sods of turf it must be, and on them, in hollows, five or six eggs. That's her, I thought, of the earth as ever. (*Turtle was Gone a Long Time*, vol. 1, p. 184)

That, and the way in which Jimmy had lived his life;

> It was how I knew him, walking behind his cows, all eleven of them in calf, so
> the walking was slow, he falling in to their way, not they falling in to his way.
> Walking behind them or sitting behind them in the night, that's where he did
> his thinking. (*Nostos*, p. 690)

What he realised, as he lived again in this house in Moyvane, was that they had
lived much of their lives in accordance with the way of the world as they found
it, 'going the way of the weed in the river', accommodating themselves to it and
not attempting to beat it into submission. They were the little matchstick people
of Kuo Shi's great painting, and from them there was much to learn. They would
become images in the parables of his upanishad.

> My father walking behind his cows, all eleven of them in calf and my mother
> coming across the yard with her cross-over apron piled with turf and on the turf,
> beige on brown, six or seven eggs and recently arrived, the swallows screaming
> in paired delight above her, and screeching at her too, letting her know that for
> the next five or six months or so the sheds were theirs not hers. (*Nostos*, p. 691)

Thinking of these images he prayed
'Walk on, Mary, walk on, Jimmy.'[14]
Walk on, Jimmy, in your journey through this life. Walk on, Mary, walk on through
whatever darkness is beyond you in the next. Walk on.

16

'A SYMPATHETIC NERVOUS SYSTEM'

Canyon Christianity; back to Connemara; Leitirdyfe and Lisnabrucka; sumpatheia
ton hollon; McCahills; building a house; Sara; a prepared spirit.

Early in 1981 his sister Brenda returned from England and as she was now available
to look after Jimmy John returned to Lodge Park in good time for the early spring
work in the garden. The year spent living with Jimmy, in spite of its sadness, had
done him good. The inner turmoil had continued to settle, he enjoyed reconnecting with family, Madeleine's in Lenamore and Phyllis' just over the road in Leitrim
Middle, and he was still in regular contact with Eileen who at that time was living
in Dublin. He had also completed his upanishad of six stories and had given some
thought to how the process they enacted might be given a physical shape, how they
might be made real in the world. He was playing with ideas as usual; he imagined
a new temple which would incorporate Bright Angel Trail, its main aisle or its
ambulatory marking the journey downwards to the floor of the Grand Canyon,
down into the savageries of human nature, there to acknowledge and accept and
forgive all destructive energies. That done, asking grace from Bright Angel, the trail,
the new aisle, would continue upwards into a new and more humble humanity.
Here in Moyvane, living with Jimmy, he had sketched it out.

This is the temple of a new Christianity, Canyon Christianity, and Jesus, given
what he had undergone in Gethsemane, is the pioneer of this path. On that agonising Holy Thursday night, the night he crossed the Kedron, the night his disciples
failed to watch with him, John would imagine that Jesus descended Bright Angel
Trail, right to the floor of the Canyon, above him all the terrors and savageries of
human evolution and human history, and there, right at the very bottom, there is
a rockpool. It is a clear night, and mirrored in the rockpool, is everything that is
above it, all the strata of the world, and above that again, the stars that are shining
in the night sky. In that pool is the challenge for Jesus. He must drink from that

pool. He must accept everything that is in it. In trepidation he pleads to be excused, 'let this chalice pass from me', but there is no avoidance, he must face his karmic human inheritance, recognise all that he humanly is, and drink. He cups his hands and drinks from the pool, accepting all that is in this 'chalice'. It is in this way that John imagines that Jesus 'harrows hell' and by so doing has opened up the path, the only possible path, to 'further and final evolution'. Ascending the path, every savage instinct that ever existed has been suffered, integrated and therefore blessed. The new Christian temple offers each individual the opportunity to walk this path, a path into one's own repressed life, into all damaging and destructive energy, into all 'sins', knowing that one shares this karmic inheritance with every being on the planet and that a suffering compassion towards oneself and all other beings is the first step on the upwards journey.

This dream, this 'work in progress' he took back with him to Lodge Park and it is highly unlikely during the next year and a half that Robert Guinness had any idea of the depths that were being explored in his utterly civilised eighteenth century gardens! The healing depths of Bright Angel Trail: Jesus drinking the rockpool cup; Jesus, still in the Garden of Olives telling Peter, who wishes to protect him, to 'put up thy sword'; Jesus healing the man whom Peter has wounded. These tremendous words, 'Put Up Thy Sword', John imagined them echoing back through millennia, echoing all the way back to the pit in Lascaux, back to what John saw as 'the primal trespass' where Palaeolithic man speared the bison bull through the genitals. Echoing forward all the way to the Mincer on the deck of the Pequod in 'Moby Dick', slicing, slicing, slicing sheaves of whale fat to melt it down to make candles, spermaceti candles, to light the world. Not, not the way to light the world. And it was back to the old question, asked in an Aztec origin myth, 'who will take on himself the burden of lighting the world?' and for John there was now only one answer:

Jesus reaching for the cup.
    I'd imagine it.
    Jesus reaching.
    And I'd think, right there we are available now again to evolution, and I'd think how good it would be if religions older than Christianity were to watch with him, in this his reaching, because it is before the fin-feet of humanity as a whole that Bright Angel Trail has opened.
    I'd picture it:
    Judaism with all its plentifulness watching with Jesus
    Islam with all its plentifulness watching with Jesus
    Hinduism with all its plentifulness watching with Jesus

Buddhism with all its plentifulness watching with Jesus
Taoism with all its plentifulness watching with Jesus
Aboriginal religions with all their plentifulness watching with Jesus
In the way that adults will sometimes need to be healed in their infancy so
do civilizations. (*Nostos*, pp. 688–9)

In the interest of that healing he imagined a thesis that he would nail to the doors of all temples that were founded on what he called 'a hatchet job'; thesis in hand he would go back to ancient Sumeria where Gilgamesh slays Huwawa and destroys the Cedar Forest; to ancient Mesopotamia and its creation myth where Marduk slays Tiamat the terrifying sea-dragon; to ancient Egypt where Atum destroys Apophis, the giant serpent of the Underworld; to ancient Greece where Zeus annihilated Typhon, the monstrous snake being; back to Canaan where Ba'll bludgeons the chaos deity Yam; back to Judea where the Hebrew god Yahweh destroys the dragon Leviathan; and back to the Bible, where in the Book of Revelations Michael the Archangel tramples Satan. Huwawa, Tiamat, Apophis, Typhon, Ba'al, Leviathan, Satan, these 'dragons' represent the powerful, frightening energies in man and in the world, which repressed do not go away. Remembering always that 'a killed dragon is not a dead dragon', on all temples based on such hatchet jobs he would pin his thesis:

To the extent that it continues its detour around who we phylogenetically are, western history will always be on the way to the next disaster of its own making.' (*Nostos*, p. 689)

In place of all of these hatchet jobs, and in the hope of preventing the next global disaster, he offered a 'Tsetsekia' in the form of Bright Angel Trail and for hero, not a murdering conqueror, but Jesus calling for an end to all swordplay. 'In commanding Peter to put up his sword, Jesus was inviting all gods and all heroes to bury the hatchet.' 'Bury the hatchet', yes, but do not attempt to bury those powerful dangerous energies. He thought of what John Keats had to say about a street brawl, something to be condemned in itself but 'the energies displayed in it are fine.'[1] Canyon Christianity must suffer, include and manage those energies.

He spent 1981 working at Lodge Park. It provided stability and routine. Eileen was in Dublin and they often met at weekends, but he was not in any position to progress the relationship. Eventually the inevitable happened, Eileen broke up with him and he was heartbroken, heartbroken but helpless. He felt that he had to let her go; he was still battling his own difficult energies, still struggling against the 'abyss' and very much aware that his need for solitude and freedom was incompatible with commitment and responsibility. It was an agonising dilemma but he believed that compromise on his part would have damaged them both. Then, within a very short space of time, his life unravelled even further.

> Out of the blue one morning Mr. Guinness and myself had a big row. It became a battle of wills. I was up against him, but more seriously I was up against me ... on the third day, he came into the garden and handed me a letter. No, he wasn't giving me the sack, but he was determined to have what I was determined to have, victory.
>
> I gathered up the tools, I put them in the barrow, I wheeled it up past him and Patsy, the farm manager, and within an hour I had packed and was gone. (*Nostos*, p. 695)

For a few nights he lodged with Patsy and Bridie Prendergast in Coolcarrigan, from there he was invited to stay with Charlotte Bielenberg and her husband Thomas O'Connell in Prosperous and 'earned my keep and my dignity' by working in the grounds of their home Caragh House. This was a short-term arrangement. Again he put an advert in *The Irish Times* and did get some replies. Charlotte drove him to a number of potential placements but, 'I'd sense that in these posh places I'd be walking on eggs, and I didn't need anyone to tell me that when I walk on eggs I break them.'[2] In spite of the fact that he had 'no job, no money, no place of my own' he decided not to risk any more breakages. He phoned Lynne.

> After the pleasantries, I told her I had been given the sack. To make sure I would hear her loud and clear, she called out, "come back to Connemara, John, come back here to us, we understand you."
>
> Two evenings later, everything more or less as I remembered it, I had settled back into a cottage mirrored in the Owenmore, the river that was soul to me when I felt I had no soul at all. (*What the Curlew Said*, p. 15)

This was the summer of 1982, almost four years since he had gone to work in Lodge Park, but it was not long before he had reconnected with neighbours and friends. On his first visit to the McCahills he had to face the gossip that his return had generated. There were rumours, some of them mocking, none of them true, and he simply had to weather them.

> I went in to see Kathleen and the girls, Mary Teresa and Noeleen. We had a lot to talk about. After an hour or so the girls retired to the living room to do their homework. And now Kathleen had me on my own. "You're a proud man, John,

she said, and you're a stubborn man, and you will always be getting the sack, always you'll be left walking the roads, and one day you will come home here to us and we'll have no place for you, and we'll watch you walking back up the road, up past Ted's place and round the turn and we'll think we have sinned against you, and do you know, John, you should never put us in that position, in the position where we will sin against you. What I'm telling you is, save for a site and build a house for yourself."

It would have been out of order to answer her.

I looked at her a long while.

She outlooked me.

She walked me to the door saying she hoped the men weren't too hard on me.

I heard beyond the laughter, I said.

I'll have to think about that one, she said.

God bless you, Kathleen.

God bless you, John. (*What the Curlew Said*, pp. 17–18)

He was home. Back in a community that cared about him even if there was 'an air of scandal' about him, even if his lifestyle was a puzzle to them. Within a month he had sourced work as a gardener, one day a week in Lisnabrucka, an Edwardian house on thirty five acres, whose owners lived in England; one day a week working for Lynne in the grounds of the Anglers Return; two days a week in Leitirdyfe, a Victorian house on forty acres which was owned by a syndicate of Dutch people, all of them environmental enthusiasts and many of them specialists in botany. The garden and grounds of Leitirdyfe were the responsibility of Victor Westhoff, a professor of botany in the University of Nijmegen. All three gardens-grounds called for a big effort. As he said, at Leitirdyfe all paths but one ran into what could only be described as woodland jungle; in Lisnabrucka, while the formal gardens were in good shape, outside them 'you wouldn't get very far with a secateurs'; and in Lynne's, while he had previously made some inroads, 'never had I encountered granite so dense and so heavy as here.'

Even so, except for lawnmowers, each of them three and a half horsepower, I worked only with old-fashioned tools, with spade and shovel and digging fork and bow-saw and secateurs and long handled cutters and pick and crowbar and sledge hammer and axe and hoe and rake. And a hand-barrow to transport things in. I had, after all, grown up on a farm that didn't have electricity or a single power tool. (*What the Curlew Said*, p. 15)

He would always remember the night at home in the kitchen when Jameen Kissane had wanted to half-sole a shoe and his mother had prevented him because the sound of the hammer would damage or even kill the 'little specks of developing life' in the eggs that a hen was hatching under the kitchen table.

> From then on, naturally and out of need, I lived by that interdiction. All in one it was my Ten Commandments. All in one, as though it had come down from the summit of Mount Sinai, it was the big Thou Shalt Not. Thou Shalt Not Make Murderous Noise In The World. (*What the Curlew Said*, p. 15)

So regardless of the toll that it took on him physically he endeavoured to live by that commandment. 'At no season of the year, least of all in spring, could I pull the string of a chainsaw and release the murderous, revving roar.' More than ever now, shaping nature as he was, he thought again about Prometheus and the dolphins.

> This I believed: there are two ways we could have gone, the way of the Titan, Prometheus; or the way of the dolphin. In the Promethean way we shape nature to suit us, in the way of the dolphin we let nature shape us to suit it. Everywhere there is evidence that we have chosen wrongly. (*What the Curlew Said*, p. 16)

There was no doubt about it, what he was doing in these gardens and grounds was Promethean, and there were times, as he axed clumps of bamboo in Leitirdyfe, when it felt like a 'hatchet job' but he would be as little Promethean as he could; the compromise was 'to live as though it mattered to not make too much noise', to do what he was doing as gently as he could, and as far as possible to let his interference be in keeping with what he sensed to be a co-operation with Nature, of benefit to the place as well as to the people it served. Attitude would be everything.

> The compromise was, to live as though it mattered to not make too much noise in the world and to continue surrendered to nature in places deeper within me than my grip on scythe or spade, than my grip on myself. (*What the Curlew Said*, p. 16)

In doing this he hoped to find a way of living ecumenically with all things. No easy task. As he struck at the bamboo he wondered how far different this was from striking at an animal. There were times when he couldn't help thinking that he might as well have been a boner in the slaughterhouse opposite the railway station in Galway.

> Waiting for a bus one day, I saw ten or twelve bullocks railed in on a ramp

outside that windowless, grey, concrete block, its interior imaginable only because it was real. They had maybe been trucked here from the fields of Athenry and they looked all out of place and stupefied. (*What the Curlew Said*, p. 37)

What terror were they feeling and what 'squealing moments' lay ahead of them? Looking at one old cow there, "away from her fields,... I couldn't help feeling that our relationship with her was all wrong. In the Christian tradition it is common to say that you can only sin against another human being or against God ... Not so. You can sin against anything, when you see anything as smaller or less than what it is you are sinning against it; when you see something only with an economic eye you are sinning against it."[3] This slaughter at the heart of civilised life he had come to terms with on a personal level some years previously by giving up meat eating, but it did not ease the pain he felt in relation to man's place at the top of the food chain and the almost universal blindness and indifference towards the cruelty which that position entails. Time and again, here in Leitirdyfe, he would ask, 'what was I doing now with an axe in my hand?'

> And yet the axe in my hand wasn't the whole story.
> There were times when my whole mind was as low as the mind of a badger to the floor of the wood. It was as if my arrogant and divisive central nervous system had become a sympathetic nervous system and sympathy in the literal sense of experiencing with, suffering with, enjoying with, living with, dying with, that above all else is who and what I was. In the sense of being ecumenical with all things, with the curlew calling below on the shore, with herons shitting on me, with badgers avoiding me, I was everything I had been over the whole course of evolution. (*What the Curlew Said*, pp. 37–8)

'A sympathetic nervous system', 'suffering with, enjoying with, living with, dying with', that word '*with*' perhaps saying it all, perhaps part of what it means 'to stay awake *with* Jesus in Gethsemane'. Cultivating a sympathetic nervous system might be the way into the wood, might provide a healing approach to the world. The pain and suffering at the heart of survival might be alleviated or at least made bearable by an inclusive compassion, based on the 'three great Greek words: *Sumpatheia ton hollon* ... which simply states that all things are in sympathy with one another.'[4] To recognise and live from that realisation might be an antidote to Titanism, it might provide a real ecumenism.

In spite of his misgivings about this wielding of axe and scythe the work in these grounds suited him. He worked alone, therefore able to lose himself completely in both the task in hand and whatever reflections that task would present. In Leitirdyfe his aim was to open up the forty acres in order to provide access to all of its riches to the botanists and naturalists who were frequent visitors. In deference to the wood itself 'all paths would be as natural as the stream or as the trail of a fox seeking new territory ... they would be in keeping with the lie of the land.'[5] They would facilitate scientists but they would preserve the magic and acknowledge the mystery of the wood. As his paths were opening up he was making comparisons with the public road that he had to cycle every morning on his way to the wood. How sterile, how utterly unimaginative and dead this concrete road versus 'the kind of wildwood that Merlin lives in.' And of course he had a poem. D. H. Lawrence again

> That I am I.
> That my soul is a dark forest.
> That my known self will never be more than a little clearing in the forest.
> That gods, strange gods, come forth from the forest into the clearing of my known self, and then go back.
> That I must have the courage to let them come and go.
> That I will never let mankind put anything over on me, but that I will try always to recognise and submit to the gods in me and the gods in other men and women.

This was the message, the concrete road might be necessary to get to Roundstone but the concrete 'single vision' of the modern mind had to be resisted and challenged, there must be an openness and acceptance of whatever strangeness lies beyond the 'known self' and the known world. Unfortunately, he believed, 'we live in a merely knowable universe. And as for our sense of ourselves, we also are merely knowable.'[6]

> I had recently walked through this wood with Professor Westhoff. Delightedly, as we walked this way and that, he filled page after page after page of his notebook with the names of what, quite clearly to him, were botanical wonders, revelations almost, not just familiar specimens ... and then we emerged, and I was disappointed thinking, he walked through the wood but he at no point walked into it. Having an educated, expert eye, he met his own knowledge but he didn't meet the wood. (*What the Curlew Said*, p. 75)

John was disappointed because the Professor, for all of his enthusiasm, had not developed a 'sympathetic nervous system', his genius not 'con-genial with the genius of the universe', he did not have what Keats calls negative capability, 'the ability to cease being yourself and to become the sparrow you are looking at.' To take the time to look, to listen, and to allow the thing you observe simply to be itself. To explain con-genial genius he quotes Yeats:

> 'I know that revelation is from the self, but from that age-long memoried self, that shapes the elaborate shell of the mollusc and the child in the womb, that teaches the birds to make their nest; and that genius is a crisis that joins that buried self for certain moments to our trivial daily mind.'[7]

It is that genius, John would say, that operates when, after wrestling with a problem late at night it defeats us and we decide to sleep on it. Effortlessly in the morning it solves itself, or that is how it seems.

> Throughout all of nature there is mind. Not neurologically lobed and con-strained, it doesn't need to resort to mental activity. Lao Tze would think of it as Tao. Uvavnuk would think of it as Silam Inua. And Yeats, I supposed, would think of it as Anima Mundi. (*What the Curlew Said*, p. 74)

The spirit of the world, the genius of nature, the 'miracling point' that he so often referred to, this was it and he was convinced that there are those who live, not just for moments, but continually from that buried self. 'Indeed that buried self is unburied in them.' He thought of these people, great artists, saints, the Buddha, Jesus, Lao Tze, mystics, healers – usually people who meditate and pray – they have access to it and, it is not that they perform miracles, 'miracles simply happen in their presence.'[8] He believed that the educated expert eye was an impediment to this 'sympathetic nervous system', to this 'buried self'. Working in Leitirdyfe, he said, sensing this 'genius' in the wood, was one way to make sure 'that I did not relapse into European common sense.'[9]

As he was living and working alone neighbours were of great importance to him and on one particular Sunday, needing to experience something of family life, he decided to call to McCahills. His walk to their new house took him past a nineteenth century fish-cannery; all that now remained of this cannery was the ice-house and he remembered Martin Halloran telling him that in the 1940s and 50s it had been the local dancehall.

> Martin Halloran once talked to me about the clouds of instinctive steam and heat that would come billowing out through the door when things within were

at their excited height. Famously, one night, Martin himself was heard calling out to May Diamond, "will you shthand shtiff aghinsht me".

The wonder of it, I thought, as I passed it now, an icehouse at a crossroads, an icehouse full of sexual fire, a thing not comely in De Valera's comely Ireland. (*What the Curlew Said*, p. 43)

Here again he recognised a genius for instinctive life still battling against the 'cultural icehouse' that the Ireland of the time had become and it saddened him to think that the battle had been lost. Still on the road to McCahills he passed Maamo's, a now closed pub that had at one time been the heart of the community and 'from everything I had heard about her Maamo was as grand, as welcoming and as warm a woman as her name suggested.' Turning into McCahills however he knew that the warmth and welcome that had existed in Maamo's was alive and well. Kathleen and Micheál, and the two girls, Mary Teresa and Noeleen, were in the kitchen when he arrived and as usual there was no fuss, just another chair pulled up to the table, conversation ranging from the weather to the local news and politics and then on to discussion with Micheál on 'one of the big philosophical questions about which he would be typically brilliant.' Later on in the afternoon he spent some time discussing *Hamlet* with Mary Teresa who was studying for her Leaving Cert. As usual it was a heart-warming visit.

On the way out I met Kathleen and Micheál coming in at the front door. Commenting on the weather, Kathleen left me with a blessing and continued on in. Micheál turned to walk down, as I thought, to the gate with me. The conversation more a search for conversation, he continued over the road with me, over past Petey Welsh's, over along by Josey's meadow, round the turn and when we were opposite the icehouse he bent down and, picking a stone off the road, the threw it into the meadow, his by inheritance for the past few years, and he said, "Now John, from where that stone landed to Lynne's wall, that's a site for you to build a house on. Kathleen and myself and the girls would love to see you having a place of your own".

A site overlooking the Owenmore River!

A house that would be mirrored in the Owenmore River!

I stood there looking at him, at a loss what to say.

"Think about it," he said. He picked up another stone and walking forward a few steps he threw it in a different direction and farther and said, "Somewhere there where it landed, that if I was you is where I would build. You'll get a good foundation there."

"Good luck to you", he said, and with that he turned to walk over home.

Having had no time to get used to the idea and having handled the whole
thing silently and awkwardly, I didn't call after him. (*What the Curlew Said*,
p. 47)

John was overwhelmed at the enormity of the gesture; in this generosity he
recognised the real sense of 'care'. He remembered Kathleen's advice to him months
earlier to save for a site, she and Micheál had now taken matters into their own
hands and it left John wondering how he could accept it. 'Am I too small a man to
accept a gift so big?' He had often remarked that giving and receiving are a complex
business; very often the most generous givers are what he termed 'mean receivers',
they make an enormous fuss about receiving. There is he would say a generosity in
accepting as well as giving, a willingness to allow others to be generous, an openness
to being indebted; he was being tested now. He was being tested in other ways as
well. What would ownership mean for him?

I needed to walk, and I did, up past the cottages, up past the big house, along by
the Well Field and out into the open world in which for some years now I had
been happy to be improvident. I had expressed the attitude in words:
    'Clear days bring the mountains down to my doorstep, calm nights give the
rivers their say, the wind puts its hand to my shoulder some evenings and then
I don't think, I just leave what I'm doing and I go the soul's way.'
    And having a house of my own, what would that mean? That I wouldn't
be as available as I used to be to the wind that bloweth where it listeth, to that
wind touching me on my shoulder? If I had a house, would I ever again shove
the fork I was working with in the soil and walk away, not caring, now again,
where the dawn broke on me or the night fell on me?
    Jesus had said: "Seek ye first the Kingdom of God and all things else shall
be added unto you." I had come to believe that in this he wasn't only talking
about divine care from beyond the universe. In this He was talking about something as immanently true of the universe as Newton's laws of gravity. (*What the
Curlew Said*, pp. 47–8)

On the other hand he was aware that his 'reliance on Divine Providence' was
already at 'some cost, moral and emotional, to his friends.' Kathleen McCahill
had spelt it out to him when he returned from Kildare, her fear that he would one
day return to them and there would be no welcome for him; equally there was
his own worry that his presence in the cottages prevented Lynne from making
better use of them; added to these concerns was the discomfort of the permanent
dampness in which he lived.

And yes, there was genius in the cottages, I loved living in them, but there was this other side to them. Lying in bed upstairs in the third cottage I only had to look up and I would see daylight between the chimney bricks and the corrugated-iron roof. And in winter when the sun hit the corrugated-iron roof around late midmorning it would melt the ice underneath it and there would be drip drop onto my bedclothes and floor. But nothing that anyone might say to me could be half as persuasive as what Kathleen had said – simply, don't leave us with the sense that we have sinned against you. That I couldn't counter. That I had no defence against.

Walking in my own door I decided that tomorrow evening after work I would go back over to talk to the McCahills, especially to the girls, Noeleen and Mary Teresa. (*What the Curlew Said*, p. 50)

This he did. With both girls insisting that the site was already his and assuring him that 'they'd be delighted' if he'd take it, and Kathleen asking him 'to pass the milk from the fridge', the matter was finalised. He was the owner of a site for a house, and returning to his cottage later that night, walking past the site he found himself thinking of Eileen. They were still friends, still in contact and he still had hope of a future with her. Other miracles were unfolding in his life. On a day when he was working in the orchard at the Angler's Lynne came to tell him that she and Simon had great news, she was expecting a baby. John's heart lifted and 'standing at the morning side of an apple tree' he addressed the new life directly: 'Keep coming', he said, 'keep coming, come out into this garden and we will have a great welcome for you.' Months later, in March 1983 Sara was born. Her birth affected John deeply. He was clearing a path in the grounds of the Angler's when Veronica, Lynne's friend, called the news to him from across the field.

I stood there, as impassively at first as Derrada Hill, and I could see her, the little wonder, and I thought I have a new neighbour and then, still picturing her, I thought, I must now be a neighbour in a new way and so, by the time Veronica reached me, we were both content to do and say the right things, outwardly we were both content to be conventionally happy, but underneath we knew, I could see Veronica knew, that something big had happened to us.

All day I felt I must be a better man than I had been.

Not just better ...

There must be shelter in me.

My arms must feel as safe as a den; a place to make for when danger threatens ...

Three mornings later Lynne gave her to me and I did take her into the den of my arms and, easing her lace shawl up over her head, I took her out through the low back door of the kitchen, out onto the flag-paved patio, up the two stone steps on to the path shadowed by azaleas and a cherry tree, along that path into the garden, along it still into the far lawn and there, under a Brewer's spruce, I brought a crumb of resin to her nose, she curled her nose, and I welcomed her into the world and, taking her among and under the great old apple trees, I touched her already adventurous head and I said, "continue in the adventure you have set out in, Sara, we'll walk a stretch or two or three of your way with you, Sara, continue with us in the adventure you have set out in, Sara".

I hoped I had founded her mind on the smell of resin, and now, a shower threatening, we took her back to the kitchen and there she was, back in Lynne's lap, our newest reason to refound the world. (*What the Curlew Said*, pp. 52–3)

In this way was Sara's spirit welcomed into the world, a world in great need of refounding, but nonetheless a world full of wonder and adventure.

Two weeks later he found himself in a new role; Lynne wanted to go to Roundstone to play badminton, and as Simon was away on the rigs, John was enlisted as babysitter. He was terrified. Hardly daring to breathe he watched her sleeping but

Sara let out a cry, only it wasn't a cry or a sigh or a wail or a whimper, never had I heard anything like it, over almost as soon as it began, and born, it had to be, from an enormity of dread. It earthquaked me into action. Going to her pram, I lifted her out into a place of mammalian safety and care far away within myself and I held her there until she returned to sleep and then, sheltering her as an Upanishad would, I took her back to my chair, and when she came in an hour or so later, that's how Lynne found us. (*What the Curlew Said*, p. 54)

Sara's cry set him thinking again about the spiritual journey. Where had this little sleeping spirit come from? Was it as Wordsworth so hopefully imagined, that 'our birth is but a sleep and a forgetting' and that 'trailing clouds of glory do we come from God, who is our home'? Or was it more complex and frightening than that? On and off over the years and particularly since his mother's death he had been reading *The Tibetan Book of the Dead* and giving consideration to the theories found there. A central concept is that the spirit, once engulfed in the world of illusion that it knows as the material world, continues 'to transmigrate from one to another existence, incarnate or discarnate, accumulating vast amounts of karma, good and bad in the process.'[10] The book outlines the three states or 'bardos' that the spirit must pass through after death. Liberation from the illusion of the mortal material world into Divine Ground is possible in all of them, particularly the first one, known as 'the chonyid bardo', but this liberation does not happen easily. For those who die 'illuded', that is in the illusion of the reality of their separate, individual personalities, who have not completed the Gethsemane and Golgotha journey in this existence, it is likely that they 'will yet again pass through all three of them [the bardos] into a new existence.'[11] Only those who have learned to live from 'the buried self', who have surrendered the ego-self and uncovered their inner 'holiness', they are the 'prepared spirits' who are ready for liberation into Divine Ground, back into God. This is completely in keeping with what Jesus had to say about entry into his Father's 'Kingdom', it is as impossible as 'passing through the eye of a needle' for those still in possession of the 'riches', the illusions of their ego selves. Unlike Narada, a prepared spirit will not have forgotten the water, will not be among the many 'who have forgotten our errand in the world.'[12]

These were difficult thoughts, frightening and challenging on the one hand; comforting and optimistic on the other. There is a journey to be undergone; an enormous journey requiring both courage and sacrifice over many lifetimes and through many 'purgatories' or bardos, but it does not lead into the arms of the 'old, mad feary father', ultimately it leads, as the Mundaka Upanishad promises:

> As rivers leaving name and form behind them
> flow into their home in the ocean
> so does the Knower, from name and form released,
> go to that Divine Person who is beyond the beyond. (*Nostos*, p. 460)

This 'movement essential' journey can begin at any time; for Sara in her new incarnation, and at any point in any incarnation when and if one sits down and waits 'for one's soul to catch up'.

17

'NOT ONE OF US BUT IS STILL WALKING IN PARADISE AT THE CORE OF OUR BEING'

Paradise as a mode of perception; water lilies; Holy, Holy, Holy; Talks; 'the living dead'; another death; Lorna; a Navajo cradle; Black Elk; Mitakuye oyasin.

Leitirdyfe and Lisnabrucka, one a Victorian estate and the other Edwardian, came to symbolise two central processes in John's thinking. In both estates he worked always from his 'sympathetic nervous system', being guided by the direction of streams and animal trails and the requirements of native vegetation, working as best he could 'as a reed moves in a river', even when that meant secateurs, scythe or hatchet. Individually however each place took on its own significance; the opening up old paths in Leitirdyfe with it heronry and badger setts becoming an image for the journey down into the Grand Canyon of human nature; in Lisnabrucka on the other hand he worked in a more open landscape. The estate bordered a lake that on clear days would mirror the surrounding mountains and on such days, he said, Connemara made purity credible to him. He was back in the world of 'Paradisal perception', of silver branch perception, of seeing things as they are in themselves, in all of their miracle and wonder. In fact, he believed, it is best not to think of Paradise as a particular place, it is instead a mode of perception, possible in any place. Perception needs to become 'admiration' and when it does 'things' become 'mirabilia', become marvels, and the perceiver becomes aware of the 'Divine Mirum' to which he or she belongs. This vision of purity, of 'genius at the heart of the universe' was no longer something that he glimpsed only occasionally, it became a reality at the core of his being, it became his truth.

Naturally the vision was challenged, as it always had been, by the 'yoga of horror' which is part of everyday reality; the lobster-pot on Inisboffin and the bitter herbs of history were never very far away, and there were regular reminders of both: the otter with a trout between its teeth; the savagery wreaked on young nestlings by the teeth of a pine martin; the sight of an eel dying in a blue plastic barrel, having been trapped on its way to the spawning grounds by submerged nets; the black iron famine pot, now a water trough, that sat in the garden of the Angler's Return; he did not have far to look to find incriminating evidence of the pain in the universe, but he was now convinced that this apparently intrinsic indifference and cruelty 'is not the whole story'.

The lake in Lisnabrucka with its water lilies in full bloom provided him with an image to counteract what Melville called 'the universal cannibalism' of sea and land, of animal and human savagery. He was aware of the significance of the lotus plant in the Hindu and Buddhist traditions and here in front of him, looking at the green lily pads on the lake with their glorious yellow blossoms, he had his own home-grown version of the lotus.

> The lotus grows in shallow water. It has its roots in mud at the bottom, it ascends through the brightening water and, having emerged, it opens out totally, almost ecstatically you would say, to the sun. Metaphorically, it is an ascent from impurity to purity. (*What the Curlew Said*, p. 81)

For John the lotus took on a double symbolism. The darkness in which it has its roots represents all dangerous repressed energies; its growth into brightness and beauty is the potential to blossom into integrated and enlightened being. Central to the image and adding to its richness is the Hindu concept of purity. The beauty that flowers on the surface has its source in the mud, the potential for beauty exists within the mud. 'Hindus', he says, 'are scandalised by our Christian belief in mortal sin, in sin that is deadly to the soul, that deadens it, that makes it dead, all the way to its core. To them, no matter how evil in no matter how many lifetimes I might have been, I continue at the core of my soul to be as pure as a drop of water on a lotus leaf.'[1] At a level, deeper than what appears, the mud itself, the source of life, is pure.

This was it. 'It is only behaviourally ... that our world is in trouble, that we are in trouble. Behind everything there is purity.' The Hindu assurance is that, however wicked, 'we continue in the core of our soul to be as pure as a drop of water on a lotus leaf ... Adam and Eve are still walking in Paradise at the core of their being. Not one of us but is still walking in Paradise at the core of our being.'[2] This is 'silver branch perception', this is 'a way of seeing no matter what thing':

> At the core of his being the Devil is still an angel still singing the heavenly hymn of praise to God. "Holy", he sings, "holy, holy, holy, Lord God of hosts, heaven and earth are full of your glory." ... At the core of his being, he sings it with

his being. At its core, that's what his being is. At its core, his being is unending praise of God. As is mine. As is yours. True, at the core of his being, of Caligula. True, at the core of his being, of Stalin. True, at the core of its being, of the hazel I am cutting back. True, at the core of its being, of the grass I walk on ... And this song of praise that the angels sing ... in Hebrew it is called the Kedushah, in Greek it is called the Trishagion, in Latin it is called the Sanctus.

In its particles, in its quavers, it is what every atom is: in its quavers it is Kedushah, it is Trishagion, it is Sanctus.

And that is what Manannán said to us, singing it to us out over the manes and heads of his horses at sea: In its quavers every atom you are made of is

KEDUSHAH

IS

TRISHAGION

IS

SANCTUS

True of the atoms of the cells of your seeing, true of the atoms of the cancer cells that are killing you. (*What the Curlew Said*, pp. 117–18)

Holy. Holy. Holy. This, as he would say again and again, is Good News. Behaviourally, and therefore morally, things can be 'out of tune', but the 'tune', what everything is at core, is a Song of Joy. This was his answer to the world of science, to a world made 'meaningless' by the theories of Big Bang and Big Crunch, an understanding wholly reliant on intellect which claims that mind or consciousness is simply matter in interaction with itself, destined for annihilation. Working in Leitirdyfe and Lisnabrucka, attuning himself to the 'genius' that he intuited, he would ask, 'How shall we sing the Lord's song in a strange land?', a world of miracles from which we have been estranged by the theories of science and mathematics; by so-called logic and reason; by the myth of progress; by the failure of the monolithic religions. Life, he was now completely convinced, was not as Macbeth had it, 'a tale told by an idiot, full of sound and fury, signifying nothing', but at its core, a song of praise, long ago recognised in the mystical tradition of all cultures. 'Modern science', he said, 'is a premature closing of our account with reality'[3] and it is therefore time for science to catch up with religion. And time for religions, as they currently are, to catch up with mystical insight.

All very inspiring when left to himself communing with lake and mountain, but what of the world in which he had to live and work? There he was, 'wheeling a rattling barrow full of rattling tools up into the wood in Leitirdyfe', ready to cut back hazels with a bow saw, very much aware that the teeth of the saw were far more murderous than anything to be found in nature. And what about the house he was about to build? Planning permission had been acquired but there was now the problem of clearing the site. He was reluctant to start but in late afternoon on November fourth 1983, Eileen's birthday, he wheeled his barrow containing spade, shovel, pick and digging fork into Josey's Meadow and started work on the foundation of a small house, 'the whole thing amounting to less than five hundred square feet.' He felt awkward and ridiculous.

> Mikie Conneely came along in his car and he stopped and I could see by the expression on his face that he was wondering, what in God's name is Moriarty up to now? I walked down to the wall and with considerable embarrassment I said, "I'm thinking of building a house, Mikie, but the fact is I only have twelve hundred and fifty pounds to my name, so the chance is that I won't get to finish it and that will mean an eyesore ruining the look of this lovely place".
>
> "No," he said, "no, not at all. Didn't I start with far, far less than you have, and look at the grand little house I have now. What you'll do is, whenever you can afford it put one block on top of another, put one slate next to another and, when it's closed in, put one board beside a board, and you'll get there."
>
> Still not convinced, I looked at him quizzically.
>
> "Never died a winter yet," he said. "God bless the work, and the workman." And with that, waving to me, he drove away.
>
> My misgivings and my embarrassment fell from me. I felt better. The work came easier to me. And it was nightfall deepening into night that stayed my hand. (*What the Curlew Said*, pp. 97–8)

That embarrassment dealt with, there was worse to come. By the following Saturday the site was cleared.

> Micheál McCahill came over to look at it.
>
> "You'll have to blast it," he said.
>
> That, because I perceived it as violation, I wanted at all costs to avoid.
>
> "No omelette without breaking eggs," Micheál said.
>
> He set about persuading me.
>
> An extremely intelligent and a knowing man, his reasons backed by arguments were difficult to counter. Particularly difficult was the seemingly inevitable fact that if you build a house on solid bedrock at one end and on infill at the other, it will settle unevenly, meaning that the walls and floors will crack, possibly quite seriously.
>
> So much, I thought walking home, for geomantic sensitivity. (*What the Curlew Said*, p. 98)

In this requirement to 'blast' the rock he believed that he was morally 'out of tune' with the way of the world, with how he felt he should live in the world. He had 'shipped oars', had attempted to go the way 'of the reed in the river', to live 'as the lilies of the field', and now he found, 'not for the first time, that I had a price. As between the melodic line of *Port na bPúcaí* and the sound of grey granite explosively blown to pieces I had chosen miserably.'[4] Was it possible to live and not be violent? He was, as always, exceptionally hard on himself. For good reasons he had accepted the site, this now meant a compromise on the creed by which he had tried to live. And yet the creed in itself was not invalid. There is a hosanna at the heart of the atom, even if that atom is being blown to pieces. It is behaviourally that things are out of tune, if this could but be recognised there might still be hope for the planet. He continued to build.

A few months later, in the spring of 1984, his life took another unusual turn. He had made the acquaintance of Fr. John O'Donohue,[5] a young curate in Rosamhil in south Connemara, and had been impressed by his 'disciplined readiness for intellectual and spiritual adventure.' Fr. O'Donohue was director of adult education in the Galway diocese and in the course of conversation had suggested that John might think of giving a talk at some time in the future. John gave a rather vague commitment, but very shortly afterwards Fr. O'Donohue contacted him with a date and time. He was unnerved. He hadn't given a public talk since leaving Canada thirteen years previously, yet he now felt that something of the journey he had gone since then could be shared.

> Back hoeing the yard after talking on the phone to Fr. John O'Donohoe, I decided I'd go for it. Mediating something of all of this in a gentle, graduating way, giving it a local habitation and a name, I would tell them a suite of six stories that I had recently composed and that I secretly thought of as an Upanishad. The worry was, I had given a copy of them to Tim Robinson, a man of exceptionally fine mind and sensibility whom I had first seen and later met in Michael John Ferron's grocery in Roundstone, and he had concluded that they could ever only have an audience of one, namely myself. To Tim, who would in time become a very great friend of mine, they amounted to mysticism and therefore to mist. Even so, this assessment of them notwithstanding, I would risk them in Galway. Hardly daring to admit it to myself, I had an Upanishad, possibly Ireland's first, to speak. It was fearful to me and dangerous. (*What the Curlew Said*, p. 61)

The following Wednesday, with this 'mist' in his heart and in his head he hitched to Galway, asking the mountains to travel with him and to keep him real.

I made it in time and ten minutes into the talk I felt that a lot of people were walking the roads of North Kerry and Connemara with me. They walked with Amanda my niece up the hilly road to her Granny's house. They walked behind his eleven cows, all of them in calf, with my father. They climbed Derrada Hill the long and the crooked way up and, from the summit, they looked out over the giftedly crooked world. They opened a door to a tinker woman dressed in a tartan shawl so radiant that it could have been the shawl of all her chakras, all of them opened. They walked drunkenly home, down along the Owenmore, with Martin Halloran. The nets of their minds and hearts hung up outside in an outhouse, they rowed themselves out into the Divine no-thing-ness in which the fishing, not fishing at all, is blessedness, is bliss. (*What the Curlew Said*, p. 61)

As with all subsequent audiences, this first one was mesmerised. Mesmerised by the message and mesmerised by the passion, humour and fluency with which it was delivered. In his presentation the 'mist', the obscurity, dissolved and his conviction of a world 'always and in everything eruptively divine' suffused the surrounding atmosphere; there was an unquestionable *draíocht* in his presence and in his performance. Within weeks there were further developments. The RTÉ presenter Andy O'Mahony came to Galway to interview Fr. O'Donohue who suggested to him that he might be interested in an interview with John. 'When he eventually did come out, on a misty day lovely for lichens, he taped enough talk for two half-hour programmes. They were broadcast some weeks later and, within days of their going out, invitations to give talks here, there and yon began to arrive.'[6] In his introduction to the radio programmes Andy O'Mahony referred to John as 'the most extraordinary man I have ever met', and this was to become a regular reaction as his fame spread. There were now constant invitations to give talks, and for as long as he was meeting new audiences he told the six stories of his Upanishad. Eventually a friend, Marie Hughes, who had invited him to talk in Dublin, arranged to have the talks taped professionally and then sold them from her house, the proceeds donated to Oxfam. 'The good thing about this', he said, 'was that I could move on to pastures new.'

It was tough going, working in the gardens for the first four days of the week and on the road hitching every Friday. From Galway I would take bus or train to wherever I had to go, Enniskillen or Cork, Carlow or Louth. On Sunday evenings I'd walk back out through Galway and, not always without embarrassment given my age, I'd turn and face the music, reaching out my hand to the passing cars. Since I was neither respectable nor a bum, people didn't know what to make of me but, over the next ten or eleven years, while I still lived in Connemara, I always managed to make it home, even if I often had to walk the last four or five miles in the dark. (*What the Curlew Said*, pp. 62–3)

Now that his 'upanishad' had taken on a life of its own, the world and landscape in which he lived and worked and the people he encountered provided an endless richness of new anecdote and imagery to elucidate his vision. Martin Halloran vehemently explaining to him that you should never talk about the dead, only about 'the living dead', Martin insisting on the truth of a story about a man who, one night on his way from Ballinafad to Glenchoaghan, saw, in the bog ahead of him, beings so grand that he could never imagine them, two troupes of them playing a game of hurling. At first he mistook them for fairy folk, but then recognised his own brother among them, and he froze in dread lest he be asked to join the dead in their game! Whatever about the existence of ghosts or fairies this little story might be used by John to question 'what has happened to the wonder-child in us?' or to guard against closing 'our account with reality', because as he would never tire of saying, in the words of JBS Haldane, 'the world is queerer than we can suppose.' It would also give rise to reflection on death. Martin's belief in 'the living dead' was echoed in the Irish language.

I marvelled at how hopefully the Irish language cares for the dead. Whereas in English we say, they are buried, in Irish we say, *tá síd curtha*, they are planted, this implying new growth in due season. And whereas in English we say, we have laid them to rest, in Irish we say, *tá síd imithe ar Shlí na Fírinne*, they have set out on the Trail of Truth, the better translation being, they have set out on the adventure of their immortality (*What the Curlew Said*, p. 63)

This 'new growth in due season', this 'adventure of their immortality' might not involve a ghostly game of hurling, but he would insist that it is a great adventure nonetheless.

I suppose there are two great adventures in life – there is the love adventure and the death adventure. Most of us I suppose enter the great love adventure in our teenage years and we remain in it a couple of decades and then we move out of that and I suppose we move into the death adventure and at this stage of my life I am beginning to imagine that the death adventure is altogether more marvellous and altogether more wonderful and altogether more tremendous than the love adventure ever was.[7]

Whatever might be the stages of that adventure, whenever he passed a grave-yard he would pray for 'the living dead'; 'I'd pray for those who are on their way home to their house in Eternity; taking time off as you do to play an odd game of hurling, may you, the living dead of this parish, prosper and flourish in the adventure of your immortality.'[8] This year, 1984, also presented him with a more personal reason for such prayers. In April word had come through to him that Jimmy was dying and so he made the journey home. On the bus from Galway he was leafing through *The Tibetan Book of the Dead* with its theory of the bardo states, he was also thinking of what Yeats had to say about the various stages of the afterlife, but

> My father's sense of what awaited him was much simpler. Sure that he had done his purgatory in this life, he was consequently sure that, no matter what, he'd find the right way in the hereafter. Only once did I hear him having doubts about it. He was however easily reassured. "Those eleven cows you have been walking behind for so long" I said, "up the road to milking in the evening and down the road after milking in the morning, they'll be there waiting for you on the other side and all you'll have to do is fall in behind them and they'll find the way for you." To which he instantly replied, "They will, the crathurs, the cows adores me." (*What the Curlew Said*, p. 150)

While John himself was uncertain and afraid for Jimmy, he decided to have faith in Jimmy's faith. Jimmy, after long years of 'thinkin', *ag smaoineamh is ag macnamh dom féin*, had prepared himself for letting go of this life, *mar go bhuil mo threabhann is mo fhuirse déanta is mo thread agam ón síon* – for my ploughing and harrowing I have done and my cattle have shelter from the rain – he knew that his work here was done. Thinking about how Jimmy had made a 'little ship of death' in his prayer for Mary after she died, John now prepared to let him go. He imagined him, 'a departing mariner, Mount Brandon sinking below the horizon behind him' and he prayed

> Go forth upon thy journey out of this world, O Christian soul
> In the name of God, the Almighty Father, who created thee
> In the name of Jesus Christ, his Son, who redeemed thee
> In the name of the Holy Spirit, who sanctifieth thee
> May thy guardian angel succour and defend thee
> May the prayers of the blessed Saints help thee
> May thy Redeemer look upon thee in pardon and in mercy
> May thy portion be peace

May thy rest be with Him this day in Paradise
Depart, O Christian soul, out of this world.

In rural Ireland custom prescribes that death belongs not to the family but to the community and that's how it was with us and our father. More than ever, as soon as he died, it was for us to surrender him to the care of our neighbours. Even Brenda who had looked after him for the past five years, her only role was to tell what our wishes were, that he would be waked that night in the house, that he would be taken to church the following evening and, after eleven o'clock Mass on the day after that again, that he would be buried in Gale Cemetery. Our role from now on was to accept condolences and go along with everything as arranged.

It was just as well that I'd had time alone with him on the bus going home. From the moment I arrived at the gate I was to a large degree passive, carried along by a community being customary. That's how it was entering the house, in the house and leaving the house, entering the church, in the church, and leaving the church, entering the cemetery, in the cemetery and leaving the cemetery. In a sense I was congregationalized, the difference between a congregation and a group being that at the heart of the former, giving it its reason to be, is a sacred ritual. In easy surrender to it over the days and nights, it was a blessing, it was requiem. My father was waked well, we did well in bringing him before God in His holy house, and we buried him well beside Mary his wife in consecrated ground.

A week or so later, back now again in my house in Connemara, he came towards me in a dream. As though we had always known what we would do, he facing me from the hereafter, I facing him from the here-and-now, we sang *The Rose of Mooncoin* together ...

Flow on lovely river, flow gently along,
By your waters so sweet sounds the lark's merry song,
On your green banks I wander where first I did join,
With you lovely Molly, the Rose of Mooncoin.

It was the song he used to silence Brosnan's Pub in Moyvane with and now by the time we got to the third verse there was no dividing line, no difference between the here-and-now and the hereafter. Whatever their burden of sorrow and separation, our songs here are the songs of Paradise.

Therese O'Mahony who lives alone on Ceim Hill above Castletownshend in West Cork once said to me that the dead aren't even the width of a spider's web away from us.

To night in a dream there was no web, no veil.

Before he turned to go, Man Walking Behind Cows looked at me and said,
I will come back in a year's time and we will sing it again.

Twenty years later I am still waiting.

But then what, where he is, is a year to him? (*What the Curlew Said*, pp. 157–9)

'Walk on Jimmy, walk on. Let the darkness of God come upon you now. You've quenched your lantern, Jimmy, the lantern of your eyes and mind, let the darkness of God come upon you now.'[9]

It was around this time that he again consulted Fr. Norbert, with a view to joining the Carmelite community as a monk. Fr. Norbert said no, John's place was to continue giving talks for as long as the invitations kept coming and people were listening, because he said, they are not listening to people in religious life anymore. He accepted that advice and asked for a blessing from Fr. Norbert, this giving him some sense of legitimacy in what he was doing. In the course of the of the following years he would weave stories about Jimmy's death into his talks; he would weave the very fabric of his own life into them, small and apparently incon-sequential events would introduce profound themes. Little Sara crossing the yard, wearing only one red shoe, and interrupting Nina, the Palomino mare at her feed of oats, would begin a story that led into a vision of hope for the world. He dared to believe that, in spite of our most un-Sapient 'hatchet-job' past, that *homo sapiens* might still be alternative to who and what we have been. This became his mission; to influence a culture, to expose the destructive mind-set at the heart of it, and to indicate a healing process. No small task and an enormous drain on his energy but he was driven by a sense of urgency; the 'doom of our white day'[10] that might yet be averted 'if only' people would listen. He had become, as he said, addicted to saving the planet. The urgency was intensified as he watched Sara grow. Looking at her he 'knew that we could be a significant species', but given our history as 'dragon slayers and pestilence bringers'[11] he worried about how she would fare in the modern world.

Very soon there was a second pressing reason for concern. In February 1985 Sara's sister, Lorna, was born and again John felt the fiercely protective instinct that is awakened by new life. Again the concern for the unsignposted road that lay ahead of her and the mystery of the road that she had already come.

I thought of Martin Halloran and myself walking home from Ballynahinch one night. I, the sober one, was all signposts that night. Having listened to me, Martin continued to look drunkenly into the dark and, still seeing nothing, called out, "Are you there, John? Are you there, John? Oh sure I know well

phere we're now, John! I know well phere we're now, John! But phere the fuck
are we?"

I don't know, Lorna. I don't know. But here you are to night with us in this
grand old house under Derrada Hill, beside the Owenmore River, in the parish
of Roundstone, in Co. Galway. Tomorrow I'll take you out and I'll show you
the yard and the garden and the river, and that marmalade cat, that one there,
he's called Tiger, and this other one, this fluffy black one, he's called Stomper,
and when Lynne puts them out at night they come over to me. And I who am
holding you, I am your Navajo Grandfather and right here in my chest I am a
Navajo cradle board for you:

> I have made a cradleboard for you,
> my child,
> May you grow to a great old age
> Of the sun's rays I made the back
> Of black clouds I have made the blanket
> Of rainbow I have made the side loops
> Of lightnings I have made the lacings
> Of river mirrorings I have made the footboard
> Of dawn I have made the covering
> Of light and high horizons and

Of Earth's welcome for you I have made the bed. (*What the Curlew Said*,
pp. 144–5)

This cradle, he said, suggests an affinity with nature, a trust in nature. 'It seems to
me, this is the cradle that we all need. No matter what age we are, young or old,
male or female, it is a cradle we should all be willing to lie down into. We would be
lying down into great creative nature, lying down into the genius of the universe. In
this cradle of light and high horizons we could receive and experience ecological
second birth.'[12] To have Lorna live in a world that offered welcome and integration of that sort, that would indeed be 'Paradise regained'. On her behalf he must
continue the battle for an alternative way of being in the world.

His house-building was also continuing, slowly but hopefully, as was his hope
for a future with Eileen. Loving Sara and Lorna as he did made him ache to be
a husband and father and yet he knew that the life he lived would not allow it;
in spite of his 'adopted' family in Connemara, his extended family in Moyvane
and many friends, at his heart's core it was a lonely and a difficult life that he had
chosen. But it was also rich and eventful and anything might happen, as he would
so often say 'we live, after all, in a world of miracles'. By 1988 he had moved into
his new house just sixty or so yards up the road from his cottage.

That I had a dry bed to get into at night and that I had dry clothes to get into in the morning and that I wasn't constantly breathing mould spores, all this was welcome. And my neighbours were glad to see a new light brightening the darkness of winter. (*What the Curlew Said*, p. 165)

Shortly after the move, completely out of the blue, he received a letter from Brian McKinnon, one of his former students in Canada. A number of them had founded a 'John Moriarty Society', they had raised some money and they wanted him to come and give some lectures in Winnipeg. John accepted but he had more than lectures in mind, and probably far more than the Canadians had bargained for.

Ever since I had read a book called *Black Elk Speaks*, I had thought of going back to North America, specifically to the Tongue River in Montana, there in the hope that I might persuade Native Americans to re-enact the world-redeeming drama in which, as a boy of nine, Black Elk had a decisive role. (*What the Curlew Said*, p. 165)

No doubt this plan to re-enact Black Elk's 'world-redeeming drama' did sound like madness to his Canadian friends, but for John, Black Elk was of enormous significance. As Black Elk begins the story of his life he insists that it is not the events of his own life that are important, 'for what is one man that he should make much of his winters?' Yes, he will tell of these things but only 'by the way', for he has a much bigger story:

It is the story of all life that is holy and good to tell, and of us two-leggeds sharing it with the four-leggeds and the wings of the air and all green things; for these are children of one mother and their father is one Spirit ...
    Now that I can see it all as from a lonely hilltop, I know it was the story of a mighty vision given to a man too weak to use it; of a holy tree that should have flourished in a people's heart with flowers and singing birds, and now is withered; and of a people's dream that died in bloody snow.[13]

At the age of nine Black Elk was granted his 'mighty vision', a vision of how to save his people, the Native American Lakota Sioux. The young boy was extremely ill and the vision could of course be dismissed as hallucination but it was so extraordinarily vivid and coherent that initially it frightened the young boy into silence. In his dream-vision Black Elk, led by magnificent horses which had come from 'the four quarters of the world', is taken to meet the Grandfathers. Black Elk intuited that these Grandfathers were not old men but the Powers of the World and as the dream progresses they give him gifts – a wooden cup 'full of water and in the water was the sky', it was the power to make live; a peace pipe with which 'you shall walk upon the earth and whatever sickens there you shall make well', the power to heal; a bow and arrow which granted him 'the power to destroy' that which would harm his people; and 'a bright red stick that was alive and as I looked it sprouted at the top and sent forth branches and on the branches many leaves came out and murmured and in the leaves the birds began to sing. And then for just a little while I thought I saw beneath it, in the shade, the circled villages of people and every living thing with roots or legs or wings and all were happy.' The bright red stick was the 'power to grow' and Black Elk was told that he must 'make it blossom'.

In this dream John saw that Black Elk was given the gifts needed to redeem the Earth, to release the creative energies that existed before 'we misappropriated and polluted and poisoned life at its source.'[14] That is how John interpreted the task imposed on Black Elk, he had been chosen by the Grandfathers as a redeemer of his people and was shown the ritual he must perform in order to save them. Black Elk was extremely troubled:

> I wondered if maybe I was only crazy, and my father and mother worried a great deal about me ...
>
> When the grasses were beginning to show their tender faces again, my father and mother asked an old medicine man by the name of Black Road to come over and see what he could do for me. Black Road was in a tepee all alone with me and he asked me to tell him if I had seen something that troubled me. By now I was so afraid of being afraid of everything that I told him about my vision and when I was through he looked at me and said, 'Ah-h-h!', meaning that he was much surprised. Then he said to me, 'I know now what the trouble is! You must do what the bay horse in your vision wanted you to do. You must do your duty and perform this vision for your people upon earth. You must have the horse dance first for your people to see. Then the fear will leave you, but if you do not do this, something very bad will happen to you.[15]

Black Elk did eventually organise the Horse Dance portion of this 'saving ceremony' but from the point of view of Native Americans their world, their Earth, was already doomed, they in themselves were powerless to re-energise it, and just as the Ghost Dance years later would fail, so too did their Horse Dance. However, John Moriarty recognised within it a reverence toward the earth and all its creatures; a belief in the creative, mysterious powers that suffuse it; and also the prospect of redemption for a planet that has become a 'wasteland'. Black Elk, a shaman of the Lakota Sioux, was according to John, 'perhaps our greatest holy man since Christ.'[16] Both were pioneers of inclusion and integration, both were potential saviours.

> Astonishingly, Black Elk became a Roman Catholic Christian. In fact, there is a photograph of him, he a Pleistocene thunder dreamer, with a rosary beads in his hands. I think of him as a new kind of Christian. A Christian who, as his name suggests, is ecumenical with elk, that meaning all animals, living and extinct. A Christian who is ecumenical with lightning. A Christian who, before he converted to Christianity, concluded the rituals he performed with the words *mitakuye oyasin*, meaning all my relatives, in other words, everything that exists, and it might well be that a ritual is effective only when it is panecumenical, only when it is in and from and with and through all things. (*What the Curlew Said*, pp. 193–4)

Mitakuye oyasin, all my relatives, words that resonated so powerfully with John that in re-imagining Jesus at the floor of the Karmic Canyon, drinking from the mirroring rockpool, these are the words he will have spoken. With all of this in mind, sustained by his defiant optimism and no doubt exasperating naivety, he did persuade David James to drive him to the Tongue River. This was the same man with whom he had seventeen years previously shared a horse-blanket in the Grand Canyon so perhaps David knew what he was in for. It was a pilgrimage and it had its difficulties but on reaching the river he did succeed in enacting a private ceremony, although not on the scale he had hoped. However, as he had always had faith in gesture, and a belief in the power of imaginative re-enactment, he was satisfied with the attempt.

> It delighted me to touch the Tongue River.
> It delighted me to pick a pebble from its bed and hold it.
> It delighted me to see the footprints of wild geese on its mudflats.
> It delighted me to cross barefoot to an island in the Tongue.
> It delighted me to think that the Horse Dance might have been per-
>   formed here on this unfenced level land in front of me.
> Coming back off the island, I went to stand there, just in case.
> Could it be that it was here somewhere that he planted the flowering
>   stick? ...
> I stood there and imagined it, picturing it as well as I could remember.
> (*What the Curlew Said*, p. 204)

He had honoured and re-energised the vision. That would have to be enough. They returned to Winnipeg and to a party being held in his honour. Invited were a number of Native Americans whom he had met at lectures in the previous weeks. One of them, a Cree Indian, asked to speak privately with him. In an otherwise empty room the Indian welcomed him to Native America and eventually, having held his gaze for what seemed like an inordinately long time, presented him with a single eagle's feather saying that he trusted him, he trusted that John was the kind of man who would honour it. From his reading of *Black Elk Speaks* John knew the significance of the feather. "This means Wakon Tonka (the Great Mysterious One) and it also means that our thoughts should rise high as the eagles do."[17] It was with a sense of great privilege that he accepted it; seventeen years previously he had failed in an attempt to engage with a Native American boatman, whose indifference he sensed as an effort to drive the Paleface back off the continent; this gift gave him the sense that he was now 'unplundering, untrespassing', and validated him in his appropriation of the native stories that he told and in his attempt to walk in the footsteps of Black Elk. Years later it also allowed him to use Black Elk's words to conclude *Nostos*. *Mitakuye oyassin* – all my relatives; another way of saying 'we-feeling'.

18

'EVEN WHERE IT IS FRIGHTFUL ... NATURE IS ALSO IMMACULATE'

Buddh Gaia; a modern childhood; Happy Christmas Satan; a transcendent Mary; Dreamtime; return to Kerry; Turtle was Gone a Long Time; seal's breathing holes; the Blackbird and the Bell; scientific fundamentalism.

The journey to the Tongue River had been an attempt to walk in the footsteps of Black Elk – he had genuinely hoped to organize a ritual re-enactment of the Horse Dance. Quite predictably he had not succeeded in that but nonetheless he returned from Canada with renewed conviction and optimism. 'Christianity', he argued, 'needs to go bush.' The new Christianity would have to be 'Native American Christianity', with the powerful imagery of Jesus descending the Grand Canyon, accepting the entire evolutionary past of humanity, recognising brotherhood and genetic inheritance with the 'four-leggeds and the wings of the air and all green things', and thereby initiating world-healing. He was convinced that a culture, actively dedicated to Canyon Christianity and to the 'panecumenical' vision of Black Elk, would be a healing and sheltering culture. It could lead to a 'New Jerusalem', a Jerusalem that would be 'the earth itself newly named, named Buddh Gaia,'[1] an Earth that would be both enlightened and divine. A vision of ourselves as enlightened beings living on a planet called Buddh Gaia, this he put forward as 'final destination' for humanity; the alternative is that 'we go on wrecking our planet.' Of one thing he was certain, 'Where there is no vision the people perish.'[2] Could he re-energise the Christian vision?

His return to Connemara meant a return to what had almost become a regular life. He was settled in his new house, he was writing, still traversing the country giving talks, finding company among neighbours and friends and taking to heart his role as godfather to both Sara and Lorna. This was his social world, but his

return was also a return to the world of Lisnabrucka and Leitirdyfe, where he
spent days every week working by himself, time when he could be immersed in
the 'paradise' that he now saw everywhere. Any morning in Connemara was 'an
immaculate morning'; so perfect was the river as he cycled past that 'a scientist who
said merely scientifically true things about it would be sinning against it.'[3]

> A bright day, today was a silver branch day in Connemara. But even if it was the
> greyest of days that still is what it would be, a silver branch day.
>   It was a joy to me and an anguish to me that silver branch perception was so
> fully and so finally established in me. (*What the Curlew Said*, p. 213)

What he saw all around him now was the hosanna, the sanctus, at the heart of
the atom, and he was able to say that 'even where it is frightful ... Nature is also
immaculate'

> It was immaculate this morning as I cycled up along the river to work.
>   It was immaculate all day in the wood I worked in.
>   As I returned at day's end with the tools, it was immaculate in the instincts
> and eyes, in the beaks and claws, of two fiercely fighting cock robins. (*What
> the Curlew Said*, p. 215)

And yet ever present was the 'anguish' at what is being done to this paradisal world.
Anguish that we look at the world in all its wonder and mystery and only see 'as
yet undiscovered facts'; anguish 'that we have reduced our originally stupendous
planet to economic size.'[4]

> But what about the hard bondage we have laid upon things, upon rivers, upon
> stones? The hard bondage of how oppressively we perceive them.
>   Every Connemara bush is a burning bush, burning with green fire in spring
> and with red fire in autumn ...
>   When we look at a tree and we see only timber we are subjecting it to the
> hard bondage of that perception. When we look at a cow and we see only milk
> and meat we are subjecting her to the hard bondage of that perception. When
> we look at ourselves and we see only workforce we are incarcerating ourselves
> in the hard bondage of that perception. (*What the Curlew Said*, p. 214)

To cleanse the modern world of 'utilitarian' perception, of 'biblical' perception, of 'scientific' perception, that would be to open the gate to the ever-present
Paradise of silver-branch perception, this was his mission and the burden of it was

both his hope and his despair. 'The pity of it, I thought. Our minds elsewhere, on other goals, we are forever driving past our paradisal lives.'[5] This was the message that he took from venue to venue during the coming years; this difficult journeying was his personal Horse Dance for the planet. The remedy for the ecological deadliness and spiritual atrophy that he saw everywhere he summarised as: 'Silver branch perception, the Orphic note and the path that Jesus pioneered.'[6] Silver branch perception is the mystical recognition of the hosanna at the heart of the atom; to live by the Orphic note is to live in harmony with the way of the world – to go as 'the reed in the river', to live without the sword; and to walk the path that Jesus pioneered is to face the 'the lobster pot' of animal nature and behaviour, to eat 'the bitter herbs' of the past, both personal and historical, and from there to learn to behave with compassion towards every living thing.

It was challenging and radical. Certainly in re-imagining Christianity he was straying very far from theological correctness; but then an academic theology that insisted on particular dogmas he saw as a major impediment to spiritual enlightenment. As he would say time and again, he was far more concerned with what Jesus did than with who he was.

> In my own eyes I am a Christian not because I believe that Jesus of Nazareth was true God and true man or that he was born of a virgin but because I seek, with God's help, to walk the path he pioneered. If it was shown to me for sure that Jesus was true God and true man, I'd say fine, I am happy to cross the Torrent with him. If it was shown to me for sure that he was but man, I'd say fine, I am happy, I am undoubtingly happy, to cross the Torrent with him.
>
> There is no adventure so great as crossing the Torrent with Jesus. (*What the Curlew Said*, p. 142)

'Crossing the torrent' is the Gethsemane journey to the Grand Canyon, it is the 'lobster pot' and 'bitter herbs' journey, it is the 'dark night of the soul' journey and it is the 'movement essential' human journey if there is to be any hope for the planet. It can be made with or without recourse to dogma; the Jesus that John talks about transcends 'all dead metaphors', transcends his biblical identity, is forever growing, and cannot be 'fenced in' by any one creed. In a conversation one evening with Kathleen McCahill, it being Shrove Tuesday and John happy to eat pancakes with the family, she began teasing him. What, she demanded, was he going to do for Lent? He hedged but she was undeterred. What would he be 'fasting from'? Finally she got her answer. He would be fasting from Christian doctrine! Or maybe re-inventing it, but that bit was left unsaid.

He might have been 'fasting from Christian doctrine' but he was undoubtedly

spreading a Christian message, a new Christianity that could incorporate stories
and mystical insights from all traditions, a Christianity that was open to and that
encouraged challenge and debate. It was inspiring and original and it found ready
and receptive audiences. He spoke to packed halls in pastoral centres, schools, community centres, convents; he spoke at retreats, at teacher conferences, at summer
schools, at literary gatherings. His friend, the poet and dramatist Aidan Matthews,
once described him as the 'Bishop of the Margins' and while that would have given
him a good laugh there is no doubt that his message resonated with many who were
disillusioned, questioning or looking for guidance, both within and without the
traditional church. What these audiences found in him was a 'bishop' with a great
sense of humour, an inspiring presence and his feet firmly grounded in the earth, who
regularly recommended that they take their own 'karmic digging fork' and set to work
on the personal journey to enlightenment, where Black Elk, the Buddha, Lao Tsu and
Jesus could all provide direction on 'the journey home to the great and sacred earth'.

During these years, the late eighties and early nineties, his personal life was
reasonably stable. He had a steady income from gardening and while he never
charged for the talks he did receive donations, at the discretion of those who invited
him, to cover his costs. Intermittently, since his house had been built, he had been
seeing Eileen and had finally asked her to marry him. Quickly 'it became clear that
it wasn't going to happen'. Within weeks of proposing to her he told her that he
needed to retire for a few months to a monastery in Greece! He knew it; he was
fooling himself, 'not about her, about me.'[7] In spite of the heartache involved he
knew that he could not marry. The life he had chosen (or that had chosen him)
could not accommodate the demands either of intimate relationship or 'normal'
social life – this appears as a persistent difficulty of the spiritual journey and is
possibly the primary rationale for monasticism, asceticism and celibacy. It is certainly the price that has to be paid by anyone who is a pioneer of this journey, in
particular for anyone who attempts it outside the protection of such shelter as that
provided by church or monastery. There were, however, compensations.

> In the best sense of the word, I lived in a neighbourhood. The challenge, even
> when there were serious disagreements and suspicions between us, was to
> continue to be neighbours. Essential to my sense of myself was that I was a
> neighbour, and mostly it worked. I would cut and save his turf for Martin
> Halloran and on a January evening, freewheeling down Arkeny Hill, I would
> look across the bog and there it would be, smoke rising from my chimney ...
> Leaving the key in my door was decisive in how I lived. (*What the Curlew Said*,
> p. 224)

The closest neighbours were of course Lynne, Simon, Sara and Lorna and it was a never-ending joy to him to be part of the lives of the two children. He would regularly babysit them and as they got older the ritual of 'making tea for John' would be followed by a game and 'always in the end a video, *Dumbo* or *The Jungle Book* or *My Little Pony* or *Care Bears* or *The Muppets*, and ... it gave them the deepest pleasure to continue explaining everything to me, and there I was, with my best friends in all world having a more modern childhood than the one I'd had.' And then to bed and a bedtime story, this time it was his turn to do the entertaining, and both would be enthralled.

> An hour or so later I'd go up to see that they were alright and I'd look at them sleeping and I'd wonder, where are they now? In their dreaming where are they? And one night I knew I could murder. I'd murder to protect them. And coming down the stairs, in a twist of it, I asked myself, how do people have the nerve to become parents and, having become parents, how do they endure it. I imagined it. If Sara and Lorna were in trouble on the far side of Derrada Hill and I couldn't get up over it I'd eat my way through the half mile of rock, schist or gneiss, to get to them. A Maam Valley of care had opened inwardly into my chest and for the first time in my life I knew that, in spite of an almost instinctive recoil from violence, I could be violent, and savage, beyond measure. And for the sake of these two children alone, I'd change the world in ways unthought of by Isaiah and Rousseau. (*What the Curlew Said*, p. 218)

He was part of a family and there were even occasional outings. One such was a train trip to Dublin six days before Christmas to see the lights and experience the excitement; their friend Mary Margaret Conneely was invited along as well and the three girls were thrilled beyond measure waving goodbye to Lynne at the station in Galway. They stayed with John's friend Marie Hughes who provided not only lavish entertainment but directed the itinerary: Grafton Street alive with Christmas lights and carol singers; a pantomime at the Lambert Puppet theatre; the Zoo; a Christmas film in the cinema; attraction after attraction until they were all exhausted. The children's excitement was infectious but it wasn't only because he was with the girls that he was having a happy Christmas.

Just as he had done with the Easter story, he was interrogating the Christmas story, imagining how it might be incorporated into the modern spiritual journey. A visit to the Christmas crib in the Dominican Priory had opened the door. This was no simple crib. It turned out to be a long succession of scenes, continuous across three rooms, each room enacting a wonder of Nature or of history, and as he walked, looking at depictions of a hen laying an egg or a cow giving suck to her calf, he was struck by the enormous significance of the birth in a stable. The importance here was not a virgin birth, an immaculate conception or a god made man, instead this 'coming down' could symbolise the birth of godliness, godliness among animals and shepherds, godliness existing at a primal level, symbolised by a child lying on straw. The child is a metaphor for the purity at the heart of all life, the hosanna at the heart of the atom, born and reborn with each new life, requiring recognition and a sheltering culture in which to flourish. Later in the evening, walking along Grafton Street with the girls, noticing the lights, 'and at the heart of every row, dipping down towards us, the star that stood still above the stable, above God coming to birth in ourselves maybe.'

> For all of us who had ears to hear, Grafton Street tonight was a Nativity Play, and whatever our role in it was, herald angel, ox, ass, Mary, Joseph, Shepherd, Orient King, could it be, I wondered, that our real role was to undergo a Nativity, each of us coming from a far-off, foreign country to see ourselves lying on a bed of straw at the core of our being?
>
> Tonight with the girls on Grafton Street I dared to believe it. I dared to believe that it is also about ourselves we are singing when we sing *Silent Night*:
> Silent night, holy night,
> All is calm, all is bright,
> Round yon Virgin, Mother and Child,
> Holy Infant, so tender and mild,
> Sleep in heavenly peace, sleep in heavenly peace.
> How far off, how long a journey by camel, are we from the Divine Ground of our being? (*What the Curlew Said*, pp. 228–9)

'God coming to birth in ourselves' this might be the true message of Christmas, and the challenge may be to undergo 'our journey, as Magi, to who we are at the core of our being.'

Within this Nativity Play is also the figure of Mary and in her story must be recognised aspects of ancient mythical traditions, in particular the motif of the virgin birth and the mythology of the mother of the dead and resurrected god, which if read as historical fact must give rise to enormous modern scepticism. However if read as symbol, which is the proper function of all myth, then just as the Christ child becomes a powerful symbol for the awakening of soul so Mary can become an equally powerful symbol for the flowering of that soul. According to Alan Watts "when myth is confused with history, it ceases to apply to man's inner life ... the tragedy of Christian history is that it is a consistent failure to draw the life from the Christian myth and unlock its wisdom."[8] John's attempt to re-interpret

the Christmas and Easter stories was an effort on his part to release at least some
of that wisdom. And so Mary can become a symbol for the perfected inner life,
'immaculate', 'full of grace' and 'blessed'; she is the lotus flower, she is the soul that
has come through all of its incarnations, through Gethsemane, through Golgotha,
she is that to which the soul aspires.

> I greeted her not as a unique but as a fully democratic possibility, thinking that
> everyone can in time be lotus-born, that everyone can in time be jewel-born,
> thinking that in time everyone can be, and will be, crowned in heaven. (*What
> the Curlew Said*, p. 82)

Again the 'crowning in heaven' is not literal; but it provides an image for a gloriously transcendent state, a state that is possible for every soul that sets out upon
the journey. With that interpretation in mind, it is possible to pray the Rosary; to
celebrate Christmas; to celebrate Easter; to re-imagine heaven; finally to emerge as
'butterfly', as 'lotus-born' on an enlightened planet newly named Buddh Gaia. 'That
surely', he said, 'is good reason to rejoice in the dead of winter.'[9] This transcendent
Mary, the Mary of the Book of Revelations, 'a woman clothed with the sun, and
the moon under her feet, and upon her head a crown of twelve stars ...,' would
replace the image of Mary with her foot on the head of the serpent, crushing it.
Instead the serpent would be included, he also pure at the core of his being. And
so, walking along Grafton Street with his three friends on this particular Christmas,
in his heart he sang, with all the choirs of angels he sang, 'Happy Christmas Satan'.
Nothing not saveable.[10]

This was his optimistic vision for the potential of the human spirit. Could this
vision provide a second chance for humanity? By following the 'path that Jesus
pioneered' into all that is terrible and terrifying, into everything that has become
'satanic', could it be possible 'to turn all cultures founded on a demiurgic hatchet
job around'? In *Moby Dick* Herman Melville had offered no hope. 'The drama's
done', it is all over for human beings if not for the planet. The chilling image of
the Mincer on the deck of the Pequod is Melville's requiem for humanity. John
Moriarty in re-imagining Christianity, dared to say, 'A new drama has begun.'
Working within the 'sheltering mythology' of this new Christianity, human beings
might eventually provide a sheltering world for the Jamaican girl and her baby, for
Sara, for Lorna and for Mary Margaret Conneely on their journey into the future.

> It was, I knew, a strange thing I was doing, asking people to jump ship and fall
> in with Jesus in the Canyon.
> What is sure is this: if we are to emerge as an astronomically, as distinct

from a locally, significant species, we have Canyon work to do. (*What the Curlew Said*, p. 246)

'Canyon work' must involve acknowledgement of how, as a species 'we so utterly and perversely violated the generative and regenerative power of Nature ... with Waste Land consequences both natural and cultural ...' He believed that, enormous as the task might be, an alternative culture is possible, his own part in it to continue to tell the newly imagined Christian story and to keep faith with the vision of 'silver branch perception' and with the possiblity of human beings who will be 'Buddh Gaian' in behaviour. But it was not only the Christian story that needed to be retold. Modern culture, 'tabloid' culture, had to be challenged and healed and this might lead to history itself being healed, if only it could be healed in its cultural roots. He was thinking in particular now of Irish history.

> Think about how troubled Ireland's history is – fighting, fighting fighting – every people that came ashore fighting the people who were previously ashore and it has been war and rumours of war ever since and I was wondering how would you heal Irish history, how would you heal Ireland, how would you unite Ireland and I asked myself do we in Ireland have a dreaming, a dreamtime,[11] and I find that we have. We have the old myths and the old legends and the old stories and I went back down to those old stories, stories that have run simul-taneously with the history, stories about Cú Chulainn, about Crom Dubh, Cúroí Mac Daire, the Paps of Danu, and I went back down into that old folk world and I wrote there ... I said if we could be united in our dreamtime, in our dreaming, then we can be socio-politically united. ... So, the first thing to do, as distinct from John Hume saying 'let's draw a line under history', I say, let's go below our troubled history altogether down into our dreamtime and see if we can be united there.[12]

For a task of that enormity talks alone would not be enough. Every evening after work in his 'gardens' he would write his re-imagined 'dreamtime' stories, finding a way of looking at them and interpreting them that invests them with a wisdom as rich and as subtle as the stories themselves. These stories became the scripts for a series of talks that he gave in All Hallows in March 1992 where he invited audiences to go 'walkabout' with him in Ireland's Dreamtime. A short time later a chance encounter with Antony Farrell of The Lilliput Press led to the publication of these pieces naturally entitled *Dreamtime*, which was launched by the then Minister for Arts, Culture and the Gaeltacht, Michael D. Higgins, at Clifden Arts Week in September 1994. Critically the book was very well received.

Fintan O'Toole commended it as a 'personal vision of a world alive to spirituality ... an enthralling reminder that religion is supposed to be about openness, daring and humility' and it was also hailed as 'one of the most extraordinary books ever published in Ireland.'[13] High praise indeed, and yet for a wider audience it proved difficult.

> Kathleen McCahill and Mary Keaney ran into each other in Ballynahinch the next day. Mary was in a right fix. "Thinking it was going to be about gardening or something", she said, "I sat down to read John's book last night, but what is it about, Kathleen? And what in God's name am I going to say to him when I meet him? Not a word of it ever did I understand!"
>
> And so it turned out. Even people who understood me when I talked gave up on it. Nothing came up off the page to them. So as not to embarrass people therefore, I rarely mentioned it to them, but, popularity or applause not my purpose, I kept going. (*What the Curlew Said*, p. 267)

Mary Keaney was right, *Dreamtime* is a difficult and challenging read but it is not obscure. Just as John's vision aims at new way of 'seeing' and a 'a new intelligence' so his writing requires a new way of reading. It could perhaps be described as 'vision literature' or 'prose poetry', where myths and origin stories not only from Ireland but from all of the world's cultures are enlisted in order to heal history, to open the 'wonder-eye in you' and so keep 'the human spirit from disintegration'.[14] The book is not sequential nor does it offer logical argument, and yet it references Descartes, Nietzsche, Freud, Einstein, Newton and puts a convincing case for the need to look beyond these great minds in order to 'bring newness of life to our Waste Land'.[15] Reading it one must learn a new vocabulary of rich imagery and in so doing one will walk imaginatively with Pwyll, Prince of Dyfed, with Ollamh Fódhla, with Conaire Mór, with St Patrick and with Oisín, with Sir Gawain and the Green Knight, with Greek gods and goddesses as well as with the Greek philosophers. Ultimately one will come to rest with the mystics, with the Buddha, with Lao Tsu, Black Elk and Jesus and with the Inuit shaman who, in an igloo in the Arctic, could speak the amazing words *sila ersinarsinivdluge*, do not be afraid of the universe. *Dreamtime* 'is a battle against the evil eye, against the *súil mildagac,* in us all ... the eye that commodifies everything, that looks at a cow and sees gallons of milk, that looks at a tree and sees cubic feet of timber' and it is 'a quest for a greater vision of the world we already live in.'[16] Undoubtedly, with all of its references and cross-references it is challenging, but there are numerous times when, to borrow an image from a writer on William Blake, 'a paragraph or even a single line will flash and strike like a lightning bolt, illuminating an entire landscape'[17] and the effort will have been repaid a hundred-fold. Twenty three years later the book is still in print and its readership is still learning.

However, while all of this was happening, life was unravelling on another front.

> Over the years in Connemara I found that as much as I needed air I needed silence and solitude and, in this regard, things had worked out well for me. Until recently. After years of lying empty and idle Maamo's Pub, which was just up the road from me, had been bought and reopened and people were coming here now from twenty to thirty miles away in all directions. Coming home from work, whether from Lisnabrucka or Leitirdyfe, I'd see signs saying, Music Tonight, and for me that meant, no sleep tonight. Three nights a week no sleep at all, other nights none till near dawn. Since I didn't wish to be a spoil-sport, there was nothing I could do about it. Given my needs, my house was a write-off. (*What the Curlew Said*, p. 239)

There was nothing for it but to sell. With the help of neighbours he located and bought another site that would offer the seclusion he needed. Planning permission secured 'I went up one day to plant some bulbs around the place. All day long I heard loud drilling noise and when I made enquiries I was told that a quarry, long since idle, had been reopened across the way. It was going to be a big operation.' He was caught. There was no way he could continue to develop the site and so he sold again. Interestingly, and ironically given his complete lack of interest in financial security, in each transaction he made a profit. Naturally this left him vulnerable to those neighbours who were annoyed with him because of the environmentalist campaigns he had been involved in. Now they had him where they wanted him and they didn't spare him – he was 'a land speculator' who came to Connemara with nothing, and look at him now! In spite of the fact that it had all happened as a sequence of reactions and not by design, this did not let him off the hook. 'If someone called me a fraud there was little I could do but agree.' He berated himself, 'why did I not become a world-renouncer in my everyday way of life as well as in insight? Why, myself unworldly, had I not walked out into unworldliness?'[18] But perhaps he had, nothing of what was happening had been either anticipated or planned, and he had no choice but to respond.

Even after he had paid Micheál McCahill for his original site he still had a substantial profit. He also had a substantial problem. What to do? Recently there had been trips to Kerry to give talks, he had relatives and friends there already and now a new circle was developing. Equally, he was formulating a new project, the possibility of a mystical hedge school, and his belief was that Kerry rather than Connemara was the more natural home for any such venture. With reluctance, but with a feeling that it was again time for change, he began to look for a site in his home county. He wanted seclusion and he wanted mountains and rivers and lakes, and with the help of friends, in particular Father Pat Moore, he settled on a site in a place called 'Coolies', at the foot of Mangerton mountain near Killarney, a place he described as 'heartbreakingly beautiful'. This time he would build a three-bedroom house, and in spite of reservations about 'wrapping twenty-three thousand pounds worth of the world's scarce resources around my own four bones' he justified it in terms of the possibility that it might eventually become the hedge school he envisaged. While the house in Kerry was being built he remained in Connemara, living during the summer months in the basement of Lisnabrucka and during the winter months in a flat adjoining the big house in Leitirdyfe.

Invitations to give talks here and there throughout the country continued to come, but recently I had been backing off, telling people that I was played out, shagged. I sensed that the mysterious weakness that had flattened me some years ago was now again coming down over me and coming up over me. Then, before I had time to properly adjust to the idea, it was clear that my time in Connemara had come to an end. Seamus O'Brien, who had been building a house for me in Kerry, phoned to tell me that, while it wasn't finished, it was habitable. ... As it happened, Pat Crowley, a friend of mine from West Cork, had come to stay with me for a few days and so it was that, having packed some things in his van one morning, we were on the way south. (*What the Curlew Said*, p. 285)

This was 1995 and he was fifty seven. In spite of the fact that there had been quite a lengthy wait between the sale of his own house and the actual move to Kerry, he had not properly reckoned on the emotional upheaval it would entail. He had been very happy in Connemara and in the end, the move was abrupt. Suitable transport, in the shape of Pat Crowley's van, became available and so he took the opportunity. Given his exhausted state this was perhaps not the wisest move, but he had sourced a job as a gardener in the Lake Hotel in Killarney which could not be put on hold. The hotel, on the shore of Loch Leine, was within hilly cycling distance of his new house, and within a few days he had begun work. By the end of the first week he knew that he was in trouble. By midday on Friday he was in a state of near collapse and had to telephone Fr. Pat Moore for a lift home. The weakness was chronic. Diagnosed by one doctor as M.E. and another as 'burnout', this didn't particularly surprise him.

I worked in three big gardens-grounds and, in each of them each day, work had to be a big day's work. I gave talks and sequences of talks around the country and this meant that I had to keep coming up with new themes, new topics, some of them a real risk and difficult and burdensome to deal with in public. I'd sit and write almost every evening and that meant standing on dangerous ground or on no ground at all in one or another of the deep places within my own psyche, a common consequence being that I was often quite spooked as I climbed the stairs to bed. I spent more time than was good for me down among the sea floors of the Karmic Canyon. Every time I went back down I hoped it would be the last but it never was. So intense sometimes was the strain that I'd think, just as a lung can collapse so can my psyche. (*What the Curlew Said*, p. 285)

Fortunately it was not psychic collapse; as Jimmy had told him years previously, ''tis in you to have a strong mind' and this strength brought him through now, but it took patience to 'sit it out'. The newness of everything did not help, he was missing his Connemara 'family' but as usual he was fortunate in his neighbours, Maisie and Mikie Brosnan, 'not knowing what to make of me, but willing, with welcome in their eyes, to give me the benefit of the doubt.'[19] As ever he was susceptible to the 'yoga of horror'. His own inner immensities, his personal failings along with the universal human condition that he called 'deinanthropus',[20] was always a source of suffering for him and he was vulnerable again now. 'Some days I'd think I'm neither physically nor metaphysically able for this. All I could do was to surrender to God's safe keeping, to the safe keeping of God as unknowable, inexperiencable Divine Ungrund, Divine Mirum.'[21] This was his 'abyss of faith', his trust in the mystical vision of a deeper and more profound sense of purpose than he could fathom intellectually. It helped him to pull through.

In spite of the weakness he was able to write for a couple of hours every day and he had a task on hands. After the success of *Dreamtime* The Lilliput Press had undertaken to publish his trilogy *Turtle was Gone a Long Time* and he needed to provide a separate introduction for each of its three volumes. In those months of slow recovery he wrote the 'Overture' to the first volume. In it he states 'I know of no other than a religious response to the stupendous risk of being human.'[22] He again returns to one of his favourite sayings 'there is surely some spark of divinity in us' and claims that it is only by 'growing' this divine spark 'that there can be any hope of evolutionary improvement'. The 'growing' of this spark requires work, call it soul work, that demands space and time. Recognising that familiar rituals and practices have, for many people, lost their power, his book is a tapestry of myths, mandalas, memories, philosophical reflections, poems and stories, all of which he describes, with his usual originality and freshness as 'seal's breathing holes'. Seals, he explains, are great divers but they cannot remain underwater indefinitely, they must come up for air. With the coming in of winter in the Arctic the ice freezes over completely; seals have adapted to this by forcing holes in the ice and they must, by constant attention, keep these breathing holes open throughout the entire season, otherwise they will drown. Human beings, he argued, need to breathe not only physically, but transcendentally, they need to allow air to that 'spark of divinity' already almost completely smothered by the ice of rationality that allows 'nothing but' hard facts. His trilogy was an attempt to open, and keep open, some 'breathing holes' in secular culture.

Fr. Pat Moore recounts a visit to him during this time. 'He was sitting by the fire, and there were bundles of papers and books on the floor all around him. He looked thin and worn out and I wanted to know if he had eaten anything or if he had food in the house, but all he wanted to do was talk about seal's breathing holes and how we might provide them, and how as a priest I should be keeping them open, and did I think maybe the Christian sacraments were breathing holes in the ice and then, on top of that, did I think that *Turtle was Gone a Long Time* was a good name for a book ... honest to God between seals and turtles I thought that one of the two of us had finally lost it!' Pat would later come to appreciate the relevance of the seal image; it became a very powerful metaphor for John in the years ahead. The movement essential journey requires these 'breathing holes'; they can take any form once they involve time and meaningful ritual of some sort that will nourish soul. It could be a traditional ritual (or that ritual re-imagined) but equally it need only involve lighting a candle or looking at a tree or listening to a river once that is done with 'self' in abeyance; not projecting anything but simply allowing 'seeing', allowing 'hearing', recognising the 'wonder' of what is out there, and recognising also that 'tat tvam assi', that art thou. A passage from Socrates, which he quotes in *Turtle was Gone a Long Time*, throws some light on the urgent need for 'breathing holes'.

Now, when a man abandons himself to his desires and ambitions, indulging them incontinently, all his thoughts of necessity become mortal, and as a consequence he must become entirely mortal, because he has nourished his mortal part. When on the contrary he has earnestly cultivated his love of knowledge and true wisdom, when he has primarily exercised his faculty to think immortal and divine things, he will – since in that manner he is touching the truth – become immortal of necessity, as far as it is possible for human nature to participate in immortality. (*Turtle was Gone a Long Time*, vol. 3, p. xvi)

By now he had accepted that his gardening days were over, his doctor had warned him about the consequences of 'squandering' his health any further, and so he had decided to concentrate on his writing and follow wherever that would lead. He had written his first poem, *In Buddha's Footsteps*, when he was nineteen and had been writing regularly ever since, although as he told Maurice O'Keeffe, he never thought of himself as a writer. 'If you asked me to this day am I a writer, I'd say no ... First and foremost I'm a normal everyday human being, the fact that I do a bit of writin' doesn't mean to say that I'm a writer ... I did it because I needed to name myself ... I had to turn in to my own psyche and try to map it ... it was a need in me.' And in his writing he says 'it was as if I was in séance with somewhere very deep in myself, moods would come down on me and I'd write from there.' In a sense, he explained, 'the writing was incidental to the thinking. And it was such strange stuff that I was writing like, you couldn't imagine that anyone would ever want to publish it, but I had to write as I felt, as I thought, and if this is difficult, so be it like. Anyway the hope was that someone looking over my shoulder, there might be the odd person, who'd find what I was saying worthwhile. But I knew what I was writing was probably both unreadable and unpublishable.'[23]

As has been seen it was both publishable and readable, but undoubtedly difficult. The talks however were absolutely accessible and as popular as ever. As his health improved he responded to requests to give retreats and presentations in venues across the country and in late 1996 he recorded a series of six programmes for RTÉ, entitled *The Blackbird and the Bell*, where he was host to a panel of writers and musicians who offered 'talk, music and musings' which could lead absolutely anywhere. The title took its inspiration from the early Irish poem *Lon Doire an Chairn*, where Oisín urges St Patrick to listen to the song of the blackbird and Patrick argues the merits of the monastic bell; John argues for synthesis, a Christianity that incorporates the pagan worldview. True to form, in the very first programme he takes the war to fundamentalism of every kind claiming that 'there isn't only a biblical fundamentalism, there's a scientific fundamentalism,' and maintains that this is a greater threat to the world than fundamentalism of any other kind. It was a programme that interrogated modern 'truths' and made him a national name; it also brought him new friends and before long he had regular visits to his home at the foot of Mangerton from people who simply wanted to hear a bit more.

His door was always open and he had time for every caller. His only request was that no car would drive beyond 'the big gate' that led to the house. He had no radio, no television and very little in the way of modern conveniences; in order not to be a nuisance to his neighbours he did find it necessary to have a telephone but that was a reluctant concession, there was not even a typewriter. All his books were written in longhand, including what eventually became the seven hundred published pages of *Nostos*. His manuscripts, now in the safekeeping of Trinity College Dublin, are remarkable for their lack of revision, even if he did once admit to being addicted to Tippex; he would wake at around 5.00 am and before getting up would think through the structure of what he would write later in the morning. Themes, motifs and images would be ready before he put pen to paper. As he wrote, the beauty of the world outside his window could often overwhelm him, could confirm for him that 'reality as a whole is immaculate, is perfect, is pure', even if 'three stone-fenced fields away a fox is ravenously killing and devouring the still bald chicks', even if that is happening it does not take from the purity that everything is at the core of its being. The modern human condition is that of exile; 'exile from what we paradisally are.'[24] His writings are an attempt to provide signposts to guide us out of that exile and breathing holes to allow us into Divine Ground.

19

'AT THIS HOUR OF MY LIFE I'M A SINGING CHRISTIAN'

Nostos; a Christian monastic hedge-school; to welcome all the crooked world; Ephphatha; Tenebrae; cancer; Liveline; What the Curlew Said; a bird's nest; an honorary doctorate; a Chinese sage; at the core of my soul the Sanctus I am.

The third volume of *Turtle was Gone a Long Time* was eventually published in 1998 and it met with the same mixed reaction as previous publications. There was critical acclaim but there was also incomprehension from friends and family. These extraordinary volumes repay the attention that they demand but they do not easily surrender the riches they contain. A number of friends, anxious that his work would gain a wider readership, suggested that he write his autobiography, and while so doing explain his thinking in the context from which it emerged. He was reluctant, the vanity of putting himself on show bothered him, but the friends, in particular Dolores O'Connor and Tim Robinson, were persistent and eventually he acquiesced. He justified it in terms of what it might mean for other people, people who like him 'had been made to fall out of their stories ... In telling it maybe others would find something of their story in my story, in which case the effort wouldn't be as narcissistic as it might otherwise be.'[1] Hence *Nostos* which was published two and a half years later in 2001, but again there was the problem of accessibility for a general readership. It was hailed by Aidan Matthews as the greatest masterpiece since James Joyce's *Ulysses*[2] but again, the myths, the references, the eccentric word coinages, all such an integral part of his thought processes that there could be no thinking, no writing, without them, were for many readers simply baffling. There is no doubt that this bothered him, he joked about it and told entertaining stories about what people said, but there was a level at which it was a serious issue. His entire life had been devoted to finding 'a better way of being in the world', to finding 'a sheltering mythology', ultimately to providing a 'lifeboat' for modern culture which would enable humanity to flourish in a flourishing world ... what chance for any of that if people could not read his books?

In spite of this he continued to write, within the next four years completing another large volume called *Night Journey to Buddh Gaia*, which although completed in 2003 was not published until 2006, Lilliput Press rejecting it until then on the grounds that much of it was repetitive of what had appeared in the previous books. This aspect of his work he would vehemently defend.

> It isn't by trying them on once in a shop that a new pair of boots will take on the shape of your feet or the shape of your walking. Similarly, it isn't in a single encounter with it that an unfamiliar idea will take on the shape of our seeing and knowing. (*Turtle was Gone a Long Time*, vol. 2, p. xxi)

As he said in interview with Maurice O'Keeffe, "I've been dealing with the same few themes all my life", themes of such enormity that there had to be room for repetition; this would allow his readers, should there be any, to become comfortable and familiar with much that can seem very strange on a first encounter. In spite of the rejection, single-minded and undaunted as ever, he continued to write and in the intervening years between the completion of *Buddh Gaia* and its publication he wrote and published *Invoking Ireland* (2005) and *Slí na Fírinne* (2006). In all of his writing he saw himself 'leading a rebellion against established power'[3] the established power of the *súil mildagach*, the evil eye which 'is our collective eye' which has analysed and commodified and poisoned everything; it is the modern mind with which 'we've harpooned wonder, we've harpooned vision', the mind that has become 'the blind and not the window'. That was the power that had to be overthrown and in its place an enlightenment, this time not political, scientific or philosophical, not with a capital letter heralding the Age Of Reason, but a spiritual enlightenment, which would in turn influence politics, science and philosophy; a new, revolutionary and enlightened Christianity.

The 'rebellion' involves a journey, a journey that might begin in a Navajo cradle

> I have made a cradleboard for you,
> my child,
> May you grow to a great old age
> Of the sun's rays I made the back
> Of black clouds I have made the blanket
> Of rainbow I have made the side loops
> Of lightnings I have made the lacings

Of river mirrorings I have made the footboard
Of dawn I have made the covering
Of light and high horizons have I made the bed.

This is the song that a Navajo man will sing as he fashions a cradle for his newborn child; 'perhaps the journey that we now need to make is a journey to this Navajo cradle, a cradle that we might all lie down in and be born again in, nurtured and nourished by the sun's rays, by the lightnings and the rainbows, by the river mirrorings and the high horizons, by the sunbeams and the clouds... And so I say, God bless the First Peoples of the world. If we are willing to listen to them, then we might, listening to them, learn to stand and to walk beautifully on the earth, reborn into and from this Navajo cradle.'[4] And perhaps that is also how we will recover 'we-feeling', 'commonage consciousness', a realization that we share this earth with other animals; that the wound we have inflicted on them, so dramatically depicted in the cave in Lascaux, needs to be healed before any other world-healing can happen, that we need, not only to say Brother Sun and Sister Moon, but that we must say Brother to all the species with which we share the planet. Before it is too late we must light a candle in the cowstall for Christmas. Unless the rebellion leads us there the Waste Land continues.

That will not of course be the whole story. If we are not to dominate and destroy, how are we to behave on a properly 'ecumenical' earth? He had another song for his revolution, again one that came from the first peoples of the world, from Uvavnuk, his Inuit medicine woman.

The great sea has set me in motion,
Set me adrift,
Moving me as a weed moves in the river.
The arch of the sky and mightiness of storms
Have moved the spirit within me,
Till I am carried away,
Trembling with joy.

Years previously, on his sabbatical in France, he had imagined Mona Lisa as a little matchstick woman walking back into the mountains she had so long ignored and obscured, singing Uvavnuk's song, finding at last her proper place in the world. Naturally his fantasy had not stopped there. He imagined a symposium of all great teachers, philosophers and scientists, from our Hebrew, Greek and Roman past; he would call them all to a banquet and then initiate a great debate. The topic would be proposed by Uvavnuk, seconded by Lao Tze:

That the weed's way of being in the river
Should be our way of being in the world. (*Turtle was Gone a Long Time*,
vol. 1, p. 7)

The weed in the river has learned to 'rhyme with reality', to go with the way, the 'tao', of the world rather than working against it, to live in it as Mary Ann Danny O' learned to live in it, where the word *wind* rhymed with *mind,* as his mother had lived in it, where the hatching hen took precedence over the sound of hammer on anvil, as his father had lived in it, walking at the pace of his cows; to live in it by going the way of the dolphin rather than the way of Prometheus, to forego all 'hatchet jobs' and to 'ship oars'. Accommodation not domination; that is the way of Uvavnuk and that is the way of the Tao. So, before he builds a bridge the Taoist will ask what imbalance in the world that bridge will cause; before he defends himself he will seek to know if he has provoked attack, if he could have prevented strife. Going the way of the weed in the river the Taoist will firstly learn to know his own nature and then seek to align it with 'the genius of the universe', better to trust that in us 'than to trust our trivial daily minds.'[5]

However a Taoist Uvavnuk rocking the Navajo cradle, neither is that the whole story. The whole story must involve the tremendous power of the river in flood, the power that no weed can withstand or flow with, the destructive annihilating power of the universe, the 'lobster pot', the trout in the teeth of the otter, the apparent indifference of the universe, the capacity of human beings to inflict suffering and to suffer pain, the heartbreak at the heart of mortal life, the nothingness of 'the cold mad feary father', can Taoism properly equip one for that? That it cannot he had learned to his cost on a day above Lough Inagh when he was 'torpedoed' by the sight of 'the skinned foreleg of a lamb' on the bare bedrock of the river. And so his *Marseillaise* could not be complete without a third song, and it was a synthesis of many songs, of the Song of Songs, of *The Song of Wandering Aenghus*, of *Fern Hill*, of the blackbird, of St. Patrick and of all the mystics – the Sanctus, 'the holy, holy, holy', the song of angels, the song of the hosanna at the heart of the atom.

To put that mystical song at the heart of modern life, this was the aim of his rebellion; that achieved then the Cradle song and Uvavnuk's song would naturally follow. Taking the fight to modern secular culture with such an extraordinary and unfashionable message was no small task; talks to small groups, no matter how enthusiastic, were unlikely to have lasting effect; books that were all but inaccessible 'oddities'[6] would not fare much better. Painfully aware of this and yet passionately convinced of the validity and urgency of what he had to say, here in Killarney, contemplating 'the blue soul of Torc mountain' he was thinking about the mystical hedge school he had envisaged before he left Connemara. It was perhaps time to make it happen. He was motivated by a number of factors, but most particularly by the sense that in his one-man rebellion he was fighting a losing battle. He remembered something from D. H. Lawrence about Europe in the Dark Ages:

Then those whose souls were still alive withdrew together and gradually built monasteries ... little communities of quiet labour and courage, isolated, helpless, and yet never overcome in a world flooded with devastation, these alone kept the human spirit from disintegration ... like little arks floating and keeping the adventure afloat ... The adventure is gone out of Christianity. We must start on a new venture towards God.[7]

This resonated powerfully with him, he might provide an oasis to keep 'the human spirit from disintegration', his hedge school could become a monastery. However he took issue with Lawrence on one point, he was adamant that 'the adventure was not gone out of Christianity', but that it needed to be radically re-imagined. He decided that his hedge school would be Christian and monastic, a renewed rather than a new venture towards God. Naturally enough friends and acquaintances were sceptical, but the man who had attempted to re-enact the Horse Dance at the Tongue River was unlikely to see any problem with establishing a monastery on a mountain in Kerry. With the help of his friend Dolores O'Connor, after much searching, he sourced a site at Lomanaugh in the Slaheny Valley on the far side of Mangerton. As usual, he had nowhere near the price of the twenty three acres that he wanted to buy, personally he had only £3,000, but with that and 'with donations from friends and from religious orders', he managed to acquire the site. On the day he concluded the deal he realised that the dream was on its way to becoming a reality; it had now also become an obligation, not only to all who had donated but to the place itself. As well as being a Christian monastic hedge school, his centre in this 'tenderly beautiful' place would also be an ecological initiative. The plantings would all be of native species, the buildings would be small and dispersed, among which would be planted occluding shrubs and trees, the intention being that nothing built would be visible even from the summits of the surrounding hills.

It was obvious that before proceeding any further he would need a great deal more money. 'At this point however, instead of going back on the road to raise the funds with which to build it in bricks I decided it would be better to build it first in words. That way, having read the thing, people would know exactly what they were funding.'[8] First of all the groundplan, which he described as 'a slightly disguised mandala' or sacred circle with an oratory at the centre, encircled by eight outer buildings to include 'cells', a library/lecture hall, reception area and pavilion. For this he had already received planning permission. It would be called Slí na Fírinne, the way of truth, and it would provide a place where those who wished to devote their lives to a renewed Christian journey could live, work, learn and pray together. It would be primarily contemplative, opening its doors at the weekend for teaching purposes but enclosed for the weekdays; the work done there would be based on the craftsmanship of the early Irish monasteries, the making of beautiful things an essential part of what the whole thing is about.

> As its description suggests it will be Christian in intention ethos and practice. In the rhythm of its day it will be monastic. In thinking of it as a hedge school we have two things in mind: we will welcome people not of the community to participate with us in our rituals, one called Ephphatha and the other called Tenebrae and, formally in lectures open to the public, we will seek to be instructed by the great Christian mystics, that in the overall context of seeking to inherit and live by the wisdom of humanity, whatever its provenance.[9]

'The wisdom of humanity, whatever its provenance', seekers after truth from whatever tradition would be welcome; in this essentially Christian hedge school there is a place for Oisín and St. Patrick, for Uvavnuk and Black Elk, for Lao Tze and the Buddha; for ritual, for poetry, for song and for stories.

With John Moriarty there would always have to be stories, stories as extraordinary as the story of Pasiphae and the Minotaur or as ordinary as the story of the handyman Bill Joyce cutting lino in Ballinahinch Castle, or of John Welsh going to midnight Mass on Christmas Eve in Moyvane. He would weave together the mythical and the mundane – and in the stories of Bill Joyce and John Welsh he would provide the Ariadne's thread that might manage the Minotaur. It was part of the six-story Upanishad that he had written in Connemara – Bill was fitting new non-slip lino behind the bar counter at the Castle. It was a tedious and tricky job and, watching him, John became convinced that Bill was not doing it well. He did his best not to intervene, not to be 'his mother's son' but the impulse overcame him and he blurted it out, 'Is there any chance now Bill', he asked, 'that you're cutting that crooked?'

> Bill kept going, slowly working away as if nothing had happened. Then, slowly drawing out the knife, he sat back on his collops, looked up at me sideways over his shoulder and said, "This is a lovely old castle, John, it's a lovely old place, and in lovely old places like this the only good way to cut anything straight is to cut it crooked" (*Turtle was Gone a Long Time*, vol. 1, p. 190)

Later that evening, walking up Derrada Hill, still bemused by Bill's answer, he had looked around 'at all the crooked world', the river glorious in its crookedness, the mountains in all their wonder, and not a straight line anywhere. And he thought about human 'crookedness', the Minotaur within himself and within all human beings, and how that Minotaur becomes demonic and destructive when attempts are made to straighten, to repress or to deny. The crooked world, in its entirety, would be welcome at Slí na Fírinne, an acceptance and acknowledgement of crookedness woven into its rituals, all of which are based on the *Triduum Sacrum*, the experience of Gethsemane, Golgotha and the Garden of the Sepulchre. In the totality of their humanity those who live there attempt to walk the path that Jesus pioneered. The golden rule is to live with passion and compassion towards every dark impulse in oneself and in others, and that includes the fox that will kill the hens, the blight that will poison the potatoes, the thief, the murderer, the sex offender, the enemy, the 'other'; every crooked thing, for 'that art thou'. That is the demand made by the Gethsemane part of the journey.

It is also part of the ritual he designed and called Ephphatha, 'Be Opened', the word Jesus used in the course of healing the man who was deaf and dumb. Add blindness, John would say, and you have the condition of modern man, blind to the 'stupendousness' of the paradisal, miraculous world in which he lives, and equally deaf, dumb and blind to the spirit that he is himself.

> In daring to open our eyes and minds to nature we will be under no sentimental illusions about it. How could we, given the fantastic infanticide that a stoat, when she finds it, will wreak upon a wren's nest?
>
> That said, there are days when we do not need to regain Paradise. We look at the mountains all around us and know that we never lost it. On such days Ephphatha isn't something we do, it is something that has already happened to us. As if we had voyaged through Fern Hill sleep, we are abroad in the first morning of the world.
>
> And every shore is heron-priested,
> And every field is a field of praise.
>
> We vindicate God as creator when we practise being in Paradise. (*Slí na Fírinne* Brochure)

Ephphatha is 'the liturgy of Opening our Eyes'[10] of developing a sympathetic nervous system in which 'we practise being in Paradise' and its goal is 'silver branch perception', a voyage to where we are.

The opening of one's eyes is an enormous and dangerous undertaking, it can lead as he had good reason to know, to the place of nihil, to the place of spiritual darkness and it is then that one will need a different ritual, the ritual called Tenebrae.

> In Ephphatha we seek to open our eyes and minds, in Tenebrae we seek to close our eyes and to go beyond mind. Tenebrae is a Latin word. Literally, in ordinary usage, it means darkness. In Christian usage it names the mystical darkness of Good Friday, the darkness, that is, of the dark night of the soul.

Tenebrae, a Christian ceremony which dates back to the ninth century, was celebrated during the last three days of Holy Week. It is the ritual in which Christianity watches with Jesus. A distinctive part of the ceremony involves the use of what is known as the Tenebrae harrow, a triangular stand which supports fifteen candles. In a darkened setting, with only the light of the fifteen candles, readings and psalms are recited or chanted. Gradually the candles are quenched, leaving alight the candle at the apex. In a church setting the harrow will then be hidden behind the altar, the service ending in total physical darkness. John saw this as 'the most mystical of rituals' which he says 'is adequate to all that we deinanthropically are.'[11] Keeping as close as possible to the spirit of it, he re-imagined and rewrote it. It is a ritual journey into oneself, into all that one is as human and as individual, guided by appropriate readings. In the first antiphons one acknowledges:

> V. In man is all whatsoever the sun shines upon and heaven contains.
> R. Also hell and all the deeps.
> V. O the mind, mind has mountains, cliffs of fall frightful, sheer, no-man fathomed.
> R. Hold them cheap may who ne'er hung there.
> V. The mind of man is capable of anything – because everything is in it.
> R. All the past as well as all the future. (*Slí na Fírinne*, p. 128)

Here he incorporates the descent into the karmic canyon, that is the starting point for the Tenebrae journey; what follows is meditations on the human condition drawn from the Bible, from modern philosophers, from the Buddha, from Taoism, from his own writings, culminating in the nothingness of the abyss, where mind and senses are of no further use, where one must move through suffering and meaninglessness to the state of 'metanoesis', of being beyond knowing, where one prays:

> Help me to be as out of your way awake, God, as I am in dreamless sleep.
> Help me to be as out of your way awake, God, as I am in dreamless sleep.

Help me to be as out of your way awake, God, as I am in dreamless sleep.[12]

In Tenebrae all our lanterns, inner and outer, are quenched and we realise that 'to seek God with our senses and understanding is to seek God with that which eclipses God.'[13] This then is the place of 'the abyss of faith', where one must rely on the testament and reassurance of all the great mystics: that there is a state that is 'beyond knowing in the human mind', a divine ground of all being, a state of no-thing-ness, where experience of God is possible. This re-imagined ritual of Tenebrae, with its quenching of candle after candle, enacts the death of the faculties of the individual, ego-centred self in order that it might enter 'the night more lovely than the dawn', the state described in the Chandogya Upnanishad 'where nothing else is seen, nothing else is heard, nothing else is thought about, there's the Fulness.' It is here that one must trust Meister Eckhart: 'God expects but one thing of you and that is that you should empty yourself in so far as you are a created human being so that God can be God in you.' This is 'the final Eureka',[14] where mysticism goes beyond scientific discovery into spiritual rebirth, the emergence of the lotus flower from the darkness of the mud, the hosanna at the heart of the atom, the river finding its way to its home in the great ocean.

The early months of 2005 were spent in refining and writing this vision; they were also months of increasing weakness and ill health, he attended a number of doctors and alternative practitioners but nothing specific was diagnosed, apart from a slightly leaking valve in his heart. That he took lightly, saying to Chris 'Jesus, three hundred euros, if I didn't have a heart condition going in I'd definitely have one coming out!' Unfortunately that diagnosis, and the earlier diagnosis of M.E., led him to neglect symptoms that should otherwise have rung warning bells. Instead he continued to work. He now had the seed of his hedge school 'built in words' and was then fortunate to make the acquaintance of Garry McMahon, a graphic design artist who had read *Dreamtime* and was anxious to learn more. On hearing of the plans for Slí na Fírinne, he offered to produce both brochure and book, and also set up a venture called Slí na Fírinne Publishing, the book its first imprint. Two beautiful publications ensued and things appeared to be going well, he was ready for the next phase of fundraising. The plan was to raise a certain amount, get things started at the site and then, once he could move there, to sell his own house to fund the remainder of the work. Life, however, with its total disregard for the best laid plans, dramatically intervened. Weakness and lethargy had turned into physical pain, but believing that he was simply suffering with a stomach ulcer he did not seek specialist help until the pain eventually expressed itself as nausea and bleeding. By then he was in a lot of trouble. By January 2006 he had a diagnosis of three forms of cancer, prostate, bowel and liver and was in urgent need of surgery. His trip home to Kerry with that information was difficult to say the least. 'Coming through the gate and walking up to my door, I looked around at the mountains and it saddened me to think and say, my homecoming, my *nostos*, is a leavetaking.'[15] He was now in the final phase of 'the death adventure'; his body had turned against itself, but he had agreed to return to Dublin for the surgery, without which he had been told that he would be dead within weeks.

He had no money, no medical card and no health insurance but friends rallied round; Marie Hughes in Dublin and Fr. Pat Moore in Duagh put the word out and the floodgates opened, he could continue treatment, thanks to the generosity of what he called 'this great Christian medicine.' Having spent his entire life being incredibly generous with any money he had ever had he was not left in need of it now. Money was never a concern for him. One of his efforts to borrow for Slí na Fírinne had run aground when the bank manager reminded him that he had only 67 euro in his own account. 'Jaysus' he said, 'that's a euro for every year of my life so far, sure maybe I'm not doin' too badly after all.' That laughing spirit was called into play now. He underwent the surgery and then headed home for recovery before the next phase of treatment; chemotherapy was needed if he was to have even a fighting chance. The next months brought a return to strength; Eileen, with whom he had remained friends, decided to give up her job and moved in to take care of him while he continued the process, begun years previously, of 'befriending' his death. 'A good way to redeem our dying', he later wrote,' is to take it into ourselves and befriend it, if possible from a long way off. The big surprise for me in this is that the death adventure enriched me at least as much as did the love adventure.'[16]

Within weeks he was on *Liveline* telling Joe Duffy and his listenership that the cancer 'had gone walkabout all over my body,' and that even though this was 'endgame' in a very real sense "to me, Joe, it isn't endgame at all. To me, it's not a terminal lounge, it's a departure lounge for me; it's a place where we depart into the hereafter. I have no doubt in the world that we continue in the hereafter and I didn't arrive at that through a process of argument or logic. It's a deep, deep knowing inside of me. I know it in immediate experience that death isn't the end of the story. What I am from conception to death isn't the whole story. My life in the universe isn't the whole story. The universe itself isn't the whole story. I know it Joe, I know, I know like, no matter how many incarnations, no matter how we die from whatever disease, I know that God is Divine Ground. So the healing is finally greater than the illness and the wonder is that when we do finally go beyond the beatific vision, when we come home to that bliss of Divine Ground, the surprise will be that in a sense we had never left it like, that's the real homecoming."

In response to Joe's observation that there did not seem to be any sense of hopelessness in him he replied that he was leaving himself open and available to miracle, that the doctors hadn't written him off as a lost cause, 'but even if the end of this is death, death isn't hopeless, it's a door through to somewhere else'. Yes, he had felt sadness, yes there is fear, but 'I have a kind of Christian faith like' and 'it's not so difficult. I'm into it now and I'm in the swing of it and in the roll of it, and people are just wonderful, Joe, wonderful – sure I suppose I'm the poorest man in Coolies an' here I am attending the Mater Private.' Callers to the programme commented not only on his courage, but on the joy and enthusiasm that he radiated and the hope that he conveyed. 'I am', he would later say, 'optimistic on both sides of death. I can understand how people mightn't believe in a god, but if you live in a deep place within yourself you will come to know that there's a hereafter and a here-before. Don't tarnish death with the diseases that bring us to it. Separate death from that. Take the word terminal out of that – it isn't terminal, you'll go on. The cancer can't lay hands on that piece of divinity that's in you.'[17] In the course of the next year that optimism sustained him. At the time of his diagnosis he had two major projects in hand, one was Slí Na Fírinne and the other was what eventually turned out to be *What the Curlew Said*, a continuation of *Nostos*, initially inspired by a request from Tim Robinson to record everything he knew about Connemara, but which turned out to be 'about Connemara as I had experienced it ... not dealing with it as objective observable fact.'[18] There was an urgency now to complete these projects, and there was also something else he wanted to do.

In the course of the interview with Joe Duffy he had made clear that he was 'a man of faith', not 'a doctrinal Christian' but that he did have a great appreciation of the role and importance of the central Christian rituals. These provide people with what he refers to as 'the beatific vision', a vision of something greater beyond their everyday routines, images of which vary from culture to culture; later, writing in *What the Curlew Said*, he told of a potent memory of a day that he and a classmate, Jim Stack, were sent from their fifth class lessons to the church in Moyvane to spend time at the exposition of the Blessed Sacrament. The sunburst of a gold and silver monstrance was on the altar, the sacred host at its crystal heart, and the boys were to kneel before it in adoration. Sunshine coming through the church window irradiated the altar turning the monstrance into 'a rayed blaze of lunar silver.' He would always remember the feeling of awe and wonder that he experienced at the sight of this splendour. 'Again and again I would go back to it in my mind and even when I had ceased to be a Christian I'd re-enter that church, I'd kneel where I knelt, hoping for irradiation by it.'[19] What the monstrance had succeeded in doing that day was to awaken or to inspire a sense of reverence, something within himself that corresponded to this external manifestation on the altar. That, he would later acknowledge, is the profound function of ritual and sacrament; seal's breathing holes that would allow spirit to awaken and flourish.

To honour that vision he now wrote *Serious Sounds*, a small beautifully produced volume, which outlines what he saw as the value of the Christian sacramental road. It was, he said, a response to Nietzsche's claim 'that nature in us grew dark because we had no road', meaning that in modern life there is no longer any ideal for which to live; John was convinced that the Christian sacraments could provide such an ideal – spiritual initiations into an enlightened vision of ourselves as 'holy, holy, holy' at the core of our being; the ideal or goal of the road to bring that 'spark of divinity' to a full flourishing. 'The Eucharist for me isn't to take something in from outside, it is to let that eternal hymn of praise sing itself outwards through me, through all that I am, good and bad ... at this hour of my life I'm a singing Christian.' In a most extraordinary way, at this hour of his life, facing his death, he appears to have found and benefitted from that 'sheltering mythology' which had been his lifelong quest. All through a difficult year of cancer treatment, even when the chemotherapy had failed and he was prescribed a drug whose effects he described 'as straight up out of hell's kitchen', his spirit remained strong. One of the side effects of the chemo resulted in what he considered 'a small miracle'. His hair had fallen out in 'fistfuls' and one day with a particularly large clump of it in his hand, instead of putting it in the bin, he threw it into the wind, thinking that 'it would join the sheep wool that is blowing about in Tim Connor's field.' Instead, carried in a different direction by the wind, he noticed that the hair got caught on a nearby fuchsia bush. A day or two later, while tipping around outside, he noticed a little chaffinch with ribs of hair in her beak. He watched her and realised what she was doing, she was lining her nest with his hair. Months later, after she had laid her eggs and reared her young in it, he retrieved it. Twigs and hair were perfectly intertwined to provide a place of shelter. The nest was placed on his personal 'altar' and would be pointed out to his many visitors. 'Will ye look at that', he would say, 'I'm already on my way back to Divine Ground!' The story of the nest became a parable of hope; even though he would soon be turning to dust, his hair was part of the fabric of new life, everything finds its way back into this Paradise of new life, and back beyond that into Divine Ground.

Somehow that wonderful hope provided him with the energy to continue his various projects. He finished writing *Serious Sounds* and *Urbi et Orbi*; he was able to cooperate in the making of a documentary about his life with the film-maker Alan Gilsenan and most importantly he gathered a group of people together to help refine the plans and the vision he had for Slí na Fírinne. These included Garry McMahon, Fr. John Joe Spring, Fr. Pat Moore, Gary McDarby and Brendan Touhy, the latter two organising a website, the launch of a collection of 13 CDs entitled

One Evening in Eden and also recording a series of interviews with him in which he expressed his "fervent yearning hope" that his dream could be realised; that even though he would not be there to oversee it, perhaps one day someone with experience of monastic life might 'walk down the road' and embrace and enable the vision. Until then he simply asked that they might each find 'a little shrine in your life and in your heart for Slí na Fírinne ... if it grows in the heart it might happen.' If it did not happen, then the site should be sold and the money returned to the donors or given to charity. Given his illness he had done all he could do by building it in words, a place where the path that Jesus pioneered might be kept open, a place that might provide an antidote to 'the craziness that we call culture',[20] a place that might provide a starting point for the Earth as Buddh Gaia.

In September of 2006 he was well enough for two big events, the conferring on him of an honorary doctorate of literature by University College Galway and the launch, at Clifden Arts Week, of *Night Journey to Buddh Gaia*. The doctorate he had found trouble in accepting; in a sense it felt as if he was capitulating to the values of a world that he had walked away from and which he felt had little time for his unorthodox and counter-cultural vision. A great friend from his Connemara years, Brendan Flynn, managed to persuade him that it was precisely for this reason that he was being honoured and eventually he agreed to be 'gowned up'. The address by Dr. Iognáid Ó Muircheartaigh, President of the University, paid tribute to him as 'the pre-eminent original, radical, and non-conformist questioner in contemporary Ireland' and acknowledged 'the extraordinary generous, humane, and utterly civilized manner in which John has lived a unique and uniquely courageous life.' In an insightful observation Dr. Ó Muircheartaigh spoke of the Chinese belief that the wise man is to be found, not walking ahead of humanity trying to guide it, but walking behind it, picking up the inestimable treasures that it leaves behind in its flight into the future. In his acceptance speech John picked up on this theme, laughing at the image of himself as a Chinese sage, his height for one thing being a prohibitive factor, but pleased at the opportunity it offered to highlight just one of the treasures that 'the myth of progress' has abandoned. He told the story of the tribesmen who had to sit and wait for their souls to catch up, and we, he said, who have also come too far too fast, should again take example from the first peoples of the world, and sit down with them – maybe then our most neglected treasure might be afforded a second chance. The applause was rapturous and he had enjoyed the day even though he did remark on the journey home 'Christ, I'm not dead at all yet and they've started the resurrection!'[21]

Planning and writing continued for the next seven to eight months, the most demanding task being the completion of *What the Curlew Said* in which, in spite of increasing weakness, he documented his life right up to the weeks before his death. There is anguish and suffering in it; there is acceptance in it; there is prayer in it – a plea for strength to build a Christian monastic hedge school – and there is a fear that he has failed. Yes, he had resisted conscription into the 'craziness of culture'; he had managed both to jump ship and at the same time, by putting himself out there in his books and in his talks, he had stayed on board to fight, but had he failed in both ventures? He felt that the probability was yes, and yet there was always the hope that by telling his story and by sharing his extraordinary thinking, he might in some small way 'have kept the adventure afloat.' With John Moriarty there would always be hope. Even as the illness went into its final stages he was able to say 'even though I am now in the shadow of the valley of death, I am a happy man.' He shared again his belief that it was not a matter of having to save his soul but of allowing his soul to save him and he shared what he called his mantras, the short prayers that he repeated again and again:

At the core of my soul, the everlasting hymn of praise to God I am.
At the core of my soul the Sanctus I am.
At the core of my soul the lotus I am.
Opened out to the love of God I am.
In the unfallen core of my soul I myself am the Paradise I walk in.

In repeating these he was doing what he had done all of those years before when he cycled the road from Moyvane to Listowel, he was singing himself into being, now with a surer sense of what he was about; he had heard the singing of the hosanna at the heart of the atom and he was allowing that to guide him home. During these final weeks he was cared for by friends and family; his sisters Madeleine and Phyllis were a constant presence. Fr.Pat Moore remembered the silence that descended on him in the last few days but Phyllis talks of the struggle it was to get him to take his medicines, he being adamant that he wanted 'to be alert going over the line'.

The most extraordinary story of those days comes from his friend Dolores and his sister Phyllis. On the day before he died Dolores spent time with him. He had been given a mild sedative because he was in a lot of pain and later in the evening, after the rosary had been said and the neighbours had left Dolores sat with him. 'I sang a few of John's songs quietly while he held my hand ... then I noticed the cross ... it was the root of a tree in the shape of a cross that John had brought from Connemara ... I was familiar with it and John had told me that when times got tough he would hold the cross to his body and pray ... now I noticed that it was trembling, vibrating. At first I thought that it might be from the heat of the radiator, but the radiator was cold. I looked and looked but could not bring myself to touch it. Then Phyllis came into the room and sat down beside me. We talked. I knew that John was conscious. I then asked Phyllis if she noticed anything, indicating the cross. She reacted straight away and said that she had noticed it early in the day and it was shaking. Not long after Madeleine put her head in and it was obvious that she too had noticed the cross. Soon after that a night nurse arrived. It was the one and only night they had a nurse. I moved out and went home leaving two very tired sisters behind me. We gathered to say the rosary the following evening. Everything was normal in the room. The neighbours left. I felt the time had come to say his leave-taking prayer. Madeleine put her head in and John lifted his arm up, pointing it forwards. Not long after that I banged on the floor for the sisters to come up. The time had come. Madeleine held John's head, Phyllis his hands and we continued the prayer. Go forth upon thy journey from this world, O Christian soul, In the name of God, the almighty Father, who created thee ... A priest walked in out of nowhere and continued the praying. The nurse came in and held a candle to John's breath as we prayed 'Depart O Christian soul out of this world' and watched the flame flicker until the last breath.'[22]

He died on the evening of Friday 1 June 2007. He was sixty nine. And so, with Mary Hegarty we say 'God bless you, John' and as you said to Mary and to Jimmy, we say to you 'walk on'. Walk on John, however long the journey of your immortality takes you, may it eventually take you home, to where everything is holy, holy, holy, and as pure as the drop of water on a lily-pad. Sanctus.

ENDNOTES

Chapter 1: 'A world below history'
1   Gabriel Fitzmaurice, *'The Boro' and 'The Cross'* (Millennium Publication, April 2000), p.8.
2   Sacrament: John developed a very broad interpretation for the word 'sacrament' and used it to mean any action that might put one in touch with what is mysterious, wonderful or potentially sacred.
3   John Moriarty, *Dreamtime* (Dublin: The Lilliput Press, 1999), p. 244.
4   Micheál Ó Muircheartaigh, *From Borroloola to Mangerton Mountain* (Penguin, 2006), p. 258.
5   *Bothántaíocht*: Irish word for the practice of 'night visiting' or 'rambling', going to neighbouring houses for sessions of song and story-telling.
6   Hedge schools: these were an alternative form of national schooling for the rural, Catholic poor in the eighteenth and nineteenth centuries who were prevented by virtue of poverty and religion from accessing any formal education. Provided by local educated men, classes were normally held in barns or in local houses, a practice which continued in some areas until as late as the 1890s.
7   Quoted by Professor John Coolahan in a lecture in Tarbert Comprehensive School, June 2012.
8   *Meitheal*: Irish word to describe a group of workers who had come together for a particular task, eg turf-cutting or threshing.
9   Ó Muircheartaigh, op. cit., p. 260.
10 John Moriarty, *Nostos, An Autobiography* (Dublin: The Lilliput Press 2001) p.20.
11 Interview with Moriarty family by Mary McGillicuddy 7/12/2013.
12 John Moriarty, *One Evening in Eden* (Audio CD Set, Lilliput Press, 2007), Six Stories Disc 1.
13 Ibid., Six Stories Disc 2.
14 Ibid., Six Stories Disc 1.
15 *Piseógs*: Old superstitious practices that have a sinister side, similar to voodoo in the Caribbean. They 'are evil magic, the working of badness on your neighbours or the taking away of his luck to add to your own'. Eddie Lenihan in interview with Caitríona Murphy in *The Irish Independent* 03/05/2011.
16 Moriarty, *Nostos*, p. 13
17 Eucharist: used here in its widest sense, meaning communion with God, not in the strictly sacramental sense of Holy Eucharist or Holy Communion.

Chapter 2: 'Horizons of longing'
1   McGraths: Near neighbours of the Moriartys.
2   Prior to 1939 the village was known as Newtownsandes – hence Newtown.
3   From the first of a series of as yet unpublished talks John gave after the publication of *Nostos* in 2001.
4   Bostoon: Irish slang for someone stupid, ignorant, boorish.
5   *One Evening in Eden*, Six Stories, Disc 1, track 6.
6   John Moriarty in interview with Maurice O' Keeffe in *Kerry Lore* on Radio Kerry 18/2/2006.
7   Perseus and Medousa: Medousa was one of the Gorgons, with hair of hissing snakes and

the tusks of a boar; all who looked at her were turned to stone. Perseus, after an adventurous and magical journey, eventually outwitted and killed her.

8   *Silent Spring* by Rachel Carson, first published in 1962, an environmental science book which brought environmental concerns to the American public and inspired the movement that eventually gave rise to the U.S. Environmental Protection Agency.

9   Ó Muircheartaigh, op. cit., p. 260.

10   Images from *Three years she grew in sun and shower*, one of the five poems that make up William Wordsworth's *Lucy* series.

11   All quotes in this paragraph from *Nostos*, p. 20.

12   A scholarship to attend teacher-training college for primary school teaching.

13   Saturn's grey chaos: image from *Moby Dick*, used to convey the terrifying sense of infinitude in a godless, purposeless universe.

Chapter 3: 'Christ, what's happening to me?'

1   *Nostos*, p. 31.

2   Second law of thermodynamics: the tendency for all matter and energy in the universe to evolve towards a state of inert uniformity, in other words the progress of the universe is towards total annihilation.

3   From the first of a series of as yet unpublished talks John gave after the publication of *Nostos* in 2001.

4   *Nostos*, p. 56.

5   *Dreamtime*, p. 24.

6   *Nostos*, p. 57.

7   Ibid., p. 50.

8   Matthew 8:20

9   Psychic topiary: topiary is the art of pruning plants to a particular shape. John imagines that our minds, our psyches, have been subjected to a similar process by the kind of education to which they have been subjected.

10   Moriarty, *One Evening in Eden*, Eden Vol. 1, Track 6, 2:10.

11   Anita Barrows, *Rilke's Book of Hours: Love Poems to God* (Penguin, 2005).

12   *Nostos*, p. vii.

13   Ibid., p. 53.

14   Ibid., p. 46.

15   From the first of a series of as yet unpublished talks John gave after the publication of *Nostos* in 2001.

16   *Dreamtime*, p. 141.

17   *Nostos*, p. vii.

18   From the first of a series of as yet unpublished talks John gave after the publication of *Nostos* in 2001.

19   'Transformed groceries': expression attributed by Moriarty to A.B Jordanski, Canadian biologist.

Chapter 4: 'A killed dragon isn't a dead dragon'

1   From RTÉ radio programme, *Dialogue*, first broadcast 1998.

2   *Nostos*, p. 63.

3   Ibid., p. 66.

4   Caryatids of the Erechtheoin: 6 sculpted female figures, which act as columns to support the porch of the Erechtheoin, also known as the Porch of the Maidens, on the Acropolis.

5   *One Evening in Eden*, Triduum Sacrum, Disc 1, Track 8, 1:40.

6   *Dreamtime*, p. 142.

7   *Nostos*, p. 74.

8   Ibid., p. 131.

9   *The Golden Bough*: title of a book by James Frazer, which is a comparative study of mythology and religion.

10 John Moriarty, *Slí na Fírinne* (Slí na Fírinne Publishing,2006), p. 107.
11 *Nostos*, p. 134.
12 Ibid., p. 101.
13 From the second of a series of as yet unpublished talks John gave after the publication of *Nostos* in 2001.
14 'I thought of three great revolutions in human affairs: Christianity, the French Revolution and the Russian Revolution. Prominent among their achievements were the stake, the guillotine and gulag' *Nostos*, p. 162.
15 *Nostos*, p. 137.
16 The Red Cow Inn, a public house on the outskirts of Dublin.

Chapter 5: 'Something right royal in us all'
1 *Nostos*, p. 566.
2 Ibid., p. 164.
3 Ibid., p. 173.
4 Ibid., p. 174.
5 *Dreamtime*, p. 84.
6 Gorgocogito: here he combines the Latin *cogito*, meaning 'I think', with the Greek *gorgos*, meaning 'dreadful', and refers to the Gorgon, Medousa, she whose look turned everything to stone. Hence 'terrible thinking', thinking which deadens everything it attempts to understand. A similar idea to Wordsworth's 'we murder to dissect'.
7 Quoted in *Dreamtime*, p. 260.
8 William James, *The Varieties of Religious Experience: a Study in Human Nature* (Penquin Classics, 1982), p. 42.
9 *Nostos*, p. 188.
10 Ibid., p. 173.
11 *The Mabinogion*: a collection of Middle Welsh prose stories, the earliest prose literature of Britain. Traditionally the stories were recited by a mabinog or bard.
12 Jack Scanlon, the man who killed the pig in the yard in Moyvane.

Chapter 6: 'Foxwoman was my Statue of Liberty'
1 *Nostos*, p. 114.
2 Genesis 1: 26–28.
3 *One Evening in Eden*, Seeking to Walk Beautifully on the Earth, Disc 2, Track 6.
4 Genesis 9: 2.
5 *Slí na Fírinne*, p. 59.
6 John Moriarty, *What the Curlew Said, Nostos Continued* (Dublin: The Lilliput Press, 2007), p. 122.
7 Empiricism: the view that all knowledge must be derived from direct experience
8 Joseph Campbell, *Primitive Mythology, The Masks of God* (Penguin, 1991 Edition) p. 28.
9 Ibid., p. 27.
10 *Nostos*, p. viii.
11 From a poem by William Blake entitled *Mock on, Mock on* in which he maintains that there is a sacred understanding of the world that is far deeper than the scientific one, the scientific explanation is no more than particles of sand, whereas the sacred understanding, 'Israels tents', shines bright.

Chapter 7: 'Be not afraid of the universe'
1 *Nostos*, p. 275.
2 *The Merchant of Venice* (V, i, ll. 56–63), quoted *Nostos*, p. 235.
3 Two quotations that appear again and again in Moriarty's writing. 'My own suspicion is that the universe is not only queerer than we suppose, it is queerer than we can suppose.' J.B.S. Haldane, *Possible Worlds and Other Papers* (1927), p 286. In *Varieties of Religious*

Experience William James writes of 'other forms of consciousness ... that forbid a premature closing of our account with reality.' Op cit. Lecture XVI.

4   In recorded conversation with Brendan Touhy, Killarney, 2006.
5   Letter from Brian MacKinnon to Moriarty family 21/7/2007.
6   From a lecture entitled *Prometheus and the Dolphin* delivered at Media Lab Europe, 2004.
Accessible on YouTube.
7   Interview with Maurice O' Keeffe in *Kerry Lore* on Radio Kerry 18/2/2006.
8   Adapted from *One Evening in Eden*, Seeking to Walk Beautifully on the Earth, Disc 1.
9   Andromeda: In Greek mythology she is chained to a rock as a sacrifice to appease the
sea-monster, hence her terrible dread.
10   John Moriarty, *Turtle was Gone a Long Time, Volume 1, Crossing the Kedron* (Dublin: The
Lilliput Press 1996), p. 51.
11   *Nostos*, p. 251.
12   Campbell, *Primitive Mythology*, p. 53.
13   Ibid., p. 350.
14   'the nothing but universe': a favourite phrase used to describe the modern scientific view of things.
It is fully explained in *One Evening in Eden*, Seeking to Stand Beautifully on the Earth, Disc 1.
15   *Turtle, Vol. 1,* op. cit., pp. x- xi.
16   Ibid., p. xi.

Chapter 8: 'The truth about things is miraculous'
1   *Nostos* p. 261.
2   Joseph Campbell, *The Masks of God, Oriental Mythology* (Souvenir Press, 2011 Edition) p. 4.
3   Upanishads: a collection of religious and philosophical texts written in India during the
first millennium BC.
4   Adapted from *Dreamtime*, pp. 72–3
5   Mennonite/Hutterite: these are Anabaptist Christian communities, somewhat similar to
the Amish, who live by the codes of their founding fathers and are particularly devout.
6   *Auto Da Fe*: the expression used for the burning of a heretic during the Spanish Inquisition.
7   *Nostos*, p. 308.
8   Ibid., p. 284.
9   Ibid., p. 287.
10   A Sanskrit phrase from the Chandogya Upanishad, variously translated as 'That art thou',
'Thou art that', 'You yourself are It'.

Chapter 9: 'Who will take upon himself the burden of lighting the world?'
1   Tomas Torquemada (1420–1498) was the Grand Inquisitor of the Spanish Inquisiton,
taxed with ridding the Catholic church of heretics.
2   *Nostos*, p. 316. He is thinking here about the power to provide a cohesive and 'a sheltering
mythology'.
3   Ibid., p. 316.
4   Ibid., p. 317.
5   Ibid., pp. 315 & 322.
6   The Book of Numbers, 31:17.
7   All quotes in these paragraphs from *Nostos*, pp. 325–328.
8   *Turtle*, Vol 1, p. 125.
9   Song Of Solomon 2:1.
10   *Nostos*, p. 336.
11   Ibid., p. 338.
12   Ibid., p. 341.
13   *Dreamtime*, p. 101.
14   Ibid., p. 100.
15   Campbell, *Oriental Mythology,* op. cit., pp 23 and 425.
16   For a full explanation of this idea see Brendan O'Donoghue, *A Moriarty Reader*, *Preparing
for Early Spring* (Dublin: The Lilliput Press, 2013), pp. 6–7.

17   Verse from the *Tao Te Ching*, quoted in *Dreamtime*, p. 102–3.
18   Verse from the *Tao Te Ching*, quoted in *Dreamtime*, p. 101.
19   From *The Tables Turned*, a poem by William Wordsworth.

Chapter 10: 'I must plant myself in wild soil'

1   See Glossary.
2   *Nostos*, p. 351.
3   He elaborates on this theme in returned to this theme in *One Evening in Eden*, Six Stories, Disc 1, track 5. 'Have we walked on the moon only because we haven't yet the grace and the courage to walk on the great and sacred earth?'
4   In his book *The Advancement of Learning* Bacon distinguishes between 'advancement local' and 'advancement essential'.
5   Quoted in *Nostos*, p. 363, from *The Oregon Trail* by Francis Parkman, first published in 1849.
6   Jon E. Lewis, *Native Americans* (Constable and Robinson, 2004), pp. 299–300.
7   John G Neihardt and Nicholas Black Elk, *Black Elk Speaks* (University of Nebraska Press, 2000 edition), p. 201.
8   *One Evening in Eden*, Seeking to walk beautifully on the Earth Disc 3, track 2.
9   *Nostos*, p. 371.
10   *One Evening in Eden*, Seeking to walk beautifully on the Earth Disc 3, track 2.
11   Sutra: a Sanskrit word which refers to texts used in Hinduism and Buddhism, a manual, textbook or scripture.
12   Genesis 28:16.
13   *Nostos*, p. 373.
14   *One Evening in Eden*, Triduum Sacrum Disc 1, track 16.
15   From Emily Bronte's poem, *No Coward Soul is Mine*.
16   Bright Angel Trail is the name of one of the many paths that lead down to the floor of the Canyon.
17   Psychic topiary: topiary is the art of pruning plants to a particular shape. John imagines that our minds, our psyches, have been subjected to a similar process by the kind of education to which they have been subjected.

Chapter 11: 'To ship oars and give the world a chance'

1   *Nostos*, p. 403. He is using the word yoga in its literal sense, meaning 'to concentrate'.
2   Ibid., p. 380.
3   'The roaring of lions, the howling of wolves, the raging of the stormy sea, and the destructive sword, are portions of eternity too great for the eye of man.' *The marriage of Heaven and Hell*, William Blake.
4   Mahayavkas are the 'Great Sayings' of the Upanishads.
5   From a poem, *Fourfold Vision* by William Blake 'May God us keep/From single vision/ And Newton's sleep!'
6   From *Auguries of Innocence* by William Blake.
7   *Nostos*, p. 411.
8   Ibid., p. 425.
9   John, 18:1.
10   *Slí Na Fírinne*, p. 3.
11   *Dreamtime*, p. 142.
12   Mark, 15:22.
13   This refers to the medieval legend that the Hill of Calvary was the burial place of Adam, hence John's frequent use of the image of Christ looking down into Adam's empty skull as a symbol of utter dereliction.
14   A reference to an incident in a miracle story told about St. Brigid who, after torrential rain, hung her wet cloak on a sunbeam to dry.

Chapter 12: 'What else can one be but an intellectual outlaw'

1   William Blake, *Milton: A Poem in Two Books,* First Book, ll. 20–21.
2   John Moriarty, *Turtle was Gone a Long Time, Volume 2, Horsehead Nebula Neighing* (Dublin: The Lilliput Press 1997), p. 185.
3   William Blake, *The Marriage of Heaven and Hell.*
4   *Nostos*, p. 450.
5   Tesserae: the tiny tiles of stone or glass used in the construction of a mosaic.
6   *Nostos*, p. 450.
7   Ibid., p. 445.
8   Bryan Appleyard, *The Brain is Wider than the Sky* (Weidenfeld, 2011) p. 3.
9   *Nostos*, p. 277.
10 *One Evening in Eden*, Eden, Disc 3, Track 2.
11 *Nostos*, p. 457.
12 Ibid., p. 459.
13 Ibid., p. 468.
14 Ibid., p. 468.
15 Ibid., p. 463.
16 Ibid., p. 479.

Chapter 13: 'What chance have we, when that's where we think we live?'

1   *Nostos*, p. 480.
2   From poem *That Nature is a Heraclitean Fire,* by Gerard Manley Hopkins.
3   *Nostos*, p. 484.
4   Mike Sayers, son of Peig, known locally as Maidhc File, Mike the Poet.
5   From *The Wind Among the Reeds.*
6   Etty Hillesum, 'There is really a deep well inside me. And in it dwells God. Sometimes I am there too. But more often stones and grit block the well and God is buried beneath. Then He must be dug out again.' J. G. Gaarlandt, *An Interrupted Life* (Washington Square Press, 1984), p. 44.
7   Aldous Huxley, *The Perennial Philosophy* (Harper Collins, 1990) p. vii.
8   *One Evening in Eden*, Six Stories, Disc 1, Track 2.
9   *Nostos*, p. 497.
10 *Turtle,* Vol 1, p. 85.
11 *Nostos*, p. 507.
12 Evelyn Underhill, *Mysticism* (Pacific Publishing Studio, 2011), p 8.
13 Ibid., p.8.
14 *Nostos*, p. 519.
15 *Nostos*, p. 522.
16 Psalm 107.

Chapter 14: 'A new Christianity?'

1 *Curlew,* p. 35.
2   From the poem *Sheep and Fog* by Sylvia Plath
3   *Nostos* p. 534.
4   Ibid., p. 572.
5   Ibid., p. 606
6   Ibid., p. 616
7   Ibid., p.618
8   Ibid., p. 617
9   Ibid., p. 62
10 Ibid., p. 636

Chapter 15: 'There is surely a piece of divinity in us, something that was before the Elements and owes no homage unto the Sun'

1   *Nostos*, p. 646.
2   Ibid., p. 648.
3   Ibid., p. 569.
4   Sir Thomas Browne, quoted in *Slí na Fírinne,* p. 6.
5   *Dreamtime*, p. 24
6   *The Proficiscere*, an eighth century Christian prayer for the dying.
7   Metanoesis: 'what is beyond the reach of the thinking mind', *A Moriarty Reader* p. 17, Brendan O' Donoghue.
8   The 'upanishad' of six stories is published in *Turtle*, Vol.1, and in the CD collection *One Evening in Eden*, Six Stories, Discs 1,2 and 3.
9   *Nostos*, p. 655.
10 Ibid., p.687.
11 Ibid., p.686.
12 Ibid., p.667.
13 Details in this paragraph from John Moriarty interview with Maurice O' Keeffe in *Kerry Lore* broadcast on Radio Kerry 13/3/06.
14 *Turtle,* Vol 1, p.189.

Chapter 16: 'A sympathetic nervous system'

1   John Keats, *Complete Poems and Selected Letters of John Keats* (Modern Library Classics, 2001) p. 555.
2   *Nostos*, p. 696.
3   *One Evening in Eden*, Seeking to Walk Beautifully on the Earth, Disc 2, track 11.
4   *Nostos*, p. 455, and *Dreamtime*, p. 239: 'With Stoics, I believe that there is a *sumpatheia ton hollon*, a universal sympathy, that runs through all things, that connects all things with all things, and it would I believe be good for all things, including ourselves, if we lived from that sympathy.'
5   *Curlew,* p. 41.
6   Ibid., p. 100.
7   Ibid., p. 76.
8   *Nostos*, p. 435.
9   *Curlew,* p. 43.
10 Ibid., p. 55.
11 Ibid., p. 55.
12 *Nostos*, p. 549.

Chapter 17: 'Not one of us but is still walking in Paradise at the core of our being'

1   *Curlew,* p.33.
2   Ibid., p. 117.
3   Ibid., p. 122.
4   Ibid., p. 99.
5   Father John O' Donohue, in later years to become the well known author of *Anam Cara* and other books on Celtic spirituality.
6   *Curlew,* p. 62.
7   *One Evening in Eden, Six Stories*, Disc 1, Track 6.
8   Ibid., p. 64.
9   John Moriarty in interview with Maurice O' Keeffe in *Kerry Lore* broadcast on Radio Kerry 13/3/06.
10 *Curlew*, p. 178, a quote from D. H. Lawrence.
11 Ibid., p. 107.
12 Adapted from *One Evening in Eden*, Seeking to Walk Beautifully on the Earth, Disc 3, tracks 13–16.

13   *Black Elk Speaks,* op. cit. p. 1.
14   *Curlew,* p. 176.
15   Ibid., p.174, a quote from *Black Elk Speaks.*
16   Ibid., p. 202.
17   *Black Elk Speaks,* p. xxvi.

Chapter 18: 'Even where it is frightful … Nature is also immaculate'
1   *Curlew,* p. 209. The name he based on the temple called Buddh Gaya built on the spot where the Buddha won enlightenment. 'Buddh' is Sanskrit for enlightened; he changed Gaya (which means 'holy city') to Gaia, the Greek name for the goddess Earth, thus suggesting a divine and enlightened Earth.
2   Ibid., p. 211.
3   Ibid., p. 212.
4   *Invoking Ireland (*Dublin: The Lilliput Press, 2005) p. 10.
5   *Curlew,* p. 199.
6   *Invoking Ireland,* p. 10.
7   Quotes in this paragraph from *Curlew,* p. 225.
8   Quoted by Joseph Campbell in *Occidental Mythology* (Penguin, 1976), p. 515.
9   *Curlew,* p. 236.
10   Ibid., p. 237.
11   Dreamtime: in the origin stories of the Australian Aborigines, the beginning of the world happens in what they call the *Altjeringa,* the 'Dreamtime'. In that time all that existed was a featureless waste but then eternal beings went walkabout and they dreamed and sang the world of mountains, trees and rivers into existence. They dreamed with the dreaming earth and so both world and culture, the culture of songline and story, was created.
12   John Moriarty in interview with Maurice O' Keeffe in *Kerry Lore* broadcast on Radio Kerry 13/3/06.
13   Fintan O' Toole in *The Irish Times* and Brian Lynch in *The Evening Press,* both quoted in the second edition of *Dreamtime,* 1999.
14   *Dreamtime,* p. 22.
15   Ibid., p. 236.
16   Ibid., pp 248–251.
17   S. Foster Damon, *A Blake Dictionary* (Thames and Hudson, 1973), p. ix.
18   *Curlew,* p. 240.
19   Ibid., p. 285.
20   The coined word 'deinanthropus' occurs regularly in his writings. He coined it as an alternative to the word *anthropus,* the Greek word for human. *Deinos,* meaning 'terrible' or 'fearful', he believed gives a better sense of the enormous capacity of human beings to 'deepen hell' for themselves and others, therefore deinanthropus, the terrifying, awe-inspiring human being.
21   *Curlew,* p. 286.
22   *Turtle,* Vol. 1, p. xvi.
23   John Moriarty in interview with Maurice O' Keeffe in *Kerry Lore* on Radio Kerry 18/2/2006.
24   *Curlew,* p. 297.

Chapter 19: 'At this hour of my life I'm a singing Christian'
1   *Curlew,* p. 309.
2   Aidan Matthews speaking to Joe Duffy on *Liveline,* on RTE Radio 1, Feb. 2006.
3   *Curlew,* p. 310.
4   Adapted from *One Evening in Eden,* Seeking to Walk Beautifully on the Earth, Disc 3, tracks 13–16.
5   *Sli Na Firinne,* p. 58.
6   *Turtle was Gone a Long Time, Volume 3, Anaconda Canoe* (Dublin: The Lilliput Press, 1998) p. xxxi.

7   Quoted in *Dreamtime*, p. 22.
8   *Curlew*, p. 329.
9   *Slí na Fírinne* Brochure.
10   *Slí na Fírinne*, p. 60.
11   Ibid., p. 126.
12   Ibid., p. 145.
13   *Turtle*, Vol. 3, p. 183.
14   *Curlew*, p. 328.
15   Ibid., p. 333.
16   Ibid., p. 336.
17   John Moriarty in conversation with Brendan Touhy, May 2007.
18   *Curlew*, p. 333.
19   Ibid., pp. 319 and 321.
20   Ibid., p. 352.
21   Story courtesy of Brendan Touhy.
22   As told to Mary McGillicuddy by Dolores O Connor and verified by Phyllis and Madeleine.

SELECT BIBLIOGRAPHY

Works by John Moriarty (in order of publication)
Dreamtime (Dublin: The Lilliput Press, 1994).
Turtle was Gone a Long Time, Volume 1, Crossing the Kedron (Dublin: The Lilliput Press 1996).
Turtle was Gone a Long Time, Volume 2, Horsehead Nebula Neighing (Dublin: The Lilliput Press 1997).
Turtle was Gone a Long Time, Volume 3, Anaconda Canoe (Dublin: The Lilliput Press, 1998).
Nostos, An Autobiography (Dublin: The Lilliput Press 2001).
Invoking Ireland (Dublin: The Lilliput Press, 2005).
Slí na Fírinne (Slí na Fírinne Publishing,2006).
Serious Sounds (Slí na Fírinne Publishing,2006).
Urbi et Orbi (Slí na Fírinne Publishing,2006).
Night Journey to Buddh Gaia (Dublin: The Lilliput Press, 2006).
What the Curlew Said, Nostos Continued (Dublin: The Lilliput Press, 2007).
One Evening in Eden (Audio CD Set, Lilliput Press, 2007).

Selected Reference Works
Campbell, Joseph. *The Masks of God: Primitive Mythology* (Penguin, 1991).
Campbell, Joseph. *The Masks of God: Oriental Mythology* (Souvenir Press, 2011).
Campbell, Joseph. *The Masks of God: Occidental Mythology* (Penguin, 1976).
Campbell, Joseph. *The Masks of God: Creative Mythology* (Souvenir Press, 2011).
Foster Damon S. *A Blake Dictionary* (Thames and Hudson, 1973).
Hornblower, Simon and Anthony Spaworth. *The Oxford Companion to Classical Civilization* (Oxford University Press, 1998).
Huxley, Aldous. *The Perennial Philosophy* (Harper Collins, 1990).
Lewis, Jon E. *Native Americans* (Constable and Robinson, 2004).
MacCulloch, Diarmuid. *A History of Christianity* (Penguin, 2009).
MacKillop, James. *Dictionary of Celtic Mythology* (Oxford University Press, 1998).
Magee, Bryan. *The Story of Philosophy* (Dorling Kinderly, 2001).
Mascaró, Juan. *The Upanishads* (Penguin Classics, 1965).
Narby, Jeremy and Francis Huxley. *Shamans Through Time* (Thames and Hudson, 2001).
Neihardt John G. and Nicholas Black Elk, *Black Elk Speaks* (University of Nebraska Press, 2000 edition).
O'Donoghue, Brendan. *A Moriarty Reader, Preparing for Early Spring* (Dublin: The Lilliput Press, 2013).
Underhill, Evelyn. *Mysticism* (Pacific Publishing Studio, 2011).
Willis, Roy. *World Mythology* (Duncan Baird Publishers, 2006).
Watts, Alan. *TAO: The Watercourse Way* (Pantheon Books, New York, 1975).

GLOSSARY

Ahab: Captain of the whale ship *The Pequod* in Melville's *Moby Dick*. He represents the destructive power of man.

Amergin: Mythological ancestor of the Irish people who came ashore singing a song of inclusion.

Andromeda: In Greek mythology she is chained to a rock as a sacrifice to appease the sea-monster, hence her terrible dread.

Anima Mundi: The world's soul.

Anodos: The way back up from the Underworld. Opposite of Kathodos.

Anthropus: The Greek word for 'Man'.

Arnold, Matthew (1822–1888): English poet and critic, and author of the poem *Dover Beach*.

Bacon, Francis (1561–1626): Elizabethan writer and philosopher who developed the concept of 'advancement local' and 'advancement essential'.

Black Elk (1862–1950): Native American medicine man of the Great Plains Oglala Sioux.

Blake, William (1757–1827): English poet, artist and mystic, best known for his *Songs of Innocence and Experience*.

Bothántaíocht: Irish word for the practice of 'night visiting' or 'rambling', going to neigh-bouring houses for sessions of song and story-telling.

Borobudur: A great Buddhist temple in Java.

Bright Angel Trail: Winding trail leading to the floor of the Grand Canyon in Arizona.

Brontë, Emily (1818–1848): English poet, novelist and mystic, author of *No Coward Soul is Mine*.

Buddh Gaia: The enlightened Earth. The name is based on the temple called Buddh Gaya built on the spot where the Buddha won enlightenment. 'Buddh' is Sanskrit for enlightened; Moriarty changed Gaya (which means 'holy city') to Gaia, the Greek name for the goddess Earth, thus suggesting a divine and enlightened Earth.

Cartesian clarity: This saying, derived from the name of the philosopher René Descartes, is used by Moriarty to describe the mindset that believes that it is possible to find a scientific and rational explanation for everything. It is the mindset that denies the possibility of 'otherness', of miracle.

Coatlicue: The terrifying Aztec Earth goddess.

Coleridge, Samuel Taylor 1772–1834: English Romantic poet, critic and philosopher, author of *The Ancient Mariner*.

Darwin, Charles (1809–1882): English geologist and biologist, best known for his contribution to the science of evolution. He wrote *The Origin of Species*.

Deinanthropus: A coined word as an alternative to the word *anthropus*, the Greek word for human. *Deinos*, meaning 'terrible' or 'fearful', gives a better sense of the enormous capacity of human beings to 'deepen hell' for themselves and others, therefore deinanthropus, the terrifying, awe-inspiring human being.

Descartes, René (1596–1650): French philosopher and mathematician, whose well-known phrase *cogito ergo sum*, 'I think therefore I am', became the bedrock of rationalism, and therefore led to the dismissal of anything that could not be proved by reason.

Divine Ground: The 'ground' of all being, out of which all things emanate. It is a mystical concept that corresponds to Anima Mundi, Sila, Tao, Brahman, God; that which is behind everything.

Dover Beach: Poem by Matthew Arnold.

Dreamtime: in the origin stories of the Australian Aborigines, the beginning of the world happens in what they call the *Altjeringa,* the 'Dreamtime'. In that time all that existed was a featureless waste but then eternal beings went walkabout and they dreamed and sang the world of mountains, trees and rivers into existence. They dreamed with the dreaming earth and so both world and culture, the culture of songline and story, was created.

Eckhart, Meister (1260–1372): Rhineland mystic.

Empiricism: In philosophy the theory that all knowledge must be derived from direct experience.

Fern Hill: A poem by Dylan Thomas.

Golgotha: The place of the skull, also called Calvary, the place where Christ was crucified.

Gorgocogito: A coined word; the Latin *cogito*, meaning 'I think', combined with the Greek *gorgos*, meaning 'dreadful', and refers to the Gorgon, Medousa, she whose look turned everything to stone. Hence 'terrible thinking', thinking which deadens everything it attempts to understand.

Ishmael: The narrator of *Moby Dick*.

Kathodos: The way down into the Underworld.

Keats, John (1795–1821): English Romantic poet.

Kedron: The stream that Jesus crossed on Holy Thursday on his way to Gethsemane, the Garden of Olives. See John 18:1.

Kwaikutl: Native American people living on the north-west coast of North America.

Lascaux: A cave in south-western France, in which there are Palaeolithic rock paintings, dating back to 15,000 BC.

Leviathan: Biblical sea monster.

Mabinogion, The: a collection of Middle Welsh prose stories, the earliest prose literature of Britain. Traditionally the stories were recited by a mabinog or bard.

Mahavakya: A great Upanishadic saying, such as 'tat tvam asi', ('that art thou').

Mag Meall: A paradisal Otherworld in Irish mythology.

Manannán mac Lir: In Irish mythology the God of the Sea.

Medousa : In Greek mythology Medousa was one of the Gorgons, with hair of hissing snakes and the tusks of a boar; all who looked at her were turned to stone.

Meitheal : Irish word to describe a group of workers who had come together for a particular task, eg turf-cutting or threshing.

Metanoesis : What is beyond the capacity of the thinking mind, beyond 'knowing'.

Minotaur: Half-bull, half-man, child of Pasiphae, who was imprisoned in the Labyrinth under the city of Knossos in Crete.

Mirum: Wonder, the 'Divine Mirum' is used interchangeably with 'Divine Ground' to describe the source of all being.

Mitakuye Oyasin: 'To all my relatives', a Native American saying, used by Black Elk, to include 'the two-leggeds and the four-leggeds'.

Nacht und nebel: 'Night and fog', German phrase used to describe the trains that carried the victims of the Nazis to the concentration camps.

Narada: The holy man at the centre of the Hindu story about the Lord Vishnu and the world of illusion.

Newton, Isaac (1643–1727): English astronomer, physicist and mathematician, principally associated with the laws of gravity and motion, who used the phrase 'nothing but' to describe rays of light.

Nietzsche, Friedrich (1844–1900): German philosopher who famously declared the death of God.

Nostos: Greek concept of homecoming, particularly after an epic journey. Moriarty uses it to suggest an ultimate homecoming to Divine Ground.

Orpheus: Mythical Greek hero whose music could overcome and soothe all savagery. Used by Moriarty as an alternative to a sword-bearing hero.

Pascal, Blaise, (1623–1662): French mathematician, inventor, theologian and mystic.

Pasiphae: In Greek mythology she was the mother of the Minotaur.

Pequod: The name of the whaling ship in Melville's *Moby Dick*. Moriarty uses the expression 'Pequod culture' to describe the modern, 'progressive' way of being in the world which is utterly exploitative and destructive of the natural environment and resources.

Perseus: In Greek Mythology, after an adventurous journey, Perseus outwits and kills Medousa.

Phylogeny, phylogenetically: The evolutionary history of an organism. Moriarty uses the word to describe all the ancient powerful energies that are latent in man as a result of his evolution from the animal kingdom and that, when erupted, cause terrifying and terrible havoc.

Piseóg : Old superstitious practices that have a sinister side, similar to voodoo in the Caribbean.

Plath, Sylvia (1932–1963): American poet, novelist and short-story writer who wrote the poem *Sheep and Fog*.

Prometheus: One of the Titans in Greek mythology who stole fire from the gods and enabled the technological progress of humanity. However Moriarty sees the theft as a defiance of the gods which has led to abuse of the technology that it enabled. Prometheus is an image for man's belief that he can 'shape the world to suit him' regardless of the cost to the planet.

Psychic topiary: topiary is the art of pruning plants to a particular shape. Moriarty uses this image to suggest that human beings have been subjected to a similar process by the kind of education to which they have been subjected.

St John of the Cross (1542–1591): Spanish mystic and author of *The Ascent of Mount Carmel*.

St Teresa of Avila (1515–1582): Spanish mystic and reformer of the Carmelite Order.

Saturn's grey chaos: image from *Moby Dick*, used to convey the terrifying sense of infinitude in a godless, purposeless universe.

Second Law of Thermodynamics: the tendency for all matter and energy in the universe to evolve towards a state of inert uniformity, in other words the progress of the universe is towards total annihilation.

Shaman: Siberian term, now used for those among the First Peoples of the Earth who were credited with the ability to communicate with another dimension of the world in order to learn about life and healing.

Sila Ersinarsinivdluge: An Eskimo phrase, which means 'Don't be afraid of the universe'.

Sila: An Eskimo concept that corresponds with *anima mundi* or 'world soul'.

Súil mildagach: Irish expression for 'the evil eye', used by Moriarty to describe the eye of progress, of consumerism, of exploitation which has become the collective eye of the modern world.

Sumpatheia ton hollon: The Stoic belief that there is a universal sympathy, that runs through all things and that therefore connects all things.

Sutra: a Sanskrit word which refers to texts used in Hinduism and Buddhism, a manual, textbook or scripture.

Takanakapsaluk: In Eskimo legend she is the mother of all the sea-beasts and lives on the floor of the ocean. In Eskimo tradition she must be treated with care and respect and kept appeased, otherwise she will withdraw her bounty from the world.

Taoism: A Chinese philosophy, based on the *Tao Te Ching* by Lao Tze, which advocates living in harmony with 'the way' of the world. Also known as Daoism.

Tenebrae: A Christian ritual which re-enacts the darkness of Good Friday, and the suffering of Christ.

Theseus: Legendary Greek hero who killed the Minotaur.

Torrent: Used by Moriarty to refer to the Kedron, the brook crossed by Jesus on his way to Gethsemane.

Triduum Sacrum: The three sacred days of Easter: Holy Thursday, Good Friday and Holy Saturday.

Tsetsekia: A ritual of the Kwaikutl people where, instead of slaying the terrifying monster, they invite in 'The Great Iakim'. It is a ceremony that incorporates the inclusion and integration of destructive energies rather than the repression and exclusion common in the Graeco-Roman tradition.

Upanishads: a collection of religious and philosophical texts written in India during the first millennium BC.

Uvavnuk: Inuit medicine woman.

Vishnu: A powerful god in the Hindu tradition, one of the three gods, the others being Brahma and Shiva, who make up the Supreme Being.

Wordsworth, William (1770–1850): English Romantic poet, author of *Ode on the Intimations of Immortality*.

Year One Reed: in the Aztec calendar this was the year in which their world was overthrown by the Spanish conquerors. For Moriarty it becomes an image for the overthrow of any creed or culture. The modern world, having lost its 'sheltering mythology' has undergone a 'Year One Reed'. It is an image for a cataclysm but could also symbolise the possibility of a new beginning. He imagines one new flag for the entire planet, a single reed, which might lead to a new enlightenment; to Buddh Gaia.

Yeats, William Butler (1865–1939): Irish poet and dramatist, founder of the Abbey Theatre and winner of the Nobel prize for Literature in 1923.